Thomas Aquinas on Seeing God

The Beatific Vision in his
Commentary on Peter Lombard's
Sentences IV.49.2

Thomas Aquinas on Seeing God

The Beatific Vision in his *Commentary on Peter Lombard's Sentences* IV.49.2

Translated and Introduced by

Katja Krause

Max Planck Institute for the History of Science
and Technical University Berlin

MEDIÆVAL PHILOSOPHICAL TEXTS IN TRANSLATION
NO. 53
RICHARD C. TAYLOR, EDITOR

Marquette University Press
Milwaukee WI 53201-3141

Manufactured in the United States of America
founded 1916

∞The paper used in this publication meets the minimum requirements of the American National Standard for Information Sciences—Permanence of Paper for Printed Library Materials, ANSI Z39.48-1992.

Cover image courtesy of the Getty's Open Content Program
Book Design by Carol Sawyer

Library of Congress Cataloging-in-Publication Data

Names: Thomas, Aquinas, Saint, 1225?-1274, author. | Krause, Katja, 1980- translator, writer of introduction.

Title: Thomas Aquinas on seeing God : the beatific vision in his Commentary on Peter Lombard's Sentences IV.49.2 / translated and introduced by Katja Krause.

Other titles: Scriptum super IV libros Sententiarum. Liber 4. Distinctio 49. Quaestio 2. English | Mediaeval philosophical texts in translation; 53.

Description: Milwaukee, Wisconsin : Marquette University Press, 2020. |

Series: Medieval philosophical texts in translation ; 53 | Includes bibliographical references and index. | Summary: "Thomas Aquinas's first eschatological account of the beatific vision 'face-to-face', as presented in his commentary on Peter Lombard's Sentences, integrates the theological discourse of his times with newly available philosophical reasoning. This book provides a translation of book 4, distinction 49, question 2 of his commentary, and comprehensively examines, in the introductions and notes, how Aquinas solved the deepest conceptual dilemmas of his predecessors"--Provided by publisher.

Identifiers: LCCN 2020017623 | ISBN 9780874622652 (paperback)

Subjects: LCSH: Peter Lombard, Bishop of Paris, approximately 1100-1160.
Sententiarum libri IV. Liber 4. Distinctio 49. | Beatific vision--Early works to 1800. | Knowledge, Theory of (Religion)--Early works to 1800. | Intellect--Early works to 1800.

Classification: LCC BX1749.P4 T56413 2020 | DDC 236/.2--dc23

LC record available at https://lccn.loc.gov/2020017623

Marquette University Press
Milwaukee

The Association of Jesuit University Presses

Matri et avae meis
hic adhuc cognoscimus sicut per aenigmas
ac avo meo
qui brevi tempore abiit illuc ubi videbimus sicut nunc videmur
maximo amore et caritate maxima
istum librum mitto.[1]

1. This dedication is inspired by a most beautiful and fitting dedication which Alfred Gideon Langley, the English translator of Leibniz's *New Essays Concerning Human Understanding* (1896) wrote for his mother, sister, and father. I came across it shortly after my grandfather, our family's ever-present guide and role model, passed away. Langley's dedication reads as follows: "To my mother and sister sometime gone where we shall know as we are known and to my father still where we see as in a mirror obscurely in deepest love and gratitude, I dedicate this book."

Contents

Preface and Acknowledgments

. . . nec umquam
esse satis potero, praestem licet omnia, gratus.
Quod loquor et spiro caelumque et sidera solis
respicio, possimne ingratus et impius esse?

(P. Ovidius Naso, *Metamorphoses*, l. 14, v. 170–173)

HOW MUCH MORE CAN WE ACCOMPLISH in our work and everyday life with the help of those who give freely! How much do we stand in debt to those who do so! With their help and with our gratitude to them, I believe, we truly are and become ever more human. It is in this spirit that I wish to express my deepest gratitude to the people and institutions that have provided me bountifully with all the means required to see this project to success.

Upon the completion of my doctoral thesis, Richard C. Taylor suggested that I embark upon a complete English translation of Thomas Aquinas's earliest treatment of the beatific vision in his commentary on the *Sentences*, d. 49, q. 2, a. 1, and invited me to publish it with Marquette University Press. I very happily accepted his suggestion and invitation, and worked on the project over the course of five years. During that time, Richard always accompanied the process with wise guidance, numerous suggestions, and ceaseless patience. Words cannot express my gratitude to him.

Many of the findings contained in the general introduction of this book were made during the writing of my doctoral dissertation at the Philosophy Department of King's College London. Peter Adamson, Thomas Pink, Maria Rosa Antognazza, and Christopher Hughes provided the most valuable advice, criticisms, and mentorship during these formative stages of my scholarship. I also received support from

King's College London and the Konrad Adenauer Foundation during this period, and I wish to thank these institutions as well.

When I was a postdoctoral fellow at Department II of the Max Planck Institute for the History of Science (MPIWG) in Berlin, my colleagues, and especially the director, Lorraine Daston, opened new ways of thinking to me about the relationship between the ideals and practices of human knowing. The fine teachings, guidance, and challenges I encountered during these two years were pivotal in shaping my future studies and in encouraging me to go beyond disciplinary boundaries and historical spaces and times. I owe special thanks to Lorraine Daston for her model of learning and scholarship, and for the privilege of receiving her insights and inspiration. My deepest gratitude also goes to Sietske Fransen, Judy Kaplan, Elisabeth Wallmann, and many more colleagues at the MPIWG for discussing my ideas with me.

I was able to continue my work on the manuscript during the academic year 2016–2017 while a lecturer at Durham University, and to present parts of it at the "Theology and Ethics Research Seminar" convened by Simon Oliver. To him and to my colleagues at the Theology Department, Lewis Ayers, Jane Heath, Christopher Insole, and Susan Royal, I am grateful for the many conversations and their general encouragement.

The following academic year I had the privilege to see my research on this book to near completion at the Science, Religion, and Culture Program under the auspices of Harvard Divinity School at Harvard University. There, I was able to discuss my work at length with Katharine Park, Ahmed Ragab, and Julia Reed, and to present parts of the manuscript at the Harvard Center for the Study of World Religions. To the head of the Center, Charles Stang Marshall, and to members of the audience I am most grateful for insightful comments and sharp questions. I am equally grateful for the conversations with Jeffrey McDonnough and Alison Simmons at the Harvard Philosophy Department. My research for that year was supported by the Deutsche Akademie der Naturforscher Leopoldina–Nationale Akademie der Wissenschaften. It is my greatest pleasure to thank them most heartily for their generous support.

Over the past years I have had the opportunity to share my work with other very dear colleagues, near and far. To them, Justin Anderson, Therese Cory, Nicola Polloni, Jacob Terneus, and Rik Van Nieuwenhove, all of whom provided most useful advice and suggestions for improving parts of the manuscript, I extend my warmest thanks. My deep gratitude also goes to Kate Sturge, my editorial assistant, and my two student assistants at the MPIWG, Fabio De Gregorio and Anina Woischnig, who have patiently and repeatedly rectified all formalities of the book. Thanks, too, to Kellyann Falkenberg Wolfe for creating the index.

To two incomparable friends and mentors, Henryk Anzulewicz and Steven Harvey, I reserve a very special debt of gratitude. They read through the whole manuscript more than once. Their innumerable comments and invaluable suggestions for improvement, their penetrating questions and thought-provoking criticisms helped me to enhance the substance of the book. Through their generosity of time, their patience and kindness, their inquisitiveness, and their genuine interest, I was able to grow immensely as a scholar and writer over the past years.

I would also like to thank Marquette University Press for publishing my book, and especially Maureen Kondrick for her seemingly endless patience and continual encouragement.

My family always inspired me throughout these years, and provided enormous moral and spiritual support. I thank my mother, Vera Krause, and my grandmother, Elisabeth Marschner, for listening to alien stories long gone, and my grandfather, Gerhart Marschner, who did not live to see the completion of this book, for his sharp questions and profound comments. It is to them that I dedicate this book with deepest gratitude and love.

Abbreviations and Symbols

ABBREVIATIONS RELATED TO TREATISES

AL	Aristoteles Latinus
BnF	Bibliothèque nationale de France
Colon.	ed. Coloniensis
CCCM	Corpus Christianorum Continuatio Mediaevalis
CCSL	Corpus Christianorum, Series Latina
CSEL	Corpus Scriptorum Ecclesiasticorum Latinorum
CUP	Chartularium Universitatis Parisiensis
Leon.	ed. Leonina
PL	Patrologia Latina
SC	Sources Chrétiennes

GENERAL ABBREVIATIONS

a.	articulus
add.	addidit
c.	capitulum
com.	commentum
d.	distinctio
ed. / eds.	editio, editor / editors
ep.	epistula
f.	folio
ibid.	ibidem
id.	idem
l.	liber
lat.	latinus
lect.	lectio
marg.	marginalia, marginalis
ms. / mss.	manuscriptum / manuscripta
n.	numerus
obj.	objectio

om.	omisit
p. / pp.	pagina / paginae
prop.	propositio
q., qla.	questio, questiuncula
ra	recto, columna a
rb	recto, columna b
resp.	responsio
sect.	sectio
sol.	solutio
sq. / sqq.	sequens / sequentes
t.	tomus
tr.	tractatus
trans.	translatus, translatio
tx.	textus
v.	versus
vet.	vetus
vol.	volumen

SYMBOLS

< >	addendum
( )	Latin original
[ ]	alternative reading

Editor's Introduction: A Vexed History Of Seeing God

I

Aims and Purposes

THOMAS AQUINAS'S YOUTHFUL THEORY of the beatific vision attests to his mastery of centuries of theological discourses. Apart from the Bible, among the authors who speak to us through his theory are Augustine, other Latin Church Fathers, the Eastern Christian authorities of Dionysius the Areopagite and John of Damascus,[1] the Aristotelian and Arabic Peripatetic thinkers such as Alexander of Aphrodisias, Themistius, Alfarabi, Avicenna, Alghazali, and Averroes, and the theologians and philosophers who preceded him at the University of Paris and in the Dominican *studia*. Yet young Thomas did not simply accumulate their discourses. He created instead his own theory on the shoulders of these giants, a theory often thought to solve the deepest dilemmas of his predecessors.[2]

But how exactly did young Thomas create his theory of the beatific vision? How did he draw on his sources? And how did he engage head-on with the debates of his near-contemporaries? The answers to these questions are the topic of the present book as a whole—a book which contains at its heart a complete English

1. Since the authorship of the *corpus Dionysiacum* by Dionysius the Areopagite, the Athenian convert of Paul the Apostle as alluded to in Acts 17:34, remained largely unquestioned during the Scholastic period, I will refer to those whom we know to be the late fifth- / early sixth-century authors pseudo-Dionysius as "Dionysius" or "Dionysius the Areopagite" throughout this book (with the exception of the bibliographic references in the footnotes). On the history of the persona of Dionysius the Areopagite, see, for instance: Corrigan and Harrington 2018 and Mainoldi 2018.

2. See, for instance: de Contenson 1959a, p. 31; de Contenson 1962, p. 409 and p. 421; Mailliard 2001, p. 221; Taylor 2012, p. 512; Torrell 1997, p. 46; Trottmann 1995, pp. 302–336; Wéber 1978, p. 25. One study that explicitly questions a direct connection of Aquinas's conception of the beatific vision with previous conceptions is de Contenson 1959b, particularly on p. 18 and p. 29.

translation of Aquinas's youthful theory of the beatific vision as presented in his commentary on Peter Lombard's *Sentences*, book IV, distinction 49, question 2, articles 1–7. Through this theory, Aquinas speaks to his readers directly and allays their thirst with his own words. Yet he does not provide in his text a reflective understanding of the historical and doctrinal contexts within which he developed it.

The aim of this introduction is precisely to offer such reflections. The introduction is intended to be read as a guidebook to the actors who preceded and surrounded Aquinas, to the debates that they conducted, to the ideas that they suggested, and to the frameworks of thought that they entertained, at times in contrast to and at times in accord with Aquinas. To some extent, the introduction will cover well-trodden territory for the expert reader. It will introduce key figures in the history of theology and philosophy from the Bible to Aquinas and beyond, in order to chart the emergence and nature of the increasingly complex discourses on the beatific vision. The goal here is not to provide a comprehensive survey of centuries of debate on this topic, but to concentrate on those historical discourses that stand in immediate connection to Aquinas's conception of the beatific vision.

These discourses help to underscore the novelty of Aquinas's conception—a novelty that can only emerge if they are read on their own systematic terms. Such a reading, engaged with the distinctive possibilities of thought present in Aquinas's predecessors, has not yet been given in the literature, the focus of which has conventionally been on portraying Aquinas's theory as that solution which met all requirements of orthodoxy.[3] This introduction, therefore, offers a complementary reading of the history of his theory of the beatific vision in that it pays particular attention to the different historical conditions under which distinctive ideas and solutions could and did in fact emerge.

---

3. See previous note.

Aquinas's commentary on the *Sentences* offers crucial insights into the sophistication of medieval learning and academia, which easily transcend the walls of the University of Paris where he began his career. Resonating from the pages of his commentary is not only his intellectual talent, but also the influence of his teacher Albert the Great, whose new, lasting, and widespread academic practices were first implemented at the Dominican study house in Cologne. Albert's introduction of Eastern Christian theology, of Aristotle's *Nicomachean Ethics*, and of Arabic Peripatetic philosophy into the theological curriculum of the Dominican friars left a deep mark on Latin thought for centuries to come, and young Aquinas was one of the first to profit from it. Yet Aquinas also embarked on his own distinctive paths, one of which was the patent intensification of his teacher's practices. In his commentary on the *Sentences*, Aquinas plainly translated much of theological doctrine into the philosophical language of Aristotelianism—a language that was introduced by Aristotle and refined by his Peripatetic followers over the centuries. Aquinas's transfiguration of the beatific vision and other key theological teachings did nothing less than allow Latin theology to join this choir of common Aristotelian expression despite cultural and religious differences. His pronounced Aristotelianism is, of course, a *topos* among medieval scholars. Yet its peculiar birth, in its manifest conversation with the Arabic Peripatetics in his commentary on the *Sentences*, remains to be fully appreciated.[4]

Of similar import is the reception history of Aquinas's commentary, its enormous popularity in circles outside academia, and

4. The literature on this general topic is ever growing. Recent studies of importance concerning the Arabic Peripatetic influences on Thomas Aquinas include: Bazán 2013, pp. 243–277; Black 2014, pp. 213–236; Brenet 2006, pp. 310–342; id. 2011, pp. 215–247; Cory 2015, pp. 607–646; Hasse 2000; id. 2010; Krause 2014; id., 2015b, pp. 175–217; Müller 2001; Oliva 2012a, pp. 397–430; id. 2012b, pp. 585–662; Taylor 2009a, pp. 187–220; id. 2013, pp. 141–183; Wirmer 2006, pp. 569–590. Aquinas's commentary on the *Sentences* in particular is generally understudied. Some key studies on this early work include: Borgo 2013, pp. 83–128; Krause 2014; Oliva 2006; id. 2012b, pp. 585–662; Taylor 2012, pp. 509–550; Tellkamp 2012, 611–640. In my forthcoming book *Aquinas's Vision of Seeing God: Arabic Philosophy and Christian Eschatology* in the new Brepols series Philosophy in the Abrahamic Traditions in the Middle Ages. I will expand in great detail upon the brief insights offered here.

its seemingly uninterrupted importance for theological thought in the centuries that followed its composition. While modern scholarship has been mostly indifferent towards the fourth book of Aquinas's commentary on the *Sentences*, it was one of his most popular works in the Middle Ages, with 217 extant manuscripts.[5] Yet while this large number of manuscripts clearly testifies to the book's influence, it is only part of the story. There is also the indirect and often overlooked influence. For example, much of Aquinas's theory of the beatific vision as presented in book IV, question 2, articles 1–4 and 7, may be found in a fifteenth-century pseudo-Thomistic treatise on the beatific vision, entitled *On the Vision of the Divine Essence*.[6] Erasing any reference to the Arabic sources, this treatise quickly found its way into the hands of the Dutch mystic Hendrik Herp (1410–1477), who first copied and inserted it into his academic Latin treatise *Eden*, and shortly thereafter amended and translated it into Middle Dutch to popularize it in his mystical guide, *Spieghel der volcomenheit* (*Mirror of Perfection*). From this later work, Aquinas's system of the beatific vision voyaged all over Europe in numerous vernacular translations, which were made over the following two centuries.[7] This single case of reception history may well attest to a wide dissemination of Aquinas's early teachings in the sea of thinkers who had access to the very many manuscripts of the fourth book of his commentary. Until this history is written, one can only imagine the true extent of the impact of Aquinas's text. Its marked importance, however, should now be manifest.

No complete English translation of this question as a whole has yet been published on the basis of the pre-critical edition of the Commissio Leonina, the best edition of the text, which is currently

5. For references, and more detail on the number of manuscripts, see section "Notes on the Text" below. Concerning matters of copying and circulating the manuscripts in the Dominican study houses (apart from the university libraries) see, for instance: Mulchahey 2008, pp. 118–147; id. 2012, pp. 577–599.

6. Pseudo-Thomas Aquinas, *De visione divinae essentiae*, Wolfenbüttel 59.1. For a reference to all the preserved mss. see: Bataillon 1964, 471–474.

7. On the immense popularity of Herp's *Mirror of Perfection* and on Herp's use of the pseudo-Thomistic treatise, *On the Vision of the Divine Essence*, see the excellent doctoral thesis by Abram (2017) and her article (forthcoming).

being prepared but is not yet available in print.[8] On the basis of the Parma edition from 1858 and with a limited pool of references, however, Beth Mortensen has recently translated the whole of book IV of Aquinas's commentary on Peter Lombard's *Sentences* in volumes 9 and 10 of the *Opera omnia* project of the Aquinas Institute.[9] This project proves highly useful, I believe, to readers who are less familiar with the Latin of Aquinas, who wish to study his earliest writings in their own right and with few references to context, and who do not necessarily require a translation on the basis of the pre-critical edition of the Commissio Leonina.

Yet one can also easily imagine the wide appeal that a new and fully annotated translation on the basis of the best Latin text available could have. For example, philosophers (in training) may wish to investigate Aquinas's theory of the beatific vision as a part of his overall theory of cognition. Historians of ideas may wish to engage with his indebtedness to his sources, or they may simply wish to stand on solid historical ground for establishing their reception histories in later thinkers. Theologians may be interested in the connections between Aquinas's youthful and mature conceptions of the beatific vision, and in comparing his teachings here to his famous treatment in the *Summa theologiae*, l. I, q. 12, or in studying its impact on twentieth-century systematic theologians such as Karl Rahner or Henri de Lubac. However diverse these contemporary interests may be, and they are certainly much more diverse than the illustrations just listed, Thomas Aquinas's youthful treatment of the beatific vision in his commentary

---

8. For more information concerning this textual basis, see "Notes on the Text" below. A partial translation of this most recent Latin edition is found in Richard Taylor's translation of a. 1 online; see: Thomas Aquinas, *In 4 Sent.*, d. 49, q. 2, a. 1 (trans. Taylor).

9. See: Thomas Aquinas (trans. Mortensen 2018). In addition, three articles of the commentary on the *Sentences* are contained in the supplement to the third part of Aquinas's *Summa theologiae*. These are equivalent to aa. 1, 2, and 5 in Aquinas's commentary on the *Sentences*, were translated into English around 1920 by the Fathers of the English Dominican Province on the basis of the Leonine edition of the *Summa theologiae* text. See: Thomas Aquinas, *The Summa Theologiae of St. Thomas Aquinas*, supplement to the third part, q. 92, a. 1–3 (trans. Fathers of the English Dominican Province). For the Latin original of the supplement, see: Thomas Aquinas, *Summa theologiae supplementum tertiae partis*, q. 92, aa. 1–3 (ed. Leon. 12, pp. 217–224). I have consulted all three English translations available for my own translation, but followed my own principles of translation as outlined in my "Notes on the Translation" below.

on the *Sentences*, l. 4, d. 49, q. 2, speaks to an interdisciplinary and general historically inquisitive audience, far broader than the scholars of medieval Scholastic philosophy and theology for whom this text by the young Aquinas should be required reading.

This introduction on the history of Aquinas's earliest theory of the beatific vision follows a largely chronological order and pays primary attention to the added layers of complexity that evolve with the arrival of new source materials. Accordingly, it begins with reflections on the key passages from the Bible; proceeds to the Latin Church Father Augustine of Hippo; and advances to the Greek Christian theologians before turning its attention to the combined assimilation history of these three theological strands of influence in Aquinas's Scholastic predecessors. After dealing with the new translations that arrived in the Paris of the thirteenth century—translations of a panoply of new Greek Christian theological and Arabic Peripatetic philosophical sources—the introduction turns to the second layer of a combined assimilation history in some of Aquinas's other Scholastic predecessors. Since some of their theorizations of the beatific vision were perceived by the Church to be as pessimistic as could be and understood as denying a direct beatific vision, the magisterium did not hesitate to intervene. The condemnations of 1241 thus form the following step of the introduction. This step is followed by a third wave of appropriations of translated material, including Robert Grosseteste's complete translation of Aristotle's *Nicomachean Ethics*, the so-called *translatio Lincolniensis*, and Michael Scot's translations of Averroes's works. Their importance for the works of Aquinas's contemporary and teacher, Albert the Great, in combination with the well-known Dionysian works will comprise the final step before the introduction addresses Aquinas's own selective approach to all these influences in the introductions to each article. It is here that Aquinas's book reaches its climax with deliberations on his systematic solution, in light of his historical indebtedness, to his initial question of whether God's substance can be seen through His essence (*per essentiam*).

II

Two Ways to God

According to the New Testament, the vision of God presents a true possibility of ultimate fulfillment to the Christian believer in a life to come. The first Epistle of John attests to this optimistic view in suggesting that "we shall see God as He is" (I John 3:2).[1] Yet earlier in the New Testament, the apostle St. Paul offers a much more pessimistic view. In his First Letter to Timothy, he suggests in so-called apophatic terms that God, "whom no man sees, nor is capable of seeing" (I Tim. 6:18), remains invisible. Some historical interpreters of St. Paul took this passage to pertain to the life to come, in particular to the heavenly vision of God. These two disparate views—contained in the New Testament and supported by similar passages in the Old Testament—shaped the historical discourses on the beatific vision over centuries from the Church Fathers to the Middle Ages and beyond, discourses that either gravitated towards the optimistic view of St. John, or, in contrast, tended towards the pessimistic view of St. Paul.[2] We will now turn to those historical discourses that were of particular relevance to Aquinas's view on the beatific vision.

1. Epistula Iohannis I 3:2 (Vulgata 2007): *carissimi nunc filii Dei sumus et nondum apparuit quid erimus scimus quoniam cum apparuerit similes ei erimus quoniam videbimus eum sicuti est.* Similar New Testament passages on the optimistic side include, for instance: Secundum Matthaeum 5:8 (Vulgata 2007): *beati mundo corde quoniam ipsi Deum videbunt.* Ad Corinthios I 13:12 (Vulgata 2007): *videmus nunc per speculum in enigmate tunc autem facie ad faciem nunc cognosco ex parte tunc autem cognoscam sicut et cognitus sum.*

2. For Old Testament passages on the optimistic side, even for rapture in this life, see, for instance: Exodus 33:11 (Vulgata 2007): *loquebatur autem Dominus ad Mosen facie ad faciem sicut loqui solet homo ad amicum suum.* Numeri 12:6–8 (Vulgata 2007): *dixit ad eos audite sermones meos si quis fuerit inter vos propheta Domini in visione apparebo ei vel per somnium loquar ad illum at non talis servus meus Moses qui in omni domo mea fidelissimus est ore enim ad os loquor ei et palam non per enigmata et figuras Dominum videt quare igitur non timuistis detrahere servo meo Mosi.*

St. Augustine of Hippo (354–430), the most influential of the Latin Church Fathers, embraced the Bible's optimistic view. In his *On the Literal Meaning of Genesis*, a commentary on the book of Genesis, which exerted pervasive influence on medieval discourses, Augustine distinguished three visions of God: a sensible vision, a spiritual vision, and an intellectual vision. Of these three, he portrayed the intellectual vision as the highest, a vision that he restricted to the raptures of Moses and St. Paul in this life, and that he granted to the blessed in the life to come. Augustine justified this restriction by the requirement of a complete separation of the mind from its body. Only on the basis of the removal from the senses does the human mind reach sufficient freedom to turn to a vision of God's substance directly.

> We rightly understand the third <heaven> to be that which is gazed upon by the mind—on the assumption that the mind has been separated, removed, entirely drawn away from the carnal senses and cleansed—so that it may, by the charity of the Holy Spirit, be granted the ability to ineffably see and hear those things which are in heaven, the very substance of God, and God, the Word through Whom all things were made.[3]

Because of his book's overall genre as a literal commentary on the Bible,[4] Augustine's reasoning here carries less of an argumentative force than a hermeneutical one. Direct noetic access to God in rapture and the vision of a future life are presented as theological doctrines that Augustine in no way queries, but simply illuminates. The Holy Spirit, the third person of the Trinity, writes Augustine in his explanations above, grants the gift of the vision of God the Father (the first person of the Trinity) and God the Son (the second person

3. Augustinus Hipponensis, *De Genesi ad litteram*, l. XII, c. 34 (CSEL 28/1, p. 432, v. 1 and v. 5–9; PL 34, p. 483): "recte accipimus <...> tertium uero <coelum> quod mente conspicitur ita secreta et remota et omnino abrepta a sensibus carnis atque mundata, ut ea, quae in illo caelo sunt, et ipsam dei substantiam uerbumque deum, per quod facta sunt omnia, per caritatem spiritus sancti ineffabiliter ualeat uidere et audire."

4. See, for instance: Greene-MacCreight 1999; Fladerer 2010.

of the Trinity). As such, the Holy Spirit could be interpreted as the decisive facilitating factor of the beatific vision. In another passage, however, Augustine describes God's form (*species*) as a facilitating factor when he reasons:

> In this <third vision> the clarity of God is seen <...> through His form (*species*): namely, <through that> by which God is whatever He is, regardless of however little the mind can take hold of Him, <the mind> that remains distinct from God, even when it has been cleansed of all earthly defect and alienated and rapt away from every body and likeness of a body.[5]

The way in which Augustine conceives of God's form (*species*) here is clearly in identity to His same-Self or His "whatness." Thus, since God is simple and the three Persons of the Trinity are one single Essence in God, Augustine's intention was apparently not to conceive of the Holy Spirit in real distinction from the divine form (*species*). His theological and philosophical explanations of the facilitating factor of the beatific vision therefore amount to the same: it is, in one way or another, God Himself that enables our vision of His very substance. Yet Augustine is quick to remind his audience that this ultimate vision has its limitations: even then, the created human mind remains a creature and is therefore capable only of a restricted vision that is necessarily limited by its own intellectual capacities, which in turn are determined by its ontological status as a creature.

These brief passages from his *On the Literal Meaning of Genesis* also reveal Augustine's theological intention. A systematic defense of his faith, as will be witnessed in Aquinas's commentary on the *Sentences*, was not on Augustine's mind, a mind in which the Bible was the sign (*signum*) that pointed to God (*res*) on the presupposition

---

5. Augustinus Hipponensis, *De Genesi ad litteram*, l. XII, c. 28 (CSEL 28/1, p. 422, v. 16.21–24; PL 34, p. 478): "in hoc <uisio tertia> uidetur claritas dei <...> per speciem scilicet, qua deus est quidquid est, quantulumcumque eum mens, quae non est quod ipse, etiam ab omni terrena labe mundata, ab omni corpore et similitudine corporis alienata et abrepta capere potest."

that God had already been known.[6] Yet despite its semiotic presentation, Augustine's optimistic view that God will be seen directly in His own substance soon became the orthodox reading of the Bible and thus the Church's doctrine in the Latin West. Aquinas, as we shall see, embraced Augustine's doctrine wholeheartedly, yet in his times, in contrast to those of Augustine, it seemed to have become necessary to defend it by means of arguments based on Aristotelian philosophical standards.

6. For this understanding, see, for instance: Augustinus Hipponensis, *De magistro*, c. 10 (CCSL 29, p. 192, v. 114–133; PL 32, p. 1214): "quod si diligentius consideremus, fortasse nihil inuenies, quod per sua signa discatur. Cum enim mihi signum datur, si nescientem me inuenerit, cuius rei signum sit, docere me nihil potest, si uero scientem, quid disco per signum? Non enim mihi rem, quam significat, ostendit uerbum, cum lego 'et sarabarae eorum non sunt commutatae.' Nam si quaedam capitum tegmina nuncupantur hoc nomine, num ego hoc audito aut quid sit caput aut quid sint tegmina didici? Ante ista noueram neque cum appellarentur ab aliis, sed cum a me uiderentur, eorum est mihi facta notitia. Etenim cum primum istae duae syllabae, cum dicimus 'caput,' aures meas impulerunt, tam nesciui quid significarent, quam cum primo audirem legeremue sarabaras. Sed cum saepe diceretur 'caput,' notans atque animaduertens, quando diceretur, repperi uocabulum esse rei, quae mihi iam erat uidendo notissima. Quod priusquam repperissem, tantum mihi sonus erat hoc uerbum; signum uero esse didici, quando cuius rei signum esset inueni, quam quidem ut dixi non significatu, sed aspectu didiceram. Ita magis signum re cognita quam signo dato ipsa res discitur."

III

WORLDS APART

IN CONTRAST TO AUGUSTINE'S VIEW, the Greek Christian theologians relevant to the discussions in the Latin West—John Chrysostom (ca. 347–407), Dionysius the Areopagite (ca. 485–518/528), Maximus the Confessor (580–662), and John of Damascus (676–749)—largely espoused the Bible's pessimistic outlook, or so it seemed. But they did so in quite different ways from one another.

Dionysius the Areopagite, a highly influential Greek Christian thinker in the Latin West and regarded as a great authority, denies any ultimate intellectual union with God on the basis of God's maximal transcendence. Since God is inconceivably other than any creature, He must be beyond all creaturely ability and power, including the angelic and human ability to understand. The hidden Self of God (Gr. *agnōstos theos*, Lat. *Deus absconditus*) remains intellectually concealed from all creatures, even in ultimate heavenly union with Him. Thus, even though ultimate union with God is possible, it occurs on a supra-intellectual level. In Dionysius's eyes, ultimate beatitude consists in a union with God that is beyond knowing Him.[1]

Yet when it comes to knowing God, Dionysius the Areopagite suggests that He does reveal Himself (Gr. *hypostasis*, Lat. *Deus revelatus*) to humans in so-called "theophanies" or "actualities." Indeed, he takes these theophanies to constitute divine intelligible revelations,

1. Pseudo-Dionysius Areopagita, *De divinis nominibus*, c. 7, sect. 24, trans. Sarraceni (Dionysiaca t. 1, pp. 385–386): "Oportet autem videre mentem nostram habere quidem virtutem ad intelligendum per quam intelligibilia inspicit, unitionem autem excedentem mentis naturam per quam conjungitur ad ea quae sunt supra ipsam. Secundum hanc igitur oportet divina intelligere non secundum nos, sed nos ipsos totos extra nos ipsos statutos et totos deificatos. Melius est enim esse Dei et non nostri ipsorum, ita enim erunt divina data cum Deo factis."

which are nothing other than "the differentiated presence of the one God in his creatures."[2] Seen in this way, his apophatic outlook on the beatific vision suggests God is knowable in His revealed Self, yet not in His transcendent Self. What this shows about Dionysius's conception of the divine essence is that it has two aspects for him: The first aspect, God's transcendent Self, translated into Latin with *Deus absconditus*, remains utterly removed from any creaturely reality. It is only accessible to creatures beyond all creaturely modality and it remains invisible even in the intellectual beatific vision. The second aspect of the divine essence, God's revealed Self, translated into Latin with *Deus revelatus*, infuses all levels of creaturely being and all modes of creaturely reality, including that of cognition.[3] God therefore can make Himself knowable or visible in the revelations of the theophanies as they radiate into creaturely cognition from God's hidden Self.

As we will see shortly, these Dionysian theophanies presented a serious challenge for Latin theologians. They were difficult to reconcile with Augustine's optimistic outlook, since Augustine and his

2. Perl 1994, p. 24.

3. Pseudo-Dionysius Areopagita, *De divinis nominibus*, c. 4, sect. 16, trans. Sarraceni (Dionysiaca t. 1, pp. 146–149): "Etenim sicut noster sol, non ratiocinans aut praeeligens, sed per ipsum esse, illuminat omnia participare lumen ipsius secundum propriam rationem valentia, ita quidem et bonum, super solem sicut super obscuram imaginem segregate archetypum, per ipsam essentiam omnibus existentibus proportionaliter immittit totius bonitatis radios. Propter ipsos substiterunt intelligibiles et intellectuales omnes et substantiae et virtutes et operationes; propter istos sunt et vivunt et vitam habent indeficientem et imminorabilem, ab universa corruptione et morte et materia et generatione mundae existentes, et ab instabili et fluxa et aliquando aliter ferente variatione elevatae, et sicut incorporales et immateriales intelliguntur, et sicut mentes supermundane intelligunt, et existentium proprie illuminantur rationibus, et rursus ad cognata propria deferunt." Id., c. 5, sect. 21, trans. Sarraceni (Dionysiaca t. 1, pp. 322–324): "Etenim boni Dei nominatio totos causae omnium processus manifestans, et ad existentia et ad non existentia extenditur, et super existentia est. Vitae autem ad omnia viventia extenditur, et super viventia est. Sapientiae vero ad omnia intellectualia et rationalia et sensibilia extenditur, et super omnia ista est." Id., c. 12, sect. 40, trans. Sarraceni (Dionysiaca t. 1, pp. 537–540): "Igitur perfectum quidem est non solum sicut per-se-perfectum, et secundum se ipsum a se ipso uniformiter segregatum, et totum per totum perfectissimum, sed et sicut superperfectum secundum omnium excessum, et omnem quidem infinitatem terminans, super omnem autem terminum extentum, et a nullo captum aut comprehensum, sed extendens se ad omnia simul et super omnia indeficientibus immissionibus et interminabilibus operationibus. Perfectum autem rursus dicitur et sicut inaugmentabile et semper perfectum, et sicut non-minorabile, sicut omnia in se ipso praehabens et supermanans secundum unam impausabilem et eamdem et superplenam et imminorabilem largitionem, secundum quam perfecta omnia perficit et propria adimplet perfectione."

followers did not endorse Dionysius's view on God's revealed Self. But his theophanies were not the only challenge. Similarly difficult to reconcile with the Augustinian position were other Greek Christian conceptions of the beatific vision, first and foremost that of John Chrysostom. In his fifteenth homily on the Gospel of St. John, a text that was translated into Latin by Burgundio of Pisa between 1171 and 1173, Latin theologians found a similar if not more apophatic view on the beatific vision. After Augustine's anagogical or tropological considerations on the Gospel of St. John, Chrysostom's homilies were the only available literal commentary on the fourth gospel in the High Middle Ages in Latin, and thus presented an important text that led to a revival of this gospel in particular.[4]

Commenting on the gospel's verse "God has never been seen by anyone" (John 1:18), Chrysostom wonders: "How does John say 'God is never seen by anyone'?"[5] In his reply, Chrysostom suggests that all witnesses of visions of God in the Old Testament, such as the visions of Isaiah, John, Ezekiel, Daniel, Moses, and Jacob, "were all condescensions <of God>, but not a vision of His plain substance."[6] Chrysostom reasons that because their prophetic visions of God all differed and had references to physical reality, such as sitting, standing, and walking, none of them could have possibly been of His substance. "The manner in which He is, however, only He alone does know."[7] However, not only are all these prophets barred from a vision of God's substance, in Chrysostom's eyes, but so are the angels and archangels. Their mission is to praise God in singing, but one does not hear from them of the substance of God.[8] Consequently, only Jesus

4. See: Dondaine 1952, p. 73.

5. Iohannes Chrysostomus, *Homiliae in Iohannem*, 15:1, trans. Burgundionis (ed. Dondaine 1952, p. 101, v. 9): "Qualiter igitur Iohannes dixit: Deum nemo uidit unquam?"

6. Ibid. (ed. Dondaine 1952, p. 101, v. 9–10): "Ostendens quoniam omnia illa condescentionis erant, non ipsius substantie nude uisio."

7. Ibid. (ed. Dondaine 1952, p. 101, v. 11–14): "Si enim ipsam uidissent naturam, nequaquam differenter eam considerassent: simplex enim quedam est et infigurabilis hec et incomposita et incircumscriptibilis. Non sedet, neque stat, neque ambulat: omnia enim hec corporum. Qualiter autem est, ipse nouit solus."

8. Ibid. (ed. Dondaine 1952, p. 101, v. 17–27): "Quia enim debebat Christus eius Filius per ueram carnem apparere nobis, desuper eos exercitabat uidere Dei substantiam sicut eis possibile

Christ, the Son of God, and the Holy Spirit see God, for "something that is a created nature, how could it possibly see what is uncreated?"[9]

When Chrysostom finally turns to the beatific vision and inquires whether the blessed will see God Himself, his answer is equally negative. Neither the blessed nor the angels will see God as He sees Himself; this vision is reserved for the Son. The blessed and angels, in contrast, will see in accordance with their capacities or natures. The blessed will see "what is possible" for them, and the angels will see "nothing other than what they always imagine of God."[10] However, these visions of God do not amount to a cognition of His substance; they do not reveal to the beholders "what He is."[11]

Chrysostom's denial was echoed over eight centuries later, almost verbatim, in the condemnations of 1241; but by then the meaning of the terms had gone through a long history of Latin reception of his and Dionysius's writings. In fact, what is immediately clear is that these two, and the other similar pessimistic discourses by Maximus the Confessor and John of Damascus concerning a divine reality utterly transcendent, did not form part of the dominating discourse in the Latin West. Augustine, as we just saw, took it for granted that God's reality is no more than His transcendent Self, a reality that exists in clear distinction from anything that would be created reality. The sharp division between the optimistic Latin discourse on the beatific

---

erat uidere: quia ipsum quodcumque est Deus non solum prophete, sed neque angeli uiderunt neque archangeli. Sed si interrogaueris eos, audies de substantia quidem nichil respondentes, gloria uero in excelsis Deo solum cantantes et in terra pax, hominibus bona uoluntas. Et si a cherubin uel seraphin concupiueris aliquid discere, misticam sanctimonii melodiam audies et quoniam plenum est celum et terra gloria eius. Si superiores uirtutes inuestigaueris, nichil aliud inuenies quam quoniam unum opus est eis laudare Deum: laudate enim eum, ait, omnes uirtutes eius."

9. Ibid. (ed. Dondaine 1952, p. 101, v. 27–28): "Solus igitur eum uidet Filius et Spiritus Sanctus. Quod autem creabilis nature est, qualiter et uidere poterit quod increabile est?"

10. Ibid. (ed. Dondaine 1952, p. 102, v. 47–53): "Quidquam igitur est quod dicitur, sicut cum dicat: beati mundo corde quoniam ipsi Deum uidebunt? Eam secundum mentem uisionem ait, et que nobis possibilis, et intelligentiam que est de Deo. Ita et in angelis dicere est, quoniam propter puram eorum et insompnem naturam nichil aliud quam Deum semper ymaginantur. Propterea et ipse rursus ait: nullus cognoscit Patrem, nisi Filius."

11. Ibid. (ed. Dondaine 1952, p. 102, v. 54–58): "Quid igitur? et omnes in ignorantia sumus, ait? Absit. Sed ita nouit nullus ut Filius. Sicut enim uiderunt eum prophete secundum capacem eis uisionem, substantiam uero nullus considerauit: ita et nunc scimus omnes Deum, substantiam uero nullus nouit quid est, nisi solus qui genitus est ex eo."

vision and the pessimistic Greek discourse on the same topic was thus ultimately grounded in two different views of divine reality, one concerning God's simplicity, the other His scope of diffusion in created reality. The critical encounter that would take place between these discourses in the thirteenth century was therefore virtually inevitable.

Yet such an encounter already occurred much earlier in the Latin West. Augustine's optimistic outlook on the beatific vision dominated the Latin West over many centuries, but the contrary pessimistic outlook was known to the Latin West as early as the sixth century. Pope Gregory I (c. 540–604), a man who was no stranger to the Eastern discourse due to his ambassadorial journeys to Constantinople, attests to such a pessimistic view in his *Moralia in Iob*. Here, he identifies "some, who pronounced that, even in that region of blessedness, God is seen by no means in His Nature, while <He is> gazed upon in His Brightness." This is a distinction which sounds exceedingly similar to Dionysius's distinction between God's transcendent Self and God's revealed Self. Yet Gregory, like many thinkers after him in the Latin West but in opposition to those in the East, insisted on a strict simplicity of God and His essence, limited to His transcendent Self. This insistence, which is evident from his reading of the Greek Christian conceptions, is a distinctly Latin way of interpretation, one with serious consequences. It led Gregory to abandon his own reading of these Eastern thinkers, and to say about their work that "without a doubt, they were misled by the imprecision of their inquiry."[12] In his own conception of the matter, Gregory instead followed the trodden path of Augustine and reasoned some lines later in his *Moralia*: "We shall <...> see God, who will be the prize of our labor, so that after the darkness of this current mortal state, we may rejoice in our likening to His light."[13]

12. Gregorius Magnus, *Moralia in Iob*, l. XVIII, c. 54 (CCSL 143A, p. 953, v. 92–98; PL 76, p. 93C–D): "Sciendum uero est quod fuere nonnulli qui Deum dicerent etiam in illa regione beatitudinis in claritate quidem sua conspici, sed in natura minime uideri. Quos nimirum minor inquisitionis subtilitas fefellit. Neque enim illi simplici et incommutabili essentiae aliud est claritas, aliud natura, sed ipsa ei natura sua claritas, ipsa claritas natura est."

13. Gregorius Magnus, *Moralia in Iob*, l. XVIII, c. 54 (CCSL 143A, p. 954, v. 133–135; PL 76, p. 94C): "Videbimus igitur Deum ipsumque erit praemium laboris nostri, ut post mortalitatis huius tenebras, accessa eius luce gaudeamus."

While Gregory circulated his Western interpretation of the pessimistic views of Greek theologians and judged them rather harshly by his own standards, some three centuries later John Scotus Eriugena (c. 815–877) fully embraced this pessimistic view. Born an Irishman, Eriugena relocated to France around 845 and became one of the successors of Alcuin of York (735–804) as the head of the Palatine School at King Charles the Bald's Carolingian court. Probably during his thirty years in this position, Eriugena got hold of a manuscript of the *corpus Dionysiacum* that had been given to the Abbey of St. Denis in the care of Abbot Hilduin (775–840) after Byzantine ambassadors had brought it to the court of Louis the Pious (778–840). Hilduin, in fact, in the 820s, became the first Latin theologian to compose a translation of Dionysius's works. Eriugena followed suit and wrote a second translation of it some thirty years later. Unlike Hilduin, however, Eriugena creatively added a number of other translations to the text of Dionysius the Areopagite, such as Maximus the Confessor's *Ambigua ad Iohannem* and Gregory of Nyssa's *De hominis opificio* (known in the West as *De imagine*),[14] all of which espoused the Eastern pessimistic outlook on the beatific vision.

Eriugena implanted into Latin theology the apophatic view that Gregory had rejected especially in his own treatise, entitled *The Division of Nature* (*Periphyseon* or *De divisione naturae*), which Pope Honorius III condemned as "heretical perversity" in 1225.[15] "We shall, therefore, not see God Himself because neither do the angels see Him, since this is impossible to any creature. <...> Yet, we shall contemplate certain theophanies made by Him in us."[16] This passage

14. See: Dondaine 1952, p. 63.

15. CUP, tx. 50 (ed. Denifle t. 1, pp. 106–107): "Nuper siquidem, sicut nobis significavit venerabilis frater noster <...> Parisiensis episcopus, est quidam liber, qui *perifisis* titulatur, inventus totus scatens vermibus heretice pravitatis. Unde a venerabili fratre nostro <...> archiepiscopo Senonensi et suffraganeis ejus in provinciali concilio congregatis justo est judicio reprobatus" (emphasis as in edition).

16. Iohannes Scotus Eriugena, *Periphyseon*, l. 1 (CCCM 161, p. 12, v. 265–269; PL 122, p. 448 C): "Non ergo ipsum deum per se ipsum uidebimus, quia neque angeli uident—hoc enim omni creaturae impossibile est; *solus* nanque, ut ait Apostolus, *habet immortalitatem, et lucem habitat inaccessibilem*—sed quasdam factas ab eo in nobis theophanias contemplabimur" (emphases as in edition).

shows how a Western reading of strict divine simplicity went beyond even the Eastern distinctions of *Deus absconditus* and *Deus revelatus*. An identification of the divine essence with its theophanies, as Eastern discourse had suggested, remained beyond Eriugena's vision. Instead, he construed the Dionysian theophanies as entities distinct from God, intelligible creaturely forms infused into the soul from God so it might contemplate Him, despite His complete hiddenness. According to Eriugena's view, therefore, it is these theophanies and not God Himself who will be known in the ultimate vision. Together with some elements of Avicennian philosophy, this view of theophanies as created objects of knowing, distinct from God, would stir intense theological debates in the thirteenth century.

Yet already in the twelfth century, Eriugena's pessimistic outlook faced some serious criticism. Hugh of St. Victor (1096–1141), a Saxon canon regular and later head of the Abbey of St. Victor in Paris, rekindled interest in Dionysius's works. He commented on Eriugena's translation of Dionysius's *Celestial Hierarchy* and on Eriugena's commentary on it.[17] Hugh displayed a thorough knowledge of the Dionysian theophanies, though he was clearly reading through the lens of Eriugena's interpretation. Yet as a traditional Augustinian who held firmly to a beatific vision face to face, he criticized both the Dionysian and the Eriugean positions in a rather polemical fashion:

> Yet, these <theophanies>, certain images, as it were, of the hidden divinity put media between the rational souls and God—higher than the mind, and lower than the divinity. And indeed, this alone is seen of God, and only in this God is seen, since He cannot be seen in Himself by any mind or soul. But these images are <images> of delusions and fantasies of vanity. While they were trying to affirm the visible and perceptible light of the divinity alone in these <theophanies>, they were determined to remove the true cognition

17. For the reception history of Dionysius's writings in Scotus Eriugena, and for Scotus Eriugena's transmission of them in Latin thought, esp. in Hugh of St. Victor, see, for instance: Beierwaltes 1987; Marenbon 1981; McEvoy and Dunne 2002; Rorem 2005; Moran 2008; Rorem 2008, pp. 601–614.

> of God and the vision from the minds of the blessed. For what does it mean that God is only seen in these images, and not seen outside of them, other than that God is never truly seen, and the truth is never seen? For if an image alone is always seen, the truth is never seen, since an image is not the truth, even though it is of the truth. Let them therefore abolish their fantasies by which they endeavor to overshadow the light of our minds; and let them not bar our God from us by the images of their own estimations. For just as nothing can satiate us besides Him, so can nothing cause us to stop us on our path to Him.[18]

Hugh of St. Victor's reasoning here is clear: in his eyes, some thinkers—Dionysius the Areopagite and Eriugena seem to be implied—suggest that God is only seen in His images, but never in His true Self. Such a vision could never constitute ultimate beatitude, as it would prevent humans from the closest possible union with God, from seeing Him face to face. But why would Hugh think that this is the case? Hugh's criticism of the theophanies rests on the same real distinction between *Deus absconditus* and *Deus revelatus* that we encountered in Gregory the Great and to a certain extent also in Eriugena. Only God's transcendent Self represents His true same-Self, while His revealed (and created) Self is utterly unlike Him. All revealed theophanies, or "images" of God, as Hugh conceives of them, therefore, constitute a reality that is no longer identical to God Himself. Like the Western tradition before him, including Eriugena's commentary, Hugh's restriction of the divine essence to His transcendence alone

18. Hugo de Sancto Victore, *Super Ierarchiam Dionysii*, l. 2 (CCCM 178, p. 444, v. 901–917; PL 175, p. 954D–955A): "Ipsa autem quasi quaedam simulachra absconditae diuinitatis inter rationales animos ac Deum media ponunt, altiora quidem mente, inferiora diuinitate, et hoc quidem solum de Deo uideri et in hoc solo Deum uideri, utpote qui in seipso a nulla mente uel animo uideri possit. Haec uero simulachra sunt errorum et fantasmata uanitatis; in quibus, dum solum diuinitatis lucem uisibilem et perceptibilem conantur asserere, ueram deitatis cognitionem et uisionem mentibus sanctis probantur auferre. Quid est enim in illis solum Deum uideri et extra illa non uideri, nisi nunquam uere uideri et uerum nunquam uideri? Si enim imago sola semper uidetur, ueritas nunquam uidetur, quoniam imago ueritas non est, etiam cum de ueritate est. Tollant ergo fantasias suas, quibus lumen mentium nostrarum obumbrare nituntur, neque nobis Deum nostrum simulachris estimationum suarum intersepiant, quia nos, sicut saciare non potest aliquid preter ipsum, ita nec sistere usque ad ipsum."

triggered a crisis of anxiety and rejection of Eastern discourse. What was in truth rejected, however, was not the Eastern outlook on the beatific vision as maintained by Dionysius and other Church Fathers. Rather, Hugh took issue with a peculiar traditional Latin reading of this outlook, a reading that he suggested himself and that was committed to a conception of God's reality restricted to His transcendent Self and therefore different from the Eastern tradition.

Hugh's commentary on Dionysius's *Celestial Hierarchy* circulated widely together with the *corpus Dionysiacum*, in a textbook for university students, and set the tone in rejecting the Greek Christian conceptions for the emerging Scholastic period. This textbook contained Hugh's polemic reading together with Dionysius's original in Eriugena's and the Sarracen's translations, and it was, in addition, accompanied by Anastasius's translations of the scholia, and excerpts from Eriugena's *Periphyseon*.[19] But already by the end of the thirteenth century, we see that, because of its popularity and widespread use, the first generation of Latin students to read this book had virtually no chance of understanding the Areopagite on his own terms. Because of all the accompanying texts which provided something like a canonical Western interpretation of Dionysius, students had to read him through the lenses of these Western interpretations. For those interpretations, it also did not matter whether the attitude they displayed towards the supposed "pessimistic" outlook in Dionysius was one of embracement (Eriugena) or one of rejection (Hugh of St. Victor). Hugh's praise of the traditional Western conception of the divine essence and his rejection of the Eastern doctrines in his own reading, together with

19. See: Dondaine 1953, pp. 117–122. As we learn from Harrington 2004, pp. 1–3, neither Hugh of St. Victor's polemic criticism of Dionysius and Eriugena, nor Pope Honorius's condemnation of Eriugena's *De divisione naturae* could prevent Latin thinkers in the thirteenth century from engaging more deeply with the *corpus Dionysiacum* and its Eastern view of the beatific vision. When a new version, compiled in the first quarter of the thirteenth century by an anonymous Dominican monk in Paris, was circulated, the *corpus Dionysiacum* even gained textbook status. Together with John the Sarracen's readable Latin translation from 1167, this edition included Eriugena's ninth-century literal translation, Anastasius's translation of the Greek *scholia* that explained Eriugena's text and matched his choice of words, excerpts from Eriugena's *De divisione naturae*, Thomas Gallus's paraphrase, and three Latin commentaries on one book of the *corpus Dionysiacum*, the *Heavenly Hierarchy*, written by Eriugena, John the Sarracen, and Hugh of St. Victor.

Eriugena's and Athanasius's similar interpretations, must have struck most of his Western readers as distrustful of the true Eastern view on *Deus absconditus* and *Deus revelatus*, such that they no longer had the choice of appreciating it in its original meaning. Yet Hugh's was not the only influential reading of the Eastern tradition that would leave its mark on High Scholasticism in the thirteenth century.

IV

Scholastic Encounters

Burgundio of Pisa's above-mentioned translation of John Chrysostom's *Homily XV on the Gospel of St. John* and John's own pessimistic outlook concerning a vision of God seem to have exerted an influence similar to that of Dionysius the Areopagite and Hugh of St. Victor's refutation of him, if not an even greater influence, on early High Scholastic theologians.[1] Alexander of Hales, Hugh of St. Cher, and Guerric of St. Quentin all developed their debates on the basis of John Chrysostom's *Homily XV*, and most of them quoted it explicitly. Yet these three theologians nonetheless differ considerably from one another in their reading of the homily—a reading which is similar to that of Hugh of St. Victor, colored by certain Western presumptions on the scope of the divine reality—as much as they differ considerably in their implicit reliance on other sources, such as Dionysius and John Scotus Eriugena. As these early High Scholastic thinkers provided important distinctions that would be found later in Albert the Great's and Thomas Aquinas's theorizations on the beatific vision, it is valuable to review briefly their debates in chronological order and mark the key shifts in their teachings.

In his early *Glossa in IV libros Sententiarum* (written between 1223 and 1227), Alexander of Hales explains that God's essence is knowable in three different ways: "through itself" (*per se*), "through a form" (*per speciem*), and "through a similitude" (*per similitudinem*). By drawing on the metaphor of light, a medieval *topos* to account for cognitive acts, Alexander clarifies to whom and under which circumstances the divine essence is knowable in these ways. He identifies the

1. See, for instance: Dondaine 1952, pp. 100ff; Classen 1974.

first of these visions of God, the vision of God through Himself, as exclusively reserved for God Himself: the divine light is the light "as it is in the sun" and it therefore remains invisible or inaccessible to all creatures.[2] In this view of a core of the divine essence reserved for God alone, Alexander's divine light *per se* here is strongly reminiscent of Dionysius's *Deus absconditus*, the transcendent divine reality that is unknowable to all creatures. Yet nowhere in this passage does Alexander mention Dionysius as a source of influence on this thought.

Alexander's second light, however—the divine light of the form (*species*) or of the glory—is accessible to creatures under the circumstances of the beatific vision in heaven. This form (*species*) or glory, as Alexander conceives of it, is a directly emitted light from God, a light that is "in the air." It is through this light that God will be seen in the beatific vision.[3] Alexander further elaborates on this emanated light in the second book of his *Gloss on the Four Books of the Sentences*, where he explains that it is only visible when mixed with air, but remains invisible in itself.[4] This light analogy clarifies

2. Alexander Halensis, *Glossa in quatuor libros Sententiarum Petri Lombardi*, l. 1, d. 1 (ed. Quaracchi 12, p. 16, v. 8–16): "Respondeo: tripliciter est videre essentiam: per se, per speciem, per similitudinem. Primo modo videt solum Deus essentiam divinam; est enim *lux inaccessibilis*. Lux autem dupliciter sumi potest: ut est in aëre, vel ut est in sole. Ut est in sole, invisibilis est; ut est in aëre, pati potest oculus eius aspectum. Sic divina essentia in se est invisibilis; ut autem in unoquoque nostrum per gloriam est, sic est visibilis, et hoc appellatur species. Vel potest videri per similitudinem quae est creatura" (emphasis as in edition).

3. See note 2 above.

4. Alexander Halensis, *Glossa in quatuor libros Sententiarum*, l. 2, d. 8 (ed. Dondaine 1952, p. 106, v. 12–29, also: ed. Quaracchi 13, p. 79, v. 11–p. 80, v. 11, Quaracchi variants are noted as [Q:]): "Sicut aer a sole illuminatus nichil aliud uidetur esse nisi lux, non quod sui naturam perdat, sed quia lux in eo <preualet> ut ipsum lucidum [Q: lucem] esse estimetur: sic humana natura Deo adiuncta Deus per omnia dicitur esse, non quod deficiat [Q: desinat] esse natura, sed quod deitatis [Q: divinitatis] participationem accipiat ut solus Deus in ea esse uideatur. Item absente luce aer est obscurus, solum [Q: solis] autem lumen per se existens [Q: subsistens] nullo sensu corporeo comprehenditur; cum uero lumen aeri miscetur, tunc incipit apparere: ita ut in se ipso sensibus sit incomprehensibilis [Q: incomprehensibile], mixtum uero aeri sensibus possit comprehendi. Ac per hoc intellige diuinam essentiam per se incomprehensibilem esse, adiuncta [Q: adiunctam] uero intellectuali creature mirabili modo apparere: ita ut ipsa diuina essentia sola in ipsa intellectuali creatura appareat. Ipsius enim ineffabilis excellentia omnium natura [Q: omnem naturam] sui participem superat, ut nichil aliud in omnibus preter ipsam intelligentibus occurrat, dum per se ipsam nullo modo appareat. Sicut enim totus aer apparet lux totumque ferrum liquefactum ignis, manentibus tamen eorum substantiis ita sano intellectu accipiendum quod omnis creatura, siue corporea siue incorporea, solus Deus <esse> uidebitur, nature integritate manente, ut Deus in se incomprehensibilis in creatura quodammodo <comprehendatur>."

Alexander's interpretation of Augustine's *per speciem* terminology as a reading of divine appearance: inasmuch as the divine essence remains enclosed in itself, it is inaccessible to any other knower than God Himself, but inasmuch as it shares its own nature by way of appearance in a medium, as a form (*species*) it becomes visible. Read in this light, Alexander of Hales's interpretation of the beatific vision is closely linked to that of Dionysius yet again. The vision through a form (*species*) implies that it is God's revealed essence that is seen, His revealed essence shared and made to appear by Him so that the creature can grasp Him. None of this conception, however, ought to be understood through the Western reading of the divine reality, which we have seen in Eriugena and Hugh of St. Victor and according to which God's revealed essence is not identical with his disclosed essence. On the contrary, Alexander here appears to be a most astute reader of the Greek Christian understanding of the divine, in interpreting it as one and the same reality under the two different aspects of *Deus absconditus* and *Deus revelatus*.

The third and lowest light that Alexander mentions at the beginning of his *Gloss on the Four Books of the Sentences*, however, the light of similitude, is different from the light in itself and the light of the form (*species*). The third light explicitly constitutes a creature, and through it, God is visible to humans in this life. Alexander's conception of the beatific vision therefore does not draw any distinction between essential knowledge of God and comprehension of God. In fact, it need not do so, because the modality of the different aspects of enclosed (divine light *per se*) and diffused (divine light of the species) divine reality already points to the difference between creaturely understanding of God and divine self-understanding. Yet at the same time, we see that Alexander reshaped the meaning of Augustine's form (*species*) in his *Gloss* to refer to an aspectual or modal diffusion of God "in the air." This is a meaning that Augustine, with his understanding of the form (*species*) as identical to God's transcendent, enclosed self, did not entertain.

Alexander's perceptive reading of the Eastern view, however, was not destined to have a substantial impact on later generations.

The Latin debates, with few exceptions, showed little interest in his reading, but rather sided with a view of the divine essence that was Augustinian in character and that became increasingly couched in Aristotelian explanations as time went on. The beginning of this lasting trend can be seen in Hugh of St. Cher's *Postil on John.*[5] Hugh (ca. 1200–19 March 1263) was a key figure in the formative period of the Dominican order, but also served high offices for the curia. In 1227, two years after joining the Dominicans, Hugh became provincial of his order in France, and in 1230 Regent Master of the Couvent St. Jacques in Paris. In 1233, Hugh was sent to Constantinople as a papal legate by Pope Gregory IX, and some eleven years later he was made Cardinal Priest under Pope Innocent IV, with his titular church at Santa Sabina in Rome. Hugh's major academic contributions were in biblical theology. In addition, he wrote the first *correctorium* of the Bible, and with the assistance of some five hundred fellow Dominicans, compiled the first concordance to it. Within this academic context, therefore, and probably at the same time that Alexander of Hales was authoring the *Glossa*, Hugh wrote his *Postils*, a work that is probably the most extreme example of an interpretation of the Greek sources through an Augustinian lens, all while using a conception of the divine essence framed in Aristotelian language.

In commenting on John the Evangelist's assertion that "no one ever sees God," Hugh lists different ways in which God can in fact be seen, in close reliance on Chrysostom's *Homily XV on the Gospel of St. John.* These are "by an understanding through creatures, also through faith, likewise through the gift of prophecy, likewise in rapture as St. Paul and Adam, <and finally> likewise in the afterlife face to face." Yet, as Hugh immediately clarifies, "in none of these ways is <God> seen in His substance. Rather, he is cognized in His act (*sub actu suo*)."[6] With this reading, Hugh unequivocally suggests that

5. Hugh of St. Cher commented on all four gospels in his postils. See: Hugo de Sancto Caro (ed. Lyon 1645).

6. Hugo de Sancto Caro, *Postille sur l'évangile de saint Jean*, c. 1, v. 16 (ed. Dondaine 1952, p. 119, v. 1, 10–14): "*Deum nemo uidit unquam.* <...> Videtur enim intellectu per creaturas; item per fidem; item per donum prophetie; item in raptu, ut Paulus et Adam; item per subiectam

God's substance and act are ontologically distinct from one another. This he corroborates in the following statement about the Fathers:

> For the Fathers were found to have seen Him thus; <their> vision happened by way of a condescension, not by way of His bare substance. For if they had seen His very substance, they would have never contemplated it in differing ways. For it is something simple, without shape, and not compounded.[7]

With this view of God's substance, Hugh is certainly in line with an Augustinian reading of the divine reality, which underscores its simplicity and inseparability into aspects. Hugh limits the divine reality as such to God's substance and disallows for an understanding of an aspect or act of God that is open to be seen by His creatures. This alone would suffice to deny that the blessed will see God's substance in the afterlife. Yet with his last reason why such a substantial vision is impossible, Hugh proposes an even more drastic apophatic view. In claiming that all blessed will see the very same of God because of His simplicity, Hugh seems to have forgotten Augustine's argument against a comprehensive view of the divine essence in the beatific vision, according to which everyone will see different features of God's substance in accordance with the different mansions to be inhabited in heaven.[8]

Be this second point as it may, Hugh's view of limitation of the divine reality to God's hiddenness is repeated later in the text. There, Hugh suggests that the evangelist

---

creaturam, ut Moyses et Iacob et alii patres; item in patria facie ad faciem, 1 Cor. 13. Nullo istorum modorum uidetur in substantia sua, sed ab actu suo cognoscitur."

7. Ibid. (ed. Dondaine 1952, p. 119, v. 14–p. 120, v. 17): "Quod enim patres leguntur eum uidisse, condescentionis fuit uisio, non nude substantie. Si enim ipsam uidissent substantiam, nunquam eam differenter considerassent: simplex enim quedam et infigurabilis et incomposita est."

8. Medieval debates about heavenly mansions ultimately go back to two biblical verses in John 14:2 and 14:23 where Jesus promises his disciples that they will dwell with him in God's house. See: Iohannis 14:2 (Vulgata 2007): *In domo Patris mei mansiones multæ sunt si quominus dixissem vobis quia vado parare vobis locum.* Iohannis 14:23 (Vulgata 2007): *Respondit Jesus et dixit ei: Si quis diligit me sermonem meum servabit et Pater meus diliget eum et ad eum veniemus et mansionem apud eum faciemus.* For the discussion in Aquinas, see: pp. 148–149 and article four, note 6, on p. 154.

> John does not intend to say that we shall, in the afterlife, contemplate God's substance in any way because this is impossible for all creatures. <...> Therefore, John intends a mirror and an enigma because, in the afterlife, we shall see God by an immediate reception of light, nonetheless, <we shall> not <see> His essence, but <we shall see Him> as glory, as goodness, as truth.[9]

Glory, goodness, and truth are apparently meant to describe in greater detail God's act, a reality that is not an aspect of God Himself in Hugh's eyes, but rather something really distinct from His substance. As a consequence, therefore, Hugh of St. Cher seems to be the Latin theologian who limits the divine essence to *Deus absconditus* and, as a result, views the divine acts as condescension rather than an aspect of the divine reality. Matters could not possibly get more apophatic in a Latin teaching of the beatific vision than at this moment.[10]

Another Latin theologian, Guerric of St. Quentin, the Dominican Regent Master of the Couvent St. Jacques in Paris from 1233–1242 just before Albert the Great took over his office, continued Hugh of St. Cher's trend of reading God's substance in Augustinian terms, but he introduced an important shift in the debates. In his commentary on the Gospel of St. John, chapter 1, Guerric clarified that Chrysostom's *Homily XV on the Gospel of St. John* ought not to be read as denying the beatific vision to the blessed. Indeed, according to Guerric, Chrysostom's statement that "not only will the prophets not see that which is God, but neither will the angels nor the archangels," was read by "some" (*quidam*) to state "that God's substance is never seen, not even by the glorified."[11] These "some," so it seems,

---

9. Hugo de Sancto Caro, *Postille sur l'évangile de saint Jean*, c. 1, v. 16 (ed. Dondaine 1952, p. 120, v. 26–28, 30–32): "<...> Iohannes non intendit dicere quod nos aliquo modo consideremus Dei substantiam in patria, quia hoc est impossibile omni creature. <...> Intendit ergo Iohannes speculum et enigma, quia in patria per immediatam acceptionem luminis aperte uidebimus Deum, non tamen essentiam, sed ut gloriam, ut bonitatem, ut ueritatem."

10. Compare Hugh's view here with Bonaventure's statement on the heretical teaching concerning the beatific vision in section VI of the general introduction, note 6, below.

11. Guerricus de Sancto Quintino, *Commentaire de l'évangile de saint Jean*, c. 1 (ed. Dondaine 1952, p. 121, v. 18–22): "Ipsum quod est Deus non solum prophete, sed neque angeli uiderunt neque archangeli; sed si interrogaueris eos, audies de substantia quidem nichil respondentes, gloria uero in excelsis Deo cantantes. Per hanc auctoritatem dixerunt quidam quod nunquam uidetur substantia, etiam a glorificatis."

included Hugh of St. Cher, but their reading is false in Guerric's eyes. The correct reading of Chrysostom's statement in his homily should rather be that the term "substance evidently corresponds to <God's> fullness."[12] With this reading, Guerric manifestly reinterprets the meaning of Chrysostom's substance in the well-known Augustinian distinction between comprehension of God's essence and cognition of God's essence, and no longer draws the ontological distinction that Hugh had drawn between God's essence and his emanated light as glory, goodness, and truth. Yet while in Augustine this distinction between comprehension and cognition was commonly applied to the blessed saint who cognizes God's essence, Guerric uses it in reference to the divine substance, and distinguishes between its fullness (which would presumably equal comprehension) and its essential features (which would presumably equal cognition of the essence).

With this reinterpretation of Chrysostom's term *substantia* by means of an Augustinian distinction, Guerric conveniently shifted the Latin engagements with the Greek Christian texts to a territory in which the theologians felt safe. No longer did he have to discuss the question of what it is of God that is seen in terms of divine aspects, which are either concealed or open; he could now discuss it in terms of the extent to which God's essence is seen and which of its features. This reinterpretation was arguably not far off from what the Greek Christian texts actually entailed. After all, divine aspects and divine features seem to amount to the same thing, granted the divine aspects are truly conceived to be divine. Yet the Greek reading, as we have seen, was different from the interpretations that most Latin readers gave these Greek texts. As a result, what could have amounted to a small disagreement in fact became a large battleground of theological negotiations for more than a decade. What is more, some of these negotiations were complicated by an additional event in the history of Latin theology, the introduction and appropriation of Avicenna's thought, particularly his *Metaphysics*.

---

12. Ibid. (ed. Dondaine 1952, p. 121, v. 24–25): "<...> substantia uidelicet secundum eius plenitudinem."

V

Avicennian Beginnings

Parallel to the views found in Hugh of St. Cher and Guerric of St. Quentin, who were reliant on Greek Christian sources, early Scholastic thought about the beatific vision saw a second group of teachings which were infused with the philosophy of Avicenna. The two major proponents of this group were William of Auvergne (1180–1249, Bishop of Paris from 1228) in his early work *On the Retributions of the Saints* (before 1230), and the anonymous author of the Douai MS 434, q. 9 (ca. 1231–1236).[1] Their views did not converge into a single explanation of the beatific vision. William's explanation in particular illustrates the struggles that early Scholastics faced in weaving philosophical insights into their theologies, and shows how meanings of terms can shift dramatically in the process. What united these two thinkers, however, was their use of some insights from Avicennian epistemology within their eschatologies, even though the manner in which they used them differed significantly.

The insights that Avicenna, the great Islamic philosopher of the eleventh century whose works were translated into Latin in the late twelfth century in Toledo, offered the Latin theologians for explaining the beatific vision ultimately derived from his discussions concerning the epistemology of separate substances, beings that exist as pure forms in the supralunary realm.[2] Avicenna's *Metaphysics*, as

1. Dondaine places the anonymous author of Douai MS 434 in the tradition of Dionysius the Areopagite, as he makes use of the *corpus Dionysiacum* in his considerations of the beatific vision and connects it to the appropriated Avicennian concepts as described. For this complementary reading, see Dondaine 1952, pp. 84–88. For other more conventional readings of the history of the role of Avicennian influences on the Latin discussions of the beatific vision, see section VI, note 3.

2. For the history of the translations of all of Avicenna's works see: Hasse 2000; Polloni 2020, pp. 15–19.

Dag Hasse has convincingly argued, played a major role in the early Latin adoptions of his epistemology, much more so than his book *On the Soul.*[3] In book 3, chapter 8, of his *Metaphysics*, Avicenna inquired how human knowledge of things, given that their intelligible forms are accidents in the intellect, can be of their quiddities or substances.[4] He explained that this is possible, but only for human knowledge of sublunary beings, not of separate substances. The latter can only exist in one mode of being; they are concrete and intelligible particulars at once. Physical things in the sublunary world, in contrast, do not possess these two ontological features simultaneously. They are either concrete and exist in the world as particulars, or they are intelligible and exist in the mind as universals. They can, therefore, be true accidents in the human intellect,[5] which stands in contrast to separate substances. Indeed, since these substances possess characteristics of both particularity and intelligibility at once, they cannot doff one of them, say particularity, and come to exist in the human mind as

---

3. Both books are parts of his encyclopedic magnum opus *Book of the Healing* (*Kitāb al-shifā'*). The reception of Avicenna's *Metaphysica* (translated by Dominicus Gundisalvi in Spain) and *De anima* (translated in 1152–1166, also in Spain) begins much later in the Latin West, fully with William of Auvergne in the 1230s, as Dag Hasse has shown. See: Hasse 2000, pp. 18–23 and 44–45.

4. Avicenna, *Liber de Philosophia prima sive Scientia divina*, t. 3, c. 8 (ed. Van Riet 1977, p. 157, v. 43–p. 158, v. 57): "De scientia quaestio est. Potest enim aliquis dicere quod scientia est acquisita ex formis eorum quae sunt exspoliatis a suis materiis, quae sunt formae substantiarum et accidentium. Sed si formae accidentium sunt accidentia, tunc formae substantiarum quomodo erunt accidentia? Substantia enim sibi ipsi substantia est; igitur quidditas eius substantia est; itaque quidditas eius non est in subiecto ullo modo, sed eius quidditas stabilis est, sive accipiatur secundum quod apprehenditur ab intellectu, sive accipiatur secundum esse extrinsecum. Ad quod dico quod quidditas substantiae substantia est sic quod in signatis est non ut in subiecto. Et haec assignatio est quidditatis substantiarum intellectarum, quoniam quidditas est cuius natura est esse in signatis non ut in subiecto, scilicet quoniam haec quidditas intelligitur res cuius esse est in signatis non ut in subiecto. Esse vero eius in intellectu secundum hanc assignationem, non est in definitione eius secundum quod ipsa est substantia."

5. Ibid. (ed. Van Riet 1977, p. 159, v. 83–160, v. 93): "Si quis autem dixerit nobis: 'iam dixistis quod substantia est id cuius quidditas non est in subiecto omnino, et posuistis quidditatem eorum quae sciuntur in subiecto,' respondebo nos iam dixisse quod non est ut in subiecto in singularibus omnino. Si autem dixerint: 'igitur iam posuistis quidditatem substantiae aliquando esse accidens, aliquando esse substantiam, quod iam prohibueratis,' dicam nos siquidem prohibuisse quidditatem aliquam in singularibus aliquando esse accidens, aliquando esse substantiam ita ut sit in singularibus aliquo egens subiecto, et in eisdem non egens subiecto ullo modo, sed non prohibuimus quod intellectum de illa quidditate intelligatur fieri accidens, scilicet cum est in anima non sicut pars."

universal accidents. Their quiddities are, rather, ontologically fixed to having both characteristics at once.[6]

This ontological dilemma did not prompt Avicenna to give up entirely on the possibility of human cognition of separate substances. Rather, he construed it as the exception to the rule, suggesting that it is not the quiddities of the separate substances that come to exist in the human mind as universals (which would be impossible), but rather ideas or similitudes of their quiddities.

> <I>t is only the ideas (*intentiones*) of their quiddities that are realized in the intellects of humans, not the <quiddities> themselves. And our judgment of them is just as the judgment of other corporeal substances that we understand, except in one regard, namely that <...> they lack nothing but that they are understood in their being as they are and the soul is sealed (*sigilletur*) by them. <...> Yet since what is found of them in us are the impressions (*impressiones*) which, without a doubt, have been made similar (*assimilantur*) to the separate substances, and this is also our knowledge of them.[7]

Avicenna's argumentative move here clearly saved the unique ontology of separate substances as much as it did human cognition as

6. Ibid. (ed. Van Riet 1977, p. 160, v. 98–p. 161, v. 10): "Sensus enim nostrae dictionis quod ipsae per se intelliguntur hic est scilicet quod ipsae intelligunt se, quamvis alia non intelligant eas, et etiam quia per se sunt spoliatae a materia et ab eius appendiciis non quod ad intelligendum eas necesse sit animae eas exspoliare. Si autem dixerimus quia hoc vel consimile est intellectum de eis omnino, vel dixerimus quia ad esse id quod intelligitur de eis non est opus nisi ut essentiae earum sint in anima, tunc iam destruxerimus essentias earum esse separatas, nec erunt ipsaemet forma animae hominis: nam si essent, profecto eveniret quod in una anima acquisita esset forma totius, et sciretur omne quod est in effectu, et esset hoc uni tantum animae; ceterae vero animae remanerent non habentes quod intelligerent, eo quod aliqua una anima susciperet eas."

7. Ibid. (ed. Van Riet 1977, p. 161, v. 14–20 and p. 162, v. 33–36): "Igitur de illis rebus non inquiritur in intellectibus humanis nisi intentiones quidditatum suarum, non ipsae; et est iudicium de eis sicut iudicium de aliis intellectis substantiis corporalibus, excepto uno, scilicet quod illae aliae egent abstractione quousque abstrahatur ab eis intentio quae possit intelligi, istae vero non egent aliquo nisi ut intelligantur esse ut sunt, et sigilletur anima per eas. <...> Sed quia quod invenitur in nobis de illis est impressiones quae assimilantur eis sine dubio, et hoc est nostra scientia de illis; hoc autem vel acquiritur nobis in nostris corporibus vel in nostris animabus." For more extended discussions concerning Avicenna's theory of human cognition of separate substances, see: Black 2014, pp. 213–236; Krause 2014, pp. 108–113.

an accident thereof.[8] This move, however, was a source of some concern for the early Latin appropriations of Avicenna's insights from this chapter in his *Metaphysics*. To grasp how William of Auvergne and the anonymous author of Douai MS 434 decontextualized and recontextualized Avicenna's ideas, we have to examine first Avicenna's own understandings of the concepts of "impressions" and their "assimilation to separate substances," and subsequently compare and contrast them to their Latin appropriations.

Following Aristotle, Avicenna operated in a philosophical framework according to which the human intellect would be likened to its object in virtue of a shared formal identity between them. This would happen in virtue of an intelligible form, possessing the same quiddity with the thing in the world, that would come to exist in the intellect. For Avicenna, quiddity refers to all essential characteristics that an object in the world and the identical intelligible form in the human intellect possess, that is, it refers to all the characteristics or definitional features that, for instance, make a human being a "rational animal" and a dog a "brute animal." The quiddity that is in the mind is nothing other than the quiddity that is in the world, only that it exists in a different mode of being in each case.

In Avicenna's eyes, what holds for these objective characteristics also extends to the "impressions" which the separate substances leave in the human intellect, with the exception, of course, that it is not their quiddities that come to exist in the human intellect, but the respective images or assimilations of them. Still, regardless of the precise ontology of the intelligible form—whether it is the very quiddity of a sublunary thing or the idea of a separate substance—Avicenna took it to determine the intellect to a formal identity with its cognized object, to share in all essential characteristics of the cognized object, and to be likened to the object in its very content.[9]

8. Ibid. (ed. Van Riet 1977, p. 163, v. 38–43): "<...> unde quia sunt impressiones animae, non essentiae illarum rerum, nec exemplum quasi illae res non remaneant existentes nec in materiis corporalibus nec animabus, tunc id quod subiectum non habet, erit id cuius multiplicatur species sine causa ex qua pendeat ullo modo: igitur sunt accidentes in anima."

9. This is particularly clear from an elision from the Arabic original. See Van Riet's Latin translation of it in the critical apparatus: ibid. (ed. Van Riet 1977, p. 158, v. 57): "57 substantia] <...>

Engaging with the concepts from Avicenna's *Metaphysics*, William of Auvergne was probably the first Latin theologian to present an eschatology that centered on the concepts of "impression" and "assimilation." Yet he did so against the background of his own Augustinian commitments, and thus considerably shifted the meaning of these concepts as found in Avicenna. William's integration of the two divergent systems in his *On the Retribution of Saints* opened by situating ultimate happiness in the perfection of the human soul, a perfection which he specified further to lie in the beatific vision. He defined the human soul's nature to be "a mirror that is potentially all intelligible objects."[10] The question is in which way this is so. The idea of the soul's potentially being all intelligibles certainly derives from Aristotle,[11] but William's blending of it with the mirror

---

(scilicet non est definitio substantiae quod est in intellectu non in subiecto sed definitio eius est quod sive sit in intellectu sive non sit tamen esse eius in singularibus non est in subiecto si autem dicitur quod intellectus etiam est de singularibus respondetur quod singulare est id quod cum ei substantia acquisita est emanant ex ea actiones eius et dispositiones eius) *add.* A." For the Arabic original and English translation thereof, see: Avicenna (ed. Marmura 2005, pp. 107–108).

10. Guilielmus Alvernus, *De retributionibus sanctorum* (ed. Hotot 1674, 316 2 H): "Dicamus igitur, quoniam cum vis intellectiva animae humanae speculum sit potentialiter omnium intelligibilium, ex necessitate perfectio ejus ultima erit, ut haec sit in effectu completo, quod est, ut sit speculum omnium intelligibilium."

11. Aristoteles, *De anima*, l. 3, lect. 1 (429a10–429a23), trans. vet. (ed. Gauthier 1985, p. 445): "De parte autem anime qua cognoscit et sapit, siue separabili siue non separabili secundum magnitudinem, set secundum rationem, et, si ad eandem est, quam habet differenciam. Et quomodo forte fit ipsum intelligere, si igitur est intelligere sicut sentire aut pati aliquid sit ab intelligibili, aut aliquod huiusmodi alterum sit. Inpassibile ergo oportet esse, susceptiua autem speciei et potencia huiusmodi est, set non hoc. Et non similiter se habere sicut sensitiuum ad sensibilia, sic intellectiuum ad intelligibilia. Necesse est itaque, quoniam omnia intelligit, inmixtum esse, sicut dicit Anaxagoras, ut imperet. Hoc autem est ut cognoscat despectum. Apparere enim prohiberet extraneum et ei obiectum. Quare neque est ipsius esse naturam neque unam. Set ad hoc quod possibilis sit uocatus anime intellectus. Dico autem intellectum quo opinatur et intelligit anima; et hic nichil est actu eorum que sunt ante intelligere." For Michael Scot's Latin translation from the Arabic, see: ibid., l. 3, tx. 1–5 (ed. Crawford 1953, p. 379, v. 1–6, p. 380, v. 1–3, p. 381, v. 1–5, p. 383, v. 1–5, p. 387, v. 1–6): "De parte autem anime per quam anima cognoscit et intelligit (utrum est differens aut non differens in magnitudine, sed in intentione) perscrutandum est de differentia que sit, et quomodo sit formare per intellectum. <...> Dicamus igitur quod, si formare per intellectum est sicut sentire, aut patietur quoquo modo ab intellecto, aut aliud simile. <...> Oportet igitur ut sit non passivum, sed recipit formam, et est in potentia sicut illud, non illud. Et erit dispositio eius secundum similitudinem: sicut sentiens apud sensibilia, sic intellectus apud intelligibilia. <...> Oportet igitur, si intelligit omnia, ut sit non mixtum, sicut dixit Anaxagoras, ut imperet, scilicet ut cognoscat. Si enim in eo apparuerit, apparens impediet alienum, quia est aliud. <...> Sic non habebit naturam nisi istam, scilicet quod est possibilis. Illud igitur de anima quod dicitur intellectus (et dico intellectum illud per quod distinguimus et cogitamus) non est in actu aliquod entium antequam intelligat."

metaphor indicates a peculiar reading. What he expressed is that the soul is essentially reflective or imitative of all things in the world, and that it therefore has the potential to be assimilated to all things in the world, including God in the beatific vision in which "we shall see Him as he is."[12]

The soul's ability to reflect and imitate here, however, was not bound to the characteristics, features, or content of the objects in the world. Assimilation of the soul to its object did not stop at the level of becoming identical to the object in a cognitive act in actuality. Rather, in William's reading, this ability of the soul entailed its assimilation to its objects on the subjective level. Assimilation to the object entailed a becoming similar or congruent to it in being, very much in line with Augustine's understanding of the mind as a similitude of God. Inasmuch as the soul or the intellect (in this connection, William used the two terms interchangeably) is assimilated to its cognitive objects, the intellect's mirror-like qualities become object-like operatively and ontologically, so that the soul is capable of reflecting and imitating its cognized object maximally. As can be seen from his text, William did not strictly distinguish between the two kinds of objective and subjective assimilation. This ultimately meant that assimilation did not entail an intransitive actualization of the intellect that would result in a formal identity brought about by a determinate intelligible form which shared the very same essential characteristics with its object, as was the case for Avicenna. Rather, assimilation of the intellect, in William's eyes, entailed an adjustment or congruence in which the intellect would be rendered capable of entering into a transitive relational act of cognition with its object that did not exist before.

William applied this same kind of understanding to the beatific vision. For him, the principle that ontological congruence is achieved through intellectual assimilation held universally true. Portraying the beatific vision as "assimilation of our intellect" to God, William

---

12. Guilielmus Alvernus, *De retributionibus sanctorum* (ed. Hotot 1674, pp. 316 2 H–317 1 A) "Intellexit autem hoc Joannes Evangelista, et expressit in tertio primae Canonicae suae dicens. Filii Dei sumus, sed nondum apparuit quid erimus, cum autem apparuerit similes ei erimus, quoniam videbimus eum sicuti est."

took this to mean that "our intellect will then be of necessity an imitation in which the similitude of the original shines forth."[13] The way in which he envisioned this ontological imitation to occur was not, as Augustine maintained, in virtue of God's sheer presence to the intellect, but rather, following Avicenna's insights, in virtue of "an impression of His similitude." This, William emphasized, was required for cognizing everything that lies outside our intellect.[14] Hence, the impression of God's similitude is not an object of cognition in William's eyes, but rather that which itself assimilates the intellect to God, and renders the intellect congruent or similar to Him in its being, to the extent that this is possible. Through this newly established congruence, the intellect is able to cognize God.[15]

---

13. Ibid. (ed. Hotot 1674, p. 317 1 A–B): "Quare visio, qua videbimus Deum, quem utique in gloria deitatis non videbimus, nisi oculo intellectus, erit assimilatio nostri intellectus ad ipsum, licet pro captu modico suo, et angustia receptibilitatis suae. Quia ergo ipse in seipso, et per seipsum exemplar est, cujus exemplum est universum, licet incomparabilis distantiae, ac similitudinis ad illum, erit ex necessitate noster intellectus tunc exemplum, in quo relucebit similitudo expemplaris illius, prout quidem et naturalis capacitas, et meritorum dignitas impum adjuverit." See also: ibid. (ed. Hotot 1674, p. 317 1 C–D): "Facies enim nostri intellectus ad faciem dicti speculi, quod et Dei facies est, et Dei vultus, sicut dicimus, applicata, atque coaptata, faciem illam repraesentabit expressa similitudine, similiter et in sequentibus: Cognoscam autem, sicut et cognitus sum. Quid est hoc dicere? nisi quemadmodum Deus verbum in seipso videt haec omnia, tanquam in speculo expressissimae, ac lucidissimae repraesentationis, sic et ego quantum ad vim intellectivam factus speculum perfectae (sicut diximus) assimilationis ad ipsum, cognoscam in meipso, quaecunque in me ipso, quaecunque in huiusmodi speculo, per irradiationem primi speculi resultabunt."

14. Ibid. (ed. Hotot 1674, p. 318 1 E–F): "Omne enim, quod sic extra animas nostras est, non apprehenditur ab animabus nostris, nisi per impressionem similitudinis suae, hinc est, quod ea quae in corporibus nostris sunt, videlicet ossa, intestina, nervi, naturaliter ignoramus, quantumcunque proxima sint nobis essentialiter, et animabus nostris, quoniam praedicto modo extras animas sunt. Haec autem omnia induximus, ut videas, quoniam non praesentia essentialis, aut propinquitas perficit cognitionem, sed impressio similitudinis, aut sigillatio animarum nostrarum <...>."

15. Ibid. (ed. Hotot 1674, p. 318 1 H–318 2 E): "<...> nos autem planius respondebimus ad hoc et dicemus, quia impressio quae fit in oculo a re visa non videtur, sed magis res a qua impressa est, et ad hunc modum se habere de formis, et impressionibus imaginabilibus et intelligibilibus, quia non ipsae imaginantur, aut intelliguntur, sed magis res, quarum sigillationes, et similitudines sunt, nisi forte quis de eis considerationem per se fecerit, quemadmodum, et nos sic loquentes facimus: sic ergo aspiciens in rem aliquam non id, quod habet in oculo, sed rem illam videt per illud, sic semetipsam intuens mens humana in gloria illa, non semetipsam proprie videt, sed Deum cujus imago, et similitudo tunc est, et repraesentatio pro modo, qui ei congruit, perfecta."

William's epistemological commitments and his combining Avicennian insights with his traditional Augustinianism no doubt contributed to an increased use of philosophical ideas in eschatology during the generations that followed. Yet his appropriation of philosophical insights did not extend to preserving the meanings these ideas had in their original contexts. Rather, the opposite was the case. William found ways of explaining the beatific vision by way of the philosophical terms "assimilation," "impression," and "similitude," but none of them carried with them the connotations of identifying the intellect with the thing in the world by way of an intelligible that is formally identical to its essence, as Avicenna wrote in his *Metaphysics*. What was at stake for William was a qualitatively sufficient agreement in ontology between the one seeing and the thing seen, a coordination in ontology for the possibility of a new cognitive relation. Thanks to this stark reinterpretation of the meaning of Avicennian concepts, William did not need to worry about mediation in the beatific vision. Directness was ensured in virtue of ontological congruence rather than intellectual identification with the object. This may explain why William never seriously questioned the directness of the beatific vision in this early work of his, and why this ontological reinterpretation of Avicenna was not a stumbling block for his theory of the beatific vision as propounded here. Yet the dilemma of mediation emerged precisely at the point where the Avicennian assimilation was no longer reinterpreted in its meaning, but appropriated and preserved by Latin thinkers in its objective meaning.

❂ ❂ ❂

The dilemma of mediation in the beatific vision triggered a new distinction in the debate between a subjective, disposing medium and an objective, representative one. After the middle of the 1230s, many theologians, including Albert the Great and Thomas Aquinas, would rely on this distinction in their own solutions to the beatific vision, which held that the blessed would be elevated by a subjective, disposing medium, but that due to God's direct presence to the intellect, there would no longer be need for an objective, representative one. What seemed to them like the natural solution to this dilemma emerged only after the early works of William of Auvergne, and appeared in exemplary fashion in the writings of the anonymous author of the Douai MS 434, q. 9.

Moving towards a more authentic reading of the Avicennian similitude in the cognizer, the anonymous author began his inquiry into the question of the beatific vision by distinguishing between an internal and an external similitude for cognizing God. Only the former would actually allow the intellect to see Him:

> By the internal similitude, we shall truly see the One showing His own Form (*ipsam speciem*) because in this similitude by which we shall be similar to Him, His original will be seen. By the external <similitude> which is not a form of the One seeing but an accident or an extrinsic sign, we shall not see Him.[16]

The anonymous author's distinction here between internal and external similitudes is not meant to indicate a local distinction, as in distinguishing between something that is in the mind and something that is outside the mind. Rather, the anonymous author meant to specify the difference in effects that these two similitudes have on the mind. The external similitude affects the powers of the intellect in actualizing its natural capacity to a determinate object of cognition that is naturally within the range of the intellect. As such, it is an accident in the intellect and an extrinsic sign pointing to or signifying an object in the world. The internal similitude, in contrast, affects the powers of the intellect in such a way that it conforms the intellect to God, that it relates it to God. This internal similitude acts very much like a qualitative change in the intellect in that it alters its

16. Anonymous, *Douai MS 434*, q. 9 (ed. Dondaine 1952, p. 108, v. 46–49): "Per similitudinem interiorem uidebimus uere demonstrantem ipsam speciem, quia in ipsa similitudine qua similes ei erimus uidebitur eius exemplar; per exteriorem que non est uidentis forma, sed accidens aut signum extrinsecum, non uidebimus." See also: ibid. (ed Dondaine 1952, p. 108, v. 33–39): "Necesse est enim similitudinem esse mediam, de qua similitudine dicitur 1 Ioh. 3: cum apparuerit similes ei erimus quia tunc cognoscemus sicut cogniti sumus. Aut per medium distans quod non est in nobis sed extra, inter nos et uisibile: sic non per medium. Ipsum enim uisibile in nobis erit et in nobis apparebit, et uidebitur ut presens sensui interiori qui informabitur a specie uisa qua uiuet et cognoscet."

natural capacity for a new and higher object of cognition, God. For the anonymous author, following Augustinian insights, the internal similitude or medium that brings about the intellectual alteration is not only cognitive, but also affective; "it is truth but also love, or a power of truth and love," and as such it is "an image or a similitude of the Trinity."[17]

As such, the similitude was not removed from God, the object of cognition. Repeatedly, the anonymous author related the metaphysics of the similitude, with its operative and relational properties, to God Himself: "The similitude of this type is not disjoined from the Truth itself, but is the very form impressed by the truth present to the mind, the image of God."[18] The conformity to God as effected by the similitude in the intellect of the blessed is not of a metaphysical nature, but rather of a relational one, in that it "is <a conformity> between them."[19] For the anonymous author, the internal similitude thus operates as a necessary link or bond to God.[20]

---

17. Ibid. (ed. Dondaine 1952, p. 110, v. 125–135): "Ex his ergo habemus secundum membrum quasi determinatum, scilicet per quod medium oportet intelligere: scilicet per medium quod est ueritas et aut amor, aut uirtus ueritatis et amoris. Sine enim omni uirtute ueritatis impossibile est ueritatem aliquam intelligere, sine uirtute amoris impossibile est diligere. Necesse est ergo ad hoc quod uideamus, quod diligamus: et ita necesse est habere uirtutem in nobis ueritatis et amoris. Ecce ymago uel similitudo Trinitatis, quod patet per nomina: uirtute enim potentia, ueritate sapientia, amore ipsa dilectio notatur. Hec uirtus quando erit in nobis et apparebit, tunc poterimus ueritatem presentem uidere quam dilexerimus. Et hoc est quod dixit Apostolus: *cum apparuerit, similes ei erimus*; non dicit *eis*, sed *ei*. Illa enim similitudo est illa uirtus" (emphases as in edition).

18. Ibid. (ed. Dondaine 1952, p. 111, v. 155–156): "<...> huiusmodi enim similitudo non separatur ab ipsa ueritate, sed est forma ipsa impressa ab ipsa presenti ueritate in mente ymagine Dei."

19. Ibid. (ed. Dondaine 1952, p. 112, v. 192 and 197–200): "Dicimus quod ista similitudo est conformitas <...>. Dicitur etiam similitudo conuenientia unius ad alium non secundum commune quod est in utroque, sed secundum quod est inter illa: sic dicitur hic similitudo non ab eo quod in illis est, sed ab eo quod est inter illos, hominem et Deum. Quod autem inter eos est, est amor <...>."

20. Ibid. (ed. Dondaine 1952, p. 108, v. 29–33): "Contendimus quod uidebitur Deus per medium. Sed hoc dupliciter contingit intelligi; quia aut per medium quod est inter potentiam naturalem anime, que est ymago Dei creata, et inter ipsam diuinam essentiam uisibilem que est ymago iuxta quam prior creata est aut similitudo: et sic uerum est quod per medium uidebimus." See also: ibid. (ed. Dondaine 1952, p. 113, v. 211–215): "Similitudo enim dicit relationem que in se nihil aliud est quam ipsa impressio, ut ita loquar, uirtutis ueri amoris ab ymagine increata; ut ymago creata sit quasi loco cere, teste Augustino, ymago increata Trinitas loco sigilli, ipsa similitudo media impressio uel infusio per quam similes erimus in gloria."

The ontology and activity of the internal similitude thus resolved, the anonymous author was free to theorize about the precise object of the beatific vision. Unquestioned for him was the avowal of a face-to-face vision.[21] The anonymous author did not side with the pessimism of Dionysian theology, even though he referenced it repeatedly.[22] Instead, in striking similarity to some ideas propounded later by Guerric of St. Quentin and Albert the Great, the anonymous pleaded for a distinction between a vision of God "as He is," which he endorsed, and a comprehensive vision, which he denied. To see God's "essence as essence," he reasoned, would amount "to comprehending in seeing Him, in such a way that nothing lies concealed, or whose ends can be encompassed." This precise formulation of the anonymous author's denial of comprehension may sound like a denial of a vision of God's essence. Yet for him, the emphasis lay on the last two terms of the phrase "essence *as essence*." Indeed, he unequivocally clarified that it concerned nothing but a denial of

21. Ibid. (ed. Dondaine 1952, p. 108, v. 40–41): "Ad illud quod obiectum est ex utraque parte, respondendum est per diuisionem. Videbimus enim *facie ad faciem* <...>" (emphasis as in edition). See also note 23 below.

22. Ibid. (ed. Dondaine 1952, p. 110, v. 111–115): "Notandum ergo quod omnis essentia intelligibilis est intelligibilis immediate, per potentiam, primo per actum; unde actus facit cognoscere potentiam, et potentia siue uirtus essentiam, cum non sint nisi tria in omni re, teste Dionysio: in tria diuiduntur secundum se supramundana ratione omnes diuini intellectus in essentiam, uirtutem et operationem." See also: Pseudo-Dionysius Areopagita, *De caelesti hierarchia*, c. 11, sect. 67, trans. Eriugenae (Dionysiaca t. 2, pp. 930–931): "<...> sed quoniam in tria dividuntur secundum se supermundana ratione omnes divini intellectus (in essentiam et virtutem et operationem), cum simul omnes aut eorum quosdam inobservate caelestes essentias aut caelestes vocamus virtutes, eos periphrastice de quibus sermo est significare nos aestimandum ex ea quae per singulos eorum est essentia vel virtute." Anonymous, *Douai MS 434*, q. 9 (ed. Dondaine 1952, p. 111, v. 147–149): "Et talis similitudo est similitudo glorie; unde Dionysius: diuine similitudinis est uirtus que aduenientia ad causam conuertit, modis iam dictis, scilicet modo ueritatis et amoris." See also: Pseudo-Dionysius Areopagita, *De divinis nominibus*, c. 9, sect. 31, trans. Sarraceni (Dionysiaca t. 1, pp. 468–469): "Et est divinae similitudinis virtus, quae advenientia omnia ad causam convertit; ista igitur dicere convenit similia Deo, et ea secundum imaginem divinam et assimilationem, neque enim ipsis Deum esse similem, quoniam neque propriae homo imagini est similis." Anonymous, *Douai MS 434*, q. 9 (ed. Dondaine 1952, p. 114, v. 267–269): "Dionysius dicens in principio ierarchie: Iesum inuocemus paternum lumen quod illuminat omnem hominem uenientem in hunc mundum, per quem ad principale lumen accessum habemus." See also: Pseudo-Dionysius Areopagita, *De caelesti hierarchia*, c. 1, sect. 55, trans. Eriugenae (Dionysiaca t. 2, pp. 729–730): "Ergo Jesum invocantes, paternum lumen, quod est quod verum est quod illuminat omnem hominem venientem in mundum, per quem ad principale lumen Patrem accessum habuimus, in sacratissimorum eloquiorum Patre traditas illuminationes (quantum possibile) respiciemus <...>."

the divine *mode* of cognizing God's essence: seeing His "essence *as essence*" would amount to an infinite mode, and thus be inappropriate for a finite (even though conformed) creature.[23]

Even though he denied the blessed the infinite mode of seeing God, the vision that the anonymous author conceded to them was extensive:

> We shall see a thing in three ways in heaven, as Augustine says in book 22 in *The City of God*: <1> God shall be known and visible to us in such a way that He will be seen in the Spirit by each and every one of us, <2> He will also seen by one in the other, <3> He will be seen in Himself, and in the new heaven and the new earth and in all things that will then be a creature. This is the three-fold way of seeing God.[24]

The third vision of the anonymous author's Augustinian distinction here would, in thinkers writing after the condemnation of 1241, arise as the beatific vision of God's essence. Thomas Aquinas

23. Anonymous, *Douai MS 434*, q. 9 (ed. Dondaine 1952, p. 110, v. 102–107): "<...> sic uidebimus Deum sicut est, non tamen essentiam ut essentiam. Aliud est totum in uidendo comprehendere, ita quod nihil lateat, aut cuius fines circumspici possunt: sic non contingit uidere Deum. Hoc enim esset modum et mensuram ponere infinito: quod absit in Deo, secundum quod dicit Gregorius quod non ad perfectum uidebitur, et quod eius essentia a nullo plene uidebitur, id est commensurabitur." Unlike the reading of the anonymous author of Douai MS 434 here, Gregory does not suggest that God's essence will not be seen as essence in his *Morals on the Book of Job*. Rather, Gregory admits that "we do not contemplate His essence fully," meaning that there will be no comprehensive vision of God. See: Gregorius Magnus, *Moralia in Iob*, l. X, c. 8 (CCSL 143, p. 547, v. 37–40; PL 75, p. 928 C): "In retributionibus autem culmine reperiri Omnipotens per contemplationis speciem potest, sed tamen ad perfectum non potest, quia etsi hunc in claritate sua quandoque conspicimus, non tamen eius essentiam plene contuemur."

24. Anonymous, *Douai MS 434*, q. 9 (ed. Dondaine 1952, p. 115, v. 299–303): "Tripliciter autem uidebimus in patria res, ut dicit Augustinus in XXII de civitate Dei, qui dicit: Deus erit nobis notus atque conspicuus ita ut uideatur spiritu a singulis nobis, uideatur ab altero etiam in altero, uideatur in seipso et in celo nouo et in terra noua et in omni que fuerit tunc creatura. Ecce triplex modus uidendi Deum." See also: Augustinus Hipponensis, *De civitate Dei*, l. 22, c. 29 (CCSL 48, pp. 861–862, v. 197–206; PL 41, p. 801): "Aut ergo sic per illos oculos uidebitur deus, ut aliquid habeant in tanta excellentia menti simile, quo et incorporea natura cernatur, quod ullis exemplis siue scripturarum testimoniis diuinarum uel difficile est uel inpossibile ostendere; aut, quod est ad intellegendum facilius, ita Deus nobis erit notus atque conspicuus, ut uideatur spiritu a singulis nobis in singulis nobis, uideatur ab altero in altero, uideatur in se ipso, uideatur in caelo nouo et terra noua atque in omni, quae tunc fuerit, creatura, uideatur et per corpora in omni corpore, quocumque fuerint spiritalis corporis oculi acie perueniente directi."

distinguishes different objects of knowing in the beatific vision much more extensively than the anonymous author, as emerges from articles four and five. Yet despite his brevity, the anonymous author had a clear understanding that the third way of seeing God would be a vision of God "in Himself," "as the cause of creatures."[25] All three visions, however, would in his eyes ultimately lead "the intellect in us to be perfected in the threefold vision in which the created image of God consists."[26] Nothing in his solution to the beatific vision, therefore, could possibly have provoked the worries of an indirect beatific vision, as they were propounded somewhat later in the condemnation. Indeed, with the exception of Hugh of St. Cher, none of the early thirteenth-century theories that have been discussed put forward an indirect vision, neither those that took their inspiration from Greek Christian theologies, nor those that took theirs from Avicennian philosophy. The concerns of an indirect vision articulated in the condemnation resulted from an imprecise reading of the insights contained in these early theories and a failure to understand accurately the distinct frameworks of thought operative in their background. Attention to detail would likely have prevented the overly simplistic and harsh condemnation of 1241. Yet given the difficulties the historical actors faced in integrating the new philosophies with their traditional theologies, this reaction was perhaps inevitable.

25. Anonymous, *Douai MS 434*, q. 9 (ed. Dondaine 1952, p. 116, v. 331–332): "Tertius modus erit secundum quod Deus uidebitur in seipso, quod erit ut causa creaturarum."

26. Ibid. (ed. Dondaine 1952, p. 117, v. 366–368): "In predicta triplici uisione perficietur intellectus in nobis triplex, in quo consistit Dei ymago creata."

VI

THE MAGISTERIUM RULES

NONE OF THE SOLUTIONS OFFERED to the question of the beatific vision in the early thirteenth century could, so it seems, satisfy the magisterium in their theological orthodoxy. On 13 January 1241, the chancellor of the University of Paris together with the acting masters of theology at the time and the Bishop of Paris, the aforementioned William of Auvergne, issued condemnations against "ten errors against the truth of theology."[1] From the censure of the first error, which concerns the beatific vision, it emerges that the condemnation understood certain recent theological writings to maintain that the divine essence will not be seen in itself by the blessed or angels in heaven.

> The first error is, that the divine essence in itself will not be seen by any human being or angel. We condemn this error, and, by the authority of William, the bishop <of Paris>, we excommunicate those who assert and defend it. On the contrary, we firmly believe and assert that God will be seen by the angels and all blessed in His essence, or rather substance, and is seen by the glorified souls.[2]

Scholars have speculated about which of the thinkers we have discussed in the previous two sections was the target of this first

1. CUP, tx. 128 (ed. Denifle t. 1, p. 170): "Isti sunt articuli reprobati contra theologicam veritatem et reprobati a cancellario Parisiensi Odone et magistris theologie Parisius regentibus anno Domini M•CC•XL dominica secunda post octabas Natalis Domini."

2. CUP, tx. 128 (ed. Denifle t. 1, p. 170): "*Primus* [error], quod divina essentia in se nec ab homine nec ab angelo videbitur. Hunc errorem reprobamus et assertores et defensores auctoritate Wilhermi episcopi excommunicamus. Firmiter autem credimus et asserimus, quod Deus in sua essentia vel substantia videbitur ab angelis et omnibus sanctis et videtur ab animabus glorificatis" (emphasis as in edition).

condemnation.[3] However, a close reading reveals that only one of them, namely Hugh of St. Cher, could have legitimately been understood to hold that God will not be seen in his essence. All the others, if they are read equitably and in light of their own systematic commitments, do not seem to fall under this condemnation. As we have seen in the previous sections, none of these positions took a negative view, and none of them suggested that God will not be seen in Himself. Nonetheless, it is true that the solutions required careful reading, especially since their systematic principles and commitments shifted from Augustinian to Greek Christian to Aristotelian. It was certainly not an easy task for the reader to pick up on the nuances of these texts, and to know in each case what the author considered to be the scope of the divine essence and what the blessed could see of it.

---

3. Dondaine 1952, p. 92 reasons, for instance: "Mais pour comprendre la réaction des maîtres parisiens, il faut dépasser l'obscur dialogue entre Augustin et Denys; il faut y percevoir les échos ou les remous d'un autre dialogue, ouvert depuis quelques décades, et qui se poursuit de plus en plus serré, entre la théologie chrétienne et la philosophie gréco-arabe. C'est, croyons-nous, ce second dialogue qui a activé la prise de conscience de certains biens propres des deux traditions théologiques, et aussi du risque encouru par la tradition latine en accueillant des apports orientaux mal assimilés." Along similar lines, de Contenson 1959a, p. 32 reasons that "certains des éléments qu'il fournit donnent consistance à l'hypothèse d'une filiation doctrinale entre l'avicennisme et la négation de la vision faciale condamnée en 1241." In the same year, de Contenson (1962, p. 421) adds: "il nous semble que ce texte <*viz.* le *De retributionibus sanctorum* de Guillaume de Auvergne> illustre et confirme l'hypothèse d'une inspiration avicennisante de l'erreur concernant la vision béatifique condamnée en 1241. <...> Certes les théologiens des générations suivantes, particulièrement un S. Albert et un S. Thomas, ne pourront se contenter de cette première tentative de l'évêque de Paris; l'insuffisance de son élaboration se manifeste assez à ce fait que, selon la logique de sa construction doctrinale, en définitive ce n'est pas véritablement Dieu lui-même qui est atteint par les bienheureux mais une certaine image ou *similitudo*" (emphasis as in original). More than one and a half decades later, Wéber (1978, p. 215) reiterates de Contenson's observations: "Mise au jour la cause des insuffisances qui affectent la noétique d'Avicenne, Thomas entreprend l'exposé d'une épistémologie fondée sur celle d'Averroès." This is also the case in Maillard's study more than two decades later (2001, p. 221): "Historiquement, Thomas peut s'être jugé plus proche d'Aristote qu'Averroès; de même, il peut s'être estimé plus fidèle à Augustin que ses contemporains augustiniens conduits malgré eux à relativiser, par leur lecture d'Avicenne, l'immédiaté de la vision bienheureuse." The same history is confirmed in Taylor (2012, p. 512): "Although we shall see Aquinas mention Avicenna only briefly, earlier theologians had used the best philosophical science of their day, the philosophy of Avicenna, to reason that the divine essence itself is beyond direct human vision. In contrast, Aquinas insists that the scriptural account asserting the direct intellectual vision of God be taken as true and not subject to any interpretive diminution or watering down as allegorical, symbolic, and so forth."

The complexity of thought found in the theological speculations subject to the condemnations could, of course, not be mirrored in the condemnations themselves. Their brevity, so it seems, left open a wide range of interpretive possibilities concerning the ontology of the divine essence. Yet they prescribed an epistemology of the beatific vision in the affirmative statement that seemed quite clear: "God will be seen <...> in His essence or rather substance." On a second look, however, this epistemology turns out to imply an ontological statement about God: If God's essence or rather God's substance will be seen, then God's essence can be interpreted to be identical to his substance.[4] If this was the implied sense of this statement, then it would seem to entail the end of a Dionysian understanding of the divine essence according to which this could extend to descending divine hierarchies of lights (*Deus revelatus*). With the possibility of such an implicit exclusion, any solution that built upon Greek Christian insights of an essential identity between *Deus revelatus* and *Deus absconditus* was obstructed by the magisterium, and hence alternative paths, explanatory principles, and frameworks were, it seems, needed.

The impact of the condemnations could be felt on at least two levels. The immediate generations of theologians to follow, among them Albert the Great, Bonaventure of Bagnoregio, and Thomas Aquinas, would all reference this ruling in their writings, though in strikingly different tones. In his *On the Four Coequals*, the first major work that Albert probably began to write in Germany and concluded in Paris before 1245, he criticized voices that mimic the magisterial ruling and complained about their simplicity:

> Concerning this <matter>, some have nonetheless erred and said that God will not be seen in heaven except as the light of the sun is seen in the air. Others, more simplistic than necessary, seem to condemn all authorities in whose <writings> it is said: 'We shall

4. The reading of this passage in the condemnation certainly depends on the interpretation of the conjunction "or" (*vel*). If it is read in an inclusive sense, then the interpretation I give above holds. If, however, it is read in an exclusive sense, then it seems sufficient to hold that either the essence of God or His substance is seen in the beatific vision, but it is not necessary to say that both of them are seen, provided there is a good explanation for how they differ.

> not see God or the substance of God and what God is.' And the perfect solution to all these matters is found in the aforementioned question.[5]

Some years later, Bonaventure took the opposite view and embraced the ruling in his commentary on the *Sentences*. In striking contrast to Albert's attitude, he now reasoned with direct reference to the condemnation that "certain people have said that God will never be seen immediately. But this position is heretical and has been condemned."[6] Aquinas followed Bonaventure's lead and wrote in a similar tone, more than one and a half decades after the ruling, that "certain people have erred by saying that God cannot be seen by any created intellect through His essence. But this position cannot be sustained because it is heretical."[7]

---

5. Albertus Magnus, *Prima pars Summae de creaturis* [*De IV coaequaevis*], tr. 4, q. 32, a. 1 (ed. Borgnet 34, p. 509): "Circa hoc tamen quidam oberraverunt dicentes Deum non videri in patria, nisi ut lumen solis videtur in aere. Alii plus quam oportet simplices omnes auctoritates, in quibus dicitur: Non videbimus Deum vel Dei substantiam et quid est Deus, videntur condemnare. Et solutio omnium horum perfecta invenitur in quaestione praedicta." This passage also plays a key role in the dating of Albert's *On the Four Coequals*, see: Anzulewicz 1999, pp. 161–172.

6. Bonaventura, *In secundum librum Sententiarum*, d. 23, a. 2, q. 3 (ed. Quaracchi 2, pp. 543–544): "Quidam namque, innitentes auctoritatibus male intellectis et rationibus sophisticis, dixerunt, Deum nunquam *immediate* videri, nec in via nec in patria. Dicit enim Chrysostomus: 'Ipsum, qui Deus est, non solum prophetae, sed nec etiam Angeli vident.' Et aliae reperiuntur auctoritates consimiles, quas male intelligentes et putantes, hoc dictum esse, quod Deus *immediate* videri non posset propter improportionabilitatem lucis increatae ad oculum mentis creatae, dixerunt, quod Deus per quasdam *lucubrationes* videri habet et in statu viae, et in statu innocentiae videbatur, et in statu gloriae. Et in illis luminosis influentiis dixerunt, Deum in his statibus videri magis clare et minus clare, secundum quod Deus se magis oculo nostro vult contemperare et clarioribus theophaniis ostendere.—Sed ista positio haeretica est et reprobata; nec immerito, quia et contra *rationem* est, cum anima quiescere perfecte non possit, donec in se ipso videat Deum; et contra sacram *Scripturam*. Nam primae ad Corinthios decimo tertio dicitur: *Tunc cognoscam, sicut et cognitus sum*; et primae Ioannis tertio: *Videbimus eum, sicut est*. Ad hoc etiam ipsum innumerae auctoritates doctorum reperiuntur, quibus omnibus adhaerendo, error iste reprobandus est; et auctoritates, si quae videantur esse pro ipso, omnes exponendae sunt, quia loquuntur de cognitione *comprehensionis*, qua dicitur aliquid cognosci totaliter; et hac cognitione Deus sibi soli cognoscibilis est, sicut in libro tertio patebit" (emphases as in edition).

7. Thomas Aquinas, *Quaestiones disputatae de veritate*, q. 8, a. 1 (ed. Leon. 22/2, p. 217, v. 128–134): "Dicendum quod circa hanc quaestionem quidam erraverunt dicentes Deum per essentiam a nullo umquam intellectu creato videri posse, attendentes distantiam quae est inter divinam essentiam et intellectum creatum; sec haec positio sustineri non potest cum sit haeretica."

Albert's reaction therefore appears to be the only voice critical of the position taken by the condemnation, whereas Bonaventure's and Aquinas's reactions unequivocally indicate a firm adherence to the prescribed orthodoxy. The attitudes displayed here are also mirrored in the solutions that each Scholastic thinker gave to the question of the beatific vision. Aquinas followed the implicit prescription of the proposed ontology of the divine essence, but Albert was less eager to do so. In these matters of theology, his commitment to theological authority, particularly to Dionysius the Areopagite and John Scotus Eriugena, whom he quoted as Maximus the Confessor, was steadfast over and above any philosophical authority.[8] Nonetheless, Albert was creative enough to find a solution that would fully avoid any potential anathema.

8. In fact, Albert clarified in his *Sentences* whose authority he would trust in which matters. See: Albertus Magnus, *Commentarii in II Sententiarum*, d. 13, a. 2 (ed. Borgnet 27, p. 247): "Unde sciendum, quod Augustino in his quae sunt de fide et moribus plusquam Philosophis credendum est, si dissentiunt. Sed si de medicina loqueretur, plus ego crederem Galeno, vel Hipocrati: et si de naturis rerum loquatur, credo Aristoteli plus vel alii experto in rerum naturis."

VII

Fresh Perspectives

THE CONDEMNATION OF 1241 marked a turning point in the theological discussions of the beatific vision. The era of diverse explanatory frameworks co-existing side by side, it seems, came to an abrupt halt. Aristotelian ideas began to play an increasingly dominant role. Different models of integration emerged in some of the earliest works written by Albert and Bonaventure.[1] Both of them favored explanatory frameworks of traditional theologies, yet began to include Aristotelian principles wherever suitable. Albert's solution, however, attempted the seemingly impossible: to integrate Aristotle's epistemology with Dionysius's theology. Albert's integration supplied Aquinas with important insights for his own solution, but, at the same time, provided sufficient material for him to part ways with his teacher.

In the wake of the condemnations, probably shortly after his arrival at the University of Paris to take up his theology studies, Albert put the final touches on some of his earliest theological writings. Among them were his *Question on the Vision of God* (one of the fifteen early theological questions that are considered authentic works),[2] a question that was likely composed slightly earlier than

1. Bonaventure's solution to the beatific vision and heavenly happiness is discussed in greater detail in: Wicki 1954, esp. pp. 35, 69–70, 83–88, 92–94, 105, 144–147, 160, 173–174; Trottmann 1995, esp. pp. 197–208.

2. Concerning the dating of the theological *Questions* absolutely and relatively speaking for the *Question on the Vision of God*, see: Fries 1993, p. xxii: "Constat igitur, licet inter hos duos locos parallelos <scil. inter *Quaestionem de visione dei* et operem *De resurrectione*> vigeat notabilis convenientia in auctoritatibus, in doctrina expositioneque, qua idem prompte agnoscitur auctor utriusque, Quaestionem de visione dei, quippe quae accuratior et limpidior sit, antecellere tractatum Alberti in opere De resurrectione contentum."

his three longer treatises *On Sacraments*, *On the Incarnation*, and *On the Resurrection* (all around 1242–1245).[3] All of these works played a significant role also for the final composition of his commentary on the *Sentences*, which Albert concluded in 1245 or 1246, and thanks to which he would then become a master of theology. Because Albert kept amending these works in Paris and incessantly worked on redacting them, it is more than likely that Aquinas was acquainted with all these works during the time that Albert taught in Paris as Regent Master.[4] As mentioned above, Albert inherited this position in 1245 from Guerric of St. Quentin, and then resigned from the post when he was sent to Cologne by the Dominican general chapter to set up one of the first three Dominican general study houses in the province, choosing his student Aquinas to accompany him.[5]

In Cologne, Albert no longer taught according to the ordinary curriculum of the Dominicans at Paris, but ventured into new territory. As Michèle Mulchahey has shown, Albert chose to devote the first two years of his teaching to the works of Dionysius, the *corpus Dionysiacum*, and the second two years to Aristotle's *Nicomachean Ethics* in their first full translation by Robert Grosseteste.[6] To say the least, these works contained ideas challenging to traditional theology. Dionysius suggested a conflicting view of Christian

3. Concerning the dating of these three theological treatises, see: Kübel 1958, pp. viii–x, here p. x: "Cum haud dubie constet eos ante summas De homine et De bono scriptos esse, has autem esse tempore priores quam Scriptum super Sententias, terminus ante quem absoluti sunt, satis certus est, quia Albertus anno 1246 in libro secundo Sententiarum exponendo videtur fuisse occupatus, ut verba eius testantur II Sent d. 6 a. 9 qla.: 'iam enim elapsi sunt mille ducenti quadraginta sex anni.'"

4. Concerning the different redactions of Albert's early theological works, see: Rigo 2005, pp. 325–374. Concerning Aquinas's use of Albert's *Questions*, see: Fries 1993, p. vii: "vel tandem eo quod Thomas de Aquino, suo in Sententias Petri Lombardi commentario et Quaestionibus disputatis de veritate occupatus, has quaestiones in promptu habebat exque his hausit citationes, obiectiones, opiniones aliorum, argumenta, solutiones, quo utcumque manifestum fit, quanti discipulus magistrum aestimaret."

5. See the excellent studies by Mulchahey 1998, pp. 255–257 and esp. p. 255 n. 127, 2008, pp. 118–147.

6. For the translations of Aristotle's works into Latin, see the classic article by: Dod 1982, pp. 45–79. For the Latin transmission history of Aristotle's works, see: De Leemans 2010, pp. 325–353. For the translations and transmission of spurious Aristotelian works, see: Williams 1995, pp. 29–51.

eschatology, including his pessimistic outlook on the beatific vision. Aristotle, together with the Arabic Peripatetic commentary tradition, likewise endorsed a rival view of human happiness, which is one reason why his books had long been banned from public reading.[7] Yet well before the revisions of the university curriculum at Paris in 1255, Albert opened his classroom to these seemingly challenging sources, with the likely intention of showing his students how they could be reconciled with traditional theology.

In the writings of this period, and even in his theological works from the Parisian years, Albert eloquently neutralized the opposition between Augustine's theology, Dionysius's apophaticism, and Aristotle's philosophy. Albert's treatment of the beatific vision is only one example of this, but it reveals in exceptional ways how the recent master of theology worked in light of a magisterial decision that was everything but easy to resolve. In his *Question on the Vision of God*, probably Albert's earliest treatment of the beatific vision, he focused on explaining the possibility of an immediate vision of God. Repeating almost verbatim the affirmative statement of the condemnation of 1241, Albert avowed at the outset that "God in heaven will be

---

7. The first official anti-Aristotelian censure was issued by the synod of Paris in 1210. It was explicitly directed against Amalric of Bena and David of Dinant and, in this context, suggested that "libri Aristotelis de naturali philosophia nec commenta legantur Parisius publice vel secreto, et hoc sub pena excommunicationis inhibemus" (CUP, tx. 11 (ed. Denifle t. 1, p. 70)). The second censure was issued by Robert of Courçon, Bishop of Paris, only five years later in 1215. It confirmed the first censure, and added Maurice of Spain as culprit. "Non legantur libri Aristotelis de *methafisica* et de *naturali philosophia*, nec *summe* de eisdem, aut de doctrina magistri David de Dinant, aut Amalrici heretici, aut Mauricii hyspani" (CUP, tx. 20 (ed. Denifle t. 1, pp. 78–79), emphases as in edition). On 13 April 1231, finally, the Bull *Parens scientiarum* was issued by Pope Gregory IX. It prohibited the Masters of Arts from drawing upon Aristotle's *libri naturales* until those books had been purged from their errors. Equally, it advised the Masters of Theology to abstain from openly drawing on these works. "Ad hec jubemus, ut magistri artium unam lectionem de Prisciano et unum post alium ordinarie semper legant, et libris illis naturalibus, qui in Concilio provinciali <*viz.* that of 1210> ex certa causa prohibiti fuere, Parisius non utantur, quousque examinati fuerint et ab omni errorum suspitione purgati" (CUP, tx. 79 (ed. Denifle t. 1, pp. 136–139, here: p. 138)). In contrast, on 16 February 1252 and 19 March 1255, this attitude of the magisterium changed profoundly. The new statutes of the Parisian faculty of arts prescribed Aristotle's works as required readings for their students; in 1252 the *Posterior Analytics* and the book *On the Soul* were prescribed (see: CUP, tx. 201 (ed. Denifle t. 1, pp. 227–230)), and on 19 March 1255 his *libri naturales* as complete corpus followed suit (see: CUP, tx. 246 (ed. Denifle t. 1, pp. 277–279)). Discussions of these censures and prescriptions in the secondary literature are vast; one of the most important studies is: Bianchi 1999.

seen through His essence by the angels and the blessed," and he added that this vision is "not such that He will present <His essence> through some mediating species as similitudes to the glorified intellects, but as He presents Himself to His very own Self."[8]

With this avowal, Albert spoke to one of the major concerns of the condemnation: the theologies that proposed a mediated vision, probably those such as that of Hugh of St. Cher. In line with William of Auvergne and the anonymous author of Douai MS 434, q. 9, but perhaps more decisively than these predecessors, Albert explained that the beatific vision required a type of subjective medium that would "sufficiently strengthen the intellect to this vision of the divine essence." This is not to be confused, he reasoned further, with a type of objective medium that would be interposed between God and the intellect and "in which God is <merely> seen through a mirror of creatures and the enigma of scriptures."[9] The concern of an Avicennian type of mediation by means of an interposed object and a resulting indirect beatific vision was thus addressed directly, very much

8. Albertus Magnus, *Quaestio de visione Dei in patria* (ed. Colon. 25/2, p. 98, v. 32–35): "Dicendum, quod deus in patria videbitur per essentiam ab angelis et sanctis, quam non mediantibus aliquibus speciebus ut similitudinibus intellectibus gloriosis obiciet, sed sicut sibi ipsi se obicit." This theme of an immediate vision of God is reiterated in Albert's later theological writings of this early period; see, for instance: id., *Super I librum Sententiarum*, d. 1, c. 2 (ed. Colon. 29/1, p. 29, v. 46–52): "Ad hoc sine praeiudicio dicimus affirmantes quidem certissime quod divina substantia videtur a beatis omnibus; qualiter autem videtur, sine praeiudicio dicimus sic quod videtur immediate per coniunctionem, ita quod deus offert se nostro intellectui per substantiam suam sicut intellectus sibi ipsi; et hoc est quod dicit Apostolus: 'Cognoscam sicut et cognitus sum.'"

9. Albertus Magnus, *Quaestio de visione Dei in patria* (ed. Colon. 25/2, p. 99, v. 23–34): "Sed quia hoc lumen <id est, lumen fidei> non adhuc sufficienter confortat intellectum ad visionem divinae essentiae sine medio specierum, quia in ipso videtur deus per speculum creaturarum et aenigma scripturarum, ideo superadditur aliud lumen, scilicet gloriae, confortans intellectum, ut divinam ipsam essentiam videre possit sine aliqua specie mediante. Sed ipsa divina essentia determinabit sui ipsius cognitionem. Et tale lumen vocat Dionysius 'theophaniam,' quae est medium in visione patriae, non sicut species emanans in intellectum a deo, in qua ut obiecto accipiatur eius cognitio, sed sicut medium confortans videntem." On media, see Aquinas's comments in article one, pp. 117–118. This theme of a subjective medium as the solution to the difficulty of an indirect vision is equally reiterated in Albert's later theological works. See: id., *Super I librum Sententiarum*, d. 1, c. 2 (ed. Colon. 29/1, p. 30, v. 59–p. 31, v. 8); id., *Super Dionysium De caelesti hierarchia*, c. 4 (ed. Colon. 36/1, p. 71, v. 20–24) as quoted in article seven, note 64. For secondary literature on Albert's conception of the light of glory or theophany, as he calls the elevation of the intellect interchangeably, see: Anzulewicz 1999, pp. 161–172; Krause 2014, pp. 152–156; Trottmann 1995, pp. 295–302; Wicki 1954, pp. 154–157.

anticipating Aquinas's reasoning in his *Sentences* later. Nonetheless, with an acute view to the difficulties present in the theological solutions of Dionysian inspiration, Albert also addressed the worry of theophanies. His reasoning concerning these potential media built on suggesting that the strengthening medium in the intellect is identical to the "light of glory." This light Albert subsequently associated with the Dionysian theophany (*theophania*), and suggested that it is "a medium in the vision in heaven, not as a species emanating into the intellect from God, in which the cognition of Him is taken from an object, but as a medium strengthening the one seeing."[10] Albert thus reexpounded the worry of an indirect vision, not only regarding the Latin Avicennian positions but also regarding the Latin Dionysian ones, and he therefore fully adhered to the affirmative statement made at the end of the condemnation of 1241 concerning the beatific vision.

Indeed, this rapprochement between separate strands of the theological debate reveals two dominant concerns in Albert's early engagement with the beatific vision. On the one hand, his reading seemed to come at the expense of the Dionysian outlook on the scope of God's essence. Albert seemed to echo silently the Augustinian and Aristotelian views on the divine essence prescribed by the condemnation, which implied that God's essence is limited in scope to what Dionysius, along with his predecessors such as Alexander of Hales, Hugh of St. Cher, and Guerric of St. Quentin, would take as God's transcendent reality, as *Deus absconditus* alone.[11] Later, in his commentaries on the *corpus Dionysiacum*, Albert paid closer attention

---

10. For the Latin, see previous note.

11. In more explicit terms, this understanding of the divine essence emerges in Albert's *On the Resurrection*, where he reads the Augustinian term *species* to refer to the divine substance or nature. See: Albertus Magnus, *De resurrectione*, tr. 4, q. 1, a. 9, § 2 (ed. Colon. 26, p. 329, v. 77–85): "Dicimus, quod visio dos est visio amati et habiti sine medio ad glorificandum. Et inquantum est sine medio, dicitur facie ad faciem; inquantum autem est sine symbolo et aenigmate, dicitur visio per speciem; species enim dicitur hic propria natura dei, secundum quod est principium ad cognoscendum suam substantiam secundum 'quid est,' Et hoc accipitur ex quadam auctoritate Maximi dicentis: 'Pretiosa in conspectu domini mors sanctorum eius' <...>." As Wicki 1954, p. 135, and Anzulewicz 1999, p. 162, have pointed out, the authority here is not Maximus the Confessor but rather Scotus Eriugena's *On the Division of Nature*. See: Iohannes Scotus Eriugena, *Periphyseon,* l. 5 (CCCM 162, p. 94, v. 2979; PL 122, 919 C).

to this point concerning *Deus absconditus*, and revisited his understanding of the divine essence in his more extended discussions of the emanated theophany.[12] In his *Question on the Vision of God*, however, the question of mediation so preoccupied Albert's discussion that related aspects of the beatific vision, particularly its epistemology and phenomenology, were mostly ignored. These aspects began to surface in his following writings.[13]

In his subsequent treatises, *On the Resurrection*, *On the Four Coequals*, and on Dionysius's *On the Divine Names*, Albert embraced the familiar Augustinian division between vision and comprehension, but strengthened its argumentative force with a key Aristotelian distinction. Cognition of a thing "as it is" (*ut est*) or "that it is" (*quia est*), Albert wrote, echoing the Stagirite, entails "seeing the being of the thing and the essence of the thing"; whereas cognition of a thing "what it is" (*quid est*) involves "seeing its proper definition including all limits of the thing."[14] This distinction served Albert to counteract the seeming limitlessness of a vision of God's essence, even though in the distinction's original context it was not intended

12. See discussion below on pp. 58–60.

13. Albert continued to solve the question of a direct vision on the basis of similar lines of reasoning to those just discussed. See, for instance: Albertus Magnus, *Quaestio de dotibus sanctorum in patria*, a. 6 (ed. Colon. 25/2, p. 110, v. 53–p. 111, v. 8): "Ad obiectum in contrarium dicendum, quod Chrysostomus intelligit, quod deum, ut est, caelestes essentiae non vident ita, quod comprehendant ipsum, quia sic ipse solus videt se. Nihilominus tamen angeli et sancti vident eum per essentiam sine medio, vident tamen sub theophaniis, ut dicit Dionysius, quae non sunt species dei, sub qua videatur ut obiectum, sed lumen gloriae confortans intellectum ad visionem divinae essentiae sine medio specierum, sicut supra habitum est in Quaestione de visione Dei." Id., *De resurrectione*, tr. 4, q. 1, a. 9, § 1 (ed. Colon. 26, p. 328, v. 47–50): "Quod concedimus dicentes, quod videbimus deum in patria, sicuti est. Sicut enim deus seipsum videt sine medio, ita sine omni medio offeret se nobis. Et haec visio erit dos animae."

14. Ibid. (ed. Colon. 26, p. 328, v. 50–57): "Sed tamen distinguendum est, quod aliud est videre deum, ut est, et aliud est videre, quid est deus, sicut aliud est videre rem, ut est, et aliud videre, quid est res. Rem enim videre, ut est, est videre esse rei sive essentiam rei; videre autem, quid est res, est videre propriam diffinitionem includentem omnes terminos rei. Et ista duo differunt, secundum quod differunt quaestiones de ipsis." See also: id., *Super I librum Sententiarum*, d. 1, c. 2 (ed. Colon. 29/1, p. 31, v. 9–19): "Ad hoc autem quod posset *quaeri*, utrum deus sit comprehensibilis, dicendum quod duplex est comprehensio, scilicet quae est tactus intellectus super terminos rei, et sic non comprehenditur. Unde Augustinus ad probam: 'Attingere deum mente possumus, comprehendere autem minime.' Est autem comprehensio quandoque perfecta consecutio alicuius ut finis, quae consecutio praecipue fit in affectu, et sic comprehenditur deus, ut dicit Apostolus ad Eph. iii (18): 'Ut possitis comprehendere cum omnibus sanctis, quae sit longitudo, latitudo, sublimitas, et profundum.'"

to do so. Indeed, this distinction between cognition of the being and essence of a thing and cognition of its definition took its inspiration from the *Posterior Analytics* at the very beginning of book II, where it connected Aristotle's discussion of demonstration in the first book with his discussion of definitions in the second.[15]

Aristotle, however, may not have been the only source of inspiration for Albert's distinction here. Some of his Scholastic predecessors discovered its worth, indeed, the worth of all four of Aristotle's scientific questions from the *Posterior Analytics*—namely, "the fact, the reason why, if it is, and what it is"—for their accounts of human cognition of God. Most prominent among them was Alexander of Hales, who identified in his *Summa theologiae* five different modes in which humans may cognize God, borrowing some of Aristotle's four scientific questions: (1) cognition of God that He is (*quia est*), (2) what He is not (*quid non est*), (3) what He is according to His substance (*quid est secundum substantiam*), (4) how He is (*qualis est*), and (5) how great He is (*quantus est*). Alexander's five modes went well beyond the division of two questions that Albert picked, since Alexander's intention was to provide a survey of all possible ways in which humans may cognize God. Albert's aim, in contrast, was simply to distinguish the beatific vision as *ut-est* cognition of God that was both direct and of God's essence, from comprehension as *quid-est* cognition of God that would amount to knowing His definition.[16]

Albert underscored the importance of this epistemological distinction even more by teasing out the psychological impact it had on the human intellect. Drawing on the example of natural cognition of

15. Aristoteles, *Analytica posteriora*, l. II, c. 1 (89b23–26), trans. Gerardus Cremonensis (AL IV.3, p. 63, v. 2–5): "Res quas querimus et res quas scimus sunt res una eadem numero. Et questionum quidem numerus est quatuor; quarum una est an hoc insit huic, et secunda quare istud insit huic, et tertia an hoc sit, et quarta quid est hoc."

16. For parallel passages in Albert's early theological works, see, for instance: Albertus Magnus, *Commentarii in IV Sententiarum*, d. 48, a. 2 (ed. Borgnet 30, pp. 654–655): "Si dicat aliquis, quod hoc est intelligendum de visione quae est in ipsa divinitatis praesentia. Contra: Augustinus dicit, quod ea quae praesentia sunt intellectui, melius videntur: sed Deus per essentiam suam modo praesens est intellectui ergo etiam modo per essentiam videtur: et tamen non surgit inde gaudium: ergo falsum est quod dicit." For more extended discussions on this matter in the secondary literature, see: Wicki 1954, pp. 134–138; Trottmann 1995, pp. 295–302; Anzulewicz 1999, pp. 161–172; Krause 2015b, pp. 203–205.

separate substances in this life, Albert reasoned that on the epistemological level, the question "if the thing is" (*si est res*) initiates inquiry into separate substances. As soon as "we cognize that a thing exists," the answer to this question is clear to us on the epistemological level. Yet on the psychological level, Albert insists, this answer translates into the intellect's making "contact with the thing" (*attingere rem*). Because the answer results in a particular mental state on the epistemological level, it equally brings about a particular psychological relation, where the intellect engages with the thing in the world. For Albert, matters did not stop here. The answer to the first question also gives rise to a subsequent question, again on the level of a mental state, and Albert considered this question to be "what a thing is." Once an answer to this second question is given, an answer which entails "cognizing the perfect definition of the thing by the limits enclosing the whole being of the thing, in such a way that nothing of the being is outside these limits," it also resulted in a psychological relation. This relation, however, by far surpassed the first. Indeed, in Albert's eyes, the epistemological comprehension of a thing occasioned a "seizing of the intellect beyond the limits of a thing"; it prompted a psychological relation in which the cognizer was perfectly joined to the cognized. However, Albert considered this perfect joining on the psychological level as much an impossibility as he took comprehension on the epistemological level to be impossible in the beatific vision. Our intellectual making contact "with His being without a medium" does in no way entail that "we comprehend Him."[17] Aristotle's epistemology thus paved the way for Albert to distinguish the beatific vision of the divine essence from the comprehension of God.

17. Id., *De resurrectione*, tr. 4, q. 1, a. 9, § 1 (ed. Colon. 26, p. 328, v. 58–72): "De simplici enim sive incomplexo quaerentes primo quaerimus, si est res, et terminatur quaestio ista, cum cognoscimus, quod res illa est et habet esse causatum causae primae; causa enim prima non ponit nisi esse et nullam differentiam addit super illud. Cognoscentes ergo hoc quaerimus, quid est res, volentes cognoscere rei perfectam diffinitionem per terminos claudentes totum esse rei, ita quod nihil sit de esse extra terminos illos. Et intellectui primae quaestionis non competit nisi attingere rem secundum intellectum. Intellectui autem secundae quaestionis competit comprehendere rem vere, secundum quod comprehensio est contactus intellectus super terminos rei. Sic dicimus de deo, quod attingimus esse ipsius sine medio per intellectum, sed nequaquam comprehendimus."

Nonetheless, the solution that Albert offered with his epistemological distinction and its psychological consequences left out one important aspect. If God is cognized "as He is" in the beatific vision, yet the blessed do not know "what He is," what exactly is it that they cognize? What is the phenomenological content of their cognition? Albert responded to these questions in an un-Aristotelian manner, resonating with the attibutive solutions found in the earlier theologies of Alexander of Hales and the anonymous author of Douai MS 434, q. 9:

> According to the being <the substance of God> is touched through any attribute whatsoever, which is the essence of God. <...> Any attribute can be the divine essence according to the fact that it is in God, namely, according to the fact that it is perceived by the intellect. The attributes are distinguished by way of the things inspected with them. And therefore, one praises God as glorious, another as wise, another as majestic.[18]

Aristotelian epistemology would have demanded a solution along the lines of assimilation between cognizer and the cognized, a noetic identification between them in which the cognizer becomes identical to the cognized, in which the cognizer cognizes the quiddity (*quid est*) of God.[19] Albert's epistemology of the beatific vision, in contrast,

18. Ibid., ad 1 (ed. Colon. 26, p. 329, v. 6–16): "Est enim substantiam dei considerare duobus modis, scilicet secundum 'quid est' et secundum esse, ut dictum est. Secundum 'quid est' non finitur a nostro intellectu, sed secundum esse attingitur per quodlibet attributum, quod est essentia dei. Et per hoc patet solutio ad sequentem rationem, quia licet attributum quodlibet sit essentia divina, secundum quod est in deo, tamen, secundum quod percipitur ab intellectu, distinguuntur attributa per connotata. Et ideo alius laudat ut gloriam, alius ut sapientiam, alius ut maiestatem."

19. It appears that much of the criticism that Albert's solution has experienced in the secondary literature is owed to this Aristotelian expectation, an expectation that would, however, be much more in line with Aquinas's way of thinking than with Albert's. See, for instance: Dondaine 1955, p. 77: "Saint Albert, Pierre de Tarentaise, Guillaume de Méliton: on aperçoit mieux maintenant l'ampleur du courant «agnostique», et la portée de la décision thomiste. Entre l'universelle vision du *quid est*, qui souriait aux augustiniens, et l'agnosticisme céleste des Albert, Tarentaise, Méliton, saint Thomas a tracé une voie moyenne qui n'est pas sans difficultés, mais qui sauve de grands biens. En réservant aux saints du ciel l'accès au divin *quid est*, il accuse mieux que ne faisait l'augustinisme le caractère surnaturel et sublime de la vision de Dieu; mais il a craint aussi, s'il réservait à Dieu la saisie de son *quid est*, de dévaluer la donnée traditionelle: *videre Deum per speciem, id est per essentiam.* Sur ce point précis, saint Thomas s'est séparé de son maître et s'est obligé du même coup à définir autrement le privilège de

remained on solidly theological ground. Hugh of St. Victor's authority supplied Albert with the analogy of light that expressed how the intellectual subject is maximally illumined by the divine presence.[20] Phenomenologically speaking, Dionysius's theophanies were explicitly turned into divine aspects or actualities seen. For Albert, these aspects were the visible aspects of His transcendent essence (*essentia*) that He made visible to the blessed—an understanding that is close enough to Dionysius's view on God's emitted reality.

Albert's solution concerning cognition of God's essence in the beatific vision thus eruditely blended Aristotelian epistemology with Dionysian theology. With the help of Aristotelian metaphysics concerning God's essence and Aristotelian epistemology concerning cognizing Him, Albert found a harmonious answer to the theological

---

Dieu." Trottmann 1995, pp. 193–194, follows Dondaine's reading and suggests with similar expectations: "Saint Albert distingue donc entre '*Videre Deum ut est,*' ce qui est le lot des bienheureux, et '*Videre quid est Deum' ce qui demeure impossible à toute créature intellectuelle.* Du coup, la vision béatifique est réduite à n'être qu'une modalité, certes moins imparfaite que celle d'ici-bas, de la connaissance de Dieu '*quia est.*' Mais Albert ne représente pas un cas isolé, la distinction se retrouve chez Pierre de Tarentaise et Guillaume de Méliton. <...> Thomas d'Aquin, rompant en cela avec son maître va proposer une solution originale, mais nous voyons que les doutes qui sont à l'origine de la condamnation de 1241 subsistent au-delà d'elle tant que la difficulté métaphysique et noétique de la connaissance de l'infini par la créature n'a pas trouvé de solution satisfaisante" (emphases as in original). See also: Trottmann 1995, p. 302. An alternative reading that is free from these Thomistic expectations and illuminates Albert's theology excellently is found in: Anzulewicz 1999, pp. 161–172.

20. Albert rejects the Aristotelian psychological solution to the question of the beatific vision. See: Albertus Magnus, *De resurrectione*, tr. 4, q. 1, a. 9, § 1 arg. 6 (ed. Colon. 26, p. 327, v. 41–50) "Item, si debeat esse visio secundum intellectum, necesse est intellectum assimilari rei intellectae; omnis enim intellectus est per assimilationem. Aut igitur intellectus assimilabitur deo secundum substantiam vel secundum habitum sive speciem aliquam formalem. Constat, quod non primo modo, quia intellectus non erit deus. Si autem secundo modo, datur [sequitur], quod non est visio nisi in theophaniis; forma enim, sive lumen, recepta ab intellectu non est deus, sed aliquid in quo et per quod cognoscitur deus." Instead of the psychological solution, he favors Hugh of St. Victor's light metaphor in his reply. With this metaphor, Albert expresses an assimilation in virtue of God's presence according to which the intellectual subject is maximally illuminated by the divine presence. See ibid., ad 6 (ed. Colon. 26, p. 329, v. 41–54): "Similiter habitum est, quod deus est in intellectu essentialiter et intimus ipsi et continens eum. Et sic, sicut intellectus convertitur supra se sine medio, ita convertitur in deum sine medio. Et hoc qualiter sit, ostendit magister Hugo de S. Victore per simile dicens: 'Sicut duo sunt: lumen et, quod suscipit lumen, corpus, et ex his duobus unum efficitur lucens, et ipsum lucens imago quodammodo est et similitudo luminis in eo quod lucet sicut ipsum lumen: ita et deus noster lumen est et verum lumen est, et ipsum lumen rationales animi mundi et puri concipiunt et ex eo lucentes fiunt et non sunt ipsi imago luminis in eo quod sunt, sed in eo quod lucent ex lumine, sicut ipsum lumen lucet.'"

dilemma of the beatific vision that struck a balance between adhering to the limitations of the magisterial decision on the one hand and to the authority of Dionysian theology on the other. Nonetheless, while Dionysius the Areopagite played the key role for Albert, he did not present a black-and-white pessimistic solution to human cognition of God. Rather, Dionysius offered a panoply of insights that, if interpreted correctly in line with the optimistic Western theology, would enrich and enhance the insights into the promise we have been given by God in the Bible.

Albert's attitude toward Dionysius's theology was intensified when he revisited the question of the enablement for the beatific vision in his commentaries on Dionysius's works, especially on his *On the Celestial Hierarchy*. Instead of conceiving of a theophany as a created intellectual enhancement for the beatific vision alone, as he had done in his previous works, Albert now recommended a second theophany relevant to the beatific vision, a theophany that is God Himself.

> <A vision is called theophany> when an object which is God is seen in the light which is God. In this way, as Hugh of St. Victor says, God Himself is in every blessed saint as light, such that He makes him His similitude by participation in Him. And the vision of God is called theophany in such a similitude. For, in this way, the same God will be the light and the object. Yet <He will be> the object as He is in Himself, and the light as participated in by the blessed.[21]

21. Id., *Super Dionysium De caelesti hierarchia*, c. 4 (ed. Colon. 36/1, p. 71, v. 12–40, translated above are v. 25–31): "Dicimus, quod theophania quattuor modis dicitur: primo modo visio, quae est per corporales formas similitudine dissimili ducentes in deum, in qua necessarium non est lumen divinum esse, sed tantum ductio in deum; secundo modo dicitur, quando lumine divino, quod non est deus, videtur aliquid quod non est deus, sicut Ieremias vidit ollam succensam lumine divino, intelligens per hoc destructionem Ierusalem; tertio modo, ut est in usu loquentium, quando in lumine divino, quod non est deus, videtur obiectum, quod vere est deus, non in lumine sicut in medio, sicut videtur res in sua imagine, sed sub lumine confortante intellectum videtur immediate deus; quarto modo, <v. 25> quando in lumine quod est deus, videtur obiectum, quod est deus, sicut dicit Hugo de Sancto Victore; sic deus ipse est in quolibet beato ut lumen quoddam, participatione sui faciens eum sui similitudinem, et in tali similitudine dei visio dicitur theophania; sic enim idem deus erit lumen et obiectum, sed obiectum, prout est in se, lumen vero, prout est participatus a beatis. <v. 32> Primis igitur duobus modis non videbitur deus in patria, et de illis tenet obiectio Magistri Hugonis; dicit enim: 'Quid est in

Albert's ultimate theophany in the beatific vision, as described in this passage, came close to Dionysius's genuine understanding of descending divine hierarchies of lights, of *Deus revelatus*. Occurring in a segment that listed altogether four different theophanies—of which the first two were simple representations and created objective truths about God, the other two the subjective enhancement, as discussed earlier, and God Himself—Albert envisioned this ultimate theophany to be present in the blessed saint as divine light, and yet to remain God substantially and as such "to be participated in by the blessed." Admittedly, his argument here could only hold if divine presence in its subject did not entail its reduction to the subject's mode of being, to its limitation, to its createdness. But it seems that for Albert, unlike for Aquinas, this was of no particular concern. As I will show in greater detail in the introductions to the individual translated articles, Albert took the metaphysical and epistemological conditions and rules that apply to this life to be of only partial relevance for the afterlife.[22] His eschatology did not have to be in line with and adhere to Aristotelian explanations used for natural

theophaniis videri et praeter illas non videri nisi numquam vere videri et verum numquam videri?' Sed aliis duobus modis erit in patria visio per theophanias, licet ipse Hugo non ponat nisi quartum, quia non attendit tertium, et ideo reprehendit alios aliter ponentes, qui tamen vera dicunt, intelligentes secundum tertium modum." Albert's reference to Hugh of St. Victor here is quoted above in section III, note 18. Albert provides the same understanding of the fourth theophany also in his commentary on the *Sentences*, book IV, which he may have concluded in Cologne at the same time of commenting on the works of Dionysius. See: id., *Commentarii in IV Sententiarum*, d. 49, a. 5 (ed. Borgnet 30, p. 670): "<...> Deus in patria aliter est in anima, et aliter in via et in omnibus: quia in patria est in intellectu lumine gloriae replens totam animam, et vitam aeternam sibi influens, secundum quod beatitudinis est objectum, ut supra dictum est: et sub illa claritate anima convertitur immediate in Deum, non accipiendo aliud ab ipso quam ipse sit: sed hoc modo unita ei in uno spiritu intelliget eum: et ideo ad hunc intellectum non est necessaria speciei assimilatio formalis quando substantialiter inest. <...> Sed in patria <...> incircumscriptum lumen deitatis quod est Deus ipse, unitur intellectui agenti, et sic effunditur substantialiter super totam animam et implet eam: et hoc modo anima plena erit ipso Deo qui est sua beatitudo."

22. We can also see this for instance in Albert's descriptions of eternal life, which stand in close connection to his understanding of the fourth theophany as quoted in the previous note. See: id., *Commentarii in IV Sententiarum*, d. 46, a. 6 (ed. Borgnet 30, p. 635): "Dicendum, quod vita gloriae et etiam gratiae per prius est in essentia. Est enim haec vita, ut dictum est, actus primae vitae in spiritum secundum influxum gloriae et beatitudinis: et sic procedit ab ipsa secundum quod ipsa est in beatis spiritibus per gloriam: et hoc in esse primo est spiritus, et secundo potentiae."

phenomena, but was largely a matter of theological authority; in this, he expressly favored Augustine and Dionysius over Aristotle. Nonetheless, Aristotle's *Posterior Analytics* came in useful for Albert for rectifying the teachings of those theologians who had strayed from the correct interpretation of theological doctrine. This attitude of Albert's contrasted sharply with the ambitions of his student, Thomas Aquinas, who would provide the most influential rationale for a solution to the question of the beatific vision built on the Greek and Arabic Peripatetic *De anima* traditions.[23]

23. In this reading of Aquinas's Aristotelian solution according to its reliance on Arabic Peripatetic insights from their *De anima* interpretations, I agree with Trottmann's observation (1995, p. 317) that "la théologie thomiste de la vision béatifique pousse ainsi au maximum les exigences, tant de la noétique aristotélicienne, que du donné de foi." Nonetheless, I hesitate to agree with it as a blanket statement, since, as I have just shown, Albert's solution is equally Aristotelian, even though it prefers the *Posterior Analytics* to the *De anima* in its explanatory value.

VIII

Untrodden Paths

What did the young Thomas Aquinas make of all these intricate debates when he wrote his commentary on the *Sentences* between 1252 and 1255? Which of the debates—be they found in his source texts or in the writings of his near contemporaries—mattered most to him? And how did he utilize them for his own youthful theorizations? In a nutshell, Aquinas's earliest solution presents a shift in the epistemology and ontology of the beatific vision. He left behind the conciliatory approach between the Greek Christian and Latin Christian sources of his predecessors, discussed in section VII, an approach that found its culmination in Albert the Great's treatment of the beatific vision. Aquinas also set aside an Avicennian explanation of the beatific vision. This, as he must have seen in other Latin predecessors, led to nothing but the renunciation of crucial Augustinian teachings and thus of the contemporary doctrine found in the magisterial affirmation of William of Auvergne. Yet it was precisely Augustine's teachings on the directness of the beatific vision and on the incomprehensibility of God that Aquinas fully embraced in his own solution, not least because of the magisterial decisions. In this way, Aquinas did not start from scratch, but placed his earliest theorization within the long history of Latin views on the beatific vision. Most crucially, though, since he no longer relied on familiar ways of explaining the beatific vision, Aquinas's contribution to its history should be seen as lying in a systematic determination of a new explanatory framework whose formulation was erected upon his use of key principles that he found in the metaphysics, psychology, and epistemology of Averroes's *Long Commentary on Aristotle's On the Soul*. I shall discuss these principles, in their peculiar formulations and formations in Aquinas's theory of the beatific vision in his *Sentences*, in my short introductions to each of the seven articles concerned with the beatific vision.

For now, it is important to situate Aquinas's theory of the beatific vision in its biographical context. As emerges in Weisheipl's and Torrell's exquisite biographies, it must have been in April of 1244 that Aquinas joined the Order of Preachers in Naples at the age of nineteen.[1] This decision stood in opposition to his family's high hopes that he would become the abbot of the famous Benedictine abbey Monte Cassino, where he had studied as a boy. As soon as his mother Theodora learned of his taking the habit of one of the newly established Mendicant orders, she sent for couriers to return him to the family home and to make him rethink his decision. Aquinas's brother Rinaldo, and Pier delle Vigne, Frederick II's counsellor at that time, assumed the task and led Aquinas back to the family's castle in Roccasecca. There, he remained under house arrest for more than a year until his family must have finally appreciated his reasoning and brought him back to the Dominicans in Naples in the summer of 1245. The best-known story about Aquinas's house arrest is arguably the episode of a prostitute who was sent to his chambers to seduce him. Yet as we learn from his historical biographer, William of Tocco, Aquinas cared considerably more about matters of spirit and learning than those of the flesh. These intellectual interests were primarily reading the Bible in its entirety and studying the systematic theological textbook which was mandatory for all theology students at this time, Peter Lombard's *Sentences*.[2]

From the Dominican priory in Naples, to which Aquinas returned in the summer of 1245, he was almost immediately sent to Rome. Weisheipl and Torrell speculate that this must have occurred because

1. Unless otherwise indicated, my historical remarks here are based on the relevant chapters in these two biographies. See: Weisheipl 1983, pp. 1–51; Torrell 2000, pp. 1–27.

2. Guillelmus de Tocco, *Ystoria sancti Thome de Aquino*, c. 10 (ed. le Brun-Gouanvic 1996, p. 110, v. 4–p. 111, v. 10): "Cui intantum spiritualis intelligentie radiis Deus miserator illuxit quod ibi Bibliam perlegit et textum Sententiarum didicit, et tractatum Fallaciarum Aristotilis, ut dicitur, compilauit, atque sorores suas sacras litteras pro presagio sui magistratus instruxit. Qui iam incipiens sua fructificare doctrina sororem suam, quam ad eum seducendum parentes miserant, ad amorem Dei et contemptum mundi suis monitionibus et exemplis induxit."

the Dominicans feared another abduction by members of his family, who, however, abstained from intervening a second time. Aquinas thus made it to Rome safely. There he met with the master of his order, John the Teuton, and both men, probably in the company of some other friars, journeyed soon thereafter to Paris, the center of Latin theological learning at that time. Although Aquinas biographers have been divided over whether he actually studied at the University of Paris before he left the city for Cologne together with Albert the Great in the summer of 1248, there seems to be sufficient evidence that he in fact did. Weisheipl and Torrell conjecture that Aquinas took classes at the Arts Faculty and possibly also at the Theology Faculty under Albert the Great, who served there as a regent master between 1245 and 1248. The strongest argument for Aquinas's studies at the Arts Faculty has been presented by René-Antoine Gauthier, who suggests that Aquinas's late commentary on Aristotle's *Nicomachean Ethics* (written in 1271/72) reveals a close acquaintance with the teachings of some Parisian arts masters of the 1240s. This acquaintance, Gauthier reasons, is particularly true for Arnulf of Provence and some anonymous authors of commentaries on the *ethica vetus* and *ethica nova*.[3] I have elsewhere pointed to a similar presence of some of these ideas in book IV of Aquinas's commentary on the *Sentences*. These concern the question of ultimate happiness, the question that immediately precedes the present question of the beatific vision.[4]

In these considerations of ultimate happiness, Aquinas establishes that it is a specific good of the human soul's theoretical intellect (*intellectus speculativus*) in initial reliance on Aristotle's teachings in the *Nicomachean Ethics*:[5] happiness lies in the active perfection of the theoretical intellect. With this intellectual part of the soul as the main subject of happiness, Aquinas places himself with ease in

3. See: Gauthier 1971, pp. xv–xvii. For an edition of the anonymous author's text of the *Lectura in Ethicam Nouam*, see: Gauthier 1975, pp. 71–141, and for the edited text: pp. 94–141. For an edition of Arnulf of Provence's *Divisio Scientiarum*, see: Arnulfus Provincialis, *Divisio Scientiarum* (ed. Lafleur 1988). For the edited text of the anonymous author's *Guide for Students*, see: Anonymous, *Le «Guide de l'étudiant»* (ed. Lafleur 1992).

4. Krause 2015a, pp. 15–56.

5. For Aquinas's view, see: Thomas Aquinas, *Commentum in quatuor libros Sententiarum*, l. 4, d. 49, q. 1, a. 1, qcc. 2–3 (ed. Parma 7/2, p. 1184). Secondary sources discussing Aquinas's

opposition to his near contemporaries. Albert the Great, for instance, favors a holistic understanding of ultimate happiness, locating it in the theoretical and practical intellects and in the will, whereas Bonaventure locates happiness in the will as its main subject. Nonetheless, unlike Aristotle, Aquinas does not present this active perfection of the theoretical intellect as a perfection of an acquired habit, which Aristotle described in his famous function argument (*ergon*) in the *Nicomachean Ethics* I.7 (1097b23–1098a16).[6] On the contrary, the conspicuous absence of any mention of an acquired habit in Aquinas and its perfectibility for happiness bears a strong resemblance to the work of the anonymous arts master of Paris's *Lectura in Ethicam nouam* and to Robert Kilwardby's *Divisio scientiarum,* even though Aquinas advocated the requirement of a divine facilitation in the form of an infused habit, the light of glory (see Article 6), for the attainment of the beatific vision.

In addition to this unusual view on the conditions for the perfection of the theoretical intellect, Aquinas also found inspiration in the early Latin commentators for yet another key teaching: his instrumentalist view of the activity of knowing God in the beatific vision. Whereas for Aristotle the very performance of the highest activity amounted to happiness in this life, Robert Kilwardby and other early arts masters of Paris, such as the anonymous author of the *Guide for Students*, proposed that the ultimate end and good is God Himself, the object of knowing. The activity of knowing Him, however, was

early conception of happiness include, for instance: Kleber 1988; Bradley 1997; Donato 2006, pp. 161–189. For Albert the Great's conception of theological happiness, see, for instance: Albertus Magnus, *De resurrectione*, tr. 4, q. 1, a. 11, § 1, ad 2 (ed. Colon. 26, p. 333, v. 50–59): "<...> quod intellectus non habet remunerationem respectu finis tenti, inquantum est tentus, sed potius respectu finis intellecti vel veri, inquantum huiusmodi. Similiter de voluntate, quae est respectu boni vel dilecti, inquantum huiusmodi. Unde cum penes fines differant actus animae, erunt tres actus respectu trium finium, scilicet respectu veri, inquantum est verum, et amati, inquantum est amatum, sive boni, inquantum est bonum, et tenti sive habiti, inquantum est huiusmodi." For secondary literature on Albert's conception of theological happiness, see, for instance: Hoye 1981, pp. 61–77; Müller 2001; Anzulewicz/Rigo 2002, pp. 388–416. For Albert's conception of philosophical happiness, see, for instance: Müller 2001; Anzulewicz/Krause 2018, pp. 158–194.

6. For general overviews of the early reception of Aristotle's *Nicomachean Ethics* in the thirteenth century, see, for instance: Wieland 1981; id. 1982, pp. 657–672.

just a means to an end for them: it was to lead the human intellect to God, who was the ultimate good and who enjoyed ultimate happiness to the highest degree.[7] Aquinas took over this view for his explanation of ultimate happiness. In short, Aquinas's interpretation of ultimate human happiness in his commentary on the *Sentences* was inspired by some key ideas which he found in his Latin predecessors at the University of Paris, even though, as is evident from these few remarks, he altered them in accordance with his own needs. Unlike these early arts masters, who had at their disposal only parts of Aristotle's *Nicomachean Ethics*, Aquinas abstained from reinterpreting the *Ethics* in its own right in a theologial vein, as many of these masters did. Indeed, he selectively used their interpretations of the *ethica vetus* and *ethica nova* for his own theory of eschatological happiness, by dissociating their views from the original context of the *Ethics* in these early commentaries and recontextualizing them to the related theme of the beatific vision.[8]

Without any doubt, however, it was Albert the Great who exerted the greatest influence on young Thomas. While Weisheipl and Torrell are not certain that Aquinas studied under Albert in Paris, they both consider it a real possibility. Upon resigning from his obligations as conventual lector in the Teutonian cities of Hildesheim, Freiburg, Regensburg, and Strasbourg, Albert served as regent master of theology at the University of Paris from 1245–1248, where he and Aquinas must have overlapped for almost three years. What was true of the lecture hall at the university must have been even truer of the Dominican convent of St. Jacques. This was the main locale where both Dominicans would have stayed during this time, probably

7. For Aquinas's view, see: Thomas Aquinas, *Commentum in quatuor libros Sententiarum*, l. 4, d. 49, q. 1, a. 1, qc. 4 (ed. Parma 7/2, p. 1183): "Respondeo dicendum ad primam quaestionem, quod beatitudo, cum sit naturaliter ab omnibus hominibus desiderata, nominat ultimum humanae vitae finem. Finis autem cujuslibet rei est operatio propria, vel per operationem propriam ad finem venit. Cum autem forma propria sit in qualibet re operationis propriae principium; forma autem propria hominis, inquantum est homo, sit rationalis anima; oportet quod vel in ipsis actibus rationalis animae beatitudo consistat, vel in his ad quae homo per actus rationalis animae comparatur. Haec autem bona animae dicuntur; unde necesse est beatitudinem ponere in bonis animae, etiam secundum philosophos."

8. For the concept of "dissociated transformations" of ideas, see: Krause 2015b, pp. 175–217.

conversed frequently, and where Albert, as a master of the Dominican study house, may have also taught Aquinas.[9] The likely close contact between Albert and Aquinas in Paris for such an extended time also appears to be a convincing historical explanation for Aquinas's early and unwavering interest in explaining key theological teachings, such as the beatific vision, by way of Aristotelian and Peripatetic philosophical insights. Indeed, at a time when Aristotle's natural works were still officially banned from the curriculum at the university, Albert was already a strong defender of Aristotelian philosophy in its usefulness for theology. In a famous quotation from his commentary on Dionysius's *Seventh Epistle*, he showed little respect for

> certain people, who have no knowledge, but wish to fight the use of philosophy in every possible way, and especially among the Preachers, where there is no one to stop them, who are, as it were, irrational animals blaspheming in those things of which they are ignorant.[10]

Albert's outspoken criticism of his seemingly prejudiced Dominican brothers may have been part of his classroom teaching while in Paris, but it certainly was immediately after the Parisian period, when he lectured on the *corpus Dionysiacum* in Cologne during the years of 1248–1252. Albert was instructed to go to Cologne by his Dominican superiors in the summer of 1248 in order to found one of four new study houses in the Dominican provinces, Heilig Kreuz. He took with him four famous Dominican students: Thomas Aquinas, Ulrich of Strasbourg, Thomas of Cantimpré, and Ambrogio Sansedoni. In the fall of the same year, Albert returned to his teaching obligations, now at Heilig Kreuz. Yet he did so in a form highly unconventional for any Dominican study house of the time. As we learn from Michèle Mulchahey's careful reconstruction of Aquinas's classroom notes of the time—notes which have been preserved in the precious manuscript Napoli, Bibliotheca Nazionale, MS I.B.54—Albert did

9. See: Mulchahey 1998, pp. 254–257; id. 2008, pp. 118–147, esp. p. 120.

10. Albertus Magnus, *Super Dionysii Epistulas*, ep. 7 (ed. Colon. 37/2, p. 504, v. 27–32): "quidam, quia nesciunt, omnibus modis velint impugnare usum philosophiae, et maxime in praedicatoribus, ubi nullus eis resistit, tamquam bruta animalia blasphemantes in his quae ignorant."

not give the two theology lectures that we would expect of a traditional curriculum: one on a book of the Bible, another on a book of the *Sentences*. Rather, he innovated instantly upon his arrival. In the first two academic years, 1248/49 and 1249/50, Albert taught his students Dionysius's apophatic theology, the *Ecclesiastical Hierarchy* and the *Divine Names*, together with book four of the *Sentences*. In the two subsequent academic years of 1250/51 and 1251/52, he went even beyond this simple replacement of biblical exegesis with Greek Christian negative theology by teaching Aristotelian philosophy in the form of Aristotle's *Nicomachean Ethics* together with books two and three of the *Sentences*.

Both of Albert's pedagogical decisions would have a fundamental and long-lasting impact on the educational policies of the Dominican study houses, and also on Thomas Aquinas's personal career as a scholar and teacher.[11] This can be seen not only in his imitation of Albert's curriculum at the Dominican study house Santa Sabina, which he himself headed in Rome between 1265 and 1268, but also in his preparation of the *Tabula libri Ethicorum*, a small index or lexicon which he instructed his secretaries to compile in 1270, some two decades after his studies in Cologne, in preparation for composing his own commentary on Aristotle's *Nicomachean Ethics*. This *Tabula* contains an index not only of the main themes discussed by Aristotle, but also of those covered by Albert in *Super Ethica*, his Cologne commentary on the *Ethics*.[12]

Young Aquinas, the bright and eager student at Cologne, would bequeath to us both a precious notebook on the Dionysius lectures of Albert the Great and his own marginal and interlinear glosses on a manuscript known today as Codex 30 of the Archiepiscopal Diocesan and Cathedral Library of the city of Cologne. This codex contains John Scotus Eriugena's translations of the *corpus Dionysiacum* in an edition that can be dated to the eleventh century. The glosses to this codex, as Maria Burger has shown in her meticulous examinations, are written

11. See: Mulchahey 2008, pp. 122–137.

12. See, for instance: Torrell 2000, pp. 229–231 and 343–344.

in young Aquinas's hand and reveal a striking overlap in content and organization with Albert's commentaries on Dionysius's corpus.[13] While these recent findings have helped scholarship to reevaluate some of the datings of Albert's commentaries on the *corpus Dionysiacum*, discussions are still ongoing concerning his first commentary, *On the Celestial Hierarchy*, which Albert may have begun at Paris, but prepared for publication with Aquinas's help at Cologne.[14]

All of these factors combined meant that the young Aquinas had a solid four-year training in Dionysian theology and Aristotelian *Ethics* under his belt when he headed for the University of Paris in the summer or fall of 1252. Still, his becoming a bachelor there was an exception. Aquinas was two years under the age, twenty-nine, prescribed to take up such a position, and he joined the University of Paris in the midst of a conflict between secular clergymen and mendicants—a good reason not to seek statutory dispensation for the Dominicans. Yet his teacher Albert went to great lengths and provided him with the strongest possible recommendation, which he urged upon the previous master general and now cardinal, Hugh of St. Cher. Finally, upon the combined support of these two esteemed clergymen, the master general of the Dominicans, John the Teuton, gave in and assigned the twenty-seven-year-old Thomas Aquinas to his first official, and at the same time highly prestigious, position, as *baccalaureus Sententiarus* in Paris.

If academic teaching at Paris already followed the schedule as described in the statutes of 1335 or later, Aquinas probably began to lecture on the four books of the *Sentences* on 9 October 1252, the day after the feast day of St. Dionysius.[15] Adriano Oliva O.P. has convincingly shown that Aquinas indeed did so in the actual order of the

13. See: Burger 2005, pp. 190–208; id. 2009, pp. 561–582.

14. See: Mulchahey 2008, p. 141 note 22; Oliva 2006, pp. 214–253, Burger 2009, pp. 572–574.

15. CUP, tx. 1188, n. 9 (ed. Denifle t. 2, pp. 692): "Item, nota, quod bachalarii in theologia qui debent legere Sententias, et illi qui habent legere Bibliam in quatuor Ordinibus Mendicantium, debent facere *principia* sua infra festum Exaltationis Sancte Crucis et festum beati Dionysii. Et presuppositio quod tot sint quod non possint complere, tamen non sit in quolibet die nisi unum principium. Et semper in primis Sancti Jacobi immediate post predictum festum beati Dionysii illi qui non fecerunt faciunt, nec legitur aliqua hora in ipsa facultate, quousque omnia predicta principia sint facta totaliter et completa. Tamen si pauciora essent principia, ita quod finita essent ante festum beati Dionysii, nichilominus non legitur in ipsa facultate a crastino Exaltationis Sancte Crucis usque ad crastinum sancti Dionysii in aliqua hora."

books over the following two academic years, before he sat down for another year or two to revise these lectures for publication.[16] Besides these ordinary teaching obligations, Aquinas also assisted with the theological disputations of the university masters and gave his own public disputations on various occasions of the academic year. All these activities were closely overseen by the Dominican regent master for foreigners in order to determine whether the young *baccalaureus* was making sufficient progress. In Aquinas's case, this was Elias Brunet, who had succeeded Albert in 1248 and remained in this position until Aquinas took over on 3 March 1256, the day that he obtained his licence to teach as a master of theology at the University of Paris. This he did with great diligence during the following three academic years until 1259, when he headed back to Naples, his original priory.[17]

As might be expected from his studies under Albert at Cologne, Aquinas's commentary on the *Sentences* was strongly indebted to the thought of his teacher. While he quotes Dionysius over 600 times and Aristotle's *Ethics* over 730 times in his commentary, some of the most striking overlaps with Albert's use of these sources occur in our present text. The notes to my translation signal the repeated concurrence between Aquinas's and Albert's use of Dionysius's teachings on the vision of God—teachings such as those we find predominantly in Albert's earliest theological writings, for instance, *On the Resurrection*, *On the Incarnation*, *Question on the Vision of God*, and his commentary on the *Sentences*. Although there is no room here to discuss this influence conclusively, the evidence strongly suggests that the young Aquinas was not only well versed in incorporating the sources he studied under Albert, but also in doing the same with Albert's own writings. It is thus all the more intriguing to ask, as I illustrate in the introductions to each article of the present question, to what extent and in which ways Aquinas left the conciliatory approach of his teacher behind and found his own innovative ways to explain how the blessed will see God through His essence.

16. See: Oliva 2006, p. 253.

17. See: Torrell 2000, p. 99.

Notes on the Text

Ever since Pope Leo XIII instigated the epistle *Iampridem considerando* of 15 October 1879, progress on the systematic and critical study of the manuscripts of Thomas Aquinas's works has been far-reaching. Under the auspices of the famous Editio Leonina (Rome 1882–1984, Rome/Paris, 1984–present), a team of editors, now at the Commissio Leonina in Paris, have published thirty of the projected fifty volumes of the critical edition of Aquinas's *opera omnia*. Aquinas's commentary on the *Sentences* (tt. 17–20) still awaits its full publication in this edition.[1]

Until we hold these volumes in our hands, every scholar working on book IV of the *Sentences* commentary wishes to have lived in eighteenth-century Barcelona, Spain. There, Aquinas's autograph is said to have been available at Santa Catalina until a fire hit the Dominican convent in 1835, the first year of the ecclesiastical confiscations of Mendizábal, and purportedly destroyed the manuscript.[2] Nonetheless, the manuscript situation is hardly dire. James Weisheipl lists 167 extant codices in the "Brief Catalogue of Authentic Works" of his monumental study *Friar Thomas d'Aquino*.[3] Winfried Fauser, the current editor of the critical edition of book IV of the *Sentences* and associate member of the Commissio Leonina, now catalogues 217 extant codices.[4]

From these, the pre-critical edition, which has been generously granted to me as textual basis for the present translation by Dr.

1. The Prologue of Book I of Thomas Aquinas's commentary on the *Sentences* has been critically edited in: Oliva 2006, pp. 301–340.

2. More information on the autograph of book IV of the *Sentences* is found in: Anzulewicz 2016, p. 7. The confiscations of 1835–1837 also affected the Dominican convent of Almagro, where a fragment of d. 15, q. 4, a. 4, sol. 2 ad 2–a. 5, sol. 3 was preserved. For the official confiscation texts concerning smaller convents such as Almagro, see: BOE núm. 211 (29 de julio de 1835), pp. 841–842 and BOE núm. 292 (14 de octubre de 1835), p. 1157.

3. Weisheipl 1983, pp. 358–359.

4. Fauser 2014.

Adriano Oliva O.P., the head of the Commissio Leonina, rests on two families of codices. The former stems from the tradition of the University of Paris in three exemplars, the latter from an Italian tradition.[5] As Dr. Oliva advises in a personal email conversation, the critical edition of book IV will probably be available within six to seven years of publication of this translation.[6]

The textual basis of this translation is, therefore, the best possible compromise currently available. As the primary textual basis for the translation, I have taken Dr. Fauser's pre-critical edition of Thomas Aquinas's commentary on the *Sentences*, book IV, distinction 49, question 2, which Dr. Oliva kindly has permitted me to use. As the secondary textual basis, I have consulted the Parma edition (1852–1873, reprinted 1948–1950, 25 volumes), and provided variants in the notes to the text whenever relevant for the argumentation.

5. Ibid.

6. Oliva, 23 Jan 2018: "Le volume ne paraîtra pas avant 6 ou 7 ans."

NOTES ON THE TRANSLATION

WHEN THE FAMOUS GERMAN PHILOSOPHER and literary critic Walter Benjamin (1892–1940) stated that "There is no muse of philosophy, nor is there one of translation,"[1] he seemed to note an important similarity between the two. Knowledge as embodied in the nine muses of Greek mythological writings ought to be skillfully mastered to perfection—a demand which is virtually impossible to fulfill in philosophy and translation alike. And even if we followed Plato or the Pythagoreans before him in subsuming philosophy under the art of μουσική,[2] as Strabo tells us, and likewise if we assumed a musical ideal of translation, we would still remain in the dark as to what skillful mastery to perfection it entailed.

Ever since the extensive vernacularizations of Greek and Latin in the Renaissance, translation theories have come to the rescue and told us about how to realize these lofty ideals in practice.[3] Yet the very ideals they have propounded have been subject to the whims of Kairos and Horae rather than to the inspiration of Euterpe and Polymnia. The Romantic period alone—the period that still bears heavily on our translation ideals—saw its own ideals change from aesthetic and stylistic paradigms, to taking "literary possession" of the translated works, to accurate renderings of the original text in cases of historical, philosophical, or scientific works.[4]

The paradox that seems to have prevailed through the ages and that makes skillful perfection of translation impossible is what

1. Benjamin 1996, p. 259.

2. Strabo, *Strabonis Geographica* l. 10, c. 3, s. 10 (ed. A. Meineke 1877): "*καὶ διὰ τοῦτο μουσικὴν ἐκάλεσε Πλάτων καὶ ἔτι πρότερον οἱ Πυθαγόρειοι τὴν φιλοσοφίαν, καὶ καθ' ἁρμονίαν τὸν κόσμον συνεστάναι φασί, πᾶν τὸ μουσικὸν εἶδος θεῶν ἔργον ὑπολαμβάνοντες. οὕτω δὲ καὶ αἱ Μοῦσαι θεαὶ καὶ Ἀπόλλων μουσηγέτης καὶ ἡ ποιητικὴ πᾶσα ὑμνητική.*"

3. See, for instance: Venuti 2000.

4. Burwick 2008, pp. 68–69.

Goethe termed "simple prosaic translation" versus "parodistic translation" and what Schleiermacher called *Paraphrase* versus *Imitation*.[5] Neither a word-for-word *Paraphrase*, which, in Schleiermacher's words, reproduces "the contents of a work with some accuracy" but dispenses altogether with "the impression made by the work," nor the *Imitation*, which "strives to be for its readers, as far as possible, everything the original provided its original readers," but which ultimately sacrifices the original's identity, would do justice to the art of the muses. Closest perhaps is what Goethe identifies as the highest form of translation. It goes unnamed in his *Notes and Queries* (*Noten und Abhandlungen*), maybe on purpose, but it demands no less a task of the translator than to familiarize his audience with the foreign text through the closest possible adherence to the original:

> In an attempt to identify with its original, a translation ultimately approaches an interlinear version and eases the understanding of the original exquisitely—through it, we are led, even driven to the original text. In this way, therefore, the whole circle which encompasses the approaching movement of the foreign to the familiar, of the known to the unknown, is ultimately closed.[6]

Nothing less than closing the Platonic circle, so Goethe seems to tells us, is the skillful mastery of translation to perfection: the translator's striving for his own identification with the original, his subsequent prophetic conveyance of it in the language of the audience in order to take them onto the same path of identification and to consimilate their life world with that of the author. Through this circular movement shines Goethe's trust in the translator's ability to perform and to enact the original in a hitherto foreign medium until this medium is molded to assume familiarity with the original. The

5. Goethe 1961, pp. 307–310; Schleiermacher 2012, p. 48.

6. Goethe 1961, p. 309: "Eine Übersetzung, die sich mit dem Original zu identifizieren strebt, nähert sich zuletzt der Interlinearversion und erleichtert höchlich das Verständnis des Originals; hiedurch werden wir an den Grundtext hinangeführt, ja getrieben, und so ist denn zuletzt der ganze Zirkel abgeschlossen, in welchem sich die Annäherung des Fremden und Einheimischen, des Bekannten und Unbekannten bewegt."

tools to be used in such a mastery, the instruments to be applied to put these lofty ideals as much into practice as humanly possible, ought to focus on all textual elements—on meaning, form, image, and style. Nothing less than all the features of the original ought to shine through the translation.

In translating Thomas Aquinas's *Commentary on Peter Lombard's Sentences*, putting this ideal into practice appears to be fraught with complexity and obstacle. Readers of the mature Aquinas in the original Latin language will be acquainted with his lucid style, his concise diction, his assertive syntax, and his succinct responses. Readers of the young Aquinas do not always meet with such an experience. Here, more than anywhere else in his oeuvre, Aquinas wrestles with ideas and thoughts contained in his sources, emulates reflections and considerations gathered from his teacher Albert the Great, and joins in agreement viewpoints of seeming divergence found in many of his near contemporaries. And yet, amidst all these entangled and engaged, demanding and dedicated pursuits, Aquinas energetically declared his own voice and dynamically expressed his own mind. The reading experience that emerges from such a powerful, intricate work should ideally emerge in translation as well. The young Aquinas should be discernible as the young Aquinas, regardless of the language in which he is read. This is why all care has been taken in the translation to remain faithful to the original in meaning, diction, and style. Yet over and above these considerations range the demands of accuracy. In the case of a Scholastic text filled with technical terminology and argumentative precision, the translator must be faithful to the text. Oftentimes, the dilemma between eloquence of translation or being as faithful as possible to the letter is no small one. However, the decision seemed to me straightforward: I considered it most appropriate to side with the Latin letter as much as the requirements of the English language would allow.

As dry and monotonous as it may appear to today's audience—widely read in sensitive and powerful expressions of centuries of world literature—I have tried, wherever possible, to reproduce the same Latin term with the same English term. I have included these terms with their translations in a glossary that follows the text, which may particularly aid cases where deviation from this practice was unavoidable. In view of the significance of Aquinas's technical terminology, I often saw eye to eye with Deferrari's dictionary, which excellently collates Aquinas's technical terms and their connotations as they emerge in his mature works.[7] For instance, as Deferrari shows, Aquinas makes use of the Latin term *in actu* to express either the dynamic and operative aspect of performing a particular action or activity (in opposition to a particular habit or a potency for a particular action or activity), or the static and ontological aspect of being in actuality (in opposition to being in potentiality). In my translation, I pay attention to the context of each use of *in actu* and translate it either with "in act" expressing the dynamic meaning, or with "in actuality" expressing the static meaning.

In the interest of readability, I have translated all Latin technical terms, even the key technical term in Aquinas's discussion "through God's essence" (*per essentiam Dei*). Aquinas makes abundant use of this technical term throughout to express the cognitive mode by which God will be seen in the life to come. The beatific vision through God's essence stands in sharp contrast with any vision through a species (*per speciem*), since only the vision through His essence provides an unmediated, direct access to the essence of God—the only essence that cannot be noetically communicated through any created intelligible species.[8] In English, this Latin term could be rendered "by the essence" or "through the essence," and it was no easy choice between emphasizing the aspect of instrumentality (in the case of "by") or an aspect of intermediacy (in the case of "through"). Either of the two takes away the precise layers of meaning contained in the Latin term *per*, which are crucial to understanding Aquinas's solution to the beatific vision. In fact, neither of the two English terms is capable of expressing the directness and immediacy that Aquinas intends to express with the Latin *per essentiam*—so I can only hope

7. See Deferrari 2004, entry: *actus*.

8. For the extended discussion on this matter, see introduction to article one.

that my readers consult these preliminary remarks carefully to grasp the impact of a translation. In all other cases, I translated the Latin *per* with the most appropriate English proposition for the context.

The pre-critical Leonine edition of the text has proven extraordinarily helpful for cross-referencing. For my translation, I checked all these references and, where the Latin reference was no longer than a few lines and was a reference made by Thomas Aquinas himself, I quoted it in the footnotes. I have included all the cross-references taken from the pre-critical Leonine edition. In some cases, however, I found that cross-references could be added. I thus made every effort to provide my own cross-references, especially to texts of Albert the Great, a key influence, as we have seen, on this text of Aquinas. Regarding the biblical quotations made by Aquinas, I always referenced the full verse as found in the Latin Vulgate. In my English translation of these biblical verses I consulted (in cases of non-literal quotation) and used (in cases of literal quotation) the Douay-Rheims translation of the Vulgate.

Thomas Aquinas's Commentary on Peter Lombard's Sentences Book IV, Distinction 49, Question 2

Overview

THE OVERALL ORDER AQUINAS gave to the text to follow, that is to question 2 of distinction 49 of the fourth book of his commentary on the *Sentences*, unfolds in seven articles. In the first article, Aquinas investigates the act of the beatific vision. His main point here is to show that this act of seeing God's essence will take place through a relation of knowing between God and the disembodied soul of the blessed exclusively reserved for this ultimate vision.

In the second and third articles together, he raises two constraints about this ultimate act of knowing. First, in article two, Aquinas dismisses the idea of a corporeal vision in favor of a purely intellectual vision. Then, in the third article, he rejects the view of a comprehensive intellectual vision of God in favor of an essential, albeit quantitatively limited, vision.

The subsequent two articles present us with two important clarifications concerning the beatific vision: In the fourth article, Aquinas introduces a discussion of different degrees to which the blessed will see God, and explains why it is that one blessed saint will see God more perfectly than another. In the fifth article, Aquinas turns to those things that the blessed will see in seeing God, and he limits these in close connection to the impossibility of comprehension as discussed in article three.

The last two articles present two discussions of the necessary conditions that have to be met in order to attain the beatific vision. In article six, Aquinas describes how the intellect has to be supernaturally raised to the beatific vision by a new intellectual disposition that is created by God Himself. In article seven, Aquinas explains why the vision of God cannot be attained in this earthly life, except miraculously and for a brief time span only, but rather must await the life to come.

TRANSLATION

In the following, we investigate the vision of God and ask seven questions about it. First, whether the blessed will see Him through His essence. Second, whether they are able to see God by the corporeal eye. Third, whether in seeing God they comprehend Him. Fourth, whether one seeing God through His essence sees Him more perfectly than another. Fifth, whether those seeing the divine essence necessarily see all the things that God sees. Sixth, whether any creature can reach the vision of God through His essence by purely natural means. Seventh, whether anyone can see God through His essence in the present life.

ARTICLE 1

THE VISION OF GOD THROUGH HIS ESSENCE

INTRODUCTION

Stretched out before the young Aquinas's inner eye and, to a certain extent, before his corporeal eye in the library or the *scriptorium* was the history of Christian thought on how God would be seen in the beatific vision. In his commentary on the *Sentences*, Aquinas pondered and considered the various accounts of the beatific vision. These ranged from the most recent treatises written by no one less than his erudite master, Albert the Great, and his Franciscan colleague, Bonaventure of Bagnoregio, to the ancient works penned by St. Augustine of Hippo, whose optimistic outlook on a direct beatific vision Aquinas unequivocally followed, and the Greek Christian tradition represented by Dionysius the Areopagite. Yet his own innovative account of this vision emerged almost exclusively within Aristotelian and Arabic Peripatetic explanatory concepts and frameworks, most prominently the principle of noetic identity between knower and known, as will become clear over the course of this article introduction. Indeed, unlike most of his Latin predecessors and contemporaries, Aquinas used a great variety of tools and insights contained in the new translations of medieval Arabic philosophy to shape his explanations of the modality of the beatific vision. At the heart of these explanations, he relied on theories which presented competing intellectualist views on ultimate happiness, including views that advocated a so-called ultimate conjunction with the separate Agent Intellect. But Aquinas paid little attention to their provocative content in his *Sentences*. Instead, he cherished the structural elements these new sources proposed in order to explain how ultimate conjunction works, and he adopted them to explain the modality of the vision of God through His essence.[1] Hence, Aquinas's theory of the beatific vision came to redefine and set new standards of reasoned justification of an age-old theological teaching. But how exactly did he map these Aristotelian and Arabic explanatory concepts and frameworks onto the world of Augustinian theology?

The initial step of rethinking the beatific vision in light of the principle of identity between cognizer and cognized, so-called noetic identity, was to present the theological denial of seeing God face to face (only to reject this denial immediately thereafter) in analogy to the philosophical denial of ultimate conjunction with separate substances. Aquinas knew the theological denial intimately from the condemnations of 1241 and the writings of his Latin contemporaries, and he learned about Alfarabi's philosophical denial from Averroes's *Long Commentary on Aristotle's On the Soul*.[2] Yet none of his contemporaries taught him to align these two—this alignment was Aquinas's own innovation.

1. In the eyes of most proponents of the clearly different theories of ultimate conjunction, human happiness is attained as a result of our own intellectual efforts and, in most cases, even in this life. For extended discussions of these theories in the secondary literature, see: Altmann 1965, pp. 47–87; Pines 1979, pp. 82–109; Davidson 1992; Taylor 1998, pp. 87–110; Black 1999, pp. 159–184; Druart 2000, pp. 259–273; Taylor 2005, pp. 29–51; Wirmer 2006, pp. 569–590; id. 2008, pp. 287–409; Taylor 2009a, pp. 187–220; id. 2009b, pp. i-cix; Druart 2011, pp. 371–379; Adamson 2012, pp. 97–122. Aquinas, of course, did not agree to either of these two conditions for the attainment of happiness. For extended discussions in the secondary literature, see, for instance: Wirmer 2006, pp. 569–590; Taylor 2013, pp. 141–183; Krause 2015b, pp. 175–217.

2. Averroes, *Commentarium magnum in Aristotelis De anima libros*, l. 3, com. 36 (ed. Crawford 1953, p. 481, v. 48–57 and p. 485, v. 180–p. 486, v. 190): "Dicamus igitur: qui autem ponit intellectum materialem esse generabilem et corruptibilem nullum modum, ut michi videtur, potest invenire naturalem quo possumus continuari cum intellectibus abstractis. Intellectus enim debet esse intellectum omnibus modis, et maxime in rebus liberatis a materia. Si igitur possibile esset quod substantia generabils et corruptibilis intelligeret formas abstractas et reverteretur idem cum eis, tunc possibile esset ut natura possibilis fieret necessaria, ut Alfarabius dixit in Nichomachia; et hoc necessarium est secundum fundamenta sapientum. <...> Et ideo videmus Alfarabium in postremo, cum credidit opinionem Alexandri esse veram in generatione intellectus materialis, quod fuit necesse apud ipsum secundum hanc opinionem opinari quod intelligentia agens non est nisi causa agens nos tantum; et hoc manifeste dixit in Nichomachia. Et est contra suam opinionem in epistola de Intellectu; illic enim dixit esse possibile

Initially, therefore, Aquinas suggested that, since most theologians and philosophers seemed to agree on the possibility for humans to attain ultimate happiness, they needed to overcome certain conceptual and argumentative difficulties. The greatest among these difficulties was to explain how a created, limited human intellect could come to know or be assimilated to or noetically become one with an intelligible object beyond its capacity, be it God in the theological case or the separate substances in the philosophical one. For some theologians and philosophers, this difficulty seemed insurmountable, and thus they ultimately resorted to a denial of the possibility for humans to attain ultimate happiness. Yet in Aquinas's eyes, such pessimism was indefensible. Augustine and Scripture, as well as human nature and teleology, spoke clearly against it.[3]

Already at this point, Aquinas's alignment of the theological and the philosophical denials of the possibility of obtaining ultimate happiness proved convenient: he could simply rely on the arguments made in his philosophical sources, rather than draw on arguments from theological authorities. The main argument he therefore gave to defend his optimism came from a reading adapted from Aristotle's *Nicomachean Ethics* X, which he found applied in the recently

---

ut intellectus materialis intelligat res abstractas; et est opinio Avempeche. Iste igitur sunt questiones ponentibus intellectum materialem esse generatum, et quod finis est continuari cum abstractis." Here and in the following, I only refer to the Latin edition of Averroes's *Long Commentary on Aristotle's De anima*, as it best connects to the historical actors discussed in this book, Thomas Aquinas, Albert the Great, and others. Nonetheless, readers should know that there is a very fine English translation available which was made from the Latin edition and which includes all Arabic fragments that are currently known to be extant. Averroes (trans. Taylor 2009).

3. Aquinas also has in mind Aristotle's brief remark in his *On the Soul*, book III, chapter 7 where Aristotle raises the question of whether it is possible for an embodied human intellect to understand things separate in being from matter. See: Aristoteles, *De anima*, l. 3, lect. 3 (431b17–19), trans. vet. (ed. Gauthier 1985, p. 478): "Vtrum autem contingat separabilium aliquod intelligere ipsum existentem non separatum a magnitudine, aut non, considerandum est posterius." As is well known, the Stagirite never returns to this question. Yet the long discussions that ensued over this question in the Greek and Arabic Peripatetic traditions must have already been known to the anonymous Latin commentator who wrote in a similar shorthand fashion to Aristotle (ibid., ed. Gauthier 1985, p. 483, v. 134–138): "Secunda dubitatio est utrum intellectus, cum non sit separabilis a magnitudine, intelliget aliquod separabilium, aut non? Et dicit quod hoc posterius dicendum est, set hoc non dicit in hoc libro. Et hoc est: *Vtrum autem*. Litteram lege sicut poteris, quia non habemus tempus exponendi eam" (emphasis as in edition).

available translations of the medieval Arabic philosophers. They had identified Aristotle's ethical teaching, namely, that happiness is located in the specifically human activity of reason with regard to the highest object of cognition, as lying in a transcendent kind of intellectual activity beyond that of scientific investigation, and they called it "ultimate conjunction."[4] Aquinas quite rightly took this to refer to the cognition of separate substances; in particular, the separate Agent Intellect. With this parallel ultimate object of cognition in hand, *viz.* God for the theologians and the separate substances for the philosophers, Aquinas could now easily rely on the teleology found in his philosophical sources, which is why he suggests in the present article that nothing but cognition of the principle of creation can fulfill human perfection and happiness:

> <S>ince understanding is the proper activity of humans to the highest degree, their happiness must be assigned to them in accordance with this activity when perfected in them. Yet, since the perfection of the one who understands, inasmuch as it is of this kind, is the very intelligible, <then> if humans do not attain a vision of the divine essence in the most perfect activity of the intellect, but <if they attain> rather something else, one has to say that something other than God beatifies humans. And since the ultimate perfection of anything consists in the conjunction to its principle, it follows that something other than God would be the efficient principle of humans. This is absurd according to us and it is similarly absurd according to those philosophers who assert that our souls emanate from separate substances, so that in the end we will be able to understand them.[5]

In this initial conclusion, which entailed that the principle of origin and of ultimate end need to be identical, Aquinas relied on the Neoplatonic egress-regress scheme together with a teleology of becoming noetically one with the ontological principle and ultimate

4. An important discussion of the history of this view is given in D'Ancona 2017, pp. 8–29.

5. See the translation, pp. 103–104.

end. Aquinas's reliance on this scheme was an argumentative move that he was well acquainted with from Albert the Great, whose works were permeated by it as the underlying key to reality as a whole and to human life in particular.[6] In this particular article, however, it served Aquinas in rethinking the beatific vision of God through His essence, as what he took to be the right explanatory model to sufficiently account for this vision. Unlike his Latin contemporaries, however, who were committed to more traditional explanatory models and took inspiration from theological models of their own tradition, Aquinas chose to appropriate three foreign philosophical models, all three of which he found in Averroes's *Long Commentary on Aristotle's On the Soul* and in Avicenna's *Metaphysics*. Nonetheless, it cannot be emphasized enough that Aquinas was instructed in understanding them by Albert the Great when he attended his lectures on Aristotle's *Nicomachean Ethics* in Cologne in 1250 and 1251 and helped compile and publish Albert's first ethics commentary, entitled *On the Ethics* (*Super Ethica*).[7] What intrigued Aquinas

---

6. See, for instance: Albertus Magnus, *De resurrectione*, tr. 4, q. 2, a. 2 (ed. Colon. 26, p. 341, v. 77–p. 342, v. 3 and p. 342, v. 17–22): "Sicut est principium vitae naturalis intrinsecum et unitum ei quod habet vitam, et hoc est anima vel spiritus, secundum quod dicimus angelos et daemones habere vitam naturae: sic est principium, quod est causa vitae aeternae, intrinsecum quidem, sed distinctum per essentiam, quia totum est intra et totum est extra; quod est deus. Unde vita aeterna est nihil aliud quam immediata participatio primi motus a principio coniuncto per modum gloriae, quod est deus. <...> Et dico 'coniuncti per modum gloriae,' quia licet a deo sit omnis vita, non tamen ab ipso solo habent hunc motum, sed etiam ab alio principio quod est creatum ab eo, sicut est spiritus vel anima, eo quod in talibus non est nisi essentialiter, praesentialiter et potentialiter, et non per modum glorificantis." For discussions in the secondary literature concerning the role the Neoplatonic scheme plays in Albert's works, see, for instance: Anzulewicz 2000a, pp. 369–396; id. 2000b, pp. 251–295; Anzulewicz / Rigo 2002, pp. 388–412; Anzulewicz 2009, pp. 219–242.

7. Guillelmus de Tocco, *Ystoria sancti Thome de Aquino*, c. 13 (ed. le Brun-Gouanvic 1996, p. 117, v. 24–27; p. 118, v. 70–74): "Cumque sic taciturnus <scil. frater Thomas> proficeret, cuius profectum opinio humana nesciret, cepit Magister Albertus librum De diuinis nominibus beati Dyonisii legere, et predictus iuuenis attentius lectionem audire. <...> Post hoc autem predictus magister Albertus cum librum Ethicorum cum questionibus legeret, frater Thomas magistri lecturam studiose collegit et redegit in scriptis; opus stilo disertum, subtilitate profundum, sicut a fonte tanti doctoris aurire potuit, qui in scientia omnem hominem in sui temporis etate precessit." As Kübel points out in the Prolegomena to Albert's *Super Ethica* (ed. Colon. 14/1, p. V, v. 52–58), the famous Codex Vat. Lat. 722 makes the same reference: "Codex Vat. Lat 722, quo hoc opus continetur, etiam refert Thomam huius operis conficiendi participem fuisse, cum f.209r dicatur: 'Istae sunt quaestiones fratris Alberti ordinis predicatorum quas collegit frater tomas de aquino.' Scriptor codicis hunc nuntium ex libro Wilhelmi de Tocco hausisse videtur."

in the three philosophical models that he examined in this first article may be reduced to a single epistemological question: How ought the ultimate intelligible form that the human intellect requires for cognizing God to be conceived in order to identify it noetically with God Himself?

The answer Aquinas gave to this question in article one certainly addresses the debates concerning the directness of the beatific vision that preoccupied thinkers before the ruling of the magisterium in 1241. But it also opened a way by which this direct cognition of God could be captured in Aristotelian terms. Indeed, Aquinas's reply to this difficult question was one closely tied to his theory of human cognition in general, a theory that was deeply inspired by Aristotelian principles.[8] Most important among these was the principle that the human knower ought to become assimilated to its object of knowing, that he or she ought to become noetically one or identical with it. In natural cognition in this life, Aquinas envisioned this to happen in virtue of a so-called "intelligible form" (*species intelligibilis*), an impression of the natures of external things onto the human intellect, generated in processes of abstraction, and formally identical in content with the essences of the things in the world. However, in Aquinas's eyes, no form generated by the human intellect, nor infused into the human intellect by God, could lead to its cognizing the uncreated divine essence, since both forms constituted effects of God, albeit in different ways. The Aristotelian principle of formal identity between the intelligible form in the intellect and the essence of the object in the world spoke indeed against the possibility of explaining the beatific vision in Aristotelian terms. How then did Aquinas manage to do so? The two philosophical models that he initially examined for explaining the beatific vision both echoed these concerns.

8. The body of secondary literature concerning Aquinas's theory of natural cognition in this life in its indebtedness to Avicenna is vast. Some studies I consider particularly helpful are: Bazán 1981, pp. 425–446; Wilder 1991, pp. 2–32; Spruit 1994, pp. 156–174; Pasnau 1997; Pannacio 2001, pp. 185–201; Smit 2001, pp. 85–118; Pasnau 2002; Perler 2004, pp. 31–105; King 2007, pp. 81–100; Brower & Brower-Toland 2008, pp. 193–243; Pasnau 2008, pp. 131–149; Cory 2013, 2015, pp. 607–646.

The first model Aquinas discussed, a model that advocated for the generation of an intelligible species by way of intellectual abstraction from things in the world, could, in his eyes, only go so far as to account for cognition of God "by an effect, and, as it were, in a mirror." Aquinas attributed his reading of the generation of intelligibles to a model advocated by Alfarabi and Avempace, according to which the attainment of ultimate conjunction with the separate Agent Intellect was possible through intricately interwoven processes of abstraction.[9] The identification of Alfarabi and Avempace as original sources of this model, as we find it in Aquinas, however, comes with a range of interpretive challenges. On the one hand, it is well known that Aquinas could not have been acquainted with either of their views on ultimate conjunction from their original works. Rather, he must have learned of them through Averroes's *Long Commentary on Aristotle's On the Soul.* What Aquinas suggests about Alfarabi's and Avempace's model here is therefore to be read with care and caution, since it is mediated through Averroes's reading, a reading that is not always fair and objective but itself often driven by peculiar theoretical commitments and interests.[10] On the other hand, Aquinas's portrayal of Alfarabi and Avempace's agreement does not match Averroes's reading in all aspects. For instance, even though Averroes portrays Alfarabi and Avempace as being in general agreement on the aspect of the human abstractive abilities, he makes no mention of Alfarabi when he explains how these abilities are realized.[11] Aquinas's clustering of the two thus has little grounding in Averroes, but seems to be more akin to Albert the Great's interpretive style, to which Aquinas had been exposed for a number of years before

9. For more extended discussions in the secondary literature, see: Wirmer 2006, pp. 569–590; Krause 2014, pp. 92–105.

10. Averroes's reading of Alfarabi and Avempace's model is found in: Averroes, *Commentarium magnum in Aristotelis De anima libros*, l. 3, com. 36 (ed. Crawford 1953, p. 490, v. 321–p. 492, v. 387). Questions concerning the disparate readings of Alfarabi's and Avempace's model by Averroes and Aquinas have been addressed in the following literature: Wirmer 2006, 569–590; Taylor 2012, 509–550; Krause 2014, 94–102, but to the best of my knowledge, they have not yet been studied in relation to Albert the Great's reception. For Albert's extended discussion of these matters, see note 15 below.

11. See Averroes citation in note 10 above.

composing his own commentary on the *Sentences*. Indeed, Albert's continuous focus was on adjusting and synchronizing philosophical views rather than pointing out their subtle differences.[12] What we find in Aquinas's invocation of these two Arabic Peripatetic philosophers, therefore, is a multilayered mediation of ideas as well as approaches to these ideas that are challenging to disentangle for any historian of philosophy.

With this in mind, the simplest way of proceeding is to look at Aquinas's peculiar reading of Alfarabi's and Avempace's views on ultimate conjunction. This suggests, most fundamentally, that they took the initial process of abstraction to begin in sense perception of sensible objects and end in the generation of intelligibles. Yet the intelligibles generated in this first-order abstraction are, ontologically speaking, themselves composed. They contain a material aspect, amounting to the referential content of the objects in the world, and a formal aspect, the very being of an intelligible or quiddity (*quiditas*). Alfarabi's and Avempace's first-order intelligibles, according to Aquinas's portrayal, thus constitute intentional forms that *possess* a quiddity, rather than that they *are* a quiddity. Still, these first-order intelligibles are not the final products of the interwoven abstractive processes that Alfarabi and Avempace suggest, according to Aquinas's reading. Rather, they have as their *telos* that intelligible that *is* its quiddity, and that is identical in its simplicity to separate substances. Any second-order stage of abstraction, as Aquinas shows Alfarabi's and Avempace's model to maintain, thus strips away any material aspect of content, any possession of a quiddity, and, at its very end, produces an intelligible that is simple, universal, and unified. This final product of all human abstractive processes, then, both shares in the formality of separate substances and enables humans to know these substances and, through this knowledge, attain ultimate happiness in this life.

12. An especially insightful example of Albert's conciliatory style of interpretation is found in the parallel treatment of Alfarabi and Avempace he provides in his commentary on Aristotle's *On the Soul*. See: Albertus Magnus, *De anima*, l. 3, tr. 3, c. 8 (ed. Colon. 7/1, p. 217, v. 78–p. 218, v. 75).

For Aquinas's theory of the beatific vision, for which he tested this model as one possible explanation, two elements proved particularly problematic. As Aquinas took the essences of material things and those of separate substances to be ontologically equivocal, he protested that the ability to cognize one never entailed the ability to cognize the other. Yet even if this ontological equivocity were nullified, Aquinas insisted that abstraction would be bound to the laws of generalization set forth in the Porphyrian Tree. Abstraction would always end in the most generic understanding of separate substances, and never ascend to an essential cognition of them. While these two protests may carry a significant philosophical force, they nonetheless appear to be out of place in the context of Aquinas's discussions of the beatific vision. Earlier in his *Sentences*, Aquinas had already clarified that this vision amounts to an intuitive noetic act which is only attained in the afterlife under the conditions of permanency, unrealizable in this life.[13] Why, then, would he revert

13. Thomas Aquinas, *Commentum in quatuor libros Sententiarum*, l. 4, d. 49, q. 1, a. 1, qc. 4 (ed. Parma 7/2, p. 1185–1186): "Beatitudo ergo cum sit finis ad quem referuntur omnia desideria, oportet quod sit tale aliquid, quo habito nihil ulterius desiderandum restet. Quilibet autem naturaliter esse desiderat, et permanere in bono quod ipse habet; et ideo ab omnibus beatitudo tale aliquid esse ponitur quod immobilitatem habeat et perpetuitatem. Sed de immobilitate et perpetuitate beatitudinis humanae aliqui diversimode judicaverunt. <...> Ab omnibus enim communiter ponitur quod felicitas, sive beatitudo, est bonum rationalis vel intellectualis naturae; et ideo oporteret quod ubi invenitur natura rationalis vel intellectualis per essentiam, et non solum per participationem, etiam beatitudo ponatur per essentiam, et non per participationem; et ideo cum in homine sit non solum aliqua redundantia intellectus, sicut est in brutis quaedam redundantia rationis, inquantum participant aliqua prudentia, ut in eorum moribus apparet, sed est in eis ratio et intellectus per essentiam; oporteret ponere quod ad veram beatitudinem quandoque pervenire possit, et non tantum ad aliquam beatitudinis participationem; alias appetitus naturalis intellectualis naturae quae est in homine, frustraretur. Beatitudo autem vera non potest poni in hac vita propter mutabilitates varias quibus homo subjacet; unde necesse est beatitudinem quae est finis humanae vitae, esse post hanc vitam. Et hoc quidem concesserunt omnes philosophi qui posuerunt animam, quae est forma humani corporis, esse intellectum per essentiam: posuerunt enim animam immortalem. Illi vero qui posuerunt animam, quae est forma humani corporis, non esse intellectum per essentiam, sed in ea esse refulgentiam quamdam intellectus qui est separatus, et unus communis omnibus, ponunt animam, quae est corporis forma, esse corruptibilem, nec pervenire ad perfectam beatitudinem, sed solum ad aliquam beatitudinis participationem, qualis dicta est. Sed haec opinio absurda est, ut patuit distinctione 16 <sic: 17>, 2 libri, quaest. 2, art. 1. Et ideo simpliciter concedimus veram hominis beatitudinem esse post hanc vitam. Non negamus tamen quin aliqua beatitudinis participatio in hac vita esse possit, secundum quod homo est perfectus in bonis rationis speculativae principaliter, et practicae secundario; et de hac felicitate Philosophus in lib. Ethic. determinat, aliam, quae est post hanc vitam, nec asserens nec negans."

to a philosophical model in such a theologically delimited context? A possible explanation may be Aquinas's acquaintance with Albert the Great's use of Alfarabi's and Avempace's views on ultimate conjunction, a use which Albert later documented in his commentary on Aristotle's *On the Soul*. This commentary, written probably between 1254 and 1257, contains a striking overlap of exposition and refutation of Alfarabi's and Avempace's supposed model of ultimate conjunction with Aquinas. The overlap of refutation, in particular, which both Latin thinkers present is nonetheless much more fitting to Albert's context, covering the question of "how divine, separate things, are understood," than to Aquinas's.[14] Whether the master's work was also available to his student Aquinas before he finished the final redaction of book IV of his *Sentences* in 1256 still remains to be determined.[15]

---

14. Albertus Magnus, *De anima*, l. 3, tr. 3, c 6 (ed. Colon. 7/1, p. 214, v. 83–84): "Qualiter intelliguntur divina, quae sunt separata."

15. For the overlap of refutation, see: Albertus Magnus, *De anima*, l. 3, tr. 3, c. 8 (ed. Colon. 7/1, p. 218, v. 76–p. 219, v. 34): "Sed unicuique potest de facili patere, quod haec ratio non valet, nisi nos concedamus, quod univoce sunt quiditates separatorum per se et quiditates eorum quae separantur ab intellectu a materia, in qua sunt. Si enim hoc esset verum, tunc eiusdem virtutis esset comprehendere utrasque. Si autem aequivoce sunt, tunc nihil valet ratio inducta. Et si dicatur neque esse aequivoce neque penitus univoce, tunc oportet etiam virtutem intellectivam variari, supposito hoc quod dicit Aristoteles in sexto Ethicorum, quod omnis cognitio quae est in anima, secundum congruentiam fit cognoscentis et cogniti. Nisi enim hoc esset verum, tunc quaelibet virtus acciperet quodcumque cognitum, et sic intellectus acciperet sensibile et sensus acciperet intelligibile, quod omnino esse non potest. Si autem daretur quiditates utrorumque esse univocas, tunc multae adhuc remanerent dubitationes. Si autem dicatur intellectus possibilis esse corruptibilis, tunc quaeretur secundum praedicta, qualiter corruptibile unitur incorruptibili; et haec quaestio est tam in possibili quam in speculativo, quia uterque ponitur corruptibilis ab Avempeche. Si autem dicatur possibilis esse incorruptibilis et separatus, tunc relinquitur quaestio, qualiter intelligit aliquid de novo, quia in incorruptibili secundum substantiam non potest aliquid fieri novum secundum formam, eo quod ex forma et materia fit unum novum. Adhuc autem, cum uterque sit separatus, quare modo intelligit et non ante, cum semper sit uno modo, quod est separatum? Adhuc autem relinquitur quaestio secundum istos, quare de separatis secundum se non sunt scientiae speculativae, sicut sunt de coniunctis. Si enim utrumque est in potestate nostri intellectus, tunc speculabimur de separatis per separata, sicut speculamur de coniunctis. Hoc autem non est verum, quoniam si aliquid parum aliquando speculamur de separatis, hoc facimus per coniuncta cum materia, sicut per motum accipimus motorem, et nescimus speculari passiones substantiae ipsius, nisi quae relatae sunt ad motum et ad corpora. Si enim est huius aliqua causa, ita quod habemus intellectum connaturalem nobis ad talia speculanda, tunc oportet, quod omnes deficiamus in scientia speculativa separatorum aut propterea, quia principia illius scientiae non sunt inventa, sicut deficimus in alchimia, aut propter hoc quod non sumus exercitati sufficienter; et utrumque horum est improbabile, quia talis defectus non esset generalis apud omnes homines. Si autem

Similarly to Alfarabi's and Avempace's model, Aquinas's testing of the second model ended in its rejection. According to this model, which Aquinas attributes to Avicenna, impressions of intelligible forms are infused into the intellect by God Himself. Yet in Aquinas's eyes they could do no more than explain cognition of "some brightness like a ray of Him" but never that of God's very essence. Aquinas borrowed this understanding of acquiring intelligible forms from Avicenna's *Metaphysics*, book 3, chapter 8, or from previous Latin readings thereof, as discussed in section V of the main introduction to this book.[16] Regardless of further intricacies of philosophical detail, however, all of which have been discussed in a few important publications,[17] Aquinas's take on this model was equally negative to that of Alfarabi and Avempace: since infused intelligibles amount to effects of God, they could not offer intellectual access to God's essence, since they could neither assimilate the human intellect to God nor yield noetic identity with God—the one requirement that had to be met for a direct and face-to-face vision of Him.

---

diceret quis, quod aliquid habent et aliquid non habent potentiam huiusmodi speculandi, tunc nos qui non habemus huiusmodi potentiam, aequivoce diceremur homines ad eos qui habent huiusmodi potentiam. Constat enim summam hominis potentiam esse perfectionem in contemplatione separatorum." I will discuss this matter in greater detail in my forthcoming book *Aquinas's Vision of Seeing God: Arabic Philosophy and Christian Eschatology*. For the dating of the two works, see: Albertus-Magnus-Institut 2011, pp. 28–31.

16. Avicenna, *Liber de Philosophia Prima sive Scientia divina*, l. 3, c. 8 (ed. Van Riet 1977, p. 161, v. 14–20): "Igitur de illis rebus non inquiritur in intellectibus humanis nisi intentiones quidditatum suarum, non ipsae; et est iudicium de eis sicut iudicium de aliis intellectis substantiis corporalibus, excepto uno, scilicet quod illae aliae egent abstractione quousque abstrahatur ab eis intentio quae possit intelligi, istae vero non egent aliquo nisi ut intelligantur esse ut sunt, et sigilletur anima per eas." Ibid. (ed. Van Riet 1977, p. 162, v. 26–35 and p. 163, v. 38–43): "Quod autem intelligimus de rebus separatis, ipsum esse illorum separatorum discrepans a nobis non est ex hoc quod nos scimus illa, sed quia nos imprimimur ab eis; quod enim nos imprimimur ab eis, hoc est nos scire eas; similiter esset etiam si formae naturales essent separatae et disciplinales separatae; quod enim tunc sciremus de eis non esset nisi quod acquireremus de eis, nec essent nobis nostrae animae quasi mutatae ad illas. Iam enim ostendimus destructionem huius alias. Sed quia quod invenitur in nobis de illis est impressiones quae assimilantur eis sine dubio, et hoc est nostra scientia de illis; <...> unde quia sunt impressiones animae, non essentiae illarum rerum, nec exemplum quasi illae res non remaneant existentes nec in materiis corporalibus nec animabus, tunc id quod subiectum non habet, erit id cuius multiplicatur species sine causa ex qua pendeat ullo modo: igitur sunt accidentes in anima."

17. See: Black 2014, pp. 159–184; Krause 2014, pp. 105–124.

What Aquinas required, therefore, was a model that could vindicate this assimilation, that could prove how noetic identity is attained. Such a vindication or proof, he thought, could be found in Alexander of Aphrodisias's and Averroes's model of ultimate conjunction with the separate Agent Intellect in its appropriated form as their conception of the beatific vision. Much has been said in the secondary literature about Aquinas's use of this model in his *Sentences* and about its subsequent fate in his later works, so there is no need to rehearse the details now.[18] Here, I shall restrict myself to discussing the two key elements that Aquinas took Alexander and Averroes to provide: on the one hand, the ontological identity of the intelligible form with God as the object of cognition; and, on the other, the composition of the human intellect with the divine essence in intentional form-matter terms to account for its presence in the intellect, yet to avoid any claims of inherence in it.[19]

The former element, the ontological identity of the intelligible form with God as the object of cognition, was the backbone of Aquinas's reworking of the Aristotelian norm of noetic identity in his account of the beatific vision:

> <S>ince in any cognition a form is necessary by which the thing is cognized or seen, the form by which the intellect is perfected for seeing separate substances <...> is the separate substance itself that is conjoined to our intellect as its form, so that it is itself what is understood and that by which it is understood.[20]

As soon as God was taken to be formally present in the intellect by taking over the *function* of an intelligible species (*qua intelligitur*) while remaining ontologically outside of the intellect as object

18. Wéber 1978, pp. 211–248; Brenet 2006, pp. 310–342; id. 2011, pp. 215–247; Taylor 2012, pp. 509–550. Other important studies concerning Aquinas's theory of the beatific vision include: Gilson 1964, pp. 67–88; Hoye 1975; Trottmann 1995; Torrell 1997, pp. 43–68; Williams 1999; Maillard 2001; Duba 2006; Waddell 2011, pp. 105–132.

19. For an extended discussion of intentional act-potency relations in the Neoplatonic tradition, see for instance: Trouillard 1967, pp. 1–17.

20. See pp. 107–108 of the translation.

of knowing (*quod intelligitur*), the intellect was immediately assimilated to God. It became noetically one with God through the functional presence of God's own essence. Aquinas thus ascribed to God a dual role: (1) that of functioning like an intelligible form for the intellect; and (2) that of being the object of cognition in the beatific vision. This dual role of God, this ontological identity of the intelligible form with God as the object of cognition, constituted the foundation from which the act of cognizing God's essence on the part of the human intellect could be established. For only if God were conceived to be in the intellect functionally with His own existential features and characteristics could He actualize it to become noetically identical with Him.

This is the model that Aquinas believed could be found in Alexander and Averroes, even though it was far from a precise match with their actual views of ultimate conjunction. In similar fashion to in Alfarabi's and Avempace's case, as discussed above, Aquinas knew Alexander predominantly through Averroes's, but also Albert's, mediations, and he appropriated ideas from their philosophical views on ultimate conjunction and happiness in this life to account for the theological teaching of the beatific vision in the afterlife. Aquinas thus paid little attention to the necessary conditions for attaining each ultimate noetic state and emphasized instead the very workings of attainment. The ontological identity of the intelligible form with God as the object of cognition as discussed above was one of the key themes in this adoption.

But there was more. Complementing the first element was the second one, which considered the composition of the human intellect with the divine essence in intentional act-potency terms to account for its presence in the intellect and yet to avoid any claims of inherence in it. This was meant to support Aquinas's adoption of this model further by forestalling worries of ontological identification between the human intellect and God. Aquinas's specification of the noetic relationship in terms of an intentional composition that is analogous to the composition of form and matter turns on what he reads to be Averroes's insight: there needs to be an underlying subject that is shared between the human intellect and the divine essence.[21] In Aquinas's reading of Averroes, this shared subject was the human soul, but in different ways from those conceived by Averroes. It was the subject of the human intellect in ontological terms, innately from its very creation *ex nihilo*. The intellect in turn related to the soul as its inherent faculty, as its *proprium*, which ontologically emanated from it in its creation. In the case of the divine essence and its inherence in the soul, though, things were different. Here, the human soul was the remote subject of cognitive or intentional conjunction, the subject whose inherent faculty, the intellect, would be actualized to perfection and determined to seeing God in virtue of the formal presence of the divine essence in it. As such, Aquinas took the divine essence to be functionally or cognitively present in the soul, but not ontologically. This unique functional presence could, in Aquinas's eyes, only be exclusive to the divine essence. God alone was sufficiently in act to be capable of acting in this way, since in Aquinas's view He was *actus purus* and as such had the possibility to act in any way.

We can gather from these brief notes and the article itself that neither the original subject matter of the beatific vision face-to-face, nor the philosophical principles that Aquinas applied to account for it, arose unaffected from their blending. Aquinas's youthful validation of the cognition of God through His essence was the result of combining optimistic Latin theological conclusions with the appropriated and reshaped philosophical principles of noetic identity and ultimate noetic conjunction with the highest intelligible object. The former consisted in his endorsement of a direct vision of God and knowledge of His substance or essence. The latter comprised the conception of an

21. See: Averroes, *Commentarium magnum in Aristotelis De anima libros*, l. 3, com. 36 (ed. Crawford 1953, p. 499, v. 567–577): "Et cum fuerit verificata nobis hec continuatio que est inter intellectum agentem et intellectum materialem, poterimus reperire modum secundum quem dicimus quod intellectus agens similis est forme et quod intellectus qui est in habitu similis est materie. Omnia enim duo quorum subiectum est unum, et quorum alterum est perfectius alio, necesse est ut respectus perfectioris ad imperfectius sit sicut respectus forme ad materiam. Et secundum hanc intentionem dicimus quod proportio prime perfectionis virtutis ymaginative ad primam perfectionem communis sensus est sicut proportio forme ad materiam."

intellectual human happiness found in noetic identity with God, an ontological identity between intelligible form and intelligible object, and an adaptation of composition in intentional act-potency terms. More than any other factor, it was the philosophical insights that Aquinas gathered from his own reading of Averroes's theory of ultimate conjunction that molded the conceptual, theoretical, and structural orientation of his theory of the beatific vision. These insights and their effect on Aquinas's theory of the beatific vision would remain the same throughout Aquinas's career, although any reference to their source would be conspicuously absent in all but one of his later works.[22]

TRANSLATION

We proceed to the first <article> as follows. It seems that the human intellect cannot attain the vision of God through His essence.

(1) Because John 1:18[23] says that: *No man hath seen God at any time*, Chrysostom also explains that not even the celestial essences, namely the Cherubim and Seraphim, have ever been able to see Him as He is.[24] But to humans only equality to the angels is promised according to Matthew 22:30: *They shall be as the angels of God in heaven.*[25] Therefore, none of the blessed will see God through His essence in the afterlife.

---

22. This has been discussed in part by: Brenet 2011, pp. 215–247.

23. Secundum Iohannem 1:18 (Vulgata 2007): *Deum nemo vidit umquam unigenitus Filius qui est in sinu Patris ipse enarravit.*

24. Iohannes Chrysostomus, *Homiliae in Iohannem*, 15, trans. Burgundionis (ed. Dondaine 1952, p. 101, v. 19–24; also in: Paris, BnF lat. 1782 f. 31vb): "<...> quia ipsum quodcumque est Deus non solum prophete, sed neque angeli uiderunt neque archangeli. Sed si interrogaueris eos, audies de substantia quidem nichil respondentes, gloria uero in excelsis Deo solum cantantes et in terra pax hominibus bona uoluntas. Et si a cherubin uel seraphin concupiueris aliquid discere, misticam sanctimonii melodiam audies <...>." See also: Albertus Magnus, *De resurrectione*, t. 4, q. 1, a. 9, §1 (ed. Colon. 26, p. 326, v. 74–p. 327, v. 4); id., *Quaestio de visione Dei in patria* (ed. Colon. 25/2, p. 96, v. 10–13); id., *Super Dionysium De divinis nominibus*, c. 1 (ed. Colon. 37/1, p. 9, v. 70–p. 10, v. 1).

25. Secundum Matthaeum 22:30 (Vulgata 2007): *in resurrectione enim neque nubent neque nubentur sed sunt sicut angeli Dei in caelo.*

(2) Furthermore, Dionysius reasons as follows in the first chapter of his *On the Divine Names*: "Cognition is only of existing things."[26] Yet everything existing is finite since it is in some determinate genus. And thus, since God is infinite, He is "above all existing things." Therefore, there is no cognition of Him, but He is above all cognition.

(3) Furthermore, Dionysius shows in the first chapter of his *On Mystical Theology* that the most perfect mode by which our intellect can be conjoined to God is insofar as it is conjoined to Him as "the unknown."[27] But what is seen through its essence is not unknown. Therefore, it is impossible for our intellect to see God through His essence.

(4) Furthermore, Dionysius says in his *Letter to Gaius the Monk* that "the darknesses lying over God," which he calls the abundance of light, "are hidden from every light and concealed from all cognition.

---

26. Pseudo-Dionysius Areopagita, *De divinis nominibus*, c. 1, sect. 1, trans. Sarraceni (Dionysiaca t. 1, pp. 9–14): "Sicut enim incomprehensibilia et incontemplabilia sunt a sensibilibus intelligibilia, et his quae in compositione sunt et figura simplicia et infigurabilia, et formatis secundum corporum figuras incorporalium intangibilis et infigurabilis formae carentia, secundum eamdem veritatis rationem superponitur substantiis quae est supersubstantialis, et mentibus, quae est super mentem unitas, et omnibus deliberationibus est indeliberabile quod est super deliberationem, et ineffabile verbo omni quod est super verbum bonum, unitas unificans universam unitatem, et supersubstantialis substantia, et intellectus non intelligibilis, et verbum non dicibile; et irrationabilitas et non-intelligibilitas et innominabilitas secundum nihil existentium existens, et causa quidem essendi omnibus, ipsum autem non existens, sicut super omnem substantiam, et sicut ipsum de seipso proprie et scienter enuntiet. De hac igitur (sicut dictum est) supersubstantiali et occulta Deitate non est audendum dicere neque cogitare aliquid praeter illa quae divinitus nobis ex sanctis eloquiis sunt expressa. Etenim sicut ipsa de seipsa in eloquiis (ut decet bonam) tradidit, ipsius quidem (quidquid est) scientia et contemplatio omnibus est invia existentibus, sicut ab omnibus supersubstanialiter segregata." See also: Albertus Magnus, *Super Dionysium De divinis nominibus*, c. 1 (ed. Colon. 37/1, p. 5, v. 71–79; p. 9, v. 53–55; p. 9, v. 76–79; p. 8, v. 34–p. 13, v. 70).

27. Pseudo-Dionysius Areopagita, *De mystica theologia*, c. 1, sect. 43, trans. Sarraceni (Dionysiaca t. 1, pp. 576–578): "Hoc autem puto significare divinissima visorum et intellectorum esse subjectas quasdam rationes subjectorum omnia excedenti, per quae praesentia ejus qui est super omnem cogitationem monstratur intelligibilibus summitatibus sanctissimorum locorum ejus superveniens. Tunc et ab ipsis absolvitur visis et videntibus, et ad caliginem ignorantiae intrat, quae caligo vere est mystica, in qua claudit omnes cognitivas susceptiones, et in non-palpabili omnino et invisibili fit, omnis existens ejus qui est super omnia, et nullius, neque sui ipsius, neque alterius, omnino autem ignoto, vacatione omnis cognitionis, secundum melius unitus, et eo quod nihil cognoscit super mentem cognoscens." See also: id., c. 1, sect. 41, trans. Sarraceni (Dionysiaca t. 1, pp. 567–569). Albertus Magnus, *Super Mysticam theologiam Dionysii*, c. 1 (ed. Colon. 37/2, p. 461, v. 82–87; p. 462, v. 38. 43–44; p. 463, v. 34; p. 464, v. 7; p. 457, v. 66–70.37–61).

And if anyone seeing God understood what He saw, he did not see Him, but something of the things that are His."[28] Therefore, no created intellect will be able to see God through His essence.

(5) Furthermore, as Dionysius says in his *Letter to Dorotheus*: "God exists as invisible because of surpassing brightness."[29] But just as His brightness surpasses the human intellect in this life, so does it surpass the human intellect in the afterlife. Therefore, just as He is invisible in this life, so will He be invisible in the afterlife.

(6) Furthermore, since the intelligible is the perfection[30] of the intellect, there must be some proportion between the intelligible and the intellect, the visible thing and vision. But we cannot accept any proportion between our intellect and the divine essence, since they are infinitely distant <from one another>. Therefore, our intellect cannot reach the vision of the divine essence.[31]

---

28. Pseudo-Dionysius Areopagita, *Epistulae*, ep. 1, sect. 48, trans. Sarraceni (Dionysiaca t. 1, pp. 606–607): "<...> et suppositae ipsius tenebrae et cooperiuntur omni lumini et absconduntur omni cognitioni. Et si aliquis videns quidem Deum intellexit quod vidit non ipsum vidit, sed aliquid eorum quae sunt ejus quae exsistunt et cognoscuntur." See also: Albertus Magnus, *De resurrectione*, tr. 4, q. 1, a. 9, §2 (ed. Colon. 26, p. 327, v. 13–16); id., *Super Dionysii Epistulas*, ep. I (ed. Colon. 37/2, p. 479, v. 62–63; p. 480, v. 68–72; p. 481, v. 83–p. 482, v. 24).

29. Pseudo-Dionysius Areopagita, *Epistulae*, ep. 5, sect. 52, trans. Sarraceni (Dionysiaca t. 1, p. 620): "Et invisibilis quidem exsistens propter excedentem claritatem et inaccessibilis idem propter excessum suprasubstantialis luminis effusionis." See also: Albertus Magnus, *Quaestio de visione Dei in patria* (ed. Colon. 25/2, p. 97, v. 43–47); id., *Super Dionysii Epistulas*, ep. V (ed. Colon. 37/2, p. 493, v. 73–74.43–55).

30. "Perfection" here is not simply meant as the actualization of the intellect resulting in an actualized intellect. Rather, it is also meant as a process, particularly when it is the perfection of a self-intellecting intellect. See, for instance: Albertus Magnus, *Quaestio de visione Dei in patria* (ed. Colon. 25/2, p. 97, v. 52–56): "Item ad idem: Intelligibilis ad intellectum aliqua debet esse proportio, sicut inter agens et patiens, perfectionem et perfectibile; sed essentia divina est improportionabilis intellectui creato, cum in infinitum distent; ergo ipso videri non potest." Id., *Super Dionysium De divinis nominibus*, c. 1 (ed. Colon. 37/1, p. 10, v. 22–27): "Hoc idem videtur per rationem. Perfectibilis enim ad perfectionem debet esse proportio; sed intelligibile est perfectio intellectus; ergo intellectus ad intelligibile debet esse proportio. Cum igitur non sit proportio alicuius intellectus creati ad deum, non potest videri."

31. See also: Albertus Magnus, *De resurrectione*, tr. 4, q. 1, a. 9, §5 (ed. Colon. 26, p. 327, v. 30–40): "Hoc idem videtur per rationem. In omni enim potentia, si debeat compleri per actum, necesse est supponi proportionem et capacitatem potentiae ad actum illum; sed finiti ad infinitum nulla est proportio vel capacitas; igitur potentia finita numquam habet compleri per actum infinitum. Sed omnis intellectus creatus est finitus; ergo non habet compleri per intelligibile infinitum. Sed deus est intelligibile infinitum. Ergo non intelliget deum. Et videre, prout hic sumitur, est intelligere. Ergo visio dei in propria substantia non erit."

(7) Furthermore, God is more distant from our intellect than any created intelligible is from the senses. But the senses can in no way reach a vision of a spiritual creature. Therefore, neither will our intellect be able to reach a vision of the divine essence.

(8) Furthermore, whenever an intellect understands something in actuality, it must be informed by a similitude of the thing understood—<a similitude> which is the principle of intellectual activity that is determined to such a thing, just as heat is the principle of heating. Therefore, if our intellect understood God, this <understanding> would have to come about through some similitude informing the intellect. Yet this cannot be the divine essence itself because a form and the thing formed must be one in being (*esse*). But the divine intelligence differs from our intellect in essence and in being (*esse*). Therefore, the form by which our intellect is informed in understanding God must be some similitude impressed onto our intellect by God.[32] But since this similitude is something created, it cannot lead to a cognition of God, except as an effect to its cause. Therefore, it is impossible for our intellect to see God except by an effect. But the vision of God by an effect is not the vision of God through His essence. Therefore, our intellect will not be able to see God through His essence.[33]

(9) Furthermore, the divine essence is more distant from our intellect than any angel or intelligence. But, as Avicenna says in his *Metaphysics*,[34] for an intelligence to be in our intellect does not mean for the essence of the intelligence to be in our intellect because in this way, the knowledge we have of the intelligences would be a substance and not an accident. But this means that an impression of the intelligence

32. See: Avicenna, *Liber de philosophia prima sive scientia divina*, t. 3, c. 8 (ed. Van Riet 1977, t. 1, p. 160, v. 94–p. 163, v. 43).

33. See: Albertus Magnus, *De resurrectione*, tr. 4, q. 1, a. 9, §1 (ed. Colon. 26, p. 327, v. 41–50): "Item, si debeat esse visio secundum intellectum, necesse est intellectum assimilari rei intellectae; omnis enim intellectus est per assimilationem. Aut igitur intellectus assimilabitur deo secundum substantiam vel secundum habitum sive speciem aliquam formalem. Constat, quod non primo modo, quia intellectus non erit deus. Si autem secundo modo, datur [sequitur], quod non est visio nisi in theophaniis; forma enim, sive lumen, recepta ab intellectu non est deus, sed aliquid in quo et per quod cognoscitur deus."

34. See: Avicenna, *Liber de philosophia prima sive scientia divina*, t. 3, c. 8 (ed. Van Riet 1977, t. 1, p. 160, v. 94–p. 163, v. 43).

is in our intellect. Therefore, God too is not in our intellect so that He may be understood by us, except inasmuch as His impression is in our intellect. But this impression cannot lead to a cognition of the divine essence because an intellect, since it is infinitely distant from the divine essence, degenerates <the divine essence> into another species, much more readily than if a white species were to degenerate into a black species. Therefore, just as one in whose sight a white species degenerates into a black species is not said to see white because of an ill-disposed organ, so too will our intellect, which only understands God through an impression of this kind, be unable to see Him through His essence.

(10) Furthermore, "In things separate from matter, the one understanding and the thing understood are the same" as is evident from <Aristotle's> *On the Soul*, book III.[35] But God is separate from matter to the highest degree. Therefore, since an intellect that is created cannot extend to becoming an uncreated essence, it will be impossible that our intellect sees God through His essence.

(11) Furthermore, <for> everything that one sees through its essence, one <also> knows "what it is" (*quid est*). But in the case of God, the intellect cannot see "what He is," but only "what He is not," as Dionysius[36] and the Damascene[37] say. Therefore, our intellect cannot see God through His essence.

---

35. Aristoteles, *De anima*, l. 3, lect. 1 (430a3), trans. vet. (ed. Gauthier 1985, p. 447): "In hiis enim que sunt sine materia, idem est intellectus et quod intelligitur." Compare to Michael Scot's translation from the Arabic: ibid., l. 3, tx. 15 (ed. Crawford 1953, p. 434, v. 2–4): "Formare enim per intellectum et formatum per intellectum, in eis que sunt extra materiam, idem sunt."

36. Pseudo-Dionysius Areopagita, *De caelesti hierarchia*, c. 2, sect. 57, trans. Eriugenae (Dionysiaca t. 2, p. 757): "Aliquando vero dissimilibus manifestationibus ab ipsis eloquiis supermundane laudatur, eam invisibilem et infinitam et incomprehensam vocantibus: et quae ex quibus non quid est sed quid non est significatur." See also: Albertus Magnus, *Super Dionysium De caelesti hierarchia*, c. 2 (ed. Colon. 36/1, p. 24, v. 80–82, p. 25, v. 13–32); id., *Super Dionysium De divinis nominibus*, c. 5 (ed. Colon. 37/1, p. 304, v. 52–65).

37. Iohannes Damascenus, *De fide orthodoxa*, c. 4, trans. Burgundionis (ed. Buytaert 1955, p. 19, v. 3–5): "Quoniam igitur est quidem Deus manifestum est. Quid vero est secundum substantiam et naturam, incomprehensibile est hoc omnino et ignotum. See also: ibid., c. 13, trans. Burgundionis (ed. Buytaert 1955, p. 59, v. 48–54) as quoted below in article three, note 1; Albertus Magnus, *De resurrectione*, tr. 4, q. 1, a. 9, §1 (ed. Colon. 26, p. 328, v. 75–83).

(12) Furthermore, everything infinite, inasmuch as it is infinite, is unknown. But God is infinite in every way. Therefore, He is unknown in every way, <and> therefore He will not be able to be seen by a created intellect through His essence.

(13) Furthermore, Augustine says in his book *On Seeing God* that "God is invisible by nature."[38] But the things that are in God by nature cannot be otherwise than they are. Therefore, it cannot be that He is seen through His essence.

(14) Furthermore, everything that exists in one way and that is seen in another way is not seen according to "what it is" (*id quod est*). But God exists in one way and is seen in another way by the blessed in the afterlife. For He exists in His own way, but is seen by the blessed in accordance with their way. Therefore, He will not be seen by the blessed according to what He is. And thus, He will not be seen through His essence.[39]

(15) Furthermore, what is seen through a medium is not seen through its essence. But in the afterlife God is seen through a medium which is the light of glory, as is evident from Psalm 35:10: *In thy*

38. Augustinus Hipponensis, *Epistulae*, ep. 147: De videndo Deo, c. 15 (CSEL 44/2, p. 311, v. 9–10; PL 33, p. 613): "deum nemo uidit umquam nec uidere potest, quoniam lucem habitat inaccessibilem et est natura inuisibilis <...>." See also: ibid. (CSEL 44/2, p. 310, v. 9–p. 311, v. 2; PL 33, p. 612): "si quaeris, quo modo dictus sit inuisibilis, si uideri potest, respondeo inuisibilem esse natura, uideri autem, cum uult, sicut uult; plurimis enim uisus est, non sicuti est, sed quali specie illi placuit apparere. si quaeris, quo modo eum uidit uel Cain sceleratus, quando de suo scelere ab illo interrogatus et iudicatus est, uel etiam ipse diabolus, quando uenit cum angelis, ut coram illo adsisteret, si beati mundo corde, quoniam ipsi deum uidebunt, respondeo non quidem esse consequens, ut etiam uideant deum, qui uoces ab eo factas aliquando audiunt; neque enim uiderunt eum, qui audierunt, quando dixit ad filium: et clarificaui et iterum clarificabo; uerum tamen non esse mirandum, si aliqui etiam non mundi corde uident deum in specie, quam uoluntas eius fecerit, latente inuisibili et apud se incommutabili manente natura." Ibid., c. 8 (CSEL 44/2, p. 293, v. 13–17; PL 33, 605): "Inuisibilis est igitur natura deus non tantum pater sed et ipsa trinitas, unus deus, et quia non tantum inuisibilis uerum etiam incommutabilis, sic apparet, quibus uoluerit, in qua uoluerit specie, ut apud eum integra maneat eius inuisibilis incommutabilisque natura." Albertus Magnus, *Quaestio de visione Dei in patria* (ed. Colon. 25/2, p. 98, v. 16–17.27–28).

39. See also: Albertus Magnus, *Quaestio de visione Dei in patria* (ed. Colon. 25/2, p. 96, v. 16–22): "Ad idem est ratio Chrysostomi ibidem: Essentia dei una et simplex est et eodem modo se habens; si ergo per essentiam videretur ab angelis et sanctis, ab omnibus uniformiter videretur et visus laudaretur; sed alii laudant eum ut maiestatem, alii ut creatorem, et diversi diversimode; ergo non videtur uniformiter, et ideo non videtur per essentiam."

light we shall see light.[40] Therefore, He will not be seen through His essence.

(16) Furthermore, God will be seen *face to face* in the afterlife as it said in I Corinthians 13:12.[41] But when we see humans face to face, we see them through a similitude. Therefore, in the afterlife, God will be seen through a similitude and thus not through His essence.

❁ ❁ ❁

(1) On the contrary it is said in 1 Corinthians 13:12: *We see now through a glass in a dark manner: but then face to face.*[42] But what is seen face to face is seen through its essence. Therefore, God will be seen through His essence by the blessed in the afterlife.

(2) Furthermore, <it is said> in 1 John 3:2: *When he shall appear, we shall be like to him: because we shall see him as he is.*[43] Therefore, we will see Him through His essence.

(3) Furthermore, <remarking> on 1 Corinthians 15:24: *When he shall have delivered up the kingdom to God and the Father,*[44] the Gloss says: "<This is> where, namely in the afterlife, the essence of the Father, the Son, and the Holy Spirit will be seen. It will be given only to clean hearts; it is the highest happiness."[45] Therefore, the blessed will see God through His essence.

(4) Furthermore, it is said in John 14:21: *And he that loveth me, shall be loved of my Father: and I will love him and will manifest*

---

40. Psalmi Iuxta LXX 35:10 (Vulgata 2007): *quoniam tecum est fons vitae in lumine tuo videbimus lumen.*

41. Ad Corinthios I 13:12, see section II of the general introduction, note 1.

42. Ibid.

43. Epistula Iohannis I 3:2, see section II of the general introduction, note 1.

44. Ad Corinthios I 15:24 (Vulgata 2007): *deinde finis cum tradiderit regnum Deo et Patri cum evacuaverit omnem principatum et potestatem et virtutem.*

45. *Glossa marg.* I Ad Cor. 15:24 (ed. Rusch, vol. IV, p. 339): "Nemo nouit patrem nisi filius et cui voluit filius reuelare, scilicet ubi essentia filii cum patre videbitur: quod solis mundis cordibus dabitur quod est summa beatitudo." See also: Petrus Lombardus, *In epistulas Pauli I Ad Corinthios* 15:24 (PL 191, p. 1679); Haymo, *In I Ad Corinthios* 15:24 (PL 117, p. 596).

myself to him.[46] But what is made manifest is seen essentially. Therefore, God will be seen essentially by the blessed in the afterlife.

(5) Furthermore, <remarking> on Exodus 33:20: *Man shall not see me and live*,[47] Gregory refutes the opinion of those who have said that "in the realm of beatitude, God can be contemplated in His brightness, but He cannot be seen in His nature," because "His brightness and His nature do not differ."[48] But <His> nature is His essence. Therefore, He will be seen through His own essence.

(6) Furthermore, the desire of the blessed cannot be altogether in vain. But the shared desire of the blessed is that they may see God through His essence, as is evident from Exodus 33:18: *Shew me thy glory,*[49] and from Psalm 79:4: *Shew us thy face, and we shall be saved,*[50] and from John 14:8: *Lord, shew us the Father; and it is enough for us.*[51] Therefore, the blessed will see God through His essence.

Response

It should be said that just as we assert according to faith that the ultimate end of human life is the vision of God, in the same way, the philosophers have asserted that the ultimate happiness of humans is to understand substances that are separate in being from matter. And for this reason, the same difficulty and disagreement on this question is found among philosophers and theologians.

---

46. Secundum Iohannem 14:21 (Vulgata 2007): *qui autem diligit me diligetur a Patre meo et ego diligam eum et manifestabo ei me ipsum.*

47. Exodus 33:20 (Vulgata 2007): *rursumque ait non poteris videre faciem meam non enim videbit me homo et vivet.*

48. Gregorius Magnus, *Moralia in Iob*, l. XVIII, c. 54 (CCSL 143A, p. 953, v. 92–98; PL 76, p. 93): "Sciendum uero est quod fuere nonnulli qui Deum dicerent etiam in illa regione beatitudinis in claritate quidem sua conspici, sed in natura minime uideri. Quos nimirum minor inquisitionis subtilitas fefellit. Neque enim illi simplici et incommutabili essentiae aliud est claritas, aliud natura, sed ipsa ei natura sua claritas, ipsa claritas natura est."

49. Exodus 33:18 (Vulgata 2007): *qui ait ostende mihi gloriam tuam.*

50. Psalmi Iuxta LXX 79:4 (Vulgata 2007): *Deus converte nos et ostende faciem tuam et salvi erimus.*

51. Secundum Iohannem 14:8 (Vulgata 2007): *dicit ei Philippus Domine ostende nobis Patrem et sufficit nobis.*

For, certain philosophers have asserted that our possible intellect can never attain an understanding of separate substances, such as Alfarabi at the end of his <commentary on Aristotle's> *Nicomachean Ethics*, even though he said the contrary in his book *On the Intellect*, as the Commentator tells us in his *<Long Commentary on Aristotle's> On the Soul*, book III.[52] And similarly, certain theologians have asserted that the human intellect can never attain a vision of God through His essence. What moves both parties to this <view> is the distance between our intellect and the divine essence or the other separate substances. For, given that the intellect in actuality is in some way one with the intelligible in actuality, it seems difficult for the created intellect to become the uncreated essence in some way. Hence, Chrysostom also says: "For how would the created see what cannot be created?"[53] The greater difficulty in this <position> is for those who assert the possible intellect to be generated and corruptible (to the extent that it is a power dependent upon the body), not only with respect to the divine vision, but also with respect to the vision of any separate substance.

But this position can in no way hold. First, because it opposes the authority of Canonical Scripture, as Augustine says in his book *On Seeing God*.[54] Second, because, since understanding is the proper activity of humans to the highest degree, their happiness must be

---

52. Averroes, *Commentarium magnum in Aristotelis De anima libros*, l. 3, com. 36 (ed. Crawford 1953, p. 485, v. 180–p. 486 v. 187): "Et ideo videmus Alfarabium in postremo, cum credidit opinionem Alexandri esse veram in generatione intellectus materialis, quod fuit necesse apud ipsum secundum hanc opinionem opinari quod intelligentia agens non est nisi causa agens nos tantum; et hoc manifeste dixit in Nichomachia. Et est contra suam opinionem in epistola de Intellectu; illic enim dixit esse possibile ut intellectus materialis intelligat res abstractas; et est opinio Avempeche."

53. Iohannes Chrysostomus, *Homiliae in Iohannem*, 15, trans. Burgundionis (ed. Dondaine 1952, p. 101, v. 27–28; also in: Paris, BnF lat. 1782 f. 32ra): "Quod autem creabilis nature est, qualiter et uidere poterit, quod increabile est?" See also: Albertus Magnus, *De resurrectione*, tr. 4, q. 1, a. 9, §1 (ed. Colon. 26, p. 327, v. 4–6); id., *Super Dionysii De divinis nominibus*, c. 1 (ed. Colon. 37/1, p. 10, v. 5–7); id., *Super Dionysii Epistulas*, ep. V (ed. Colon. 37/2, p. 495, v. 22–23).

54. Augustinus Hipponensis, *Epistulae*, ep. 147: De videndo Deo, c. 5 (CSEL 44/2, p. 285, v. 4–17; PL 33, p. 601): "scimus posse deum uideri, quoniam scriptum est: Beati mundo corde, quoniam ipsi deum uidebunt. an forte non debui dicere 'scimus' sed 'credimus,' quoniam deum nec corpore aliquando uidimus sicut hanc lucem nec mente sicut ipsam in nobis, qua id credimus, fidem, sed tantum quia scriptum est in ea scriptura, cuius fideles sumus, quod uerum sit minime dubitamus? apostolus tamen Iohannes cum tale aliquid diceret: Scimus, inquit, quia, cum apparuerit, similes ei erimus, quoniam uidebimus eum, sicuti est. ecce scire se dixit, quod

assigned to them in accordance with this activity when perfected in them. Yet, since the perfection of the one who understands, inasmuch as it is of this kind, is the very intelligible, <then> if humans do not attain a vision of the divine essence in the most perfect activity of the intellect, but <if they attain> rather something else, one has to say that something other than God beatifies humans. And since the ultimate perfection of anything consists in the conjunction to its principle,[55] it follows that something other than God would be the efficient principle of humans. This is absurd according to us and it is similarly absurd according to those philosophers who assert that our souls emanate from separate substances, so that in the end we will be able to understand them. Hence, according to us, it must be asserted that our intellect will attain the vision of the divine essence at some point, and that, according to the philosophers, it will attain to a vision of the essence of the separate substances. But how this can occur remains to be investigated.

For some, such as Alfarabi and Avempace, have posited that it is because of our intellect's understanding of any intelligible whatsoever that it reaches the vision of the essence of a separate substance.[56] They proceed to show this in two ways, of which the first is this: Just as the nature of a species (*natura speciei*) is only diversified in diverse individuals inasmuch as it is conjoined to its individuating

---

nondum factum fuerat nec uidendo sed credendo cognouerat. recte itaque diximus: 'Scimus posse deum uideri,' quamuis eum non uiderimus, sed diuinae auctoritati, quae sanctis libris continetur, crediderimus."

55. Here, Thomas most likely draws on his teacher Albertus Magnus, for whom the Neoplatonic motive of *exitus—perfectio—reductio* was the leading concept of all created reality. For secondary literature on this topic, see: Anzulewicz 2000a, pp. 369–396; id. 2000b, pp. 251–295; id. 2009, pp. 219–295; Anzulewicz/Rigo 2002, pp. 388–416.

56. See, for instance: Averroes, *Commentarium magnum in Aristotelis De anima libros*, l. 3, com. 36 (ed. Crawford 1953, p. 486, v. 185–187 as quoted in note 52 above; p. 487, v. 221–234): "Dicamus igitur quod Avempeche multum perscrutabatur in hac questione et laboravit in declarando hanc continuationem esse possibilem, in sua epistola quam vocavit Continuationis Intellectus cum Homine; et in libro de Anima et in aliis multis libris videbitur quod ista questio non recessit ab eius cogitatione, neque per tempus nutus unius oculi. Et nos iam exposuimus illam epistolam secundum nostrum posse. Hoc enim quesitum valde est difficile, et cum talis fuit dispositio Avempeche in hac questione, quanto magis alterius hominis! Et verbum Avempeche in hoc est firmius aliorum, sed tamen occurrunt ei questiones quas narravimus. Et oportet nos narrare hic vias istius hominis, sed primo quod expositores dixerunt in hoc." Ibid. (ed. Crawford 1953, p. 490, v. 322–p. 493, v. 399).

principles, so too is the form understood by humans only diversified in me and in you inasmuch as it is conjoined to the different imaginative forms. And for this reason, when our intellect separates off the form understood from the forms of the imagination, the understood quiddity remains which is one and the same for different people who understand it. And the quiddity of a separate substance is of this kind. And for this reason, when our intellect attains the highest grade of abstraction of any quiddity of an intelligible, it understands the separate substance by this <abstracted> quiddity which is similar to it.

The second way is that it is natural for our intellect to abstract a quiddity from all intelligibles that possess a quiddity. Therefore, if a quiddity that <our intellect> abstracts from a particular thing possessing a quiddity is a quiddity that does not possess a quiddity, in understanding it, <our intellect> will understand the quiddity of a separate substance that is of such a disposition. <This is the case> because separate substances are subsisting quiddities that do not possess quiddities.[57] For, as Avicenna says: "The quiddity of each simple <being> is itself simple."[58] Yet, if the quiddity abstracted from this particular sensible thing is a quiddity that possesses a quiddity, it is natural for the intellect to abstract that quiddity. And in this way, since this does not proceed to infinity, <our intellect> will arrive at the quiddity that does not possess a quiddity by which a separate quiddity is understood.

Yet this way seems insufficient. First, because the quiddity of a material substance that the intellect abstracts is not of the same nature (*ratio*) as the quiddities of separate substances.[59] And in this way,

57. See: Wirmer 2006, pp. 569–590.

58. Avicenna, *Liber de philosophia prima sive scientia divina*, t. 5, c. 5 (ed. Van Riet 1980, t. 2, p. 274, v. 57): "Quidditas autem omnis simplicis est ipsummet simplex <...>."

59. See: Averroes, *Commentarium magnum in Aristotelis De anima libros*, l. 3, com. 36 (ed. Crawford 1953, p. 493, v. 400–410): "Nos autem dicamus: si autem hoc nomen *quiditas* dicatur de quiditatibus rerum materialium et de quiditatibus intellectuum abstractorum modo univoco, tunc propositio dicens quod intellectus innatus est abstrahere quiditates in eo quod sunt quiditates erit vera; et similiter si dicere intellecta esse composita et individua composita fuerit univocum; si autem equivocum, tunc demonstratio non erit vera. Quomodo autem est valde difficile; manifestum est enim per se quod hoc nomen *quiditas* non dicitur de eis pura univocatione neque pura equivocatione" (emphases as in edition).

because our intellect abstracts quiddities of material things and cognizes them, it does not follow that it cognizes the quiddities of separate substances, and especially the divine essence which is, to the highest degree, of a different nature (*ratio*) compared to any created quiddity. Second, because, provided it were of the same nature (*ratio*), nonetheless the quiddity of a separate substance would not be cognized by the quiddity of a composite thing, except according to the most remote genus which is substance. Yet this cognition is imperfect unless it were to arrive at the properties of the thing. For, one who cognizes a human being only inasmuch as it is an animal, does not cognize it except in a qualified way (*secundum quid*) and in potency. Much less does one cognize it if one only cognized the nature of substance in it. Hence, to cognize God or other separate substances in this way is not to see the divine essence or the quiddity of a separate substance, but it is to cognize through an effect and, as it were, in a mirror.

And for this reason, another way of understanding separate substances is asserted by Avicenna in his *Metaphysics*, namely, that the separate substances are understood by us through "the intentions of their quiddities,"[60] <intentions> that are certain similitudes of <the separate substances> not abstracted from them because they are themselves immaterial, but impressed by them onto our souls.

But to us, this way too seems insufficient for the divine vision that we seek. For, it is obvious that whatever is received into something, is in it after the mode of the recipient. And for this reason, the similitude of the divine essence impressed in our intellect by it will be <there> after the mode of our intellect. Yet the mode of our intellect is insufficient for the perfect reception of the divine similitude. This insufficiency of a perfect similitude, however, can occur in as many ways as dissimilarity is found. For in one way, a similitude is insufficient when form is participated according to the same nature (*ratio*) of species, but not according to the same mode of perfection, just as the similitude of something with little whiteness is insufficient compared to something with much whiteness. In another way

60. Avicenna, *Liber de philosophia prima sive scientia divina*, t. 3, c. 8 (ed. Van Riet 1977, t. 1, p. 161, v. 14–p. 163, v. 43).

it is still more insufficient, when it does not attain the same nature (*ratio*) of the species, but only to the same nature (*ratio*) of the genus, just as the similitude between something that is yellow in color and something that is white in color. In another way, it is still more insufficient, when it extends to the same nature (*ratio*) of the genus, but only according to analogy, just as the similitude of whiteness relates to a human being inasmuch as each of them is a being (*ens*). And in this way, every similitude received into a creature is insufficient compared to the divine essence.

Yet, in order that sight cognizes whiteness, a similitude of whiteness must be received in it according to the nature (*ratio*) of species, though not according to the same mode of being. For a form has one mode of being in the senses and another in the thing outside the soul. For, if the form of yellow came to be in the eye, the eye would not be said to see whiteness. And similarly, in order that the intellect understand some quiddity, a similitude of the same nature (*ratio*) of species must come to exist in it, even though perhaps the mode of being is not the same in each of them. For no form that is in the intellect or in sense is a principle of cognition according to the mode of being (*modus essendi*) it has in each of them, but according to the nature (*ratio*) that it shares with the external thing. And in this way, it is evident that God can in no way be understood through any similitude received into a created intellect in such a way that His essence would be seen immediately. Hence, some who assert that the divine essence is only seen in this way, said that this essence will not be seen, but only some brightness, like a ray of His. Hence, this mode too is insufficient for the divine vision that we seek.

And for this reason, another mode should be taken, which also some philosophers have asserted, namely Alexander and Averroes in the third book of <the *Long Commentary on Aristotle's*> *On the Soul*.[61] For, since in any cognition a form is necessary by which the thing is cognized or seen, the form by which the intellect is perfected

---

61. Averroes, *Commentarium magnum in Aristotelis De anima libros*, l. 3, com. 36 (ed. Crawford 1953, p. 481 v. 58–p. 485, v. 169; p. 495, v. 462–471; p. 496, v. 488–p. 500, v. 616). See also: Alexander Aphrodisiensis, *De intellectu et intellecto* (ed. Théry 1926, pp. 76–77, 79, 81).

for seeing separate substances is not the quiddity that the intellect abstracts from composite things, as the first opinion said. Nor is it some impression left by a separate substance in our intellect, as the second opinion said. Rather, it is the separate substance itself that is conjoined to our intellect as its form, so that it is itself what is understood and that by which it is understood. And whatever may be the case for other separate substances, we nonetheless must take this mode for the vision of God through His essence because by whatever other form our intellect may be informed, it could not be led to the divine essence through it.

This, however, must not be understood as if the divine essence were the true form of our intellect, or as if one thing were made from it and our intellect absolutely (*simpliciter*), as <is the case> in natural things from natural form and matter. Rather <it must be understood> that the proportion of the divine essence to our intellect is as the proportion of form to matter. For, whenever two things (of which one is more perfect than the other) are received in the same recipient, the proportion of one to the other (namely, of the more perfect to the less perfect) is as the proportion of form to matter, just as light (*lux*) and color are received into the diaphanous, <and> light is related to color as form to matter.[62] And in this way, when the intellectual power (*uis intellectiua*, here referring to the light of glory) is received in the soul and the divine essence itself is indwelling, albeit not in the same mode, the divine essence will be related to the intellect as form to matter.

And that this is sufficient for the intellect to be able to see the divine essence through its essence can be shown in the following way. For, just as one being is made absolutely (*simpliciter*) from a natural form by which it has being (*esse*) and from matter, so too there comes to be one thing in the understanding from a form by which the intellect understands and from the intellect itself. Yet in natural things, it is impossible for a self-subsistent thing to be the form of some matter

62. See: Averroes, *Commentarium magnum in Aristotelis De anima libros*, l. 3, com. 36 (ed. Crawford 1953, p. 499 v. 571–574): "Omnia enim duo quorum subiectum est unum, et quorum alterum est perfectius alio, necesse est ut respectus perfectioris ad imperfectius sit sicut respectus forme ad materiam."

if the thing possesses its own material part because it is impossible for matter to be the form of something. But if this self-subsistent thing is form alone, nothing prevents it from being made the form of some matter and from coming to be the <principle> "whereby a thing is" (*quo est*) of the composite itself, as is evident in the case of the soul. Yet in the case of the intellect, the intellect itself in potency must be taken as matter and the intelligible species as form, and the intellect understanding in actuality will be as the composite of both of them. Hence, if there were some self-subsistent thing that had nothing in itself but what is intelligible in itself, such a thing would by itself be able to be the form by which an intellect understands. Yet any given thing is intelligible to the extent that it is in actuality, not to the extent that it is in potency, as is evident from Aristotle's *Metaphysics*, book IX.[63] And an indication of this is that one must abstract the intelligible form from matter and all properties of matter. And for this reason, since the divine essence is pure actuality (*actus purus*), it will be able to be the form through which an intellect understands, and this will be the beatific vision. And for this reason, the Master says in distinction 1 of book II of his *Sentences* that the union of the soul to the body is a certain "equivalent of the blessed union by which the spirit will be united to God."[64]

Replies to Objections

(1) To the first, therefore, it should be said that the authority can be explained in three ways, as is evident from Augustine's book *On Seeing God*.[65] In one way, <it can be explained> such that a corporeal

63. See: Aristoteles, *Metaphysica*, l. IX, c. 9 (1051a29–31), trans. media (AL XXV 2, p. 181, v. 14–17): "Quare palam quia potestate entia ad actum ducta inveniuntur; causa vero quia intelligentia est actus; quare ex actu potentia, et propter hoc facientes cognoscunt {posterius enim generatione secundum numerum actus}."

64. Petrus Lombardus, *Sententiae in IV libris distinctae*, l. 2, d. 1, q. 6 (ed. Grottaferrata, p. 334, v. 15–18): "Secundo autem dici potest quod ideo Deus voluit eam corpori uniri, ut in humana conditione ostenderet novum exemplum beatae unionis quae est inter Deum et spiritum, in qua diligitur *ex toto corde* et videtur *facie ad faciem*" (emphases as in edition).

65. Augustinus Hipponensis, *Epistulae*, ep. 147: De videndo Deo, c. 6 (CSEL 44/2, p. 295, v. 1–p. 297, v. 2; PL 33, pp. 605–606).

vision by which nobody has ever seen nor will ever see God in His essence is excluded, as will be said. In another way, such that an intellectual vision of God through His essence is also excluded from those that live in this mortal flesh. In another way, such that a vision of comprehension is excluded from a created intellect. And Chrysostom understands it in this way. Hence, he adds: "The Evangelist calls the knowledge of this the most certain contemplation and comprehension so much as the Father has of the Son."[66] This is also the understanding of the Evangelist. Hence, he adds: *The only begotten son who is* etc.,[67] wanting to prove the Son to be God by a comprehensive vision.

(2) To the second, it should be said that just as God, by His infinite essence, exceeds all existent things that have determinate being, so too is His cognition by which He cognizes above all cognition. Hence, the proportion of our cognition to created things is the same as the proportion of divine cognition to Its essence. Yet for a cognition, two things come together, namely, the one who cognizes and the thing by which <something> is cognized. Yet the vision by which we will see God through His essence is the same as the vision by which God sees Himself from the standpoint of the thing by which it is seen. <This is> because just as He sees Himself through His essence, so will we see Him too. But, from the standpoint of the one who cognizes, a difference between the divine intellect and ours is found: For in <the act of> cognizing, the thing that is cognized (*quod cognoscitur*) follows the form by which we cognize because we see the stone by the form of the stone.[68] But the efficacy in cognizing

66. Iohannes Chrysostomus, *Homiliae in Iohannem*, 15, trans. Burgundionis (ed. Dondaine 1952, p. 102, v. 56–59; also in: Paris, BnF lat. 1782 f. 32ra): "Ita et nunc scimus omnes Deum, substantiam uero nullus nouit quid est, nisi solus qui genitus est ex eo. Notionem enim hic certissimam dicit considerationem et comprehensionem et tantam quantam Pater de Filio." See also: Albertus Magnus, *Super Dionysium De divinis nominibus*, c. 1 (ed. Colon. 37/1, p. 10, v. 44–48).

67. Secundum Iohannem 1:18, see p. 95.

68. See: Aristoteles, *De anima*, l. 3, lect. 4 (431b28–432a2) trans. vet. (ed. Gauthier 1985, p. 484): "Necesse autem aut ipsa aut species esse. Ipsa quidem enim non sunt: non enim hic lapis in anima est, set species. Quare anima sicut manus est: manus enim est organum organorum, et intellectus est species specierum et sensus est species sensibilium."

follows the power of the one who cognizes, just as when, someone has strong vision, he sees more sharply. And for this reason, we will see the same that God sees in this vision, namely, His essence, but not in such an efficacious way.

(3) To the third, it should be said that Dionysius speaks there of the cognition by which we cognize God in this life through some created form by which our intellect is informed for seeing Him. But, as Augustine says, God escapes every form of our intellect because, whatever form our intellect takes in, this form does not reach the nature (*ratio*) of the divine essence.[69] And for this reason, He cannot be accessible to our intellect. But we cognize Him most perfectly in this life inasmuch as we know Him to be above all that our intellect can take in. And in this way, we are conjoined to Him as to something unknown. But in the afterlife, when we will see Him through the form that is His essence, we will be conjoined to Him as to something known.

(4) To the fourth, it should be said *that God is light* (*lux*) as is said in I John 1:5.[70] Yet emanated light (*lumen*) is an impression of

69. Aquinas's supposed quotation here of Augustine: "Deus, qui omnem formam subterfugit, intellectui pervius esse non potest," rather summarizes what Augustine talks about in his *Sermon* 117, see: Augustinus Hipponensis, *Sermones ad populum*, sermo 117, c. 2, n. 3 (PL 38, pp. 662–663): "Ineffabiliter potest intelligi: non verbis hominis fit ut intelligatur. Verbum Dei tractamus, et dicimus quare non intelligatur. Non nunc dicimus ut intelligatur, sed dicimus quid impediat ne intelligatur. Est enim forma quaedam, forma non formata, sed forma omnium formatorum: forma incommutabilis, sine lapsu, sine defectu, sine tempore, sine loco, superans omnia, existens omnibus et fundamentum quoddam in quo sint, et fastigium sub quo sint. Si dicis quia omnia in illo sunt, non mentiris. Dictum est enim ipsum Verbum Sapientia Dei: habemus autem scriptum: *Omnia in Sapientia fecisti*. Ergo in illo sunt omnia: et tamen quia Deus est, sub illo sunt omnia. Dicimus quam incomprehensibile sit quod lectum est: tamen lectum est, non ut comprehenderetur ab homine, sed ut doleret homo quia non comprehendit, et inveniret unde impeditur a comprehensione, et removeret ea, et inhiaret perceptioni incommutabilis Verbi, ipse ex deteriore in melius commutatus. Non enim Verbum proficit aut crescit accedente cognitore: sed integrum, si permanseris; integrum, si recesseris; integrum, cum redieris; manens in se, et innovans omnia. Ergo est forma omnium rerum, forma infabricata, sine tempore, ut diximus, et sine spatiis locorum. Quidquid enim loco capitur, circumscribitur. Forma circumscribitur finibus, habet metas unde et quousque sit. Deinde quod loco capitur et mole quadam et spatio distenditur, minus est in parte, quam in toto. Faciat Deus ut intelligatis" (emphasis as in edition). Aquinas was most likely familiar with this supposed quotation from: Alexander Halensis, *Summa fratris Alexandri*, l. 1, c. 333 (ed. Quaracchi 1, p. 492) or from: Bonaventura, *In primum librum Sententiarum*, d. 22, q. 1 (ed. Quaracchi 1/1, p. 390).

70. Epistula Iohannis I 1:5 (Vulgata 2007): *et haec est adnuntiatio quam audivimus ab eo et adnuntiamus vobis quoniam Deus lux est et tenebrae in eo non sunt ullae.*

<the source of> light (*lux*) in something illuminated. And because the divine essence is of another mode than every similitude of Him impressed on an intellect, he says that "divine darkness covers all illumination." <This is> because the divine essence, which he calls darkness, remains unrevealed (*non demonstrata*) by an impression in our intellect due to the excess of its brightness. And from this it follows that "He is concealed from all cognition." And therefore, whosoever of those seeing God takes something into his mind, this is not God but something of the divine effects.

(5) To the fifth, it should be said that the brightness of God, even though it exceeds every form by which our intellect is now informed, does nonetheless not exceed the divine essence itself, which will be like a form for our intellect in heaven. And for this reason, even though <His brightness> is invisible now, it will nonetheless be visible then.

(6) To the sixth, it should be said that even though the finite and the infinite can be in no proportion to one another, because the excess of the infinite over the finite is indeterminate, nonetheless, there can be a proportionality between them which is a similitude of proportions. For just as finite is equated to finite, so too is infinite to infinite. Yet in order that something be cognized entirely, there sometimes must be a proportion (*proportio*) between the one who cognizes and the thing cognized. <This is> because the power of the one who cognizes must be equal to the cognoscibility of the thing cognized, but equality is a certain proportion. At other times, however, the cognoscibility of the thing exceeds the power of the one who cognizes, as is the case when we cognize God, or vice versa, as is the case when He cognizes creatures. And then, a proportion between the one who cognizes and the thing cognized is not required, but only a proportionality (*proportionalitas*), so that just as one who cognizes is related to <the act of> cognizing, so too the cognoscible thing is related to the fact that it is cognized. And such proportionality is sufficient in order that the infinite be cognized by the finite, or vice versa.

Or, it should be said that proportion, according to the original meaning of the term, signifies the relation (*habitudo*) between two quantities, according to determinate excess or equality. But it is applied beyond this <meaning> to signify any relation (*habitudo*) of one thing to another. In this way, we say that matter must be proportionate to form. And in this way too, even though it is finite, nothing prevents our intellect from being said to be made proportionate to the vision of an infinite essence, yet not to its comprehension because of its immensity.

(7) To the seventh, it should be said that similitude and diversity (*distantia*) can be taken in two ways. One is according to agreement in nature, and in this way, God is more distant from the created intellect than a created intelligible is from sense. The other is according to proportionality, and in this way the opposite holds because sense is not proportionate to cognizing something immaterial, whereas intellect is proportionate to cognizing anything immaterial. And this similitude is required for cognition, but not the first. <This is> because it is well known that the intellect which understands a stone is not similar to it in natural being, just as also sight apprehends honey <to be> red and bile <to be> red, although it does not apprehend honey <to be> sweet. For the redness of honey agrees more with <the color> of bile, inasmuch as it is visible, than the sweetness of honey with <the taste> of bile.

(8) To the eighth, it should be said that in the vision by which God will be seen through His essence, the divine essence itself will be like a form of the intellect by which it understands. Yet, it is not necessary that they become one thing according to being absolutely (*esse simpliciter*), but only that they become one with regard to what belongs to the act of understanding, as has been said above.

(9) To the ninth, it should be said that we do not support Avicenna's assertion concerning this point because he is also refuted by other philosophers concerning what he understands of the cognition of separate substances. These, <he asserts>, are cognized through the manner (*habitus*) of the theoretical sciences and the similitudes of other things. And he suggests, therefore, that this shows that knowledge is not a substance in us, but an accident. And yet, even though

the divine essence is, according to the character (*proprietas*) of its nature, more distant from our intellect than the substance of an angel, nonetheless, it has more of the nature (*ratio*) of intelligibility because it is pure actuality without any admixture of potency—<a fact> that does not affect other separate substances. Nor will the cognition by which we will see God through His essence be in the genus of accident from the standpoint of Him who will be seen, but only with regard to the act of the one understanding, which will neither be the substance of the one understanding nor of the thing understood.

(10) To the tenth, it should be said that a substance separate from matter understands itself and understands other things. And in both ways, the authority cited can be verified. For, since the essence of a separate substance is intelligible in actuality in its own right because it is separate from matter, it is well known that, when a separate substance understands itself, the one understanding and the understood are the same in every way. For it does not understand itself through some intention abstracted from itself, just as we understand material things. This seems to be the understanding of the Philosopher in his *On the Soul*, book III, as the Commentator suggests in the same passage.[71] Yet, inasmuch as it understands other things, the intellect in actuality comes to be one with the thing understood in actuality inasmuch as the form of the thing understood comes to be the form of the intellect, inasmuch as the intellect is in actuality. <This is> not such that it is the essence of the intellect, as Avicenna proves in his *Book on the Soul*,[72] because the essence of the intellect remains one

71. For the Latin translations of Aristotle's *On the Soul*, see note 35 above. Averroes, *Commentarium magnum in Aristotelis De anima libros*, l. 3, com. 15 (ed. Crawford 1953, p. 434, v. 17–20): "Et dixit: *Formare enim per intellectum*, etc. Idest, et necesse est ut sit intellectum per intentionem in eo, quia formare per intellectum et formatum idem sunt in rebus non materialibus."

72. Avicenna, *Liber de anima seu Sextus de naturalibus*, pars 5, c. 6 (ed. Van Riet 1968, t. 2, p. 147, v. 16–p. 148, v. 39): "Dicemus ergo ultimam partem huius divisionis esse veram. Impossibile est enim dici hanc formam esse in anima in effectu perfecte, et non intelligi ab ea in effectu perfecte; sensus enim de hoc quod eam intelligit non est nisi quia forma existit in ea; unde impossibile est corpus esse thesaurum eius. Et impossibile est etiam essentiam animae esse thesaurum eius: hoc enim quod est thesaurus eius nihil aliud est nisi quia forma intellecta existit in ea et nos sic intelligimus. Non est autem sic apprehensio formae; apprehendere etenim formam non est thesauri sed tantum retinere: alterius etenim virtutis est apprehendere. Formas autem memoratas et formatas esse in aliquo non est ipsas apprehendere, sicut formas

under two forms after it understands two things successively, just as prime matter remains one under different forms. Hence, the Commentator too compares the possible intellect to prime matter in this regard in his <*Long Commentary on* Aristotle's> *On the Soul*, book III.[73] And thus, it in no way follows that our intellect becomes the divine essence in seeing God, but <it follows> that the divine essence is related to it as its perfection and form.

(11) To the eleventh, it should be said that these authorities and all those similar to them must be understood with regard to the cognition by which we cognize God in this life, on the basis of the previous account.

(12) To the twelfth, it should be said that the infinite taken privatively is said to be unknown, insofar as it is of this kind, because it is said by the removal of the completion (*complementum*) from which the cognition of a thing derives. Hence, the infinite is reduced to matter as subject to privation as is evident from <Aristotle's> *Physics*, book III.[74] But the infinite taken negatively is said by the removal of

---

sensibiles esse in aliquo non est sensus: unde corpora in quibus sunt formae sensibilium non sunt apprehendentia; apprehensionem vero secundum quod est virtutis apprehendentis, necesse est fieri ab eo in quo solet imprimi ipsa forma aliquo modo impressionis. In memoriali autem et formali non imprimuntur formae nisi secundum quod sunt instrumenta, et habent corpus retinens ipsas formas propinquum gerenti virtutem apprehendentem, quae est imaginatio et aestimatio, ita ut consideret eas cum vult, sicut retinent formam sensatam circa sensum, ad hoc ut acquirat eam sensus cum voluerit. Hoc autem potest intelligi in memoriali et formali, non in anima: formam enim intellectam esse in anima hoc est quod apprehendi eam; item adhuc postea declarabimus in sapientia prima quod haec forma non est per se existens."

73. Averroes, *Commentarium magnum in Aristotelis De anima libros*, l. 3, com. 5 (ed. Crawford 1953, p. 387, v. 27–p. 388, v. 32): "Et cum ista est diffinitio intellectus materialis, manifestum est quod differt apud ipsum a prima materia in hoc quod iste est in potentia omnes intentiones formarum universalium materialium, prima autem materia est in potentia omnes iste forme sensibiles non cognoscens neque comprehendens." Ibid. (ed. Crawford 1953, p. 409, v. 654–p. 410, v. 663): "Tertia autem questio (et est quomodo intellectus materialis est aliquod ens, et non est aliqua formarum materialium neque etiam prima materia) sic dissolvitur. Opinandum est enim quod iste est quartum genus esse. Quemadmodum enim sensibile esse dividitur in formam et materiam, sic intelligibile esse oportet dividi in consimilia hiis duobus, scilicet in aliquod simile forme et in aliquod simile materie. Et hoc necesse est in omni intelligentia abstracta que intelligit aliud; et si non, non esset multitudo in formis abstractis."

74. Aristoteles, *Physica*, l. 3, c. 7 (207b35–208a2), trans. vet. (AL VII 1,2 p. 132, v. 7–10): "Quoniam autem cause divise sunt in quadrifariam, manifestum est quod sicut materia infinitum causa est, et quod esse quidem ipsius privatio est, per se autem subiectum continuum et sensibile est."

limiting matter because form too is in some way limited by matter. Hence, the infinite in this way is cognoscible in itself to the highest degree. And in this way, God is infinite.[75]

(13) To the thirteenth, it should be said that Augustine speaks of the corporeal vision by which He will never be seen. And this is evident from what precedes in the passage: "For, no one has ever seen nor can ever see God in the way in which visible things, which can be named, are seen."[76] And His nature is invisible, just as it is also incorruptible. Yet, just as He is being (*ens*) to the highest degree in his nature, so too is He intelligibility to the highest degree. That He is sometimes not understood by us, however, arises from a deficiency

---

75. It is most likely that Aquinas found this distinction applied to the same context in Bonaventure, who, in his commentary on the *Sentences* distinguishes infinity by negation into two different kinds: infinity privatively, which does not apply to God, and infinity negatively, which applies to God. See: Bonaventura, *In primum librum Sententiarum*, d. 43, a. 1, q. 2 (ed. Quaracchi 1/2, 769–770): "Potest ergo dupliciter dici infinitum, scilicet a parte *negationis*, et similiter a parte *finis*. A parte *finis*: nam finis dicitur dupliciter, uno modo, quod est *complementum*; et sic infinitum dicitur per privationem complementi, et hoc modo infinitum dicitur in materia et in genere substantiae et in aliis generibus; et hoc modo non cadit in Deo, quia ipse est perfectissimus. Alio modo finis dicitur *terminus*, sicut finis agri, et sic infinitum dicitur quod caret termino et statu.—Et hoc potest esse dupliciter secundum *negationem*, quia potest intelligi *privative* et *negative*: *privative*, quia non *habet* terminum, sed tamen *natum est* habere, propter hoc quod habet esse limitatum, et hoc modo dicit *incompletionem*, et non est in Deo. Alio modo *negative*, quod *non habet* terminum nec *est natum* habere: et hoc modo ponitur in Deo propter summam immensitatem." A similar distinction is also found in Bonaventure's *On the Mystery of the Trinity*, see: Bonaventura, *De mysterio trinitatis*, q. 4, a. 1 (ed. Quaracchi 5, p. 80–81): "Intelligendum igitur, quod *infinitum* dicitur dupliciter, scilicet *privative* et *negative*. Secundum quod dicitur *privative*, sic privat *actum* et relinquit *aptitudinem*; et hoc modo dicitur *infinitum* quod est *natum finiri*, non tamen est finitum, et sic sonat in incompletionem.—Secundum autem quod dicitur *negative*, sic *simpliciter removet finem* sive finitatem; sed hoc dupliciter habet intelligi secundum duplicem acceptionem *finis*. Dicitur enim *finis-terminus*, *finis-complementum*" (emphases as in edition). See also: Alexander Halensis, *Glossa in quatuor libros Sententiarum Petri Lombardi*, l. 1, d. 8 (ed. Quaracchi 12, p. 110, v. 18–21): "Infinita: non sumitur privatorie, secundum quod infinitum dicitur in quantitate aptum natum habere transitum et non habens; sed negative, scilicet non aliunde ens finitum, sed finiens alia." Ibid., l. 1, d. 37 (ed. Quaracchi 12, p. 374, v. 15–21): "Respondeo: infinitum dupliciter accipitur. Uno modo accipitur negative, alio privative, secundum quod infinitum est aptum natum finiri, non habens finem. Secundum hunc ultimum modum non est verum de Deo nec sunt immediata finitum et infinitum. Secundum vero primum modum est verum quod non finitur per locum actu vel potentia." Closely related to this distinction between privative and negative divine infinity is the distinction between quantitative and virtual infinity, which Aquinas takes up as his main argument against comprehension of the divine essence in article three below.

76. See objection thirteen above, p. 100.

in us. Hence, that He may be seen after He was not seen by us is not due to a change in Him but in us.

(14) To the fourteenth, it should be said that God in heaven will be seen by the blessed *as He is*,[77] if this refers to the mode of what is seen. For God will be seen by the blessed to possess that mode which He has. But, if the mode refers to the one cognizing, He will not be seen as He is because the efficacy of the created intellect for seeing will not be the same as the efficacy of the divine essence with regard to what is understood.

(15) To the fifteenth, it should be said that a medium is found in three ways in the corporeal vision (*visio*) and in the intellectual vision. The first is a medium "under which" (*sub quo*) <something> is seen, and this is what perfects sight (*visus*) for seeing in general without determining sight to any specific object, just as corporeal light relates to corporeal sight, and the light of the agent intellect relates to the possible intellect. The second is a medium "by which" (*quo*) a thing is seen, and this is the visible form by which either of the two sights is determined to a specific object, just as by the form of the stone for cognizing a stone. The third is a medium "in which" (*in quo*) a thing is seen, and it is that by whose beholding sight is led to another thing, just as in beholding a mirror, <sight> is led to the thing represented in the mirror, and in seeing the image it is led to the thing that is depicted in the image. And in this way, the intellect too is led to the cause through a cognition of the effect, or vice versa.

However, in the vision of heaven there will be no third medium, so that God may be cognized through species of other things, just as He is cognized now, in the sense in which we are said to *see in a mirror now*.[78] Nor will there be a second medium there because the divine essence itself will be that by which our intellect will see God, as is evident from what has been said above. But there will be there

77. Epistula Iohannis I 3:2, see section II of the general introduction, note 1.

78. Ad Corinthios I 13:12, see section II of the general introduction, note 1. Douay-Rheims translates *speculum* with 'glass' here (Douay-Rheims The Vulgate Bible 2010–2013). In the context in Aquinas's works, it is, however, best to stick to the simpler translation of 'mirror.'

the first medium which will elevate our intellect to be able to conjoin to the uncreated essence in the aforementioned way. But on the basis of this medium, the cognition is not said to be mediated because it does not stand between the one who cognizes and the thing cognized, but it is what gives the power of cognition to the one who cognizes.

(16) To the sixteenth, it should be said that corporeal creatures are not said to be seen immediately, except when that which can be conjoined to sight in them is conjoined to it. Yet by reason of their materiality, they are incapable of conjunction through their essence. And for this reason, they are seen immediately when the similitude of them is conjoined to the intellect. God, however, is capable of conjunction to the intellect through His essence. Hence, He would not be seen immediately except if His essence were conjoined to the intellect. And this immediate vision is called 'the vision of the face.'[79]

Furthermore, the similitude of a corporeal thing is received into <the power of> sight according to the nature (*ratio*) by which it is in the thing, even though this is not according to the same mode of being (*modus essendi*). And for this reason, the similitude leads to that thing directly. Yet it is impossible that any similitude lead our intellect to God in this way, as is evident from what has been said above. And because of this, it is not similar.

---

79. Ibid.

ARTICLE 2

On the Impossibility of Seeing God with Corporeal Eyes

INTRODUCTION

What kind of vision is the beatific vision not? The answer Aquinas gives to this question is developed in articles two and three. The first constraint that Aquinas introduced in article two to his rather optimistic outlook on the beatific vision was aimed at casting off what he considered a false understanding of it, an understanding that would take vision literally in the corporeal sense. For Aquinas, God, as pure act, as completely immaterial and incorporeal being, could never be seen in a vision bound by physical conditions, be they earthly or heavenly. With this line of reasoning, he denied that the resurrected body could see God, a denial that was not commonly shared by his contemporaries,[1] and he limited the corporeal vision of the blessed

1. For Albert the Great, conjunction with God in eternal life is comprehensive inasmuch as it concerns all parts of the human soul and body. The picture he draws is that the intellect is conjoined to God in accordance with its two natural faculties, the agent intellect and the passive intellect. But the corporeal senses, external as well as internal, are equally conjoined to God inasmuch as they receive an influx from the intellect. Hence, they see God through the influx of the intellect. This may not be a face-to-face vision, but it is nonetheless a vision that is directly informed by the face-to-face vision that the intellect possesses. For the whole section in which Albert discusses these matters that he counts as belonging to eternal life, see: Albertus Magnus, *De resurrectione*, tr. 4, q. 2 (ed. Colon. 26, p. 340, v. 15–p. 345, v. 69). The passages concerning Albert's view on how the senses are informed by the intellect in their cognition in the afterlife are as follows: ibid., tr. 4, q. 2, a. 3 (ed. Colon. 26, p. 342, v. 83–87): "Ad id quod contra hoc est, dicendum, quod deus replebit totam animam et totum corpus gloria. Et ideo talis coniunctio harum potentiarum ad fines suos est supra vires animae, et efficit eam deus in ipsis potentiis." Ibid., tr. 4, q. 2, a. 4, § 1 (ed. Colon. 26, p. 343, v. 32–35 and 42–43):

to seeing God's glory "in sensible creatures and much more in the body of Christ" (reply to objection six in the present article).

As in the previous article, Aquinas took maximal inspiration from carefully selected Aristotelian principles. One of them is emphasized in this article and entails that one cannot have physical sensation that reaches beyond the physical realm. The other principle, which substantiated this insight, was presented earlier by Aquinas in his *Sentences*. It suggested that the specific nature of sense and even its activity ought to remain similar prior to and post resurrection. Aquinas introduced this principle of what I call "continued specific activity" in a context close to that of this article when he inquired into the question "whether the bodies of the blessed will be passible upon their resurrection" or whether they will be impassible and insusceptible of sensation.[2] In reply to this thorny question, Aquinas sided with the negative and suggested that the resurrected bodies will be insusceptible of sensation. This, it seems, was predominantly because of the unchangeable conditions of the afterlife.

Yet his negative reply provoked a serious dilemma for his Aristotelian commitments. If the senses are thought to be insusceptible of sensation, then they no longer seem to be in act in the resurrected

---

"Sine praeiudicio dicimus, quod sensus non erunt ibi sicut hic, sed erit deus replens sensus per modum gloriae; et sensibile, quod distinguit sensum, descendet ab intellectu. <...> Et sic etiam patet, qualiter actus sensuum principiantur a deo, et sic sunt vitae aeternae." Ibid., tr. 4, q. 2, a. 4, § 2 (ed. Colon. 26, p. 344, v. 11–23): "Sed in futuro ab intellectu certo ipsius rei incipit cognitio, et ideo formae sensibiles, quae ponuntur circa illud, ponuntur circa certum. Et ideo in tali compositione non accidit error. Unde patet, quod necessarium est, quod incipiat ab interiori. Et hoc credo esse intellectum Augustini in libro De spiritu et anima, ubi dicit quod 'sensus vertetur in rationem, ratio in intellectum, intellectus in intelligentiam'; verti enim sensum in rationem nihil aliud est nisi verti sensum ad rationem, ut sicut modo sensus est principium cognitionis rationalis, ita tunc cognitio rationalis efficiatur principium sensus." Bonaventure already explicitly objects to Albert's solution in his *Sentences,* and does so with arguments similar to those that Aquinas will use in the present article against Albert. See: Bonaventura, *In quartum librum Sententiarum*, d. 49, pars 2, sect. 1, a. 3, q. 2 (ed. Quaracchi 4, p. 1020): "Ad hoc dixerunt aliqui, quod non est receptio *ab extrinseco*; sed anima omnium quae vult videre species facit in oculo, et videt, quia tunc ordo erit commutatus, quia non erit receptio veniens ab inferiori, sed a superiori.—Sed haec solutio non potest stare; primum quidem, quia perverteretur ordo, cum species spiritualis fieret corporalis, perfectum fieret imperfectum; secundo, quia ita videret absentia, ut praesentia, ita oculis clausis, sicut apertis" (emphasis as in edition).

2. Thomas Aquinas, *Commentum in quatuor libros Sententiarum*, l. 4, d. 44, q. 2, a. 1 (ed. Parma 7/2, pp. 1083–1089): "Utrum corpora sanctorum post resurrectionem erunt passibilia."

body. Indeed, according to Aristotle, "to sense is to have a certain passion," and to be in the state of impassibility implies the contrary.[3] To solve this dilemma, Aquinas reviewed a number of replies that his contemporaries had given to similar questions. Most prominently among them, he featured Albert the Great's reply in his solution—a reply that was diametrically opposed to Aquinas's cherished principle of continued specific activity, since it suggested that in the glorified body the activity of sensing is other than in this life. Albert took the actualization of vision to change from receiving impressions of sensible species in this life to emitting them in the afterlife.[4] Yet Aquinas took pains to argue directly against Albert's preference for change in sensation, and in so doing relied upon the principle of continued specific activity:

> Upon the resurrection <of the body>, the specific nature will remain the same in human beings, and in all their parts. Yet, the nature of sense is of such a kind that it is a passive power, as the Philosopher shows in book 2 of his *On the Soul*. Hence, if upon the resurrection the blessed were to sense by emitting and not by receiving, sense would not be in them as a passive power. And in this way, it would not be of the same species with the sense that it is now, but it would be some other power given to them. For just as matter never becomes form, so a passive power never becomes active.[5]

---

3. Aristoteles, *De anima*, l. 2, lect. 21 (424a1), trans. vet. (ed. Gauthier 1985, p. 399): "sentire enim pati quoddam est." Compare for Michael Scot's Latin translation from the Arabic: ibid., l. 2, tx. 11 (ed. Crawford 1953, p. 313, v. 1): "Sentire enim est aliquod pati quoquo modo."

4. Albertus Magnus, *Quaestio de sensibus corporis gloriosi*, a. 1, ad 1 (ed. Colon. 25/2, p. 114, v. 2–6): "Aliter tamen solverunt quidam dicentes, quod sensus ibi erit extramittendo tantum. Sed quia hoc non competit nisi visui et neque etiam visui necessario probatur convenire, ideo relinquo." See also note 5 below for Aquinas's and Bonaventure's criticisms.

5. Thomas Aquinas, *Commentum in quatuor libros Sententiarum*, l. 4, d. 44, q. 2, a. 1, qc. 3 (ed. Parma 7/2, p. 1086): "Quidam enim dicunt, quod quia gloriosa corpora erunt impassibilia, et propter hoc non receptibilia peregrinae impressionis, et multo minus quam corpora caelestia; non erit ibi sensus in actu per receptionem alicujus speciei a sensibilibus, sed magis extra mittendo. Sed hoc non potest esse: quia in resurrectione natura speciei manebit eadem in homine et in omnibus partibus ejus. Hujusmodi autem est natura sensus, ut sit potentia passiva, ut in 2 de Anima (text. com. 51 et 121) probat Philosophus; unde si in resurrectione sancti sentirent extra mittendo, et non recipiendo, non esset sensus in eis virtus passiva; et sic non esset ejusdem speciei cum sensu qui nunc est, sed esset aliqua alia virtus eis data: sicut enim materia nunquam

Aquinas's solution to the dilemma he had created for himself followed upon this passage and suggested that there was one kind of change, the so-called spiritual change, that does not alter the nature of the recipient, but rather renders sensation in act by itself.[6] But the reason that Aquinas could provide this solution was his purist commitment to an Aristotelian understanding of sense perception pre and post resurrection, which he could only develop on the basis of the principle of continued specific activity.

These purist commitments are a constant factor in the present article, albeit implicitly. Aquinas's reliance on the famous Aristotelian distinction between proper sensibles and common sensibles in order to explain post-resurrection sense perception catches the eye of the reader immediately.[7] The Stagirite certainly did not intend this

---

fit forma, ita potentia passiva nunquam fit activa." Bonaventure, too, already noted this difficulty in Albert's position in his *Sentences*. See: Bonaventura, *In quartum librum Sententiarum*, d. 49, pars 2, sect. 1, a. 3, q. 2 (ed. Quaracchi 4, p. 1020): "Secunda positio est, quod est sensus, sed non est intus suscipiendo, sed extra mittendo virtutem, quia non recipiet, sed influet.—Sed ista adhuc non potest stare, cum cognitio sit in unione, et organa sint maxime habilia ad recipiendum."

6. Thomas Aquinas, *Commentum in quatuor libros Sententiarum*, d. 44, q. 2, a. 1, qc. 4 (ed. Parma 7/2, p. 1086): "Et ideo dicendum est cum aliis, quod sensus corporum gloriosorum erit per susceptionem a rebus quae sunt extra animam. Sed sciendum, quod organa sentiendi immutantur a rebus quae sunt extra animam, dupliciter. Uno modo immutatione naturali, quando scilicet organum disponitur eadem qualitate naturali qua disponitur res extra animam quae agit in ipsum; sicut cum manus fit calida et adusta ex tactu rei calidae, vel odorifera ex tactu rei odoriferae. Alio modo immutatione spirituali, quando recipitur qualitas sensibilis in instrumento secundum esse spirituale, idest species sive intentio qualitatis, et non ipsa qualitas; sicut pupilla recipit speciem albedinis, et tamen ipsa non efficitur alba. Prima ergo receptio non causat sensum per se loquendo, quia sensus est susceptivus specierum in materia praeter materiam, idest praeter esse materiale quod habebant extra animam, ut dicitur in 2 de Anima (text. 121); et haec receptio immutat naturam recipientis, quia recipitur hoc modo qualitas secundum esse suum materiale. Unde ista receptio non erit in corporibus gloriosis, sed secunda quae per se facit sensum in actu, et non immutat naturam recipientis."

7. See, for instance: Aristoteles, *De anima*, l. 2, lect. 12 (418a7–19), trans. vet. (ed. Gauthier 1985, p. 294): "Dicendum autem est secundum unumquemque sensuum de sensibilibus. Dicitur autem sensibile tripliciter, quorum duo quidem per se dicimus sentire, unum autem secundum accidens; duum autem aliud quidem proprium est uniuscuiusque sensus, aliud uero commune omnium. Dico autem proprium quod non contingit altero sensu sentiri, et circa quod non contingit errare. Vt uisus coloris et auditus soni et gustus humoris; tactus autem plures habet differencias, set in unaquaque iudicat de hiis et non decipitur; quoniam color est, neque quoniam sonus. Set quid est coloratum, aut ubi, aut quid est sonans, aut ubi. Huiusmodi quidem igitur dicuntur propria uniuscuiusque. Communia quidem sunt motus, quies, numerus, figura, magnitudo; huiuscemodi enim neque uni sensui sunt propria, set communia omnibus. Tactus enim motus quidam est sensibilis et uisus." For Michael Scot's Latin translation from the

distinction for post-resurrection explanations of sense perception, but his point for this life was that there are two kinds of sensible properties: (1) those that are exclusive to one sense organ, such as color for sight, or sound for hearing; and (2) those that are common to all senses and accompanying the proper sensibles, such as motion, rest, and all conditions related to magnitude. For Aquinas, this distinction played an important role in considering post-resurrection sense perception. Nonetheless, it was of secondary relevance and subordinate to yet another key distinction, a distinction that divided sense perception of physical objects into "sense perception by itself" and "sense perception by accident." As we shall see, Aquinas aligned these two distinctions with each other to conclude that a corporeal beatific vision is impossible.

For Aquinas, sense perception by itself—under which category he included Aristotle's proper sensibles and common sensibles—necessarily and without exception relied on a corporeal organ. Aquinas insisted that sensibles bound by proper and common physical properties, such as color, sound, magnitude etc., could only be received by a recipient that is physical too; hence invoking what I would call the "principle of proportionality."[8] Therefore, it was the irrevocably physical ontology of proper and common sensibles that accounted for their reception by the corporeal senses. But it also proved responsible for a bottom-up process of cognizing: proper and common sensibles had to be gathered through the senses, brought together by manifold cognitive processes in the internal senses, so as

---

Arabic, see: ibid., l. 2, tx. 63–64 (ed. Crawford 1953, p. 224, v. 1–15 and p. 226, v. 1–4,): "Et antequam incipiamus loqui de unoquoque sensuum, loquamur de sensibilibus. Dicamus igitur quod sensibile dicitur tribus modis, quorum duo dicuntur sentiri per se, et tertius accidentaliter. Et alter duorum proprius est unicuique sensuum, et alter est communis omnibus. Et est dicere *proprius* quem non potest alter sensus sentire, et illud quod impossibile est ut ei contingat error, v. g. visus apud colorem, et auditus apud vocem, et gustus apud saporem. Sensus autem plures modos uno habet, sed unusquisque eorum iudicat ista, et non errat in colore quis color sit, neque in voce que vox sit, sed in colorato quid est et ubi est, et in audito quid est et ubi est. Quod igitur est tale est *proprium*. <...> Communia autem sunt motus et quies et numerus et figura et quantitas. Ista enim non sunt propria alicui, sed communia eis omnia; motus enim sentitur tactu et visu."

8. See the introduction to article six, where this principle again plays an important role in Aquinas's argumentation.

to ultimately render possible the abstraction of a universal intelligible species by the intellect.

Yet in Aquinas's eyes, there existed another category of sensibles, things "sensed by accident," whose ontology and effect on the cognitive process was rather different. Aquinas insisted that these sensibles could be cognized instantly, not just sensed, since they involved properties included in the universals in the intellect and in the inner sense of the cogitative power. Indeed, when a particular person—Aquinas uses the example of Socrates—is heard speaking, he or she is also instantly identified as being alive. The property of "being alive" is perceived in the proper and common sensibles, but not in itself. Rather, in itself it is contained as a universal in the intellect, and, in a way, seems to be imposed upon a sense object when it is sensed. Aquinas therefore opposed the movement of cognition for these "sensibles by accident" (including names, relations, and basic ontological properties such as being alive) to the proper and common sensibles, and conceived of the former as coming through top-down cognition. More important still seems to be the fact that these properties bridged the gap between the divided line of physical and intellectual objects; they were contained in the universal and yet instantly applicable to and sensed in any sensed particular. In this way, Aquinas aligned these two distinctions. Their application to the beatific vision followed in the next argumentative step.

When it came to denying a corporeal beatific vision, Aquinas followed a similar order of arguments. The first, which addressed sense perception by itself, was easy. None of the physical properties of proper and common sensibles could possibly be compatible with seeing God, since He is *actus purus* in His own nature, and as such ontologically devoid of any physical properties. The second, considerably more sophisticated, was Aquinas's reasoning concerning sense perception by accident. He now suggested, perhaps unexpectedly, that God could be sensed by accident in two ways. Neither of these, however, must be understood to apply to the beatific vision itself. Rather, Aquinas conceived of them as corporeal visions accompanying the purely intellectual beatific vision. Indeed, he did not propose that God could thus be sensed in Himself as He was seen in Himself;

rather He could be sensed in His glory in the bodies of the blessed and in Christ's body. God's glory, however, was far from identical with God's essence in Aquinas's eyes. Similarly, Aquinas reasoned that God could be perceived and identified immediately in sensing all physical creatures because of His presence in the intellect in the beatific vision. Aquinas intended this understanding of perceiving God Himself in the proper and common sensibles to be analogous to the top-down cognition that intellect and cogitative power perform on particular sense objects in this life, as when they impose a universal property upon a sense object when it is sensed. The vision of God in His essence, therefore, imposed upon sense perception of common and proper sensibles some properties of His essence that could not be cognized in these sensibles before knowing Him intellectually.

In sum, contrary to many of his predecessors and contemporaries, Aquinas insisted on a universal applicability of select Aristotelian concepts for solving the theological question of what the beatific vision is not.[9] In article two, these concepts involved the principle of continued specific activity, albeit implicitly; and along with it, the distinction between proper and common sensibles, as well as the principle of proportionality between recipient and received object. With his insistence on these Aristotelian principles, Aquinas attempted to preserve a core identity of the human nature after the resurrection. But this came at a price. Albert the Great had allowed for a change in the modality of the activity of seeing corporeally, hence God's essence could be seen

9. Despite his harsh criticisms of Albert, as quoted earlier, Bonaventure also opted for a non-Aristotelian solution. Unlike Aquinas, he reasoned that it is the heavenly gifts (*dotes*) of luminosity (*luminositas*) and lightness (*levitas*), which become properties of the resurrected body, that reduce the senses of sight and touch to act. See: Bonaventura, *In quartum librum Sententiarum*, d. 49, pars 2, sect. 1, a. 3, q. 1 (ed. Quaracchi 4, pp. 1018–1019): "Dicendum, quod *posse sentire* est ex coniunctione potentiae cum organo bene disposito, *sentire* vero ex coniunctione ipsius cum obiecto. Quoniam igitur ibi erunt potentiae iunctae organis bene dispositis, ibi erunt omnes *potentiae* sentiendi. Quoniam vero *obiecta* omnium sensuum non erunt in gloria, sed quorundam; ideo *quidam* erunt in *actu suo*, *quidam* vero *non*.—Obiecta enim *quorundam* sensuum sunt *proprietates absolutae*, quae reperiuntur in corpore glorificando, utpote color visus, et levitas ipsius tactus; et quia corpus gloriosum resurget cum luminositate et levitate, erunt ibi obiecta duorum sensuum; ideo isti sensus erunt in suis actibus. Obiecta vero *aliorum* sensuum non sunt *proprietates corporis glorificandi* nec *proprietates abolutae*, sed *emanationes* a corporibus, ut odor et sonus et sapor; et quia non erunt in patria" (emphases as in edition).

corporeally too. Yet Aquinas insisted on an identical activity and thus had to deny a corporeal vision of God's essence. Nonetheless, his idea evolved around enlarging the scope of objects that the activity of corporeal vision could include: God's glory could be sensed by accident in corporeal objects, and the intellect could impose certain properties of God onto these sense objects per se.

TRANSLATION

We proceed to the second article as follows. It seems that the blessed will see God with their corporeal eyes after the resurrection.

Objections

(1) For the glorified eye will possess greater power than the nonglorified eye. But blessed Job saw God with his own eye as in Job 42:5: *With the hearing of the ear, I have heard thee, but now my eye seeth thee.*[10] Therefore, all the more will the glorified eye be able to see God through His essence.

(2) Furthermore, <as is written in> Job 19:26: *And in my flesh I will see my God, my savior.*[11] Therefore, it seems that God will be seen with corporeal eyes in heaven.

(3) Furthermore, when he speaks of the <power of> sight of the glorified eyes, Augustine says the following in his *The City of God*, book 22, chapter 29: "A greater power will belong to those eyes, not so that they may see more sharply—as some ascribe to the sight of serpents or eagles, for whatever acuity of discernment these animals possess, they can see nothing more than bodies—but so that they may see incorporeal objects."[12] Yet, any cognitive power that is of

10. Iob 42:5 (Vulgata 2007): *Auditu auris audiui te, nunc autem oculus meus uidet te.*

11. Iob 19:26 (Vulgata 2007): *In carne mea uidebo Deum.* Note that neither the Vulgate nor the Douay-Rheims translation includes *salvatorem meum* or 'my savior' as is the case in Aquinas's citation of the verse (Douay-Rheims The Vulgate Bible 2010–2013).

12. Augustinus Hipponensis, *De civitate Dei*, l. 22, c. 29 (CCSL 48, p. 859, v. 109–114; PL 41, p. 799): "vis itaque praepollentior oculorum erit illorum, non ut acrius uideant, quam quidam perhibentur uidere serpentes uel aquilae (quantalibet enim acrimonia cernendi eadem quoque animalia nihil aliud possunt uidere quam corpora), sed ut uideant et incorporalia."

incorporeal nature can be elevated to the vision of God. Therefore, the glorified eyes will be able to see God.

(4) Furthermore, the difference of corporeal to incorporeal is the same as the inverse. But the incorporeal eye can see corporeal objects. Therefore, the corporeal eye can see incorporeal objects. And likewise, the same <follows> as before.

(5) Furthermore, in book V of his *Morals on the Book of Job* 4:16: *There stood one whose countenance I knew not* etc., Gregory says as follows: "Humans, had they been willing to keep the precept, would have become spiritual in their flesh, but by sinning, they became carnal also in their minds." But because they had become carnal in their minds, as is said in the same passage, "they cognize only those things that they take into their minds through the images of the body."[13] Therefore, when humans are spiritual in their flesh too, which is promised to the blessed after their resurrection, they will also be able to see spiritual things in their flesh. And likewise, the same <follows> as before.

(6) Furthermore, humans can be beatified by God alone. Yet, they will be beatified not only with regard to the soul, but also with regard to the body. Therefore, they will not only be able to see God by the intellect, but also by the flesh.

(7) Furthermore, as God is present to the intellect by His essence, so too will He be present to the senses, because He will be "all in all," as is said in I Corinthians 15:28.[14] But He will be seen by an intellect because His essence will be conjoined to it, as was said above. Therefore, He will also be able to be seen by the senses.

❂ ❂ ❂

13. Gregorius Magnus, *Moralia in Iob*, l. V, c. 34 (CCSL 143, p. 261, v. 1–2.10–13; PL 75, pp. 712–713): "Stetit quidam cuius non agnoscebam uultum. <...> Homo enim, qui si praeceptum seruare uoluisset, etiam carne spiritalis futurus erat, peccando factus est etiam mente carnalis ut sola cogitet quae ad animum per imagines corporum trahit." Iob 4:16 (Vulgata 2007): *Stetit quidam cuius non agnoscebam vultum imago coram oculis meis et vocem quasi aurae lenis audivi.*

14. Ad Corinthios I 15:28 (Vulgata 2007): *Cum autem subiecta fuerint illi omnia, tunc ipse Filius subiectus erit illi qui sibi subiecit omnia, ut sit Deus omnia in omnibus.*

(1) On the contrary, Ambrose says <in commenting> on Luke 1:11: "Neither is God sought by the corporeal eye, nor captured by sight, nor touched by touch."[15] Therefore, God will in no way be seen by the corporeal senses.

(2) Furthermore, Jerome says: "Neither can the carnal eyes behold the Godhead of the Father, nor that of the Son, nor that of the Holy Spirit. But the mental eye alone can of which it is said: 'Blessed are the pure in heart,' etc."[16]

(3) Furthermore, Jerome says again: "Incorporeal things are not seen by corporeal eyes."[17] But God is incorporeal to the highest degree, therefore, etc.

(4) Furthermore, in his book *On Seeing God* Augustine says: "No one ever has, neither in this life nor in the life of the angels, seen God as He is in Himself in the way of these visible objects which are discerned by a corporeal vision."[18] Yet, the life of the angels is called 'blessed life' in which those who have risen will live. Therefore, etc.

(5) Furthermore, as Augustine says: "Humans are said to be made in the image of God because they can fix their eyes upon God."[19] But humans are made in the image <of God> with regard to the mind,

---

15. Ambrosius, *Expositio euangelii secundum Lucam*, l. 1 (CCSL 14, p. 20, v. 419–421; PL 15, p. 1624): "<...> nec corporalibus oculis deus quaeritur nec circumscribitur uisu nec tactu tenetur nec auditur adfatu nec sentitur incessu." See also: Secundum Lucam 1:11 (Vulgata 2007): *Apparuit autem illi angelus Domini stans a dextris altaris incensi.*

16. Hieronymus, *Commentariorum in Esaiam* III, l. 3, c. 6 (CCSL 73, p. 85, v. 54–58; PL 24, pp. 94–95): "Ad quod respondebimus, non solum Patris diuinitatem, sed ne Filii quidem et Spiritus sancti, quia una in Trinitate natura est, posse oculos carnis aspicere; sed oculos mentis, de quibus ipse Saluator ait: *Beati mundo corde, quoniam ipsi deum uidebunt*" (emphasis as in edition).

17. Augustinus Hipponensis, *Epistulae*, ep. 147: De videndo Deo, c. 23 (CSEL 44/2, p. 330, v. 12–14; PL 33, p. 621): "namque, sicut alibi idem Hieronymus breuiter ac ueraciter definiuit, 'res incorporalis corporalibus oculis non uidetur.'"

18. Ibid., c. 11 (CSEL 44/2, p. 303, v. 4–6; PL 33, p. 609): "deum enim nemo uidit umquam uel in hac uita, sicuti ipse est, uel etiam in angelorum uita, sicut uisibilia ista, quae corporali uisione cernuntur."

19. Id., *De Trinitate*, l. 14, c. 4 (CCSL 50A, p. 190, v. 8–10; PL 42, p. 1040): "ac per hoc si secundum hoc facta est ad imaginem dei quod uti ratione atque intellectu ad intelligendum et conspiciendum deum potest."

and not with regard to the flesh.[20] Therefore, they will see God by the mind and not by the flesh.

Response

I answer that it should be said that something is sensed by corporeal sense in two ways: in one way in itself (*per se*), in another accidentally (*per accidens*). In fact, what is sensed by itself can affect corporeal sense by itself. Yet, something can affect sense by itself inasmuch as it is sense, or this particular sense inasmuch as it is this sense. What affects sense in the second way, however, is called 'proper sensible,' as color is for sight, and sound is for hearing. Yet because sense, inasmuch as it is sense, makes use of a corporeal organ, it can only receive something corporeally: for everything that is received in something is in it in the mode of the recipient. And for this reason, all sensibles affect sense, inasmuch as it is sense, insofar as they have magnitude. And for this reason, magnitude and everything accompanying it, such as motion, rest, number and the like, are in themselves called 'common sensibles.'

Yet, what is sensed accidentally is something that does not affect sense, neither inasmuch as it is sense, nor inasmuch as it is this sense. But it is conjoined to the things that affect sense as such, such as Socrates, the son of Diarius, a friend, and the like.[21] These are cognized in themselves in the universal by the intellect; but in the particular by the cogitative power in humans; and by the estimative power in all other animals. Yet, external sense is said to sense things of this kind, even though accidentally. <This is the case> when, from what

20. See: Genesis 1:27 (Vulgata 2007): *Et creavit Deus hominem ad imaginem suam ad imaginem Dei creavit illum masculum et feminam creavit eos.*

21. Aristoteles, *De anima*, l. 2, lect. 12 (418a21–25), trans. vet. (ed. Gauthier 1985, p. 294): "Secundum accidens enim hoc sentitur, quoniam albo accidit hoc quod sentitur, unde et nichil patitur, secundum quod huiusmodi est, a sensibili. Sensibilium autem secundum se propria proprie sunt sensibilia et ad que substancia apta nata est uniuscuiusque sensus." Compare for Michael Scot's Latin translation from the Arabic: ibid., l. 2, tx. 65 (ed. Crawford 1953, p. 227, v. 1–7): "Accidentaliter autem dicitur in re quod est sensibilis, quasi sit album Socrates; iste enim non sentitur nisi accidentaliter; accidit enim albo quod fuit iste. Et ideo non patitur a sensibili secundum quod est sic. Ea autem que sunt sensibilia per se et propria sunt sensibilia in rei veritate; et sunt ea que sentire est nata substantia cuiusque sensuum."

is sensed by itself, the apprehensive power, to which it belongs to cognize the cognized thing by itself, apprehends immediately without doubt and discursion, just as we perceive someone to be alive from the fact that he speaks. Yet when it is otherwise, the senses are not even said to perceive such an object by accident.

Therefore, I say that God can in no way be seen by corporeal sight or sensed with any other sense as a thing that is visible in itself, neither here nor in heaven. For, if what pertains to sense[22] is removed from it, it will not be sensed. And similarly, if what pertains to sight, inasmuch as it is sight, is removed from sight, it will not be seen. Therefore, since sense, inasmuch as it is sense, perceives magnitude, and sight, inasmuch as it is a sense of this kind, perceives color, it is impossible that sight perceive something that is neither color nor magnitude, unless it were called sense equivocally. Therefore, since sight and sense will be in the same species in the glorified body, it will be impossible that the divine essence be seen as a thing that is visible in itself.

Yet it will be seen as a thing that is visible accidentally while, on the one hand, corporeal sight will contemplate the whole glory of God in bodies, especially in glorified <bodies> and to the highest degree in the body of Christ. And on the other hand, the intellect will see God so clearly that God will be perceived in things that are seen corporeally, just as life is perceived in the act of speaking. For although our intellect will not see God from His creatures then, it will nonetheless see Him in His creatures which are seen corporeally. And this way, by which God can be seen corporeally, is suggested by Augustine at the end of his *The City of God*, book 22, chapter 29, as is evident to those who have considered his words carefully. For, he says the following: "It is highly credible that we shall then see the mundane bodies of a new heaven and a new earth in the same way as we, with the clearest perspicuity, will see God, who is present everywhere and who governs all corporeal things, not as we now perceive intellectually the invisible things of God but rather in such

22. Sense (*sensus*)] in Leon.; *inquantum est sensus* is added in the Parma edition.

a way that when we look at humans presently, we do not have to believe that they are alive but we will simply see."[23]

Replies to Objections

(1) To the first, therefore, it should be said that the word of Job is understood as concerning the spiritual eye of which the Apostle says in Ephesians 1:18: *The eyes of your heart enlightened.*[24]

(2) To the second, it should be said that this authority must not be understood <to mean> that we shall see God by our carnal eyes, but <that> because we exist in the flesh, we shall see God.

(3) To the third, it should be said that Augustine speaks as someone inquiring in the words above and conditionally, as is evident from what was said before: "Accordingly, they will be of an altogether different power, if that incorporeal nature will be seen through them," and then he adds "accordingly, the power" etc., and subsequently he settles <the matter> as above.[25]

(4) To the fourth, it should be said that all cognition comes to be through some separation from matter. And for this reason, the more a corporeal form is separated from matter, the more it is a principle of cognition. And therefore, it is the case that a form existing

---

23. Augustinus Hipponensis, *De civitate Dei*, l. 22, c. 29 (CCSL 48, p. 861, v. 182–193; PL 41, p. 800): "ualdeque credibile est sic nos uisuros mundana tunc corpora caeli noui et terrae nouae, ut Deum ubique praesentem et uniuersa etiam corporalia gubernantem per corpora quae gestabimus et quae conspiciemus, quaqua uersum oculos duxerimus, clarissima perspicuitate uideamus, non sicut nunc inuisibilia Dei per ea, quae facta sunt, intellecta conspiciuntur per speculum in aenigmate <et> ex parte, ubi plus in nobis ualet fides, qua credimus, quam rerum corporalium species, quam per oculos cernimus corporales. Sed sicut homines, inter quos uiuentes motusque uitales exerentes uiuimus, mox ut aspicimus, non credimus uiuere, sed uidemus." This passage is also quoted by: Iohannes Pecham, *Quaestiones de beatitudine animae et corporis*, q. 5, pars 46 (BFSMA 28, p. 505, v. 16–21).

24. Ad Ephesios 1:18 (Vulgata 2007): *inluminatos oculos cordis vestri.*

25. Augustinus Hipponensis, *De civitate Dei*, l. 22, c. 29 (CCSL 48, p. 859, v. 102–104, 109–114; PL 41, p. 798): "Longe itaque alterius erunt potentiae, si per eos uidebitur incorporea illa natura, quae non continetur loco, sed ubique tota est. <...> vis itaque praepollentior oculorum erit illorum, non ut acrius uideant, quam quidam perhibentur uidere serpentes uel aquilae (quantalibet enim acrimonia cernendi eadem quoque animalia nihil aliud possunt uidere quam corpora), sed ut uideant et incorporalia." See also objection three above and the end of the response below.

in matter is in no way a principle of cognition, but in our sense, it is in some way inasmuch as it is separated from matter, and in our intellect still better. And for this reason, the spiritual eye from which the impediment to cognition is removed can see a corporeal thing. Yet it does not follow that the corporeal eye, in which the power of cognition is insufficient since it participates in matter, can cognize perfectly the objects of cognition that are incorporeal.

(5) To the fifth, it should be said that although a mind that was made of carnal flesh is unable to think without receiving from the senses, it nonetheless thinks things in an immaterial way. And similarly, sight must always apprehend corporeally what it apprehends. Hence, it cannot cognize things that cannot be apprehended corporeally.

(6) To the sixth, it should be said that happiness is the perfection of humans insofar as they are humans. And because humans are not humans due to their body but rather due to their soul—though the body is essential to humans inasmuch as it is perfected by the soul—for this reason, human happiness principally consists in an act of the soul. And from it, a certain overflow passes to the body, as is evident from what was said in distinction 44.[26] Nonetheless, a certain happiness of the body will be ours inasmuch as it will see God in sensible creatures and especially in the body of Christ.

(7) To the seventh, it should be said that the intellect is able to perceive spiritual things; the corporeal power of sight, however, is not. And for this reason, the intellect will be able to cognize the divine essence conjoined to itself; the corporeal power of sight, however, will not.

26. See: Thomas Aquinas, *Commentum in quatuor libros Sententiarum*, l. 4, d. 44, q. 2, a. 4, qc. 3 (ed. Parma 7/2, p. 1099): "<I>deo melius est ut dicatur quod claritas illa causabitur ex redundantia gloriae animae in corpus. Quod enim recipitur in aliquo, non recipitur per modum influentis, sed per modum recipientis; et ita claritas quae est in anima ut spiritualis, recipitur in corpore ut corporalis; et ideo secundum quod anima erit majoris claritatis secundum majus meritum, ita etiam erit differentia claritatis in corpore."

ARTICLE 3

On the Impossibility of Comprehending God

INTRODUCTION

Following his discussion of the first constraint of the beatific vision—the denial of a corporeal vision of God—Aquinas now turns to the second constraint, the denial of a comprehensive vision of the divine essence. This issue of comprehensiveness, together with the question of how exactly the divine essence is known, was the subject of heated debates, diverse interpretations, and even magisterial rulings just before Aquinas's times, as we have seen in the general introduction. But how exactly did Aquinas tackle the question of how to deny a comprehensive vision a good decade after the decisive ruling of 1241?

Already in the eight objections and the four *sed contrae* that precede his reply, Aquinas grounded his theory on philosophical terms and principles. His intention in so doing was to preserve the transcendence of divine simplicity and infinity on the one hand, and yet, on the other, to grant creatures limited noetic access to the simple and infinite divine essence in the beatific vision. In a marked contrast to his predecessors' ways of accounting for this difficulty, Aquinas provided his systematic clarification of the beatific vision in its precise intellectual limitations by seamlessly continuing his discussions along philosophical lines.

Aquinas's reply in article three begins with an etymological elucidation of the term "to comprehend" (*comprehendere*), which he identifies as "to seize immediately" (*prendere*) and "to enclose" (*capere*). In Latin, all three terms express, with very similar connotations, the taking hold of another, the appropriation of another into one's own possession, the containment of another in one's own reality, and the binding of another on all sides. Possibly the Damascene provided a source of inspiration for Aquinas concerning God's incomprehensibility, especially in terms of highlighting the conditions of contingency in his *On the Orthodox Faith*:

> What can be circumscribed is comprehended by place or time or comprehension; but what cannot be circumscribed is not limited by any of these things. Therefore, what cannot be circumscribed is God alone, the One who is without beginning and without end, and the One who limits all things, and the One who is not limited by any comprehension. For He alone is incomprehensible and without limits, cognized by no one, yet He alone is the One who contemplates Himself.[1]

Despite Aquinas's familiarity with and use of the Damascene's *On the Orthodox Faith*—we can gather this from the third *sed contra* argument—he did not choose to quote this passage, but another one that simply suggests in less elaborate terms: "That the substance of God is incomprehensible, is indubitable to those who believe in the Holy Scripture."[2] Nonetheless, it is highly likely that Aquinas knew the passage here for explaining God's incomprehensible nature from his teacher Albert, who, in his *On the Resurrection*, quoted it in precisely this context.[3]

Whatever the historical reality may have been, the second argumentative step which Aquinas took was the decisive one in defending God's incomprehensibility, for it spelled out the distinction

---

1. Iohannes Damascenus, *De fide orthodoxa*, c. 13, trans. Burgundionis (ed. Buytaert 1955, p. 59, v. 48–54): "'Circumscriptibile quidem est quod loco vel tempore vel comprehensione comprehenditur; incircumscriptibile vero quod nullo horum continetur. Igitur incircumscriptibilis quidem solus est Deus, sine principio et sine fine ens, et omnia continens et nulla comprehensione contentus. Solus enim est incomprehensibilis et interminabilis, a nullo cognitus, ipse vero solus sui ipsius est contemplator."

2. See translation below, p. 142.

3. For the parallel passage where Albert quotes the Damascene, see: Albertus Magnus, *De resurrectione*, tr. 4, q. 1, a. 9, § 1 (ed. Colon. 26, p. 328, v. 75–83).

between a physical and an immaterial understanding of comprehension. He conceived of physical, or material, comprehension in terms of spatial or "dimensive quantity," whereas he construed intellectual comprehension in terms of "virtual quantity."[4] This distinction had long been employed as a standard to explain divine infinity by Aquinas's predecessors and contemporaries: Alexander of Hales, Richard Fishacre, Bonaventure, and Albert the Great speak to its widespread application.[5] But, in contrast to their uses, Aquinas expanded its use

4. A parallel text in Aquinas which highlights the distinction of dimensive and virtual quantity with regard to the angels, and how they can be said to be in a place, is found in Thomas Aquinas, *Quodlibet I*, q. 3, a. 1 (ed. Leon. 25/2, p. 181, v. 23–31): "Dicendum quod qualiter angelus sit in loco corporeo, considerari potest ex modo quo corpus est in loco. Est enim corpus in loco per contactum loci; contactus autem corporis est per quantitatem dimensiuam, que in angelo non inuenitur, cum sit incorporeus, set loco eius est in eo quantitas uirtualis. Sicut igitur corpus est in loco per contactum dimensiue quantitatis, ita angelus est in loco per contactum uirtutis."

5. In the context of divine infinity, this distinction between quantitative and virtual infinity seems to have appeared as early as in Richard Fishacre's commentary on the *Sentences*: Richard Fishacre, *Commentarium in librum I Sententiarum*, d. 2, c. 1, ad objecta 1–5 (ed. Ermatinger 1958, p. 226, v. 285–297 and p. 227, v. 322–331): "Ad objecta circa tertium problema probantia quod infinitum et simplex repugnant, sciendum quod infinitum intelligi potest dupliciter, scilicet quantitative et virtualiter, licet proprie secundum Aristotelem infinitum dicatur in quantitatibus tantum. Dico ergo quod illae quinque rationes verum concludunt de infinito quantitative, et tale infinitum non compatitur secum simplicitatem in eodem. Infinitum autem virtualiter intelligi potest dupliciter, sicut et plus et minus de virtute. Plus enim de virtute intelligimus, cui additum est aliquid de virtute. Et tunc infinitum virtualiter est cui additum est de virtute infinities. Et de sic intellecto infinito virtualiler verum concludunt dictae quinque rationes. Tale enim infinitum virtuale non compatitur secum simplicitatem. <...> Si ergo dicatur infinitum virtualiter non propter infinitam additionem virtuti, sed propter infinitam elongationem ab impedimentis et a materia, patet quod sic infinitum virtualiter non repugnat, immo congruit magis simplicitati. De sic autem infinito non tenent dictae quinque rationes, ut patet inspicienti. Quia ergo Deus in se simplex est et carens compositione cum alio, ut sit pars compositi, patet quod est infinitus virtualiter, non propter additiones virtutis factas in infinitum, sed potius quia in infinitum elongatus est ab impedimentis et materia, cum sit substantia omnino separata." For secondary literature, see Sweeney 1998, pp. 384–411. We find a similar distinction of Augustinian provenance, quantity of mass (*quantitas molis*) versus quantity of power (*quantitas virtutis*), in Bonaventure's *On the Mystery of the Trinity*: Bonaventura, *De mysterio trinitatis*, q. 4, a. 1 (ed. Quaracchi 5, p. 81): "Est enim terminus secundum *quantitatem materialem*, et est terminus secundum *quantitatem spiritualem*; prima dicitur *quantitas molis*, secunda *quantitas virtutis*. *Infinitum* igitur per abnegationem *termini circa quantitatem molis* semper dicit aliquam incompletionem aliquo modo, vel actu, vel potentia, quia dicit recessum a simplicitate. Talis enim quantitas non simul stat cum simplicitate in eodem et secundum idem, et tale infinitum numquam est actu, sed solum potentia, actu autem finitum. Infinitum vero per abnegationem *termini circa quantitatem virtutis* non dicit aliquam imperfectionem, sed summam perfectionem, quia non repugnat simplicitati, immo non potest esse nisi in summe simplici; et tali modo Scripturae auctoritas et fidei confessio ponunt infinitatem sive immensitatem in ipso Deo simplicissimo" (emphases as in edition). The identification

to the context of the beatific vision. He may have been discontent with the explanatory alternatives at the time of writing his commentary on the *Sentences*. Some authors, for instance, defended God's incomprehensibility by referencing Augustine's distinction without further argumentation, while Albert the Great drew creatively on the epistemology contained in Aristotle's *Posterior Analytics*, and, at the same time, provided Aquinas with his ontological distinction of dimensive versus virtual quantity.[6]

In Aquinas's (as in Albert's) eyes, dimensive quantity referred to an extension in space: it expressed the physical condition of being spread out three-dimensionally in height, width, and depth, and being able to relate to another in this physical sense. Hence, dimensive comprehension implied a relation of complete physical confinement or enclosure, in which the contained is entirely confined or enclosed in

---

of the two distinctions can be found in Albert's commentary on the *Sentences*, see: Albertus Magnus, *Commentarii in I Sententiarum*, l. 1, d. 19, a. 1 (ed. Borgnet 25, p. 512): "Dico, quod in divinis est aequalitas: et bene concedo, quod in divinis non potest esse quantitas dimensiva, quam Augustinus vocat *quantitatem molis*: sed est ibi quantitas virtutis" (emphasis as in edition). For further uses of this distinction in Albert's discussions of divine infinity, see: ibid., l. 1, d. 19, aa. 1–4 (ed. Borgnet 25, pp. 511b-516b); ibid., l. 1, d. 20, a. 7 (ed. Borgnet 25, p. 553); ibid., l. 1, d. 31, a. 10 (ed. Borgnet 26, p. 114).

6. For Albert's epistemological solution, see, for instance: Albertus Magnus, *De resurrectione*, tr. 4, q. 1, a. 9, § 1 (ed. Colon. 26, p. 328, v. 47–72): "Quod concedimus dicentes, quod videbimus deum in patria, sicuti est. Sicut enim deus seipsum videt sine medio, ita sine omni medio offeret se nobis. Et haec visio erit dos animae. Sed tamen distinguendum est, quod aliud est videre deum, ut est, et aliud est videre, quid est deus, sicut aliud est videre rem, ut est, et aliud videre, quid est res. Rem enim videre, ut est, est videre esse rei sive essentiam rei; videre autem, quid est res, est videre propriam diffinitionem includentem omnes terminos rei. Et ista duo differunt, secundum quod differunt quaestiones de ipsis. De simplici enim sive incomplexo quaerentes primo quaerimus, si est res, et terminatur quaestio ista, cum cognoscimus, quod res illa est et habet esse causatum causae primae; causa enim prima non ponit nisi esse et nullam differentiam addit super illud. Cognoscentes ergo hoc quaerimus, quid est res, volentes cognoscere rei perfectam diffinitionem per terminos claudentes totum esse rei, ita quod nihil sit de esse extra terminos illos. Et intellectui primae quaestionis non competit nisi attingere rem secundum intellectum. Intellectui autem secundae quaestionis competit comprehendere rem vere, secundum quod comprehensio est contactus intellectus super terminos rei. Sic dicimus de deo, quod attingimus esse ipsius sine medio per intellectum, sed nequaquam comprehendimus." For Albert's ontological solution as probably used and extended here by Aquinas, see: id., *Super I librum Sententiarum*, d. 1, c. 2 (ed. Colon. 29/1, p. 30, v. 30–38): "Infinitum in quantitate est, ut dicit Philosophus, cuius partes accipienti semper est aliquid extra accipere. In spirituali autem natura increata non est infinitum in quantitate molis sed virtutis, quia quantitas virtutis dividitur ad extra secundum ea in quae potest. Et ideo intellectus attingens deum attingit ipsum, ita quod multum et infinitum virtutis semper est extra ipsum, et quia virtus sua est essentia sua, ideo etiam immensitas essentiae est extra intellectum."

what contains it, such as "wine in a barrel" or water in a bottle. Dimensive excess, however, implied a relation of material surplus, overload, or transgression in favor of the contained. It is the contained that overstepped or extended beyond what contains it. But this overstepping and extending beyond was to be understood in an ontologically horizontal way, where the contained exceeds in amount, but not in degree.

Virtual quantity, on the other hand, referred to the extension of qualities or powers (*virtutes*) according to Aquinas: it expressed the operative condition of being able to perform certain actions in virtue of possessing particular powers, and of being able to relate to another, predominantly an object of understanding, in this operative sense. Hence, virtual comprehension implied a relation of virtual confinement or enclosure in which the contained is entirely mastered by or subsumed under the power that performs its actions upon it. For instance, when the definition of man, "rational animal," was completely enclosed by the human intellect, it was not only known but comprehended. Virtual excess, however, implied a relation of intellectual or operational superiority in favor of the object over its subject. It was the understood object that surpassed or transcended the power of understanding in its intelligibility. It transgressed the constraints of these powers in a vertical rather than a horizontal fashion, overstepping the power in degree, but not in amount. For instance, by way of definition, humans could know of an angel that it exists (*quod est*), but not what it is (*quid est*).

But why would Aquinas maintain that humans cannot understand angels by way of their definition, let alone God? Why would Aquinas wish to hold that there are certain objects that transgress the constraints of the human power to understand? This epistemological point about virtual faculties and their noetic relations to their objects was grounded in a metaphysical hierarchy of being, a hierarchy which was well known to Aquinas from the Porphyrian Tree and the *Isagoge* of Porphyry.

Indeed, Aquinas thought that while the powers or faculties of the human soul ground its virtual quantity, it is the essence of the human soul that grounds the power (*virtus*) in its nature, capacity, and scope of activity. Or put more generally: Any power is ontologically demarcated by the specific being that is expressed in the essence of its possessor. The human rational power, for instance, is ontologically determined by the essence of a human being, by the nature that makes a human being what it is—a nature that was also captured in the definition "rational animal." Similarly, the animals' sentient powers are ontologically determined by their essence or quiddity, and they too can be captured in the definition "irrational animal." Correspondingly, each species of being is given its fixed ontological place in the hierarchy of beings that begins on the level of "substance," the highest genus (*summum genus*), and ends on the level of particular individuals. Human beings are creatures which fall on one side of the tree. As rational, animate, extended substances, or "rational animals," their ability to comprehend, that is to seize and to enclose an object of knowing into their own reality, is circumscribed by this ontology. Objects that do not display lower or equal characteristics, whose rank on the Porphyrian Tree is, in whatever way, beyond the ontology of the human being, exceed the virtual quantity of human understanding. In his reply, Aquinas gives two examples from the mathematical realm: a line and an infinite number. Since these objects of knowing are not bound to physical reality, since they are infinite in their essential characteristics, since their quantity transcends the virtual quantity of the human capacity to understand, they cannot be seized or enclosed by the human intellect and thus cannot be comprehended.

For the human soul, even for the disembodied and glorified human soul, this means that its powers are grounded in the essence of being human, and that they remain bound to it even in disembodiment and glorification. The reality of its createdness and creaturely powers does not cease in the ontological respect.[7] When, therefore, God becomes the object of cognition in the beatific vision in His own uncreated reality, there is an immediate ontological asymmetry between knower and known. In Aquinas's eyes, however, this

7. See also Aquinas's reply to objection six in the translation below.

asymmetry does not preclude the knower from an epistemological access to its object; the light of glory renders this access possible, as we shall see in article six. Nonetheless, the ontological asymmetry between the disembodied and elevated human soul results in a qualitative and quantitative limitation with regard to the scope and extent to which God can be grasped in His essence. This then is Aquinas's first word, an ontological word, on the incomprehensibility of God's essence even for the blessed.

TRANSLATION

We proceed to the third article as follows. It seems that when the blessed in heaven see God, they comprehend Him.

Objections

(1) <For as is said in> I Corinthians 9:24: *So run that you may comprehend!*[8] This running, however, is for a prize. Therefore, the comprehension of God is the prize of merit that is granted to the blessed.

(2) Furthermore, Augustine says in his book *On Seeing God*: "The whole is comprehended in seeing because it is seen in such a way that nothing of it be concealed to the one seeing."[9] But if God is seen by someone, nothing of Him is concealed to the one seeing because, since He is simple, it is impossible that something of Him be seen and something else be concealed. Therefore, God is comprehended by anyone who sees Him.

(3) Furthermore, everything that is seen entirely (*totum*) and completely (*totaliter*) is comprehended. But the whole of God is seen

8. Ad Corinthios I 9:24 (Vulgata 2007): *sic currite ut comprehendatis.* The Latin *comprehendere* is rendered as 'to obtain' in English in the Douay-Rheims translation (Douay-Rheims The Vulgate Bible 2010–2013). Given the theme of the article, I changed the English translation here to 'to comprehend.'

9. Augustinus Hipponensis, *Epistulae*, ep. 147: De videndo Deo, c. 21 (CSEL 44/2, p. 295, v. 3–4; PL 33, p. 605): "totum autem comprehenditur uidendo, quod ita uidetur, ut nihil eius lateat uidentem." See also: Albertus Magnus, *De resurrectione*, tr. 4, q. 1, a. 9, § 1 (ed. Colon. 26, p. 328, v. 73–74).

entirely and completely by those who see His essence because the whole of God is entirely nothing but His essence. For, any of His modes is His essence too.[10] But His essence cannot be seen unless it is itself seen as a whole and completely. Therefore, He is comprehended by all those who see His essence.

(4) Furthermore, as is said in <Aristotle's> *On the Soul*, book III, the intellect understands itself and other things in the same way.[11] But as Augustine says in his book *On Eighty-Three Different Questions*, "anything that understands itself comprehends itself."[12] Therefore, anything that understands another comprehends it. But anyone who sees the divine essence, understands it. Therefore, anyone comprehends it.

(5) Furthermore, everything that is cognized as 'what it is' (*quid est*) is comprehended because it is cognized, as it were, by its definition.[13] "Yet something is comprehended whose ends can be seen from all

---

10. With this passage, Aquinas seems to refer to previous Latin discussions concerning the beatific vision and the distinction they make between divine modes that can be seen (*Deus revelatus*) and the transcendent core of the divine essence (*Deus absconditus*), which remains invisible. See general introduction, sections III and IV.

11. Aristoteles, *De anima*, l. 3, lect. 1 (430a2–5), trans. vet. (ed. Gauthier 1985, p. 447): "Et ipse intelligibilis est sicut intelligibilia. In hiis enim que sunt sine materia, idem est intellectus et quod intelligitur: sciencia namque speculatiua et quod speculatiuum est, idem est." Compare to Michael Scot's translation from the Arabic: ibid., l. 3, tx. 15 (ed. Crawford 1953, p. 434, v. 1–5): "Et est etiam intelligibilis, sicut intellecta. Formare enim per intellectum et formatum per intellectum, in eis que sunt extra materiam, idem sunt. Scientia enim speculativa et scitum secundum hunc modum idem sunt." See also article one, note 35.

12. Augustinus Hipponensis, *De diversis quaestionibus octoginta tribus*, q. 15 (CCSL 44A, p. 21, v. 2; PL 40, p. 14): "Omne quod se intellegit conprehendit se."

13. For this position, see: Albertus Magnus, *De resurrectione*, tr. 4 q. 1, a. 9, § 1 (ed. Colon. 26, p. 328, v. 47–72), as quoted above in note 246 in this introduction of this article. See also: id., *Super Dionysium De divinis nominibus*, c. 1 (ed. Colon. 37/1, p. 10, v. 64–72): "Dicimus, quod substantiam dei, 'quia est,' omnes beati videbunt; 'quid' autem sit, nullus intellectus creatus videre potest. Cum enim cognitio 'quid est' sit principalis causarum, oporteret, si cognosceretur 'quid est,' ut circumspicerentur termini essentiae eius. Et sic totum esse eius clauderetur in intelletu creato; et ita intellectus creatus esset maior deo, cum omne claudens sit maius eo quod clauditur: quod absurdum est." Id., *Super Dionysii Epistulas*, ep. 5 (ed. Colon. 37/2, p. 495, v. 33–43): "Concedimus, quod intellectus creatus non potest perfecte attingere ad deum, ita ut nihil de cognitione ipsius maneat extra eum, sed sub quadam confusione iungitur ei quasi excedenti, eo quod non potest de ipso accipi 'quid,' quia non habet terminationem, neque 'propter quid,' quia non habet causam, neque 'quia' determinatum, quia non habet causam remotam nec effectum proportionatum; et ideo nec in via nec in patria videtur de ipso nisi 'quia' confusum, quamvis ipse deus videatur clarius vel minus clare secundum diversos modos visionis et videntium."

sides," as Augustine says in his book *On Seeing God.*[14] But everything that is seen in its essence is also cognized in its whatness (*quid est*). Therefore, anyone who sees the essence of God comprehends Him.

(6) Furthermore, quantity of action corresponds to quantity of form, which is the principle of action. For, the quantity of heating corresponds to the quantity of heat. But the form which is the principle of cognition is that by which the one cognizing cognizes. Therefore, the mode by which cognition is had, corresponds to the mode of cognition. But that by which God is cognized is nothing other than His essence, as was said above, and this is infinite. Therefore, the vision is infinite too, and therefore, the divine essence can be comprehended, even though it is infinite.

(7) Furthermore, if the divine essence cannot be comprehended, that is only due to an excess in its brightness. But an excess of a cognitive object prevents cognition insofar as it impairs the cognitive power, which occurs only in the senses, but not in the intellect. This is evident from what is said in Aristotle's *On the Soul*, book III, that he who understands the highest things is no less able to understand the lowest things, but more so, whereas the contrary occurs in the senses.[15] Therefore, since the divine essence is seen by the intellect alone, as has been said, it seems that an excess of divine brightness does not prevent the comprehension of the divine essence.

(8) Furthermore, the divine essence is comprehensible to any intellect since God comprehends Himself. Therefore, if God cannot be

14. Augustinus Hipponensis, *Epistulae*, ep. 147: De videndo Deo, c. 21 (CSEL 44/2, p. 295, v. 3–5; PL 33, p. 605): "totum autem comprehenditur uidendo <...> cuius fines circumspici possunt."

15. Aristoteles, *De anima*, l. 3, lect. 1 (429b3–4), trans. vet. (ed. Gauthier 1985, pp. 445–446): "set intellectus, cum aliquid intelligat ualde intelligibile, non minus intelligit infima, set magis." Compare for Michael Scot's translation from the Arabic: ibid., l. 3, tx. 7 (ed. Crawford 1953, p. 417, v. 6–9): "intellectus autem, cum intellexerit aliquod forte intelligibilium, tunc non minus intelliget illud quod est sub primo, immo magis." See also: Averroes, *Commentarium magnum in Aristotelis De anima libros* l. 3, com. 36 (ed. Crawford 1953, p. 488, v. 251–257): "Si vero posuerimus quod intellectus non est admixtus materie, tunc certe ille sermo erit verus, scilicet quod illud quod est magis intelligibile magis comprehenditur; quoniam quod comprehendit minus perfectum (ex eis comprehendentibus que sunt non admixta materie) necesse est ut comprehendat perfectius, et non econtrario."

comprehended by the human intellect, this will be due to a defect of that intellect. But the light of glory removes every defect from the intellect, since also every defect of the body is removed by the glory. Therefore, those who will see God in the light of glory will comprehend Him.

❂ ❂ ❂

(1) On the contrary, Augustine says in his book *On Seeing God* "no one whosoever comprehends God's plenitude at any time, neither by the eyes of the body, nor by the mind."[16]

(2) Furthermore, as Augustine says in his book *On Eighty-Three Different Questions*: "What comprehends itself, determines itself (*finitum est sibi*)."[17] Therefore, what comprehends another, determines it to itself. But God cannot be determined to any created intellect. Therefore, no created intellect can comprehend God.

(3) Furthermore, the Damascene says in <*On the Orthodox Faith*>, book 5: "That the substance of God is incomprehensible, is indubitable to those who believe in the Holy Scripture."[18]

(4) Furthermore, anything that comprehends something is either greater than or equal to it. But a created intellect cannot be greater than or equal to God. Therefore, it cannot comprehend Him.

Response

It should be said that 'to comprehend' means 'to seize immediately,' as it were, namely, 'to enclose.' And for this reason, what is

---

16. Augustinus Hipponensis, *Epistulae*, ep. 147: De videndo Deo, c. 8 (CSEL 44/2, p. 294, v. 21–22; PL 33, p. 605): "dei plenitudinem quisquam non solum oculis corporis sed vel ipsa mente aliquando comprehendit."

17. Id., *De diversis quaestionibus octoginta tribus*, q. 15 (CCSL 44A, p. 21, v. 2–3; PL 40, pp. 14–15): "quod autem se conprehendit finitum est sibi."

18. Iohannes Damascenus, *De fide orthodoxa*, c. 5, trans. Burgundionis (ed. Buytaert 1955 p. 22, v. 4–6): "Quoniam vero unus est Deus et non multi, hiis quidem qui divinae credunt Scripturae non dubium est." Aquinas quotes this passage as translated above with deviation from the original as we have it in the critical edition.

comprehended properly, is seized at once, namely, with everything that belongs to it. Hence, anything that is comprehended must be enclosed in the one comprehending it. Yet something that is enclosed is properly confined by the one confining it. And for this reason, what is comprehended must be confined by the one comprehending it. Yet, just as something is said to be confined by another corporeally—because it does not exceed the one confining it in any way according to dimensive quantity, as wine in a barrel—in this way too something is said to be confined by another spiritually which is put under its power and exceeds it in no way. And for this reason, a cognized thing is said to be comprehended by cognition when it stands under the actuality of the cognitive power and does not exceed it. Every excess, however, is according to some quantity. Yet according to this quantity, a cognizable thing is said to exceed a cognitive potency inasmuch as the cognizable thing is beyond it (*ab ipsa*).

Sensible objects, however, are cognized according to dimensive quantity because in cognizing, the senses employ corporeal organs by which they cognize all sensible things that are reduced to dimensive quantity. <Sensible objects are cognized> also according to virtual quantity (*secundum quantitatem virtualem*), as is evident from the proper sensibles which are qualities. And for this reason, comprehension by the senses is prevented due to the excess of dimensive quantity, just as one is prevented from comprehending the whole earth, and also due to the excess of virtual quantity, just as one is prevented from comprehending the brightness of the sun. For the power of the eye for cognizing it is not as great as is the brightness of the sun that is a cognizable thing.

The intelligible, however, is not cognized by the intellect under the aspect of dimensive quantity except by accident, namely, inasmuch as the intellect takes it from the senses. From this it follows that one understands together with space and time. And accordingly, the intellect is prevented from the comprehension of an intelligible due to an excess of quantity, just as it is prevented from the comprehension of a line or an infinite number. But when it is spoken of in its own right, the intelligible is compared to the intellect according to the measure (*ratio*) of virtual quantity because the proper object of the intellect is the quiddity (*quid*). And for this reason, in things that are separate from the senses, the intellect's comprehension is only prevented by an excess of virtual quantity. And this is the case when an intelligible is more cognizable than the intellect can cognize or cognizes, just as one who knows the conclusion 'the triangle has three angles' by probable reasoning, namely because it is maintained in this way by common opinion. <Yet> one does not comprehend it, not because one sees part of it and does not see another part of it, but because the mode by which one cognizes it falls short of the mode by which it is cognizable. For a triangle is cognizable by demonstration.

The divine essence, however, is cognizable through its own Truth, but the intellect is able to cognize it through the intellectual light that is in it <*viz.* the intellect>. Yet, the Truth of the divine essence exceeds the light of any created intellect.[19] And for this reason, it is impossible that <a created intellect> see God as perfectly as He is visible. And from this it follows that no created intellect can comprehend God.

Replies to Objections

(1) To the first, therefore, it should be said that the Apostle speaks of the comprehension of glory, namely by which it comes to pass that the soul encloses in itself all that belongs to its perfection in glory. And according to this, it is said to comprehend the glory, even though it never comprehends the divine essence intellectually. Or, comprehension there means the very attainment of having God because comprehension is said to follow upon hope.[20]

---

19. The long solution Aquinas provides here is clearly anticipated by its short version in Albert the Great's commentary on the *Sentences*. See note 5 above.

20. Aquinas may be thinking here of Boethius's definition of ultimate happiness, which Albert the Great provides as what he considers to be the correct understanding of heavenly happiness in his *Commentary on the Sentences*. See: Albertus Magnus, *Commentarii in IV Sententiarum*, d. 49B, a. 6 (ed. Borgnet 30, p. 674–675): "Ad haec solvenda praenotandum est, quod *beatitudo* dicitur multipliciter, et non aequivoce, sed secundum prius et posterius. Dicitur autem secundum statum perfectionis viae, et secundum statum perfectionis patriae. <...> Beatitudo autem secundum statum patriae est inhaerere Deo, et in ipso habere omnia quae appetuntur: et sic diffinitur a Boetio beatitudo" (emphasis as in edition).

(2) To the second, it should be said that Augustine maintains two things about the definition of comprehension. One of them excludes an excess of the cognizable thing over the power of the one cognizing, in accordance with dimensive quantity. And with regard to this, he says: "What is seen in such a way that nothing of it is concealed from the one seeing." Yet the other excludes an excess in accordance with the quantity of power (*secundum quantitatem virtutis*). And with regard to this, he says: "Or, whose ends can be surveyed."[21] For the ends of a thing will be surveyed when the one seeing attains the end of the vision by perfectly seeing.

(3) To the third, it should be said that the blessed will see the whole divine essence in heaven but not completely. <This is> not in such a way that there is some mode in God that they would not see, or that there is some mode in their intellect that is not turned to God. But <it is> because the mode by which they are turned to the cognition of God is not the same mode by which God is a cognizable object. And it is this inequality that is disclosed when it is said that the divine essence will not be seen completely. For the adverb 'completely' neither refers absolutely to the mode of the one seeing, nor absolutely to the mode of the thing seen. But <it refers> to the mode of the one seeing in relation to the thing seen. For this adverb determines the vision according to which the one seeing is related to the thing seen.

(4) To the fourth, it should be said that when something understands itself, the mode of the cognizer is the same as the cognized object. And for this reason, if something understands itself, it comprehends itself. Yet the mode of the cognizer is not the same as the cognized object when the intellect understands something other than itself. And for this reason, it is not similar.

---

21. Augustinus Hipponensis, *Epistulae*, ep. 147: De videndo Deo, c. 21 (CSEL 44/2, p. 295, v. 3–5; PL 33, p. 605): "quod ita uidetur, ut nihil eius lateat uidentem, aut cuius fines circumspici possunt." Also quoted in: Bonaventura, *De scientia Christi*, q. 6 (ed. Quaracchi, t. 5, p. 34): "quod dicit Augustinus ad Paulinam de videndo Deo: 'plenitudinem Dei nullus non solum oculis corporis, sed nec ipsa mente aliquando comprehendit; aliud est enim uidere, aliud uidendo totum comprehendere, quandoquidem id uidetur, quod praesens utcumque sentitur; totum autem comprehenditur, quod ita uidetur, ut nihil eius lateat uidentem, aut cuius fines circumspici possunt.'"

(5) To the fifth, it should be said that someone cognizes what a thing is by the same mode by which he cognizes the essence of the thing because the very essence is the quiddity of the thing.[22] And for this reason, only one who comprehends what a thing is, comprehends its essence. Hence, just as the blessed will see the divine essence but will not comprehend it, so too they will see what God is but will not comprehend Him. And in this way, God will not be seen by those in the same way as a thing is seen by its definition whose essence is comprehended.

(6) To the sixth, it should be said that an action is attributed not to the form alone which is the principle of action, but to the composite, just as heating <is attributed> to what is hot and not to heat alone. And for this reason, an action must be measured not only with reference to the form that is the principle of action, but also with reference to the subject of the form. But a form that is not self-subsistent does not have another mode from the mode of its subject because it has being (*esse*) only inasmuch as it is the actuality of its subject. And for this reason, the measure of the form is the measure of the composite. But a form that subsists by itself has one mode inasmuch as it is some subsistent thing and another mode according to which it is the actuality of such a subject. And this mode is taken after the measure which the perfectible attains as perfected by such a form. And the action is measured from this mode.

The divine essence, however, subsists by itself. And for this reason, the vision that comes to be in the created intellect through it is not measured after the infinite mode belonging to the essence in itself, but after the mode by which the intellect attains its perfection by it. But <the intellect> attains to this inasmuch as it is conjoined to it by the light of glory which is finite. And for this reason, the vision is finite on the part of the one seeing.

(7) To the seventh, it should be said that the brightness of God is called the truth of His essence by which He is cognizable, just as the sun

22. For a more extended discussion in the secondary literature, see: Krause 2015b, pp. 175–217.

is cognizable by its brightness. And even though it does not prevent comprehension by corruption of the intellect, it nonetheless prevents it due to its excess, because it cannot happen that a created intellect attains a cognition of the divine essence as perfectly as it is cognizable.

(8) To the eighth, it should be said that glory perfects nature and does not destroy it. And for this reason, the light of glory does not remove the imperfection that is due to the state of nature (*de ratione nature*), such as that it came to be from nothing (*ex nihilo esse*). But because of this, the created intellect lacks the possibility of comprehension. And for this reason, it cannot even attain comprehension by the light of glory.

ARTICLE 4

On One Seeing God More Perfectly than Another

INTRODUCTION

In the present article, Aquinas will review the question of different degrees of vision that the blessed have of the divine essence, and connect it with the question of different mansions which he discussed earlier in his *Sentences*. The earlier question considered the reasons that the blessed dwell in different mansions, or, as Aquinas preferred to phrase it, the reasons that they were subject to different grades of happiness:

> The principle of different mansions and different degrees of happiness is twofold, namely proximate and remote. The proximate is a different disposition which will be in the blessed, on the basis of which a difference in perfection is reached among them in the activity of happiness. But the remote principle is the merit through which the <blessed> conform to such a happiness. In the first way, however, the mansions are distinguished according to the charity of heaven: The more perfect it will be in some, the more capable it renders them of the divine clarity. According to this increase the perfection of the divine vision will be increased. Yet in the second way, they are distinguished according to the charity of this life. For our action does not take what is meritorious from the very substance of the action, but from the habit of the power alone by which it is informed. The power for meriting, however, is in all powers

> from charity, which takes its end before the object. And therefore, the difference in meriting can be reduced entirely to the difference of charity. And in this way the charity of this life will distinguish the mansions by way of merit.[1]

In Aquinas's eyes, the main reason for the different mansions was the amount of charity that the blessed possessed at two moments in time in their being: (1) in the state of the afterlife, and, prior to that, (2) in their life on earth. The different mansions represented the different spiritual post-resurrection abodes or degrees of connection with the divine that the blessed enjoyed, and these degrees were dependent upon the amount of charity earned and possessed by the individual saint.

This traditional theological view of attaining happiness through earned and possessed charity contrasted strongly with the philosophical view of attaining happiness through developing one's intellectual excellence. Perhaps Aristotle himself, but before him certainly Plato in the myth of the *Republic*, and after him the Greek and Arabic Peripatetic sages, insisted on a vertically acquired route to happiness by way of strictly governed intellectual pursuits. On the basis of their specific nature, humans were thus envisioned to attain happiness through the laborious study of the whole body of philosophical wisdom. The pursuit of the moral life, however, was excluded in exclusively intellectual construals, since it simply served the intellectual life as a preparatory stage or necessary condition for what truly mattered: intellectual development and perfection. The ideal of

---

1. Thomas Aquinas, *Commentum in quatuor libros Sententiarum*, l. 4, d. 49, q. 1, a. 4, qc. 4 (ed. Parma 7/2, p. 1196): "Ad quartam quaestionem dicendum, quod principium distinctivum mansionum, sive graduum beatitudinis, est duplex; scilicet propinquum et remotum. Propinquum est diversa dispositio quae erit in beatis, ex qua contingit diversitas perfectionis apud eos in operatione beatitudinis; sed principium remotum est meritum quo talem beatitudinem consecuti sunt. Primo autem modo distinguuntur mansiones secundum caritatem patriae; quae quanto in aliquo erit perfectior, tanto reddet eum capaciorem divinae claritatis, secundum cujus augmentum augebitur perfectio divinae visionis. Secundo vero modo distinguuntur secundum caritatem viae. Actus enim noster non habet quod sit meritorius ex ipsa substantia actus, sed solum ex habitu virtutis quo informatur. Vis autem merendi est in omnibus virtutibus ex caritate, quae habet ipsum finem pro objecto; et ideo diversitas in merendo tota revertitur ad diversitatem caritatis; et sic caritas viae distinguet mansiones per modum meriti."

an intellectualist teleology, however, promoted not only the requirement of individual efforts to be undertaken in this life, but also the advancement of a seemingly hubristic intellectual elitism. Only the few—those who were capable of leaving behind the external obstacles, of taming the internal desires, and of mastering the *corpus* of philosophical wisdom, and only those who moreover enjoyed ample opportunities for education, fortunate circumstances of good teachers, the economic wherewithal, etc.—could attain ultimate happiness on the rocky road of intellectual ascent.

For the theologian Aquinas, however, charity in its two forms mattered most, and, as is well known, Aquinas vehemently rejected the intellectual elitism of his sources in his mature writings, such as *De unitate intellectus*. These forms of charity, as we have seen above, were constructed to work in different ways by Aquinas. Heavenly charity was static, a stable disposition which determined the degree of happiness that was possessed in heaven by the blessed. Earthly charity, in contrast, was dynamic, related to human action, built on an acquired habit in the powers of the human soul. In virtue of its repeated use in action, it was thought to determine the degree of heavenly happiness remotely. Yet despite these differences, both charities precede what is the essence of happiness in Aquinas's eyes, the beatific vision: earthly charity precedes happiness temporally, heavenly charity logically. For it is only in the afterlife that happiness through the beatific vision is reached, and it is through the amount of heavenly charity that the degree of access to the divine clarity is granted, and the degree of perfection of the beatific vision is determined. Heavenly charity, like the earthly charity that the blessed possess in degrees of more or less in accordance with their earthly actions, thus also comes in different degrees. Each blessed saint has his individual access to seeing God's essence in virtue of possessing heavenly charity, and this Aquinas conceived of in terms of more or less. But it was also the case that each individual blessed saint could be subject to an increase in heavenly charity, which could render his vision more perfect, an issue that is closely linked to article five.

Aquinas's argument to support his conclusion in article four takes its anacrusis from a philosophical principle that he most likely derived from Albert the Great's commentary on the *Sentences*: "The principle of action is the form by which the action happens, the measure of action must be taken from this part."[2] An understanding of

2. See Response below. See also: Albertus Magnus, *Commentarii in II Sententiarum*, d. 26, a. 11 (ed. Borgnet 27, p. 466): "Si dicas, quod una numero forma est dans esse, et principium actionum sequentium esse: et ita uno numero est forma dans esse bonum, et quod agit actiones sequentes virtutem. Istud ridiculosum est, et ex magna ignorantia Philosophiae naturalis dictum. Cum enim forma est principium actionum consequentium esse: aut ipsa in se una manens est principium omnium illarum actionum, aut diversis principiis quae causantur ab ea in composito vel in substantia." Albert probably took inspiration for formulating this principle from Averroes's *Long Commentary on Aristotle's On the Soul*. See: Averroes, *Commentarium magnum in Aristotelis De anima libros*, l. 1, com. 89 (ed. Crawford 1953, p. 119, v. 14–p. 120, v. 44): "Cum contradixit sermonibus Antiquorum de anima, incepit hic declarare quod primo considerandum est de anima de numero actionum eius diversarum in genere; deinde utrum omnes proveniant ab una virtute, scilicet ab anima, aut agit unamquanque actionum eius diversarum in genere per virtutes diversas aut secundum diffinitionem et subiectum aut secundum diffinitionem tantum. Et dixit: *Et quia anima* etc. Idest, et quia anima habet quinque actiones aut passiones diversas in genere, quarum una est scire et existimare, secunda sentire, tertia desiderare et velle, quarta moveri in loco, quinta augeri et minui et nutriri, utrum quelibet istarum actionum diversarum in genere sunt totius anime, ita quod per eandem naturam intelligit et sentit et movetur in loco et desiderat et nutritur et universaliter agit et patitur unoquoque aliorum motuum, aut non agit aut patitur unoquoque eorum nisi per virtutes diversas et membra diversa et membra communia eis convenientia? Hec igitur opinio est Aristotelis. Non enim opinatur quod facit diversas actiones per virtutes diversas et unica membra tantum, neque per unicas virtutes et membra diversa tantum, neque etiam per virtutes diversas et membra diversa tantum; sed opinatur quod facit per virtutes diversas et membra unica, scilicet principalia, et membra diversa. Et hoc intendebat cum dixit: *per virtutes diversas et membra diversa*; idest, cum hoc quod agit cum membris convenientibus; quoniam si sic non intelligetur, erit idem cum sermone Platonis. Deinde dixit: *Utrum vita est in uno istorum*, etc. Idest, et perscrutandum est, cum hoc, utrum illud quod dicitur vita est in una aliqua istarum quinque virtutum, aut in pluribus una, aut in omnibus" (emphases as in edition). Averroes here comments in Michael Scot's Latin translation from the Arabic: Aristoteles, *De anima*: ibid., l. 1, tx. 89 (ed. Crawford 1953, p. 119, v. 1–13): "Et quia anima habet cognoscere et sentire et existimare et etiam appetere et velle et universaliter modos desiderii, et etiam animal habet per animam motum in loco et etiam augmentum et complementum et diminutionem, utrum unumquodque istorum est totius anime, et per ipsam totam intelligit et sentit et movet et facit alios motus et actiones et patitur, aut non agit neque patitur nisi per membra diversa actiones et passiones diversas? Et utrum vita est in una istarum aut in pluribus una aut in omnibus, aut habent aliam causam?" Compare for the Latin *translatio vetus* from the Greek: ibid., l. 1, lect. 14 (411a26–411b5), trans. vet. (ed. Gauthier 1985, p. 134): "Quoniam autem cognoscere anime est et sentire et opinari, adhuc autem concupiscere et deliberare et omnino appetitus, fit autem et secundum locum motus in animalibus ab anima, adhuc autem et augmentum et iuuentus et detrimentum, utrum toti anime horum unumquodque insit, et omnibus intelligimus et sentimus et aliorum unumquodque facimus et patimur, aut partibus alteris altera? Et uiuere igitur utrum in aliquo horum sit uno aut in pluribus aut in omnibus, aut et aliqua alia causa?"

how Aquinas envisioned form to be the principle and measure of action may be gathered from a reply that he gave in his discussion of the sacraments earlier in his *Sentences*:

> Action only befits self-subsistent things. And for this reason, it is neither matter that acts nor form, but the composite. Nonetheless, <the composite> does not act by reason of matter but by reason of form, which is actuality and the principle of action. And because quantity is tied to (*tenet se*) the part of matter and quality to the part of form, quantity only acts by mediating quality, which is the principle of action in itself.[3]

While Aquinas takes action to derive from the composite, he takes form to be the principle of action in the sense of being the actuality of the whole composite being. As such, form is tied to the category of quality and controls the action of matter, which is tied to the category of quantity. Hence, form is not that which acts, but is that which limits and controls action as its sovereign principle.

Although Aquinas advocates this understanding of form as a principle and measure of action in the present article as well, he modifies his understanding here slightly in distinction to the general principle. Drawing on a sharp ontological divide between form as a principle in the immaterial realm and form as a principle in the material realm, Aquinas took "the measure of action" to differ in forms existing in each of the two realms. The decisive factor for the amount of strength for an action in the physical realm is the capacity to receive a given form, just as in the passage above. If something is heated by the form of heat, it simply receives the form of heat and can thus act on this basis. For instance, a pot that has received the form of heat can actively heat a soup. It is important to note here that any given physical form that has come to inhere in a subject does not

3. Thomas Aquinas, *Commentum in quatuor libros Sententiarum*, l. 4, d. 12, q. 1, a. 2, qc. 1 (ed. Parma 7/2, p. 657): "Respondeo dicendum ad primam quaestionem, quod agere non est nisi rei per se subsistentis; et ideo neque materia agit neque forma, sed compositum; quod tamen non agit ratione materiae, sed ratione formae, quae est actus, et actionis principium. Et quia quantitas se tenet ex parte materiae, et qualitas ex parte formae; ideo quantitas non agit nisi mediante qualitate, quae est per se actionis principium."

subsist on its own.[4] In contrast, the decisive factor in the immaterial realm, Aquinas suggests, is the ability of any subsistent form to be subject to another subsistent form. This ability corresponds closely to the ontological rank of each subsistent form involved: the more alike two subsistent forms are, the more the one can be subject to the other, as there is a resemblance in receptive capacity.

In the subsequent step, Aquinas argues that the same understanding of the immaterial realm equally applies to the cognitive realm: it is the capacity of a cognitive power for cognizing that determines the extent to which any given cognitive agent could be subject to an intelligible form. In cognition in this life, Aquinas takes this capacity to be expressed by the power of the agent intellect in its activity of rendering potentially intelligible forms intelligible in actuality. This implies that in its natural ability, the human intellect is subject to the potentially intelligible forms. In cognition in the afterlife, however, this cognitive capacity is taken to be expressed by the power of the light of glory, the "new intellectual disposition" as Aquinas will call it in article six. Rather than rendering potentially intelligible forms intelligible in actuality, as the light of the agent intellect does, the light of glory's activity consists in rendering the human intellect a proper subject to the cognition of the divine essence.[5] Here,

---

4. An important parallel passage that makes explicit reference to the inherence of a form as the principle of action is found in Thomas Aquinas, *Scriptum super libros Sententiarum*, l. 1, d. 32, q. 1, a. 1 (ed. Mandonnet I, p. 743): "Sed quia cujuslibet actionis principium est aliqua forma inhaerens, ideo aliquid potest dici agens duobus modis; vel ipsa actione, quae denominat agentem, et non est principium ejus; vel forma, quae est principium actionis in agente, et secundum quid principium agentis; sicut dicimus ignem moveri sursum motu proprio et levitate."

5. In his *Disputed Questions on the Truth*, Aquinas takes up this line of reasoning again and suggests in similar fashion that "any cognition whatsoever is according to the mode of the form which is in the cognizer" (*quaelibet cognitio sit secundum modum formae quae est in cognoscente*). See: Thomas Aquinas, *Quaestiones disputatae de veritate*, q. 2, a. 6 (ed. Leon. 22/1, p. 65, v. 46–47). Later in the same work, rejecting comprehension of the divine essence in the beatific vision, Aquinas qualifies the way in which a blessed intellect is subject to the divine essence and suggests that "even though the divine essence is in some way like the form of the intellect, it nonetheless is not seized by the intellect except according to the mode of the intellect seizing it. And because the action here is not only that of the form but also that of the agent, for this reason the action cannot be as perfect as a form is perfect which is the principle of action, since there is a defect on the part of the agent." See: Thomas Aquinas, *Quaestiones disputatae de veritate*, q. 8, a. 2, ad 3 (ed. Leon. 22/2, p. 222, v. 176–183): "<S>ed divina essentia, quamvis quodam modo sit ut forma intellectus, non tamen capitur ab intellectu nisi secundum

Aquinas seems to understand activity in a more passive sense than when applied to the agent intellect because the form that ultimately causes the intellect of the blessed to become subject to the beatific vision, namely God, is of the most formal, *viz.* actual, form in its nature (*actus purus*), in opposition to the particularized and materialized forms of natural human cognitive activities. Most important for our purposes, however, is that the light of glory, the new form which comes to inhere in the intellect of the blessed as result of God's formal-efficient causality, is received according to different degrees by the blessed—degrees that depend, as we have seen, upon the amount of heavenly love that each blessed possesses. Hence, in Aquinas's eyes, the conclusion to draw was clear: the more heavenly love a blessed possesses, the greater the quantity of the light of glory that comes to inhere in the intellect of the blessed saint, the more clearly he will see God.[6]

TRANSLATION

We proceed to the fourth article as follows. It seems that of those who see God through His essence, one does not see Him more perfectly than another.

Objections

(1) <This is> because, as Augustine says in his book *On Eighty-Three Different Questions*, one cannot understand the same thing

---

modum intellectus capientis; et quia actio non est tantum formae sed etiam agentis, ideo non potest esse ita perfecta actio sicut est perfecta forma quae est principium actionis cum sit defectus ex parte agentis."

6. Unlike in most other articles translated and discussed in this book, Aquinas could not have found inspiration for his reasoning here among the usual suspects of his Latin predecessors or contemporaries, such as Alexander of Hales, Bonaventure, and Albert the Great. To the best of my knowledge, none of them seems to have discussed the different mansions or different degrees of the beatific vision in a similar Aristotelian fashion. A text that may have been inspiring for his discussion here, but that would require further research, can be found in: Avicenna, *Liber de philosophia prima sive scientia divina I–IV*, tr. 4, c. 2 (ed. Van Riet 1977, p. 205 v. 94–p. 206 v. 24).

more than another.[7] But the divine essence will not be seen except intellectually. Therefore, one will not see it more fully than another.

(2) Furthermore, something is seen more perfectly the more distinct the similitude of the thing seen comes to be in the one who sees. But there will not be a more distinct similitude by which God may be seen in one than in another among those who see God through His essence because the same essence is in all of them. Therefore, one will not see Him better than another.

(3) Furthermore, the one from whom more impediments to vision are removed sees better. But no impediment to vision will remain in anyone. Therefore, all will see God equally.

(4) Furthermore, all the blessed will see God *as He is*, as is evident from I John 3:2.[8] But He cannot be seen better than *He is*. Therefore, one will not see Him better than another.

(5) Furthermore, the best way of cognizing God is <the way> by which He is seen through His essence. But nothing can be better than the best. Therefore, of those who see God through His essence, one cannot see Him better than another.

❂ ❂ ❂

(1) On the contrary, humans are taken up into the same rank as the angels. But the superior angels see God more clearly than the inferior angels, as is evident from Dionysius's *On the Celestial Hierarchy*.[9] Therefore, among humans too, some will see God more clearly in glory than others.

---

7. Augustinus Hipponensis, *De diversis quaestionibus octoginta tribus*, q. 32 (CCSL 44A, p. 46, v. 11; PL 40, p. 22): "Utrum rem ullam alius alio magis intellegat, atque ita eiusdem rei per infinitum eat intelligentia. Quisquis ullam rem aliter quam ea res est intelligit fallitur; et omnis qui fallitur, id in quo fallitur non intellegit. Quisquis igitur ullam rem aliter quam est intellegit, non eam intellegit. Non ergo potest quidquam intellegi nisi ut est. Nos autem aliquid ita ut est intellegimus, uelut hoc ipsum nihil intellegi, quod non ita ut est intellegitur. Quare non est dubitandum esse perfectam intellegentiam, qua praestantior esse non possit, et ideo non per infinitum ire quod quaeque res intellegitur, nec eam posse alium alio plus intellegere."

8. Epistula Iohannis I 3:2, see section II of the general introduction, note 1.

9. Pseudo-Dionysius Areopagita, *De caelesti hierarchia*, c. 5, sect. 61, trans. Eriugenae (Dionysiaca t. 2, pp. 823–824): "Dicimus autem quia per omnem sanctam dispositionem excellentes

(2) Furthermore, human happiness consists essentially in the vision of God. But some will be happier than others, as was said above.[10] Therefore, some will see Him more clearly than others.

(3) Furthermore, God will be seen by the blessed in the light of glory as is said in Psalm 35:10: *In thy light we shall see light.*[11] But some will be filled more abundantly by this light than others. *For star differeth from star in brightness, so also is the resurrection of the dead*, as is said in I Corinthians 15:41–42.[12] The brightness of the body, however, will indicate the brightness of the mind. Therefore, some will see God more clearly than others.

---

quidem ordines habent inferiorum dispositionum illuminationes et virtutes, non autem participantes excellentium se sunt ultimi. Igitur sanctissimos excellentissimarum essentiarum ordines angelos vocant theologi, etenim sunt manifestatores et ipsi divinae illuminationis." Id., c. 6, sect. 62, trans. Eriugenae (Dionysiaca t. 2, pp. 832–833): "Trinum ergo hunc ornatum quasi unam et aeque ordinatam et vere primam hierarchiam communis noster magister ait, qua non est alia Deiformior, et per se praeoperantibus Divinitatis illuminationibus immediate intentior." Id., c. 8, sect. 64, trans. Eriugenae (Dionysiaca t. 2, pp. 879–880): "Etenim sapientes circa sacras nostras immolationes aiunt per se ipsas lucentes divinorum plenitudines, per alteros contemplativarum participationum esse perfectiores; sic aestimo et angelicorum ordinum immediatam participationem primo in Deum extentorum perfectiorem esse per medietatem perfectorum." Id., c. 10, sect. 66, trans. Eriugenae (Dionysiaca t. 2, pp. 917–920): "Connexa est itaque sic ipsa quidem honorabilissima circa Deum animorum dispositio, ex perfectiva illuminatione ordinata, in eam immediate ascendendo occultior et manifestior Divinitatis illuminatione purgatur et illuminatur et perficitur: occultior quidem, tamquam invisibilior et magis simplificata et unificata; manifestior vero, ut ante data, et primo lucet, et universalior, et magis in eam, ut oportet, forma effusa. Ab ipsa autem iterum proportionaliter secunda, et a secunda tertia, et ex tertia secundum nos hierarchia, secundum ipsam beneornantis ordinationis legem in harmonia divina et analogia ad simul omnis boni ornatus superprincipale principium et consummationem hierarchice reducitur. Manifestatores autem omnes sunt et angeli eorum qui ante ipsos sunt: ipsi quidem honorabilissimi Dei moventis; proportionaliter autem ceteri ex Deo motorum." See also: Albertus Magnus, *Super Dionysium De caelesti hierarchia*, c. 5. 6. 8. 10 (ed. Colon. 36/1, p. 78, v. 67–69; p. 88, v. 81–84; p. 132, v. 75–78; p. 156, v. 71–77).

10. See: Thomas Aquinas, *Commentum in quatuor libros Sententiarum*, l. 4, d. 49, q. 1, a. 4, qc. 2 (ed. Parma 7/2, pp. 1194–1195).

11. Psalmi Iuxta LXX 35:10, see article one, note 40.

12. Ad Corinthios I 15:41–42 (Vulgata 2007): *stella enim ab stella differt in claritate sic et resurrectio mortuorum.* Douay-Rheims translates *claritas* with 'glory' (Douay-Rheims The Vulgate Bible 2010–2013). Aquinas, however, clearly distinguishes between *claritas* and *gloria*, which is why I translate *claritas* with 'brightness' and *gloria* with 'glory.'

Response

It should be said that, since the principle of action is the form by which the action happens,[13] the measure of action must be taken from this part. Yet, this measure is different in subsistent forms than in other forms, as was said before.[14] For in other forms, the quantity of strength in action corresponds to the quantity of what is received of a form in a subject, such as of heat in what is hot. In subsistent forms, however, the quantity of strength corresponds to the subject put under a form to a greater or lesser extent. Yet, a cognitive power is put under a form by which it cognizes inasmuch as it has a power of cognizing. For what renders the power of sight capable of seeing is what renders it receptive for the similitude of color. Yet, just as the possible intellect comes to be capable of cognizing natural cognitive objects by the natural light of the agent intellect, in this way it comes to be capable of the vision of the divine essence by the superadded light of glory. Hence, the mode in which our intellect is put under the divine essence as its intelligible form is taken according to the quantity of the received light. And consequently, the mode of perfection in the activity of such a form is the principle, namely in the vision of God through His essence. And for this reason, some of the blessed will see Him more clearly than others, since they are more abundantly filled by the light of glory than others.

Replies to Objections

(1) To the first, therefore, it should be said that one cannot understand the same thing more than another, if the term 'more' entails a mode that is on the part of the thing understood. For it is impossible that someone understands a thing only if he understands that this

13. For possible sources of this principle, see the introduction to this article.

14. See article three, reply to objection six (p. 146). There Aquinas reasoned to the contrary that "an action is attributed not to the form alone which is the principle of action, but to the composite, just as heating <is attributed> to what is hot and not to heat alone. And for this reason, an action must be measured not only with reference to the form that is the principle of action, but also with reference to the subject of the form."

thing has the mode it has. For if he ascribes another mode to the thing, he errs and does not understand; and Augustine sees it in this way. But if the term 'more' refers to a mode which is on the part of the one understanding, in this way one can understand better than another inasmuch as his cognition is more limpid of one and the same cognitive object.

(2) To the second, it should be said that, although the similitude of God through which one blessed saint cognizes Him is not more distinct in his intellect than in the other—because any given one sees Him through His essence—nonetheless, the intellect of the one is put more perfectly under the form by which he understands than the intellect of the other. And in this way, one understands Him more perfectly than the other.

(3) To the third, it should be said that the intensity according to which something is said to be more or less is not caused by withdrawal of the contrary alone, but also by attainment of the limit, as is evident from the intensity of corporeal light. And likewise, spiritual light also extends more to one blessed saint than to another by virtue of his greater assimilation to God, even though nothing contrary to the light is found in any of them.

(4) To the fourth, it should be said that since all blessed are said to see God as He is, the term 'as' entails a mode that is on the part of the seen thing and not on the part of the one seeing. For anyone will see God's being (*esse*) in the same mode by which He is. But nonetheless, the mode of the one seeing will not be equal to the thing seen in its mode, but infinitely distant. And in this way, it will be possible that the mode of one seeing Him is less distant than the mode of another.

(5) To the fifth, it should be said that seeing God through His essence is the most perfect mode of cognizing Him in accordance with His genus, but it is nonetheless possible that a greater or lesser extent be found in this genus; just as fire is most subtle in the species of bodies, and one fire is nonetheless found to be subtler than another.

ARTICLE 5

On the Impossibility of Seeing All Things that God Sees

INTRODUCTION

Much of what Aquinas had to say about God's understanding of all things other than Himself seems, at first sight, incompatible with creaturely understanding of them, even in the beatific vision. Comprehension of the divine essence, as we saw in article three, was taken to be impossible for a finite intellect, and so is the cognition of all that God knows. But in important ways, God's knowledge and creaturely cognition of all things in God were nonetheless closely related in Aquinas's eyes. While he made much of the ontological realities and consequent distinctive characteristics that separated creature and creator—for instance, divine immutability versus creaturely mutability, divine actuality versus creaturely potentiality, divine infinity versus creaturely finitude—some of these characteristics of divine understanding served as an ideal for creaturely understanding of all things other than God in Him. Paramount among these characteristics was that of divine infinity. God's own understanding of all things other than Himself is by way of two different types of infinity: knowledge of vision (*scientia / notitia visionis*) and knowledge of a simple intelligence (*scientia / notitia simplicis intelligentiae*), a position that Aquinas had already defended in the first book of his *Sentences*, where he discussed God's noetic infinity in detail.[1] Creaturely understanding of these things, as

1. See: Thomas Aquinas, *Scriptum super libros Sententiarum*, l. 1, d. 39, q. 1, a. 2 (ed. Mandonnet 1, pp. 922–924). See also note 4 below with excerpts of this passage.

much as it might be limited by its finite ontology, could at least aspire to divine-like knowledge of vision; yet knowledge of a simple intelligence was categorically impossible. Indeed, in article five, Aquinas did nothing less than honor the capacity of creaturely intellectuality in the beatific vision by granting it the possibility of knowing all things other than God in the same way as Christ Incarnate knew them naturally in this life, despite the fact that this knowledge could not be of the same perfection. This ultimate crowning of creaturely understanding in the beatific vision, however, would have to wait until the Last Judgment. Until then, creaturely understanding of other things than God in the beatific vision would still increase.

Yet in Aquinas's eyes, nothing could comprise a nobler goal of human nature and existence than to share fully in one of the infinite ways of divine knowing. Indeed, he used one key characteristic of divine infinity in article three as the grounds for denying comprehension to creatures in the beatific vision: the infinity of virtual quantity in God. Here he applied another key characteristic, the two kinds of infinities of God's knowing other things than Himself. Aquinas was well acquainted with these views on divine infinite knowing from his near contemporaries. Discussions in the commentaries on the *Sentences* by Albert the Great and Bonaventure show acquaintance with distinctions similar to those in Aquinas, between knowledge of vision and knowledge of a simple intelligence.[2] Aquinas's answer was thus

---

2. Albertus Magnus, *Commentarii in I Sententiarum*, d. 39A, a. 4 (ed. Borgnet 26, p. 296): "Ad hoc dicunt quidam, quod triplex est scientia, scilicet intelligentiae, et visionis, et approbationis: et *scientia intelligentiae* est, qua intelligitur res simpliciter. *Visionis* autem scientia est, quae transit super res secundum quod sunt vel non sunt sub differentia hujus compositionis vel illius. *Approbationis* autem scientia est, quae est de bonis quorum Deus auctor est. Sed contra hoc objicitur: Illa scientia quae dicitur *intelligentia*, aut est finita per intelligibilis rationem idealem, aut non. Si dicas, quod sic: sed unicuique ideae respondet ideatum, vel potest respondere: ergo illi ideae quae est infiniti, respondet ideatum, vel potest respondere: ergo infinitum potest esse actu: quod ego intelligere non possum, si est verum" (emphases as in edition). See also: ibid., l. 3, d. 14, a. 1 (ed. Borgnet 28, p. 255); id., *Summa theologiae* Pars I, tr. 15, q. 60, m. 4, a. 1 (ed. Borgnet 31, pp. 615–616). Bonaventura, *In primum librum Sententiarum*, d. 39, a. 1, q. 3 (ed. Quaracchi 1/2, p. 691) For an earlier and similar, yet not identical version of this distinction, see also: Alexander Halensis, *Summa fratris Alexandri*, l. 1, p. 1, inq. 1, tr. 5, sect. 1, q. unica (ed. Quaracchi 1, p. 264): "Scientia Dei tribus modis accipitur. Uno modo pro approbatione, Psalm. 4: *Novit Deus viam iustorum*. Alio modo pro simplici notitia, sed hoc duobus modis: absolute, non connotando existentiam

embedded in the living debates of his times, siding with Bonaventure against his teacher Albert, who vehemently rejected this distinction.

Yet, unlike his contemporaries, Aquinas linked the discussions on divine infinite knowing to his discussions of the possibilities and limitations of the beatific vision. He applied them to the two related questions of comprehension of the divine essence, as we saw in article three, and understanding of things other than God through His essence in the present article. This application would indeed have a long history. In the fifteenth- and sixteenth-century debates concerning indulgences, the question would be invoked by Catholic thinkers in favor of these remissions of purgatorial punishment. The Augustinian monk John of Paltz (ca. 1445–1511), for instance, reasoned in his *Coelifodina*—a work written in Erfurt in 1490, at the same Augustinian monastery that Martin Luther would join in July 1505—that the blessed in heaven would be unable to see God by knowledge of a simple intelligence due to their finite nature, yet, in accordance with their perfection, they would know Him increasingly by knowledge of vision.[3] John of Paltz explicitly referenced this distinction from Aquinas's *Sentences*, a sure sign that the Augustinian convent of Erfurt had access to this work by Aquinas.

---

rei scitae, Psalm.: *Scientiae eius non est numerus*; alio modo connotando, secundum quod dicit Eccli. 5: *A Domino Deo, antequam crearentur, cuncta cognita sunt, et post perfectum* etc., et hoc modo significatur, ut quidam dixerunt, divina scientia ut visio, quasi transiens super rem. Primo modo bona dicuntur subiecta divinae scientiae; secundo modo bona et mala, entia et non-entia; tertio modo, bona et mala, sed entia tantum secundum aliquod tempus, praesens, praeteritum vel futurum. Et secundum hoc scientia Dei tripliciter dicitur: scientia approbationis, intelligentia, visio. Dicendum ergo ad quaestionem quod scientia Dei non augetur, scita tamen bene possunt augeri" (emphases as in edition).

3. Johannes von Paltz, *Coelifodina* (ed. Burger/Stasch 1983, p. 242, v. 1–15): "Diceret quis consequenter: Si sancti et angeli vident, 'in verbo,' 'omnia praesentia, quae hic,' actualiter aguntur, quaeritur, an aliqui sancti videant cum deo aliqua praeterita et futura. Respondetur secundum sanctum Thomam super distinctionem 49 Quarti, quaestione 9, articulo 1 <sic>, quod deus dupliciter aliqua videt, scilicet notitia visionis et notitia simplicis intelligentiae. Notitia visionis videt omnia, quae sunt, fuerunt er erunt, tamquam praesentia. Et illa notitia vocatur ideo visionis, quia sicut visione corporali videmus praesentia, sic dominus deus ista notitia videt ea, quae sunt, fuerunt et erunt tamquam praesentia, quia secundum Boethium in aeternitate omnia sunt praesentia, quia nihil est praeteritum vel futurum. Notitia autem simplicis intelligentiae videt non solum ista, sed etiam omnia possibilia ab eo fieri. Sed quia illa sunt infinita et omnis creatura est finita, igitur nulla creatura videt omnia illa, alias comprehenderet eius potentiam infinitam, quod est impossibile naturae finitae. Sed anima Christi videt omnia, quae deus videt notitia visionis. Deinde alii, quantum fuerit quis perfectior, tanto plura videt."

Whatever its reception history, the distinction that Aquinas drew reveals important insights into God's infinite knowledge. God, as Aquinas already explained in book I of his *Sentences*, intellectually exercises dominion over two infinite scopes of objects: (1) Those things that were, are, or will be (things in created actuality at some moment in time); and (2) those things that never were, are, or will be, but that could be potentially (things never in created actuality). The former, Aquinas explained, God knows in the potency of their causes as well as in their own being (*esse*) through the so-called "knowledge of vision." The latter, God knows only in the potency of their causes through the so-called "knowledge of a simple intelligence."[4] Knowledge of a simple intelligence is, however, exclusive to God alone. The reason Aquinas gave was that these potential yet never actual things are identical with God's essence, undistinguished from His simplicity and oneness. No created intellect could comprehend the divine essence, as Aquinas argued in article three, and therefore only the actual things are knowable to created intellects.[5]

4. Thomas Aquinas, *Scriptum super libros Sententiarum*, l. 1, d. 39, q. 1, a. 2 (ed. Mandonnet 1, pp. 922–923): "Respondeo dicendum, quod Deus dicitur scire aliquid dupliciter; vel scientia visionis, secundum quod videt res quae sunt vel erunt vel fuerunt non solum in potentia causarum suarum, sed etiam in esse proprio; vel scientia simplicis intelligentiae, secundum quod scit ea quae nullo tempore sunt, esse in potentia causarum suarum. De hac igitur loquendo, Deus non potest scire aliquid aliud ab his quae scit; quia nihil potest esse aliud ab his quae sunt et quae possunt esse. Loquendo autem de scientia visionis de qua hic Magister loquitur, sic potest aliquid aliud videre ab his quae videt, secundum quod potest ei quod habet esse in potentia sua tantum, dare esse in propria natura." See also: ibid., l. I, d. 39, q. 1, a. 3 (ed. Mandonnet 1, pp. 925–926); ibid., l. 1, d. 40, q. 2, a. 1, ad 1 (ed. Mandonnet 1, p. 948); ibid., l. 3, d. 14, q. unica, a. 2, qc. 2 (ed. Moos 1933, p. 447, n. 89–p. 448, n. 93, as quoted in excerpts in notes 5 and 6 below).

5. Ibid., l. 3, d. 14, q. 1, a. 2, qc. 2 (ed. Moos 1933, p. 447, n. 91–p. 448, n. 92): "Sed *ea quae* nec sunt nec erunt nec fuerunt, et tamen *potuissent esse vel fuisse vel futura esse*, cum in seipsis non sint, nullam in seipsis distinctionem habent, nec sunt nisi in potentia ipsius Dei, in qua unum sunt. Unde non possunt esse respectus diversi secundum quos distinguantur rationes horum possibilium. Et ideo haec non cognoscit Deus per ideas distinctas, sed per cognitionem suae potentiae, in qua sunt. Et ideo dicitur haec cognoscere *simplici intelligentia*, quia intelligere est concipere etiam ea quae non sunt extra concipientem. 92.—Sed quia omne quod agit aliquid vel potest agere, agit illud secundum quod est ens actu; ideo impossibile est quod aliquis sciat omnia quae ex aliqua causa possunt produci, nisi comprehendat entitatem ejus. Et quia nullus creatus intellectus comprehendit essentiam divinam, ideo nullus intellectus creatus potest scire omnia quae Deus facere potest. [Et haec sunt illa quae Deus scit simplici intelligentia.] Sed ea quae sunt vel erunt vel fuerunt, deficiunt ab infinitate divinae potentiae, quia plura facere posset. Unde non prohibetur aliquis intellectus creatus cognoscere ea omnia; sed unusquisque tanto plura eorum in Verbo cognoscit, quanto perfectius Verbum intuetur" (emphases as in edition).

Indeed, concerning these things Aquinas took a rather positive stance: Christ Incarnate (in His human soul) may not share in God's knowledge of a simple intelligence, as Aquinas reasoned in book III of his *Sentences*, because His soul is created and thus unable to share in the knowledge undistinguished from the divine simplicity. Nonetheless, Christ naturally shares in God's knowledge of vision, as this concerns things in actual existence:

> And because the soul of <Incarnate> Christ contemplates the Word most perfectly among creatures, it attains the end of their cognition, namely that it knows all things which will be and were, not only those that are made, but also those that are known and said. And because it comprehends any created essence whatsoever, it therefore knows all things which are in potency of any seminal creature whatsoever, in the same way by which God knows those that are in His power. Therefore, it should be said that in this way, Christ sees all things in the Word which the Word sees.[6]

Impossible for any creature in its state of nature, knowledge of the vision became a possibility, albeit a remote one, for angels and humans alike in their state of blessedness:

> The knowledge of the angels and of the souls of the blessed can be augmented until Judgment Day <...>. And in this state, it will be possible for all to cognize all things that God has known in His knowledge of the vision.[7]

Through this conclusion to the present article, Aquinas explicitly linked his discussion of the beatific vision to those of divine knowledge and Christ's knowledge. But to reach this conclusion, he simply

6. Ibid., l. 3, d. 14, q. 1, a. 2, qc. 2 (ed. Moos 1933, p. 448, n. 93) "Et quia anima Christi perfectissime inter creaturas Verbum intuetur, ad terminum hujus cognitionis pervenit, scilicet quod scit omnia quae sunt, erunt vel fuerunt, non solum facta, sed cogitata vel dicta. Et quia comprehendit quamlibet essentiam creatam, ideo scit omnia quae sunt in potentia seminali creaturae cujuscumque, eo modo quo Deus scit quae sunt in potentia sua. Sic igitur dicendum est quod videt in Verbo omnia quae videt Verbum."

7. See translation below on pp. 171–172.

drew on the distinction between God's knowledge of vision and God's knowledge of a simple intelligence that we saw earlier, and categorically denied knowledge of a simple intelligence for all creatures. Were a created intellect capable of sharing in God's knowledge of a simple intelligence, in knowledge of His own virtual quantity, Aquinas suggests, "it would be of the same quantity of perfection in understanding as the quantity of the divine power in producing its effects."[8] Whatever the elevation of any created intellect by way of the new disposition of the light of glory, the ontology of a creature, which Aquinas took to remain in the beatific vision, demanded a lesser quantity of perfection than the ontology of God. No creature is immutable, simple, and infinite as God is, and hence no creature can share in the immutable, simple, and infinite knowledge of Him. Aquinas's denial of comprehension by denying knowledge of a simple intelligence to creatures ought to be understood to involve an absolute denial of their access to God's creative practical knowledge as much as to the exercise of His will to create or not to create. In short, it is on the basis of ontological grounds that these two realms of divine noetic infinity had to remain inaccessible to creatures.

None of these matters played a part in the other type of divine noetic infinity, God's knowledge of vision. Compared to His knowledge of a simple intelligence, the question of sharing in God's knowledge of vision was more nuanced, and Aquinas needed to tread carefully. We learn from him that some of his near contemporaries took this kind of knowledge to be available to the blessed at any given time of their beatific vision. But Aquinas was not convinced. Other Church authorities, such as St. Jerome, suggested to the contrary:

> We have discerned the future that God decreed in His mind once upon a time, and that has now reached its perfection due to the fact that we see it. And in this way, the crucifixion of Christ benefitted

8. See Response, p. 171 below.

> not only us, but also the angels and all powers in heaven, and it disclosed to them a mystery they were unaware of before.[9]

Aquinas followed this path of authority in his solution, and did so once again for reasons that spoke against a comprehensive vision: God as the cause of creation may be seen in His essence, but not all of His effects in actuality require to be known, which would presuppose that God is comprehended as their cause. Even if all these effects in actuality were known by some angels—Aquinas considered this to be a possibility in his reply to objection one—then these effects could at least not be known perfectly in all their features and characteristics. Negating comprehension of all divine effects through knowledge of vision, therefore, implied two different things: either some effects in actuality remain unknown in the beatific vision, or if all effects are known, some of their characteristics remain unknown. Consequently, when Aquinas denied knowledge of vision to all blessed before "the ultimate state of things," he also denied to them comprehension of the second type of infinity of divine knowing. Those creatures who saw the divine essence nonetheless remained precluded from God's knowledge of the whole of creation in all its extension in the time-space continuum, as well as of the completeness of divine providence over all of creation.

With this cautious reasoning against a knowledge of vision at the outset in the beatific vision before the Last Judgment, Aquinas linked his discussion in article five to the different degrees of seeing God that he had presented previously in article four. The more effects of God are seen in the beatific vision, the more clearly His essence is seen; this implies that those who see God's essence more clearly see more of Him too. This, then, ought to be understood as a convertibility between qualitative and quantitative knowing in the beatific vision. Even more so, understanding the effects in God's essence makes it possible in Aquinas's eyes that the blessed teach

---

9. Hieronymus, *Commentarius in Epistolam ad Ephesios*, l. 2, c. 3 (PL 26, p. 515): "Quam olim Deus futuram in sua mente decreverat, et nunc esse perfectam ex eo quod videmus, agnoscimus. Crux itaque Christi non solum nobis, sed et angelis cunctisque in coelo virtutibus profuit, et aperuit sacramentum quod antea nesciebant."

one another and augment knowledge among themselves in this way until, at the end of time, all of them will have acquired the same knowledge of vision that Christ has naturally and that God has of Himself, as was outlined above. This ultimately optimistic view constituted the endpoint, the climax of the beatific vision for Aquinas, in which nothing more can be reached, attained, or acquired by a created intellect. Indeed, one of the divine noetic infinities would ultimately become accessible to the blessed, namely, knowledge of the whole of creation and knowledge of divine providence over it. But this, so it seems from the 'time' after Judgment Day, would no longer arouse any worries concerning creaturely intervention in divine action in creation.

TRANSLATION

We proceed to the fifth article as follows. It seems that the blessed, who see God through His essence, see all things that God sees in Himself.

Objections

(1) Because, as Isidore says in his book *On the Highest Good*: "The angels know all things in the Word of God before they arise."[10] But the blessed will be equal to the angels, as is evident from Matthew 22:30.[11] Therefore, the blessed too will see all things in seeing God.

(2) Furthermore, Gregory says in his *Dialogues*, book IV: "Because there all gaze upon God with common clarity, what is it that they may not know there, where they know the One who knows all things?"[12] Yet, he speaks of the blessed who see God through His essence. Therefore, those who see God through His essence cognize all things.

10. Isidorus Hispalensis, *Sententiae* (*De summo bono*), l. 1, c. 10, n. 17 (CCSL 111, p. 34, v. 111; PL 83, p. 556): "Angeli Verbo Dei cognoscunt omnia antequam in re fiant."

11. Secundum Matthaeum 22:30, see article one, note 25.

12. Gregorius Magnus, *Dialogorum libri IV*, l. 4, c. 34 (SC 265, p. 116, v. 49–51; PL 77, p. 376, <c. 33>): "Quia enim illic omnes communi claritate Deum conspiciunt, quid est quod ibi nesciant, ubi scientem omnia sciunt?"

(3) Furthermore, as is said in Aristotle's *On the Soul*, book III: "When an intellect understands the highest things, it can understand the lowest things even more."[13] But the highest intelligible is God. Therefore, He augments the power of the intellect in understanding to the highest degree. Therefore, the intellect that sees Him understands all things.

(4) Furthermore, the intellect is prevented from understanding something only inasmuch as it exceeds it. But no creature exceeds the intellect that sees God because, as Gregory says in his *Dialogues*, book II, "to the soul that sees its Creator all creatures come to be marginal."[14] Therefore, those who see God through His essence will cognize all things.

(5) Furthermore, every passive potency that is not reduced to actuality is imperfect. But in the possible intellect of the human soul, there is a potency, passive as it were, for cognizing all things because the possible intellect is that "in which all things are made," as is said in <Aristotle's> *On the Soul*, book III.[15] Therefore, if it did not understand all things in the state of happiness, it would remain imperfect, which is absurd.

(6) Furthermore, whoever sees a mirror, sees the things that are reflected in the mirror. But in the Word of God, all things are reflected as in a mirror because the Word is the measure (*ratio*) and similitude of all things. Therefore, the blessed, who see the Word through His essence, see all created things.

(7) Furthermore, as is said in Proverbs 10:24: *To the just their desire shall be given.*[16] But the blessed desire to know all things because

13. Aristoteles, *De anima*, l. 3, lect. 1 (429a31-b4), trans. vet. (ed. Gauthier 1985, pp. 445–446): "Sensus enim non potest sentire ex ualde sensibili, ut sensus ex magnis sonis neque ex fortibus coloribus et odoribus neque uidere neque odorare; set intellectus, cum aliquid intelligat ualde intelligibile, non minus intelligit infima, set magis."

14. Gregorius Magnus, *Dialogorum libri I–III*, l. 2, c. 35 (SC 260, p. 240, v. 51, PL 66, p. 200): "animae uidenti creatorem angusta est omnis creatura."

15. Aristoteles, *De anima*, l. 3, lect. 2 (430a14–15), trans. vet. (ed. Gauthier 1985, p. 459): "huiusmodi quidem est intellectus in quo omnia fiunt."

16. Proverbia 10:24 (Vulgata 2007): *desiderium suum iustis dabitur.*

"all humans desire to know all things by nature,"[17] and nature is not abolished by the glory. Therefore, cognition of all things will be given to them by God.

(8) Furthermore, ignorance is a certain penalty of the present life. But all penalties will be lifted from the blessed by the glory. Therefore, all ignorance will be too. And in this way, they will cognize all things.

(9) Furthermore, the happiness of the blessed is primarily in the soul and secondarily in the body. But the bodies of the blessed will be reformed in glory to the similitude of the body of Christ, as is evident from Philippians 3:21.[18] Therefore, their souls too will be perfected to the similitude of the soul of Christ. But the soul of Christ sees all things in the Word, as was said <earlier> in book III, distinction 14.[19] Therefore, all the souls of the blessed too will see all things in the Word.

(10) Furthermore, like the senses, intellect also cognizes all things with whose similitude it is informed. But the divine essence discloses any thing more distinctly than any other similitude of the thing. Therefore, since the divine essence becomes like the form of our intellect in the blessed vision, it seems that the blessed who see God see all things.

(11) Furthermore, the Commentator says in his <*Long Commentary on Aristotle's*> *On the Soul*, book III, comment 36 that, if the agent intellect were the form of the possible intellect, we would understand all things.[20] But the divine essence represents all things more clearly than the agent intellect. Therefore, the intellect that sees God through His essence cognizes all things.

---

17. Aristoteles, *Metaphysica*, l. 1, c. 1 (980a21), trans. media (AL XXV 2, p. 7, v. 3): "Omnes homines scire desiderant natura."

18. Ad Philippenses 3:21 (Vulgata 2007): *qui reformabit corpus humilitatis nostrae configuratum corpori claritatis suae.*

19. Thomas Aquinas, *Scriptum super Sententiis Magistri Petri Lombardi*, l. 3, d. 14, a. 2, qc. 2 (ed. Moos 1933, p. 447 n. 89–p. 448, n. 93, as quoted in excerpts in notes 5 and 6 above).

20. See: Averroes, *Commentarium magnum in Aristotelis De anima libros*, l. 3, com. 36 (ed. Crawford 1953, p. 499, v. 581–p. 500, v. 616): "Quoniam hoc posito, continget necessario ut intellectus qui est in nobis in actu sit compositus ex intellectis speculativis et intellectu agenti ita quod intellectus agens sit quasi forma intellectorum speculativorum et intellecta speculativa

(12) Furthermore, because the inferior angels do not understand all things now, they are illuminated by the superior angels concerning the things they do not know. But after the Last Judgment day, one angel will not illumine another angel. For then, "all predominance will cease," as the Gloss to I Corinthians 15.24 says.[21] Therefore, the inferior angels will know all things then, and for the same reason, all the other blessed, who see God through His essence <will too>.

* * *

(1) On the contrary, as Dionysius says in his *Ecclesiastical Hierarchy*, chapter VIII, the superior angels purge the inferior angels of ignorance.[22] Yet, the inferior angels see the divine essence. Therefore, an angel that sees the divine essence can be ignorant of some things. But the soul will not see God more perfectly than an angel. Therefore, the souls that see God need not see all things.

---

sint quasi materia. Et per hunc modum poterimus generare intellecta cum voluerimus. Quoniam, quia illud per quod agit aliquid suam propriam actionem est forma, nos autem agimus per intellectum agentem nostram actionem propriam, necesse est ut intellectus agens sit forma in nobis. Et nullus modus est secundum quem generetur forma in nobis nisi iste. Quoniam, cum intellecta speculativa copulantur nobiscum per formas ymaginabiles, et intellectus agens copulatur cum intellectis speculativis (illud enim quod comprehendit ea est idem, scilicet intellectus materialis), necesse est ut intellectus agens copuletur nobiscum per continuationem intellectorum speculativorum. Et manifestum est quod, cum omnia intellecta speculativa fuerint existentia in nobis in potentia, quod ipse erit copulatus nobiscum in potentia. Et cum omnia intellecta speculativa fuerint existentia in nobis in actu, erit ipse tunc copulatus nobis in actu. Et cum quedam fuerint potentia et quedam actu, tunc erit ipse copulatus secundum partem et secundum partem non; et tunc dicimur moveri ad continuationem. Et manifestum est quod, cum iste motus complebitur, quod statim iste intellectus copulabitur nobiscum omnibus modis. Et tunc manifestum est quod proportio eius ad nos in illa dispositione est sicut proportio intellectus qui est in habitu ad nos. Et cum ita sit, necesse est ut homo intelligat per intellectum sibi proprium omnia entia, et ut agat actionem sibi propriam in omnibus entibus, sicut intelligit per intellectum qui est in habitu, quando fuerit continuatus cum formis ymaginabilibus, eis omnia entia intellectione propria."

21. *Glossa marg.* I Ad Cor. 15:24 (ed. Rusch, vol. IV, p. 333b). See also: Petrus Lombardus, *In epistulas Pauli I Ad Corinthios* 15:24 (PL 191, p. 1679). Haymo, *In I Ad Corinthios* 15:24 (PL 117, p. 597).

22. Pseudo-Dionysius Areopagita, *De caelesti hierarchia*, c. 8, sect. 64, trans. Eriugenae (Dionysiaca t. 2, pp. 877–878): "Has habens Deiformes proprietates media caelestium animorum dispositio purgatur quidem et illuminatur et perficitur (quemadmodum dictum est) a divinis illuminationibus inditis sibi secundo per primam hierarchicam dispositionem, et per mediam illam secunda manifestatione delatis." Ibid. (Dionysiaca t. 2, pp. 881–882): "Hoc enim est omnino divina taxiarchia divinitus promulgatum per prima secunda divinis participare illuminationibus." See also: Albertus Magnus, *Super Dionysium De caelesti hierarchia*, c. 8 (ed. Colon. 36/1, p. 131, v. 81–83, p. 132, v. 80–81).

(2) Furthermore, Christ alone has *the spirit not by measure* as is said in John 3:34.[23] But it befits Christ, inasmuch as He has the spirit without measure, to cognize all things in the Word. Hence, it is said in the same passage that the Father *hath given all things into his hand*.[24] Therefore, it befits no one but Christ to cognize all things in the Word.

(3) Furthermore, the more perfectly a principle is cognized, the more of its effects are known through it. But some of those who see God through His essence will cognize God, who is the principle of all things, more perfectly than others. Therefore, some will cognize more things than others. And in this way, not everyone will know all things.

Response

It should be said that God, in seeing His own essence, cognizes all things that are, were, or will be. And this is called cognizing by knowledge of vision because, in similarity to the corporeal vision, He cognizes things as if present. Besides, in seeing His essence, He cognizes all things that He can make, even though He never has made them, nor ever will. Otherwise, He would not perfectly cognize His own power. For a power can only be cognized if its objects are known.[25] And this is called cognition by knowledge of a simple intelligence.

Yet it is impossible that some created intellect, in seeing the divine essence, cognize all things that God can make. For the more perfectly a principle is cognized, the more things are known in it, just as, in a single principle of demonstration, someone who is of a sharper nature sees more conclusions than someone who is of a

---

23. Secundum Iohannem 3:34 (Vulgata 2007): *non enim ad mensuram dat Deus Spiritum*. In this passage, Aquinas supplements the subject of the Vulgate text, 'God' (*Deus*), by 'Christ,' and the verb 'to give' (*dare*) with 'to have' (*habere*), which is why his Latin version of the Scripture citation reads as follows: "Solus Christus habet 'spiritum non ad mensuram,' ut dicitur Ioh. III." I have followed Aquinas's adaptations in my translation above.

24. Secundum Iohannem 3:35 (Vulgata 2007): *Pater diligit Filium et omnia dedit in manu eius*.

25. See: Aristoteles, *De anima*, l. 2, lect. 6 (415a18–20), trans. vet. (ed. Gauthier 1985, p. 204): "Priores enim potenciis actus et primi secundum rationem sunt."

slower nature. Therefore, since the quantity of the divine power is seen in the things it is able to do, if some intellect were to see all things in the divine essence that God can make, it would be of the same quantity of perfection in understanding as the quantity of the divine power in producing its effects. And in this way, it would comprehend the divine essence, which is impossible for any created intellect. Yet <there is> a single created intellect <that> cognizes, in the Word, all things that God knows by knowledge of the vision, namely the soul of Christ, as was already said in book III, distinction 14.[26]

But there is a twofold opinion concerning the others who see the divine essence. For some say that all those who see God through His essence see all things that God sees by the knowledge of vision. But this is against the assertions of the blessed who hold that the angels are ignorant of some things.[27] Nonetheless, according to faith, it is certain that they all see God through His essence.

And for this reason, others say that all but Christ, even though they see God through His essence, nonetheless do not see all things that God sees because they do not comprehend the divine essence. For it is not necessary that he who knows the cause knows all its effects, unless he comprehends the cause, which does not befit any created intellect. And for this reason, for anyone seeing God through His essence, the more things he beholds in His essence, the more clearly he intuits the divine essence. And it is for this reason that one of them can instruct another about these things. And likewise, the knowledge of the angels and of the souls of the blessed can be augmented until Judgment Day, just as the other things too which

---

26. See objection nine above.

27. See, for instance: Hieronymus, *Commentarius in Epistolam ad Ephesios*, l. 2, c. 3 (PL 26, p. 514): "Juxta donum gratiae Dei, quae data est Apostolo, ut evangelizaret ininvestigabiles divitias Christi et doceret in gentibus mysterium quod a saeculis fuerat ignoratum; idcirco idipsum sacramentum ei est revelatum, ut non solum gentibus, sed et principatibus et potestatibus per Ecclesiam manifesta fieret multiplex sapientia Dei, quae juxta propositum veterum saeculorum olim destinata, nunc consummata videtur in Christo. Si autem principatibus et Potestatibus in coelis, quas sanctas ministrasque Dei accipere debemus (licet quidam principem aeris istius et angelos jius interpretentur), ignota fuit multiplex sapientia Dei, quae nunc eis per Ecclesiam revelata est, quanto magis patriarchis et prophetis ignota fuit, quos supra non ignorasse mysterium Christi, sed ita ut apostolos, nescisse monstravimus?"

belong to the accidental reward. But it will not advance beyond this because then it will be the ultimate state of things. And in this state, it will be possible for all to cognize all things that God has known in His knowledge of the vision.

Replies to Objections

(1) To the first, therefore, it should be said that what Isidore says—that the angels know all things in the Word before they arise—cannot refer to those things that God knows by the knowledge of a simple intelligence alone because they will never come to be. But it must refer only to those things that God knows by the knowledge of vision. And even of these things, <Isidore> does not say that all angels cognize them all, but perhaps some of them do; and even those who cognize all things do not cognize them perfectly. For in one thing many intelligible attributes (*rationes*) must be considered, such as its different properties and relations to other things. And it is possible that, when the same thing is known jointly by two, one discerns more attributes than the other, and one takes these attributes more easily from the other. Hence, Dionysius too says in chapter 8 of his *Celestial Hierarchy* that the inferior angels are taught the attributes of the knowable things by the superior ones.[28] And for this reason, the angels, who cognize all creatures, need not participate in all <attributes> that can be understood in them.

(2) To the second, it should be said that the word of Gregory shows that the sufficiency for beholding all things in the blessed vision comes from the divine essence through which He sees all things, <and> which <for the blessed> is the medium by which He is seen. But <the fact> that not all things are seen is due to the deficiency of the created intellect which does not comprehend the divine essence.

(3) To the third, it should be said that a created intellect does not see the divine essence according to the proper mode of the very essence,

---

28. For the passage in Pseudo-Dionysius Areopagita, see note 22 above. See also: Albertus Magnus, *Super Dionysium De caelesti hierarchia*, c. 8 (ed. Colon. 36/1, p. 131, v. 81–83).

but according to its own proper mode which is finite. Hence, its efficacy, in cognizing through the aforementioned vision, need not be amplified infinitely to cognizing all things.

(4) To the fourth, it should be said that deficiency of cognition does not only come from the excess of the cognitive thing over the intellect, but also because it is not conjoined to the intellect whereby it is the measure (*ratio*) of the ability to conjoin,[29] just as sight sometimes does not see a stone because the species of the stone is not conjoined to it. Yet even though the divine essence itself, which is the measure of all things, is conjoined to the intellect of the one who sees God, nonetheless, it is not conjoined to it as the measure of all things, but insofar as it is the measure of some. And one who gazes at the divine essence more fully, perceives more of these things.

(5) To the fifth, it should be said that when a passive potency is perfectible by several orders of perfections, if it is perfected by its ultimate perfection it is not called imperfect, even if some of the preceding dispositions are missing. Yet every cognition by which a created intellect is perfected is ordered to the cognition of God as to an end. Hence, even if those who see God through His essence were to cognize nothing other than God, they would have a perfected intellect. Nor is it more perfect because it cognizes something else within Him, except until it sees Him more fully. Hence, Augustine says in his *Confessions* V: "Unhappy is he who knows everything," namely <all> creatures (*creaturas*), "but who does not know Thee; but happy is he who knows Thee even if he does not know them. He who knows Thee and these things, is not more blessed because of them, but he is blessed because of Thee alone."[30]

(6) To the sixth, it should be said that 'mirror' is something voluntary; and just as He will disclose Himself to whom He wills, so too will He

29. By *ratio conjungibilis* Thomas means the actualizing or perfective form in the intellect which establishes the relation between the subject and object of cognition.

30. Augustinus Hipponensis, *Confessionum libri tredecem*, l. 5, c. 4 (CCSL 27, p. 60, v. 2–5; PL 32, p. 708): "Infelix enim homo, qui scit illa omnia, te autem nescit; beatus autem, qui te scit, etiamsi illa nesciat; qui uero et te et illa nouit, non propter illa beatior, sed propter te solum beatus est."

disclose in Himself what He wills. This is dissimilar to a material mirror, which does not have it in its power to be seen or not to be seen.

Or (*vel*), it should be said that in a material mirror both the thing and the mirror are seen under their proper form, even though the mirror is seen through a received form from the thing, but a stone <is seen> through its proper form reflected in another thing. And for this reason, one thing is cognized by the same nature (*ratio*) as is the other. But in the uncreated mirror, something is seen through the form of the mirror itself, as an effect is seen through the similitude of its cause and conversely. And for this reason, not everybody who sees the eternal mirror must see all things that are reflected in this mirror. For it is not necessary that he who sees the cause see all its effects, unless he comprehends the cause.

(7) To the seventh, it should be said that the desire of the blessed by which they desire to know all things will be fulfilled only by seeing God, just as their desire by which they long for the possession of all good things will be fulfilled by possessing God. For just as God, by possessing perfect goodness, suffices for their affection, and they by possessing Him possess all good things in a certain way, so too does the vision of Him suffice for their intellect, as it is said in John 14:8: *Lord, shew us the Father; and it is enough for us.*[31]

(8) To the eighth, it should be said that 'ignorance' properly speaking expresses privation, and in this way is a punishment. For, ignorance in such a way is nescience of things that must be known, or that are necessary to be known. Yet the knowledge of the blessed will not be wanting any of these things in heaven. Sometimes, however, 'ignorance' is taken in general for any kind of nescience. And in this way, the angels and the blessed will be ignorant of certain things in heaven. Hence, Dionysius says that the angels are purged of their ignorance.[32] Yet in this way, ignorance is not a penalty but rather a

31. Secundum Iohannem 14:8, see article one, note 51.

32. See: Pseudo-Dionysius Areopagita, *De caelesti hierarchia*, c. 7, sect. 63, trans. Eriugenae (Dionysiaca t. 2, pp. 853–860). See also: Albertus Magnus, *Super Dionysium De caelesti hierarchia* c. 7 (ed. Colon. 36/1, p. 110, v. 74–82; p. 111, v. 78–84).

kind of lack; nor is it necessary that every such deficiency be undone by the glory. For likewise, it can also be said that there is a deficiency in Linus[33] that he did not attain the glory of Peter.

(9) To the ninth, it should be said that our body will be conformed to the body of Christ in glory according to similitude, not equality. For it will be as bright as the body of Christ, but not equally. And similarly, our soul will have glory similar to the soul of Christ, but not equally. And in this way, it will have knowledge just as the soul of Christ, but not to the extent that it would know all things like the soul of Christ.

(10) To the tenth, it should be said that although the divine essence is the measure (*ratio*) of all cognizable things, it will nonetheless not be conjoined to any created intellect inasmuch as it is the measure of all things. And for this reason, the argument does not follow.

(11) To the eleventh, it should be said that the agent intellect is a form proportionate to the possible intellect, as the potency of matter is proportionate to the power of a natural agent, such that everything that is in the passive potency of matter or the possible intellect is in the active power of the agent intellect or the natural agent. And for this reason, if the agent intellect becomes the form of the possible intellect, the possible intellect must cognize all things to which the power of the agent intellect extends. Yet the divine intelligence is not a form proportionate to our intellect in this way, and for this reason it is not similar.

(12) To the twelfth, it should be said that nothing prevents us from saying that after Judgment Day, when the glory of humans and angels will be wholly consummated, all blessed will know all things that God knows by the knowledge of vision, yet in such a way that not all may see all things in the divine essence. But the soul of Christ will see all things therein fully, as He also sees them now. Yet others will see more or fewer things therein, according to the degree by which

33. It is possible that Aquinas refers to Pope Linus here, who was most likely the second Bishop of Rome in 67–79 AD and successor of Peter.

they will cognize God. And likewise, the soul of Christ will illumine all other souls with those things that He sees before all others in the Word. Hence, it is said in Apocalypse 21:23 that *the glory of God hath enlightened the city* of the blessed, *and the Lamb is the lamp thereof.*[34] And similarly, other superior <intellects> will illuminate inferior ones, yet not by a certain new illumination as if the knowledge of the inferior be augmented by it, but by a certain continuation of illumination, as, for instance, if one understood the sun to illuminate the air while being at rest. And for this reason, it is said in Daniel 12:3 that *they that instruct many to justice will shine as stars for all eternity.*[35] Yet the supremacy of order is said to have ceased with regard to the things that are now exercised over us by their ordained ministries, as is evident from the Gloss on the same passage.[36]

---

34. Apocalypsis Iohannis 21:23 (Vulgata 2007): *nam claritas Dei inluminavit eam et lucerna eius est agnus.* Note that Aquinas adds the term *communitas* to the original Vulgate text. I inserted Aquinas's addition into the Douay-Rheims translation (Douay-Rheims The Vulgate Bible 2010–2013).

35. Daniel 12:3 (Vulgata 2007): *qui ad iustitiam erudiunt multos <fulgebunt> quasi stellae in perpetuas aeternitates.* The insertion of *fulgebunt* follows Aquinas's citation of the text.

36. *Glossa* I Ad Cor. 15:24, see above objection twelve and article one, note 44, for the verse in the Bible. See also: Rabanus Maurus, *Enarrationes in Epistolas Pauli XI*, 1 Cor. 15:24 (PL 112, pp. 146–147).

ARTICLE 6

On the Impossibility of Seeing God by One's Natural Powers

INTRODUCTION

In article six, Aquinas revisited the question of conditions or requirements that have to be met for the disembodied soul to engage in the beatific vision. Earlier in his *Sentences* (bk. 4, d. 49, q. 1, a. 1), Aquinas had reached the conclusion that two preliminary conditions had to be met before he could begin to talk about the last or ultimate condition (which he does in article six). The first concerned the disembodiment of the human soul; the second, its existence under the conditions of a-temporality.[1] While the first condition implied that the soul was now liberated from any reliance on sense experience for its cognitive activities, the second entailed that it could perform these now purely intellectual activities under the condition of external stability or immutability. Yet even though these two preliminary conditions captured what could be described as the soul's freedom from the contingencies of earthly existence—contingencies that were exercised upon it by space and time while embodied—they were insufficient in Aquinas's eyes for the soul to reach knowledge of the essence of God.[2]

1. See: Thomas Aquinas, *Commentum in quatuor libros Sententiarum*, l. 4, d. 49, q. 1, a. 1, qcc. 1–4 (ed. Parma 7/2, pp. 1181–1186). For a more detailed discussion concerning this question of the two preliminary conditions, see: section VIII of the general introduction and Krause 2015a, pp. 15–56.

2. See introduction to article seven, where Aquinas inquires into "whether God can be seen through His essence in this life," and where he faces these difficulties of the preliminary conditions again.

In the present article, Aquinas thus insists that the soul transcends those cognitive limitations which accrue to it despite its disembodied state of being under the stable circumstances of the afterlife. These limitations first and foremost concern the scope of objects which the disembodied soul can cognize without God's facilitation, a scope that Aquinas took to be limited to other creatures. In contrast to human knowing in this life, however, the soul's disembodiment already made it possible to widen the scope of cognitive objects from essences that belong to embodied creatures to essences that belong to all creatures, including angels or separate substances.[3] Nonetheless, Aquinas explicitly excluded God's essence, the essence of the Creator of all there is, from this scope of cognitive objects.

One prominent way by which he justified this exclusion was to insist on the principle that any given activity follows upon the being of the subject that performs it. Hence, since in Aquinas's eyes the human person is composed of body and soul in its being as an embodied subject, its activity of cognition must follow upon its embodiment; and this is exactly the reason that Aquinas took the scope of cognitive objects in this life to be limited to the essences that belong to material things. Similarly, since the disembodied soul is free from the conditions of corporeality and mutability in its being, its activity of cognition can now follow upon its disembodiment; and this is the reason that Aquinas took its scope of cognitive objects to involve all creatures. This principle already played a crucial role in Aquinas's reasoning in article two, and there I called it the "principle of proportionality."[4] When it came to explaining the beatific vision as the ultimate intellectual activity of the disembodied and glorified soul, however, Aquinas could no longer utilize this principle. Indeed, it is at this point that the principle had to be suspended

3. Concerning the natural knowledge of disembodied souls, see: Thomas Aquinas, *Scriptum super Sententiis Magistri Petri Lombardi*, l. 3, d. 31, q. 2, a. 4 (ed. Moos 1933, pp. 995–997); id., *Commentum in quatuor libros Sententiarum*, l. 4, d. 50, q. 1, a. 3 (ed. Parma 7/2, pp. 1249–1251). For discussions concerning this theme in the secondary literature, see, for instance: Pegis 1974a, pp. 131–158; id. 1974b, pp. 1–15; Wippel 2000, pp. 114–140; Cory 2018.

4. See introduction to article two above.

in order to account for the way in which the beatific vision could be reached. The ultimate condition to be met for the beatific vision, therefore, had to show how the disembodied soul's being as a creature would be preserved, despite the fact that its cognitive ability would be raised beyond any creaturely limitations so as to cognize God's essence.

The only being who, in Aquinas's eyes, was able to suspend this principle of proportionality and to enable the soul for the vision of God's essence was, of course, God Himself. In a grace-giving, facilitating act, so Aquinas reasons in the present article, God confers the so-called "light of glory" upon the soul of the blessed saint, a conferrence that enhances its ability to know God Himself. This is typically how most scholarship describes Aquinas's view.[5] Yet even though he used the term "light of glory" (*lumen gloriae*) toward the end of article six, a closer look at his argument reveals that he preferred another term to guide his theorization, namely "disposition" (*dispositio*). This term he used to express much more precisely, especially in view of the accounts of his near contemporaries, what he took the "light of glory" to be in its own constitution and how he took it to act upon the intellect of the disembodied soul: its purpose was to literally dispose the human soul in such a way that it may be affected by the divine essence in the beatific vision. But what precisely does this mean?

So far, we have already taken note of one key characteristic that this disposition has: its purpose is to increase the soul's cognitive ability beyond its own proper mode and to raise it to knowing God's essence. Yet the term "disposition" also illustrates that Aquinas envisioned it to be a created and new quality which would permanently take hold in the soul's intellectual faculties. As such, he saw it as a qualitative accident in the soul, which according to Aristotle's *Categories* is a property or an attribute that may or may not belong to

5. See, for instance: Garrigou-Lagrange 1943, pp. 306–381; Cunningham 1955, p. 203; Gilson 1964, pp. 67–88; Hoye 1975, pp. 274–280; Wippel 1992, p. 288; Williams 1999; Torrell 2001, pp. 167–202; Hankey 2004, pp. 149–178; White 2006, pp. 64–68; Bender 2007, pp. 264–266; Jenkins 2007, pp. 141–144; Waddell 2011, pp. 105–132; Blankenhorn 2015, pp. 291–294.

a subject, but does not change anything about its subject's essence.[6] The disposition for the beatific vision, therefore, already expressed on the nominal level that this disposition is a property in the disembodied soul that does not change anything about its nature.

With his conception of the disposition as a kind of qualitative accident, Aquinas easily preserved the constraint that the disembodied soul would remain the self-same creature in the beatific vision: not even the act of cognizing God would have any altering effects upon the soul's nature. Yet the term "disposition" also expressed that this new qualitative accident would not change anything about the arrangement of the soul's intellectual faculties. According to Aquinas, these faculties, the so-called proper accidents (*propria*), flow from the intellectual soul's essence at the moment of its creation *ex nihilo*, and they express its natural ability to act as an intellectual soul. As such, as principles of the specific activity of cognizing, they too were required to remain identical in their constitution. Hence, all the soul could possibly receive in virtue of the new disposition is a cognitive ability that would extend its scope of cognizing beyond the realm of creatures. And this is precisely how the new disposition acted upon it. At the same time, the new disposition had to be "supernatural" (*supra naturam*). For neither did it follow the principle of proportionality between the disembodied soul's being and activity, nor was it a property that was natural to the soul upon its creation, nor was it a naturally acquired property through the activities of its faculties, as acquired habits are.

The term "disposition," therefore, was most carefully chosen by Aquinas to express that the divine facilitation must be understood as a created, new, qualitative accident in the soul's intellectual faculty

6. See, for instance: Aristoteles, *Categoriae*, c. 5 (4a10–20), trans. Boethii (AL I 1–5, p. 12, v. 4–13): "Maxime autem proprium substantiae videtur esse quod, cum sit idem et unum numero, contrariorum susceptibile est. Et in aliis quidem nullis hoc quisquam habeat proferre quae non sunt substantiae, quod unum numero contrariorum erit susceptibile; ut color, quod est unum et idem numero, non erit album et nigrum, nec eadem actio et una numero erit mala et bona; similiter autem et in aliis quaecumque substantiae non sunt. Ipsa vero substantia, cum sit una et eadem numero, contrariorum susceptibilis est; ut quidam homo, unus et idem cum sit, aliquando albus aliquando niger fit, et calidus et frigidus, et improbus et probus." See also: Aristoteles, *Categoriae*, c. 8 (8b25–9a27), trans. Boethii (AL I 1–5, p. 23, v. 22–p. 25, v. 8).

whose purpose is to widen the intellectual faculty's scope of cognition for the uncreated object, God. As we have seen earlier, in the discussion of article one, the subsequent act of the beatific vision ensued instantaneously upon this widening of the soul's cognitive scope, and it was brought about by God's Self-same essence in an act of purely formal causality (as opposed to the efficient causality exercised by endowing the soul with the new disposition).

Aquinas thus determined the intimate relation between the new disposition and the act of the beatific vision in its systematic meaning. The disposition has priority in nature, not priority in time, over the act of the beatific vision; that is, the disposition is the last necessary condition for the soul—apart from its disembodiment and existence under the stable conditions of eternity—for attaining the beatific vision. Had Aquinas not made use of the term "disposition" here, which, in its meaning, entails many of the ontological and operative Aristotelian commitments he held, he would have certainly had to do much more explaining, particularly with regard to his use of the term "light of glory." In fact, Aquinas fully reshaped the connotation of the term "light of glory" by situating it in the argumentative context driven by the term "disposition": the term "light of glory" became coextensive in meaning and application with the term "disposition." This connection between the two terms expressed the new philosophical meaning, inspired once again by Averroes's *Long Commentary on Aristotle's On the Soul* as outlined below in this article introduction, that Aquinas implemented in this context of divine facilitation for the beatific vision vis-à-vis the theorizations of his near contemporaries. For none of his contemporaries used these terms in this way.[7]

As an example, Aquinas's teacher and closest interlocutor, Albert the Great, who has been credited with coining the term "light of glory,"[8] relied on it and embedded it in a web of the Dionysian terms, such as "theophany" and "deiformity," and Augustinian terms

7. See: Krause, forthcoming.

8. See: Wicki 1954, pp. 154–157.

such as "similitude" and "participation."[9] Yet his theorizations were far from expressing the same view by this term that Aquinas did by reshaping its meaning through a predominant reliance on the term "disposition" at the heart of his theorizations. Albert operated in a different, Neoplatonic framework of thought. According to this framework, the light of glory had neither to be created nor to constitute a qualitative accident in the soul's intellectual faculties alone. Rather, for Albert, it could be both a created accident in the soul and an emanated, uncreated enhancement of the soul that is identical to God. Similarly, the light of glory could take hold in the soul's intellectual faculties, more precisely in the faculty of the agent intellect, as much as it could diffuse from there into the entire essence of the soul.[10] A full explanation of the precise theorization which Albert provided, and the grounds upon which he built it, would go beyond the scope of this brief introduction. Suffice it to say here that Albert relied on rather different assumptions than Aquinas's Aristotelian ones.[11] It must, however, be emphasized that this difference of assumptions did not render Albert's theorization of the light of glory less intelligible. It just presented another avenue of thought, another framework of explanation that was available in the thirteenth century to explain the beatific vision in all its facets.[12]

---

9. See: Krause, forthcoming.

10. See: Albertus Magnus, *De resurrectione*, tr. 4, q. 2, a. 5 (ed. Colon. 26, p. 344 v. 76–82 and p. 345, v. 2–6): "Dicimus, quod uterque intellectus immediate coniungitur deo. Sicut enim est videre in duobus luminibus, quod ipsa quidem secundum substantiam manent distincta et uniuntur in illuminando, sic intellectus agens distinctus secundum essentiam ab intellectu divino unitur ei in illuminando possibilem in gloria. <...> Et sic patet quod deus ut illuminans immediate coniungitur agenti et ut res intellecta immediate coniungitur possibili. Et in his duabus coniunctionibus est actus vitae aeternae secundum intellectum." Id., *Quaestio de visione Dei in patria* (ed. Colon. 25/2, p. 99, v. 9–13.23–25.26–29): "Medium vero ex parte videntis est lumen intellectus agentis habens virtutem lucis intrinsecae et extrinsecae, quia et intelligibilia in potentia facit intelligibilia actu et illustrat intellectum possibilem confortans ipsum in sua visione. <...> Sed quia hoc lumen non adhuc sufficienter confortat intellectum ad visionem divinae essentiae sine medio specierum, <...> ideo superadditur aliud lumen, scilicet gloriae, confortans intellectum, ut divinam ipsam essentiam videre possit sine aliqua specie mediante." Id., *Commentarii in IV Sententiarum*, d. 49, q. 5, ad 1 (ed. Borgnet 30, p. 670) as quoted in section VII of the general introduction, note 21.

11. For a more extended discussion, see: Krause, forthcoming.

12. See section VII of the general introduction.

What we can see thanks to this difference in frameworks is that Aquinas, in all likelihood, reacted to Albert's view of the light of glory and composed his own theorization in marked contrast to his teacher. Aquinas's main interest, which we have already seen in our discussions of article one and find confirmed here, was to account for the beatific vision within an explanatory framework based on Aristotelian principles. To this end, he found the term "disposition" most useful, a term which, to close this brief summary, found a similar structural meaning in Averroes's *Long Commentary on Aristotle's On the Soul.*[13] Averroes used this term in a context vastly different from Aquinas's theorizations of the beatific vision. His context was the natural attainment of happiness in this life through knowledge acquisition in all the sciences. Aquinas left this context behind in its entirety, while extracting the term "disposition" in its structural meaning and creatively integrating it into a new context, namely that of the beatific vision, with the goal of communicating his new explanation of it to his Latin contemporaries.

TRANSLATION

We proceed to the sixth article as follows. It seems that some created intellects, by their own natural powers, can see God through His essence.

---

13. The context within which Averroes used the term "disposition" was his critical discussion of Alexander of Aphrodisias's view on ultimate conjunction with the separate Agent Intellect in this life. Averroes charged Alexander with an inconsistency in explaining the cause of this ultimate conjunction: any natural explanation of conjunction presupposes the acquisition of a new "disposition" in the human intellect, a disposition that it did not possess before. This, of course, was convenient for Aquinas's purposes, since the disposition of the light of glory for the beatific vision had to be new. For Averroes's reading of Alexander of Aphrodisias's view on conjunction, see: Averroes, *Commentarium magnum in Aristotelis De anima libros*, l. 3, com. 36 (ed. Crawford 1953, p. 481, v. 48–p. 482, v. 80), quoted in excerpts in article one, note 2. For Averroes's criticism of Alexander, see: ibid. (ed. Crawford 1953, p. 485, v. 170–179): "Sed huic contingit questio predicta, et est quod hoc quod modo est forma intellectui qui est in habitu, postquam non erat, provenit ab aliqua dispositione facta de novo in intellectu qui est in habitu que est causa quare ille intellectus est forma intellectui qui est in habitu postquam non erat. Et si ista dispositio non est receptio in intellectu qui est in habitu ad intellectum agentem, quid ergo est ista dispositio? Quoniam, si fuerit receptio, continget ut generatum recipiat eternum et assimiletur ei, et sic generatum fiet eternum; quod est impossible." I have previously argued for Aquinas's conceptual inspiration from this source in: Krause 2015b, pp. 175–217 and in Krause, forthcoming.

Objections

(1) For, according to the opinion of many, the angels were created in their natural powers alone.[14] But at the beginning of their creation, the angels saw things in the Word, as Augustine says in his *The Literal Meaning of Genesis*,[15] and this is called their morning cognition. Therefore, a created intellect, by its own natural powers, can see God through His essence.

(2) Furthermore, good and bad angels have nothing in common except their natural powers. But the bad angels see God through His essence, which is evident from that which is pronounced in Job 1:6 and 2:1: *When the sons of God came to stand before the Lord, Satan was also present among them.*[16] According to Gregory, however, those angels are called assistants of God who enjoy by the most intimate contemplation.[17] Therefore, the angels can see God through His essence by their own natural powers.

---

14. Petrus Lombardus, *Sententiae in IV libris distinctae*, l. 2, d. 3. q. 4 (ed. Grottaferrata, p. 343, v. 15–p. 344, v. 19). See also: Albertus Magnus, *Commentarii in II Sententiarum*, d. 3, q. 12 (ed. Borgnet 27, pp. 82–85); id., *Summa theologiae*, l. 2, q. 4, a. 18 (ed. Borgnet 32, pp. 222–223).

15. See: Augustinus Hipponensis, *De Genesi ad litteram*, l. II, c. 8 (ed. CSEL 28/1, p. 43, v. 25–28; p. 44, v. 5–p. 45, v. 4; PL 34, pp. 269–270): "conditio uero caeli prius erat in uerbo dei secundum genitam sapientiam, deinde facta est in creatura spirituali, hoc est in cognitione angelorum secundum creatam in illis sapientiam; <...> Neque enim sicut pecora solo sensu corporis uident angeli haec sensibilia; sed si quo sensu tali utuntur, agnoscunt ea potius, quae melius nouerunt interius in ipso dei uerbo, a quo inluminantur, ut sapienter uiuant, cum sit in eis lux, quae primo facta est, si lucem spiritualem in illo die factam intellegimus. quemadmodum ergo ratio, qua creatura conditur, prior est in uerbo dei quam ipsa creatura, quae conditur, sic et eiusdem rationis cognitio prius fit in creatura intellectuali, quae peccato non tenebrata est, ac deinde ipsa conditio creaturae. neque enim sicut nos ad percipiendam sapientiam proficiebant angeli, ut inuisibilia dei per ea, quae facta sunt, intellecta conspicerent. qui ex quo creati sunt, ipsa uerbi aeternitate sancta et pia contemplatione perfruuntur atque inde ista respicientes secundum id, quod intus uident, uel recte facta adprobant uel peccata inprobant. Nec mirum est, quod sanctis angelis suis in prima lucis conditione formatis prius deus ostendebat, quod erat deinceps creaturus. neque enim intellectum dei nossent, nisi quantum ipse monstrasset. quis enim cognouit intellectum domini? aut quis consiliarius illi fuit? aut quis prior dedit illi, et retribuetur ei? quoniam ex ipso et per ipsum et in ipso sunt omnia. ex ipso ergo discebant angeli, cum in eis fieret cognitio creaturae deinceps faciendae, ac deinde fieret in genere proprio."

16. Iob 1:6 (Vulgata 2007): *cum venissent filii Dei ut adsisterent coram Domino adfuit inter eos etiam Satan.* Iob 2:1 (Vulgata 2007): *cum quadam die venissent filii Dei et starent coram Domino venisset quoque Satan inter eos.*

17. See: Gregorius Magnus, *Moralia in Iob*, l. 2, c. 3 (ed. CCSL 143, p. 60, v. 1–p. 62, v. 44; PL 75, pp. 556–557).

(3) Furthermore, those who can see what is less intelligible can also see what is more intelligible, as the Commentator says in his <commentary on Aristotle's> *On the Soul*, book III.[18] But the divine essence is more intelligible than material objects, which are only intelligible because we make them intelligible. Yet because God Himself is free from matter in every way, He is intelligible in His own right. Therefore, since we see material creatures by our own natural powers, it seems all the more that we will be able to see God through His essence by our own natural powers; and this seems to be especially the case for the angels.

(4) Furthermore, as is said in Aristotle's *On the Soul*, book III: "Just as sight is related to a visible object, so too is the intellect related to an intelligible object."[19] But sight is prevented from vision only by something in one of four ways. In the first way, due to the corruption of sight, as when there is some spot on the pupil. This cannot be said of the angelic intellect even in its natural state because they are "pure and the brightest mirrors," as Dionysius says <in chapter IV of his *On Divine Names*>.[20] In another way, <sight is prevented> due

---

18. Averroes, *Commentarium magnum in Aristotelis De anima libros*, l. 3 com. 7 (ed. Crawford 1953, p. 418, v. 33–35): "Et dixit: *sed intellectus, quando intellexerit aliquod forte*, etc. Idest, intellectus autem, cum intellexerit aliquod forte intelligibile, tunc facilius intelliget intelligibile non forte" (emphasis as in edition). It should be noted that in his long commentary on Aristotle's *De anima*, Averroes maintains the opposite of how Aquinas reads him here. For Averroes, the scope of the intelligible objects which an intellect understands can be inferred from the intellectual power of that intellect. Hence, if there is an intellect that can understand what is more intelligible, this intellect can also understand what is less intelligible. In contrast, Aquinas's reading of this passage concentrates on the activity that the intellect performs in order to understand its object (and connected to this, it concentrates on the intellect's effort to render its object intelligible). Hence, since it is harder to understand something less intelligible than something more intelligible—because the less intelligible object has to be rendered intelligible—an intellect that has the ability to understand what is harder to understand (i.e. the less intelligible object) also has the ability to understand what is easier to understand (i.e. the more intelligible object).

19. Aristoteles, *De anima*, l. 3, lect. 1 (429a17–18); trans. vet. (ed. Gauthier 1985, p. 445): "sicut sensitiuum ad sensibilia, sic intellectiuum ad intelligibilia." Compare for Michael Scot's Latin translation from the Arabic: ibid., l. 3, tx. 3 (ed. Crawford 1953, p. 381, v. 4–5): "sicut sentiens apud sensibilia, sic intellectus apud intelligibilia."

20. Pseudo-Dionysius Areopagita, *De divinis nominibus*, c. 4, sect. 20, trans. Sarraceni (ed. Dionysiaca t. 1, p. 269): "imago Dei est angelus, manifestatio occulti luminis, speculum purum, clarissimum." See also: Albertus Magnus, *Super Dionysium De divinis nominibus*, c. 4 (ed. Colon. 37/1, p. 264, v. 85–86); ibid. (ed. Colon. 37/1, p. 265, v. 51–p. 267, v. 54, esp. p. 267, v. 30–46):

to the absence of the visible object. Yet this cannot be said in regard to what has been proposed because God is present to every intellect since He fills all things. In the third way, <sight is prevented> because something visible is not visible in actuality, as colors in darkness; for they only come to be visible in actuality through light. This also cannot be said in regard to what has been proposed because God is visible in His own right, since He is intelligible light (*lux*), as is evident from John 1:9.[21] In the fourth way, <sight is prevented> due to the excellence of the object which corrupts the senses. This also has no place in regard to what has been proposed. For the excellence of an intelligible object does not destroy the intellect as the excellence of a sensible object would destroy sense, as is said in Aristotle's *On the Soul* III.[22] Therefore, there is nothing that would prevent a created intellect from being able to see God through His essence by its own natural powers.

(5) Furthermore, any given object is cognized through its similitude. But an angel, according to its own nature, is an expressed similitude of God Himself, as Dionysius says in chapter IV of his *On Divine Names*, since an angel is "the image of God, the manifestation of the hidden light," that is, of the divine <light>.[23] Therefore, an angel can see God through His essence by its own proper nature.

(6) Furthermore, in the *Book of Causes* it is said that "every intelligence understands what is above it inasmuch as it is caused by

---

"Et accipiuntur omnes secundum similitudinem ad speculum corporale, quod manifestat aliquam formam. Si quantum ad essentialia, aut est susceptibilitas ipsa formae, et sic dicitur *speculum,* aut remotio a partibus opacis, et sic dicitur *purum,* aut est dispositio formalis tenens se ex parte materiae, faciens ad manifestationem, et sic dicitur *clarissimum.* Si autem accipitur per remotionem extrinsecus impedientis, aut illud est obscurans speculum in superficie et tantum per contactum, ita quod per se redit claritas, et sic dicitur *incontaminatum,* aut est profundius inhaerens, obtenebrans polluendo, sicut lutum immundat speculum, quae quidem immunditia per se non recedit statim, sed facile abstergitur, et sic dicit *incoinquinatum,* aut etiam serpit in profundissimum et inficiendo sicut macula, quae est ex inspectione menstruatae, quae etiam non facile abstergitur, et sic dicit *immaculatum*" (emphases as in edition).

21. Secundum Iohannem 1:9 (Vulgata 2007): *Erat lux vera quae inluminat omnem hominem venientem in mundum.*

22. Aristoteles, *De anima,* l. 3, lect. 1 (429a31-b4), trans. vet. (ed. Gauthier 1985, pp. 445–446): "Sensus enim non potest sentire ex ualde sensibili, ut sensus ex magnis sonis neque ex fortibus coloribus et odoribus neque uidere neque odorare; set intellectus, cum aliquid intelligat ualde intelligibile, non minus intelligit infima, set magis."

23. See note 20 above.

it."[24] But every created intellect by its nature is caused by God. Therefore, it can see God through His essence by its natural powers.

(7) Furthermore, it belongs to the immensity of the divine generosity that it shares with a creature everything of which <that creature> itself is capable. But a creature is capable of the gift that it may be able to see God through His essence by its own natural powers. For it can attain the vision of God through His essence by the light of glory. This is because light is superadded to nature in such a way that it could also be imparted to nature by God. Therefore, it has been bestowed to any creature that, by its own natural powers, it may attain the vision of God through His essence.

(8) Furthermore, the Commentator says in the beginning of the *New Metaphysics* that, if an intelligible were not understood by any intellect, this intelligible would exist in vain.[25] But it is absurd to say that the divine essence is an intelligible in vain. Therefore, some intellect can see it by its own nature.

❂ ❂ ❂

(1) On the contrary, it is said in Romans 6:23: *The grace of God, life everlasting.*[26] But the vision of God through His essence is eternal life as is evident from John 17:3: *This is eternal life: that they may know thee, the only true God, and Jesus Christ, whom thou hast sent.*[27] Therefore, it is only through grace that one can attain the vision of God through His essence.

---

24. *Liber de causis*, prop. 7 (8) (ed. Pattin 1966, p. 152, v. 6.15–16): "Omnis intelligentia scit quod est supra se <...> et scit quod illud quod est supra se est causa ei."

25. Averroes, *In Metaphysica*, l. 2, c. 1 (ed. Venetiis 1562, VIII.28 K; ed. Darms 1966, p. 54, v. 21–24). For the title *New Metaphysics* here, see: G. Vuillemin-Diem, *Praefatio*, in: Aristoteles, *Metaphysica*, I-IV.4, Trans. Iacobi sive 'Vetustissima' cum Scholiis et Trans. Composita sive 'Vetus' (ed. AL XXV 1–1a, p. xii): "Iisdem paene annis <1220–1230> Michaël Scotus latinum ex arabico fecit Averrois Commentarium Magnum quod per particulas disiectos libros Metaphysicae II, I.5–10, III–X, XII.1–10 (usque ad 1075b11) praebet; quae particulae ordine in unum conexae et sine intervallis vel commentario saepe descriptae 'Metaphysicae Novae' titulo saeculo iam decimo tertio donatae sunt."

26. Ad Romanos 6:23 (Vulgata 2007): *Gratia autem Dei vita aeterna.*

27. Secundum Iohannem 17:3 (Vulgata 2007): *Haec est autem vita aeterna, ut cognoscant te solum verum Deum et quem misisti Iesum Christum.*

(2) Furthermore, what is granted for love (*caritas*) as a reward, cannot be attained by natural powers since this love is also above nature. But the vision of God through His essence is granted for love as a reward, as is evident from John 14:21: *And he that loveth me, shall be loved by my Father, and I will manifest myself to him.*[28] Therefore, no one can attain the vision of God through His essence by their own natural powers.

(3) Furthermore, nature together with grace is stronger than nature alone. But the blessed, when they were in limbo, did not see God through His essence even though they possessed grace. Hence, it is said in their person in Tobit 5:12: *What manner of joy shall be to me, who sit in darkness, and see not the light of heaven?*[29] Therefore, it is even less possible for one to attain this vision by means of sheer natural powers.

(4) Furthermore, it is also the order of causes that is in accordance with the order of effects. For the nobler an effect, the nobler the cause. But among all things that can be beyond a pure creature, the greatest is that it see God through His essence. Therefore, the cause of this cannot be nature, but God alone Who is the highest cause of all.

Response

It should be said that in order for an intellect to see God through His essence, the divine essence must be united with our intellect in some way as its intelligible form.[30] Yet a form is conjoined to what is perfectible only when it has the dispositions by which it is rendered disposed to be affected (*susceptivum*) by such a form; as the

28. Secundum Iohannem 14:21, see article one, note 46. The Vulgate and Douay-Rheims editions add "and I will love him" (*et ego diligam eam*) before "and I will manifest myself to him" (*et manifestabo ei me ipsum*) (Douay-Rheims The Vulgate Bible 2010–2013). Aquinas, however, elides this phrase.

29. Tobiae 5:12 (Vulgata 2007): *Quale mihi gaudium erit qui in tenebris sedeo et lumen caeli non video.*

30. In his response, Aquinas talks about "our intellect" (*intellectui nostro*) whereas in article six as a whole, including the remainder of the response, he talks about all created intellects, including angelic intellects. This imprecise reference should not be over-interpreted.

body is united to the soul only when it has the proper dispositions to receive (*suspiciendam*) the soul.[31] Hence, in order for the intellect to be united with the divine essence in said way, there must be in it something like a disposition which prepares it for the said union. And this is the light by which the intellect is perfectly disposed (*perficitur*)[32] for seeing God through His essence.[33]

Yet this disposition cannot be natural to any created intellect. For the ultimate disposition for a form, according to the same reason (*eadem rationem*), is received into what is perfectible and the form itself, in such a way that if one is natural, the other is too. For what is perfectible by its ultimate disposition for the form, attains to the form itself. The form, however, which is the divine essence, exceeds all natural faculties and capacities. For a power and its proper act are always taken in the same genus. Hence, potency and act divide any given genus of being, as is evident from Aristotle's *Physics*, book III.[34] And thus, the faculty or the power of a creature extends only to the form of its own genus. And in this way, the divine essence that is outside every genus exceeds the natural faculty of any created intellect. And for this reason, the ultimate disposition, which is for the union of the intellect with such an essence, exceeds every faculty of nature. Hence, it cannot be natural but must be above nature.

---

31. The Latin verb *suscipere* here is translated with the two different English terms 'to be affected' and 'to receive.' This is because in the case of the human soul, a proper reception occurs which brings about a new substance, or, to be precise, the ontological composite of a human being. In the case of God as the intelligible of the human intellect, however, no new substance is brought about and no accident inheres in the human soul. Rather, God conjoins Himself to the intellect and functions as its form, as is evident from Aquinas's explanations in article one.

32. Although Aquinas writes *perficitur* in the Latin, which would require "perfected" as literal translation, I chose to translate it with the phrase "perfectly disposed" in view of the context. In fact, the light of glory is like a disposition for Aquinas: it disposes the intellect for the act of the beatific vision.

33. The terms which Aquinas uses in this passage to describe the light of glory, "by way of a disposition" (*per modum dispositionis*), "perfectly disposed" (*perficitur*), and the argument in the following passage, which explains that the light of glory must be supernatural, are inspired by Averroes's critical discussions of Alexander of Aphrodisias's conception of ultimate conjunction. For these discussions, see: Averroes, *Commentarium magnum in Aristotelis De anima libros*, l. 3, com. 36 (ed. Crawford 1953, p. 481, v. 58–p. 485, v. 179).

34. Aristoteles, *Physica*, l. 3, c. 1 (201a9–10), trans. vet. (AL VII 1.2, p. 98, v. 13–14): "Diviso autem secundum unumquodque genus hoc quidem ἐντελεχείᾳ esse alio autem potentia."

And this disposition is the light of glory of which it is said in Psalm 35:10: *In thy light we shall see light.*[35]

In accordance with its natural faculty, however, the created intellect can attain the cognition of God through created forms, either infused into it or acquired by it. But this cognition is neither the vision of Him through His essence, as is evident from previous considerations, nor is 'what He is' (*quid est*) known through it, but only 'that He is' (*quia est*) and 'what He is not' (*quid non est*).

Replies to Objections

(1) To the first, therefore, it should be said that, in their original condition, the angels did not see the Word through His essence. Nonetheless, they saw It through a created similitude, namely, through their own nature, which is a similitude of God. And this is the case whether they are taken to be created in grace or not, so long as they are not taken to be created in glory. Hence, the evening cognition by which they cognize themselves in their proper nature precedes the morning cognition in them by which they cognize things in the Word. This is clear because the first day has evening without morning.

(2) To the second, it should be said that the devil is not said to have appeared before God as if he had seen Him through His essence, but because he was seen by God, and because God's providence extends to him just as it does to the good angels, in the way in which we say that those things stand before us that are subject to our providence. Hence, "to appear before" or "to serve" are said equivocally.

(3) To the third, it should be said that something can be more intelligible in itself but still less intelligible to another intellect. This is evidently the case with our intellect. For the faculty of our intellect is limited to sensible forms that come to be intelligible in actuality by the agent intellect because in this way the phantasms are related to our intellect

35. Psalmi Iuxta LXX 35:10, see article one, note 40.

as the sensible things to the senses, as is said in <Aristotle's> *On the Soul*, book III.[36] And for this reason, our intellect must be naturally led to all objects that it understands through sensible forms, as Dionysius also says.[37] And because the separate substances, which are in themselves intelligible to the highest degree, exceed the genus of sensible forms, for this reason, our intellect is found to be insufficient for cognizing them. Because of this, it is said in <Aristotle's> *Metaphysics*, book II, that our intellect is related to what is most manifest by nature as the eye of the night owl is to the sun.[38]

The natural faculty of the angelic intellect, however, even though it is not limited to sensible forms, is nonetheless limited to created forms that are of its genus. And for this reason, just as our intellect is insufficient for the cognition of separate substances, so is the angelic intellect all the more insufficient for the vision of God through His essence, according to its natural faculty. The assertion of the Commentator, however, must be understood as regarding created intelligibles.[39]

---

36. Aristoteles, *De anima*, l. 3, lect. 6 (431a14–17), trans. vet. (ed. Gauthier 1985, p. 477): "Set intellectiue anime fantasmata ut sensibilia sunt <...>; ex quo nequaquam sine fantasmate intelligit anima." For Michael Scot's translation from the Arabic, see: ibid., l. 3, tx. 30 (ed. Crawford 1953, p. 468, v. 1–6): "Et in anima sensibili inveniuntur ymagines secundum modos sensuum. <...>. Et ideo nichil intelligit anima sine ymaginatione."

37. Pseudo-Dionysius Areopagita, *De caelesti hierarchia,* c. 1, sect. 56, trans. Eriugenae (ed. Dionysiaca t. 2, p. 735): "Quoniam neque est possibile nostro animo ad non-materialem illam ascendere caelestium hierarchiarum imitationem et contemplationem, nisi ea quae secundum ipsum est materiali manuductione utatur <...>." See also: Albertus Magnus, *Super Dionysium De caelesti hierarchia*, c. 1 (ed. Colon. 36/1, p. 13, v. 37–42): "*Quoniam neque possibile est nostro animo*, idest intellectui, *ascendere ad illam non-materialem imitationem et contemplationem caelestium hierarchiarum,* quia contemplando eas imitamur, *nisi utatur ea materiali manuductione quae secundum ipsum est,* idest repraesentatione materialium sibi connaturali" (emphases as in edition).

38. Aristoteles, *Metaphysica*, l. 2, c. 1 (993b9–11), trans. Iacobi (AL XXV. 1–1a, p. 36, v. 12–14): "Sicut enim noctuarum lumina ad lunam habent quod est secundum diem, sic nostre anime intellectus ad natura manifestissima omnium." In the Greek original, Aristotle speaks of a bat rather than a night owl, but in the Latin translation of James of Venice, the Greek original *νυκτερις / νυκτεριδος* was rendered with Latin *noctua*. This passage was of crucial importance for Albert the Great's early theory of human cognition, to which the young Thomas Aquinas is deeply indebted. See, for instance: Albertus Magnus, *De incarnatione* (ed. Colon. 26, p. 181, v. 3–7). For secondary literature concerning this important passage in Albert and Aquinas, see: Steel 2001.

39. See objection three, p. 185, above for reference.

(4) To the fourth, it should be said that the created intellect is not prevented in its ability to see God naturally through His essence by a deficiency in the divine essence, as if it were in its own right not intelligible in actuality, but <it is prevented by a deficiency> on the side of the created intellect. First, <this is> due to a deficiency of the created intellectual power whose natural faculty is limited to created being (*ens*). Nonetheless, this deficiency differs in angels and in humans in accordance with their natural powers as they must be considered. For in the angelic intellect, no deficiency is found from the nature (*ratio*) of its genus, but in comparison to an intellect outside its genus, namely the divine <intellect>. For it possesses every perfection owed to the genus of intellect by which it is confined only insofar as it is a created intellect. For the uncreated intellect is outside <any> genus. But the human intellect also suffers from a defect in accordance with the nature (*ratio*) of its genus because in it the intelligible light is obscured. Hence, Isaac <Israeli> says that its nature (*ratio*) arises in the shadow of intelligence.[40] Second, this <deficiency> is due to the absence of the intelligible. For even though the divine essence is present in everything, it is nonetheless not present in any intellect as intelligible form. This occurs only when there is a disposition in the intellect sufficient for it to be capable of a union with the divine essence as with an intelligible form. Third, this is due to the excess of brightness of the divine essence beyond any form through which the created intellect naturally understands. And likewise, as a

40. Isaac Israeli, *Liber de definicionibus* (ed. Muckle 1937–1938, p. 313, v. 25–27): "Sublimiore ergo animarum gradu et meliore ordine est anima racionalis, quoniam ipsa in horizonte intelligenciae et ex umbra eius generata est." Aquinas may well have been familiar with this quotation from Albert. See for instance: Albertus Magnus, *De homine* (ed. Colon. 27/2, p. 15, v. 7–13); ibid. (ed. Colon. 27/2, p. 75, v. 61–66; p. 155, v. 31–34; p. 409, v. 1–6); id., *Commentarii in I Sententiarum*, d. 25C, q. 1, a. 1, ad 2 (ed. Borgnet 25, p. 626): "Ad Aliud dicendum, quod rationale dicitur communiter, et proprie. Communiter prout per prius et posterius est in divina, angelica, et humana natura: et tunc rationalis natura discretiva veri et falsi, et boni et mali: proprie autem sumitur prout dicit Isaac, quod ratio incipit in umbra intelligentiae, quia intelligentia accipit in intellectu deiformi. Ratio autem inquirens, et studens, et discursitans (ut dicit Dionysius) habet acceptiones propter majorem sui obtenebrationem, et ideo cadit in diffinitione hominis: et est differentia divisiva animalis. Verum est tamen, quod Gregorius in Homilia Epiphaniae vocat Angelum animal rationale: sed hoc alibi expeditum est, quod dicitur animal non a natura animalis, sed potius a vi animalis, ut videtur velle Dionysius quia vim habet discretivam sensibilium et rationalium."

consequence, a created intellect is insufficient for the vision of God through His essence, even though the immensity of the divine essence does not corrupt the intellect, but rather strengthens it.

(5) To the fifth, it should be said that the created intellect can attain the cognition of God through some created similitude from its own natural powers. But this cognition is not the vision of God through His essence, as was shown above.

(6) To the sixth, it should be said that the effect retains a similitude of its cause. And from this it follows that an intelligence naturally cognizes its cause from the similitude that it has to it. But this is not the vision of God through His essence, as was said.

(7) To the seventh, it should be said that nothing whatsoever that is superadded to a creature can be of the constitution of its nature. For what belongs to the property of a superior nature cannot be shared with an inferior nature so that it possesses it naturally, unless <this inferior nature> is turned into a superior nature. Just as it cannot be shared with the diaphanous medium that it become luminous in the absence of light, unless it becomes itself luminous, even though light is shared with it by a luminous body. Yet it is the property of the uncreated intellect to be determined (*determinari*) to the uncreated intelligible form. And for this reason, the light by which the intellect is united with the uncreated intelligible form can be shared with the created intellect, but not such that it might possess this light naturally unless it were turned into an uncreated intellect. And this is impossible.

(8) To the eighth, it should be said that even if no intellect were to understand the divine essence, neither by nature nor by grace, the divine essence would not be an intelligible in vain. This is because it understands itself and because it does not exist because of another. Yet for something to be in vain happens only for those things that are because of another which they do not attain.[41]

---

41. Here Aquinas refers to those intelligibles that are infused into the human mind (or into the angelic mind) and thus caused intelligibles (rather than the uncaused divine essence). These caused intelligibles, however, do not and cannot sufficiently represent the divine essence, since they are less formal and thus less intelligible. These intelligibles, then, are in vain since they do not disclose the essence of God to the knowing intellect.

ARTICLE 7

On the Impossibility of Seeing God in This Life

INTRODUCTION

The discussion of the beatific vision that the blessed will enjoy in the afterlife in virtue of the new disposition of the light of glory was closely related to the question of whether it was also possible to enjoy such a vision already in this life on the basis of natural means. If it were possible, ultimate happiness would be attainable here and now and, perhaps even more drastic a thought, on the basis of one's own means and merits.[1] For Aquinas such a scenario was simply impossible, although, at this stage of his career, not one that required solid refutation.[2] Happiness, he proposed in a dramatic statement

1. For the century-long Latin discussions of the theme of divine visions in this life, and the different turns it took, see Wicki 1954, pp. 161–174.

2. Nonetheless, Aquinas was well aware of the fact that Albert the Great developed his thoughts in this direction in his lectures at Cologne between 1248 and 1252, commenting on the *corpus Dionysiacum* and Aristotle's *Nicomachean Ethics* (see section VII of the general introduction). Concerning Albert's teachings on intellectual development and ultimate happiness in these works, see: Albertus Magnus, *Super Dionysium De divinis nominibus*, c. 4 (ed. Colon. 37/1, p. 133 v. 71–74): "cum a Philosophis distinguatur quadruplex intellectus, scilicet agens, possibilis, formalis et adeptus, videtur, quod debuerit distinguere istos quattuor intellectus <...>." Id., *Super Ethica*, l. 10, lect. 1 (ed. Colon. 14/2, p. 708 v. 4–15): "Boethius dicit in libro de consolatione philosophiae: 'Felix, qui potuit boni fontem visere lucidum, felix, qui potuit gravis terrae solvere vincula.' In quibus verbis trahitur et tangitur tota materia huius decimi libri; bonum enim maxime est illud quod per se bonum est et ad quod alia ordinantur, et hoc praecipue est perfecta operatio intellectus speculativi, quae dicitur felicitas contemplativa." In his commentary on Aristotle's *On the Soul* (ca. 1254), Albert is even more explicit, see: id., *De anima*, l. 3, tr. 3 c. 11 (ed. Colon. 7/1, p. 221 v. 73–p. 222 v. 9.24–26: "intellecta speculata dupliciter fiunt in nobis; quaedam enim fiunt in nobis per naturam, ita quod non accipimus ea

at the beginning of his reply to article seven, is an ultimate end, and this life is unquestionably devoid of it. In support of his statement, Aquinas cited Aristotle's *Nicomachean Ethics* as his authority, where the philosopher described happiness as an activity that is

> in accordance with the highest virtue. Yet this will certainly be of the best thing. <...> For this activity is also the best thing. For the intellect is also <the best thing> of those which are in us, as are the cognoscible objects pertaining to the intellect. But it is also the most continuous. For we can also contemplate (*speculari*) more continuously than we can act in any other way.[3]

With this reference, Aquinas linked his reply here to an earlier discussion in his *Sentences*, as discussed in the introductions to articles one and six. There, he had identified happiness to lie in the disembodied human soul alone rather than in the human being in this

per aliquid vel ab aliquo doctore nec per inquisitionem invenimus ea, sicut sunt 'dignitates demonstrationum primae,' quae sunt prima et vera, ante quae omnino nulla sunt, quae non scimus ex sensu, nisi inquantum terminos cognoscimus, notitia autem terminorum non facit notitiam principiorum nisi per accidens. Quaedam autem speculata fiunt in nobis per voluntatem, quia scilicet studemus inveniendo et audiendo a doctore, et haec omnia fiunt intellectu agente influente eis intelligibilitatem, et faciendo haec intellecta secundum actum esse intellecta intellectus agens coniungitur nobis ut efficiens. Et quia omnibus his influit intellectualitatem et denudationem, sunt omnia sibi similia in hoc quod separata sunt et nuda; et ideo in omnibus his accipit continue intellectus possibilis lumen agentis et efficitur sibi similior et similior de die in diem. Et hoc vocatur a philosophis moveri ad continuitatem et coniunctionem cum agente intellectu; et cum sic acceperit omnia intelligibilia, habet lumen agentis ut formam sibi adhaerentem, et cum ipse sit lumen suum, eo quod lumen suum est essentia sua et non est extra ipsum, tunc adhaeret intellectus agens possibili sicut forma materiae. Et hoc sic compositum vocatur a Peripateticis intellectus adeptus et divinus; et tunc homo perfectus est ad operandum opus illud quod est opus suum, inquantum est homo, et hoc est opus, quod operatur deus, et hoc est perfecte per seipsum contemplari et intelligere separata. <...> Et tunc homo perfectus et divinus effectus est ad suum opus, inquantum homo et non animal est, perficiendum <...>." The development of Albert's teachings on intellectual perfection in this life has been excellently summarized in: Anzulewicz 2003, pp. 165–218.

3. Aristoteles, *Ethica Nicomachea*, l. 10, c. 8 (77a12–13 and 77a19–21), trans. Grosseteste: recensio pura (AL XXVI 1–3, p. 358, v. 25–26 and p. 359, v. 3–5): "Si autem est felicitas secundum virtutem operacio, racionabile secundum optimam. Hec autem utique erit, optimi. <...> Optima et enim hec est operacio. Et enim intellectus, eorum que in nobis, et cognoscibilium, circa que intellectus. Est autem continuissima. Speculari et enim possumus continue magis quam operari quodcumque." Ibid., trans. Grosseteste: recensio recognita (AL XXVI 1–3, p. 576, v. 10–11 and 18–21): "Si autem *felicitas est* secundum virtutem operacio, racionabile secundum optimam; hec autem utique erit optimi. <...> Optima et enim *hec* operacio; et enim intellectus eorum que in nobis et cognoscibilium circa que intellectus" (emphases as in edition).

life; and in an activity attained in virtue of the infused new disposition of the light of glory, rather than on the basis of acquired virtues, as Aristotle had intended it. In this discussion, however, it was not Aristotle alone, as most of the secondary literature has for some time maintained, but rather some early Parisian commentaries on the two incomplete translations of Aristotle's *Nicomachean Ethics* (the so-called *Ethica vetus* and *Ethica nova*) that seem to have aided Aquinas's seemingly unusual connection of Aristotle's *Nicomachean Ethics* with the Christian understanding of heavenly happiness.[4]

Aquinas's explicit reliance on Aristotle to reason for ultimate happiness in the afterlife may thus come as no surprise to learned historians of medieval philosophy, but it was not the only way to use the Stagirite in this context. Albert the Great, around 1247, was the first Scholastic thinker to have access to the full translation of the *Nicomachean Ethics* made by Robert Grosseteste. He opted for a contrary interpretation in his *Sentences*. According to Albert, Aristotle did not speak about heavenly happiness. Rather, he and the Peripatetic philosophers, such as Alfarabi and Averroes, were concerned solely with the different states of earthly happiness.[5] The authority

4. For this discussion as a whole, see: Thomas Aquinas, *Commentum in quatuor libros Sententiarum*, l. 4, d. 49, q. 1, a. 1, qcc. 1–4 (ed. Parma 7/2, pp. 1181–1186). For an extended discussion of this theme including references to other secondary literature, see: Krause 2015a, pp. 15–56.

5. Albertus Magnus, *Commentarii in IV Sententiarum*, d. 49B, a. 6 (ed. Borgnet 30, pp. 674–675): "Ad haec solvenda praenotandum est, quod *beatitudo* dicitur multipliciter, et non aequivoce, sed secundum prius et posterius. Dicitur autem secundum statum perfectionis viae, et secundum statum perfectionis patriae. Secundum statum autem viae dicitur tripliciter, scilicet proprie, large, et per causam. *Proprie* autem dicitur dupliciter, scilicet secundum virtutem moralem, et secundum virtutem intellectualem: et ideo Aristoteles in *Ethicis* facit duos libros de *felicitate*: primum enim fecit de felicitate morali, secundum autem de felicitate intellectuali. <...> Et Alpharabius in commento Arabico dicit, quod impotentia et paupertas et infortunia pronepotis contristant beatitudinem, et ita impediunt optimum actum beati. <...> Felicitas enim contemplativa dicitur dupliciter, scilicet secundum esse, et secundum suum maximum posse. Et secundum esse quidem consistit in perfectione actus intelligentiae speculativae cum delectatione contemplationis quae non habet contrarium, sicut expresse probatur in ultimo capite libri X *Ethicorum*; perfectio autem speculativae intelligentiae est praecipue in simplicium substantiarum speculatione et substantiae primae. Secundum autem maximum suum posse habet praedictam speculationem cum remotione impedimenti intus et extra et sic virtutes morales conferunt ad beatitudinem contemplativam, et abundantia exteriorum, et locus solitarius et liber, et hujusmodi. Et propter hoc dicit Averroes in commento, quod est felicitas eremitarum" (emphases as in edition).

who for him most aptly explained the reality of ultimate happiness was Boethius, and in reliance on Boethius's *Consolation of Philosophy*, Albert identified ultimate happiness as "an adherence to God in whom all desired things are had."[6] Albert, therefore, separated the two realms of philosophical and theological happiness nicely in accordance with his separation of the sciences, which he began in the second book of his *Sentences*.[7]

The consequences of the lasting connection that Aquinas drew between the Aristotelian principles discussed in this introduction and Christian eschatology were far-reaching for his conception of happiness, as emerges from the present article. As a general rule which allowed for no exceptions, Aquinas insisted that without the *sine qua non* condition of the new disposition—that is, the light of glory—ultimate happiness, which for him consisted in the vision of God in His essence, would be impossible. Since the new disposition could not be natural to humans or angels but had to be supernatural (*supra naturam*), as seen in the previous article, the attainment of happiness, too, was impossible on the basis of natural dispositions inhering in creatures. Indeed, Aquinas took creaturely cognition to be limited to the scope of the activity with which these natural

6. Ibid. (ed. Borgnet 30, p. 675): "Beatitudo autem secundum statum patriae est inhaerere Deo, et in ipso habere omnia quae appetuntur: et sic diffinitur a Boetio beatitudo."

7. Id., *Commentarii in II Sententiarum*, d. 14, a. 6 (ed. Borgnet 27, p. 266): "Alibi etiam disputatum est de ista materia multum et prolixe: et ibi secuti sumus dicta quorundam Magistrorum theologiae, qui voluerunt opiniones naturalium ad theologiam reducere dicendo quod Angeli deserviunt Deo in motibus caelorum, et quod illi ab eis *animae* dicuntur: sed nihil ita secure dicitur, sicut quod sola Dei voluntate moveantur, et natura propria non contrariante motui" (emphasis as in edition). An extended discussion of this passage is found in: Anzulewicz 2009, pp. 219–242, esp. pp. 219–220. A similar picture already emerges indirectly from Albert's conception of the science of theology at the beginning of the first book of his *Sentences*, see: id., *Super I librum Sententiarum*, d. 1, c. 1 (ed. Colon. 29/1 p. 10, v. 3–p. 15, v. 61, and esp. p. 14, v. 41–55): "Ad primum ergo quod obicitur dicendum quod ista scientia principalissime dicitur sapientia, eo quod ipsa est de altissimis et altissimo modo, quia de deo et per principia fidei; aliae autem sapientiae, quae a philosophis sunt inventae, et si sapientiae dicantur, quia sunt de altis, non tamen sunt altissimo modo, sed potius per principia, quae sub ratione sunt. Sic dico etiam quod ipsa sola libera est vel aliis liberior; dicitur enim scientia libera, sicut dicit Philosophus, sicut homo liber, scilicet quia gratia sui et non propter alterum est. Et hoc est propter scitum, quod quaeritur in illa, quod per se desideratum est. Hoc autem praecipue deus est, quem omnes scire scientia beatificante desiderant, et ideo libera est, quia hoc scitum non quaeritur propter aliud, sed propter se."

dispositions were endowed innately; and he allowed for no transcending or surpassing of these innate limitations.

What we can gather from Aquinas's argument concerning the importance of the correct disposition is twofold. On the one hand, it was once again ontology that proved responsible for the static boundaries of activities. These activities were, in the human case, limited to the constraints of knowing through intelligible forms that were ultimately derived from sense experience, and, in the angelic case, limited to the intuitive constraints of knowing through co-created or infused species. On the other hand, it was the notion of disposition that played the central role in his justification of the general rule. The importance of Aquinas's creative reliance on Averroes's *Long Commentary on Aristotle's On the Soul* is thus even greater than it seemed from articles one and six.

While the general rule thus allowed for no exceptions on the natural end in this life, Aquinas nonetheless allowed for God to overrule it miraculously. Miracles such as a virgin birth, the burning of fire in water, corporeal agility under a state of heaviness, or corporeal inviolacy under conditions of great harm all constituted divine intervention against the ordinary course of nature. This course, as Aquinas explained, was bound to the natural dispositions inherent in creatures, dispositions which supplied them with a given range of possibilities for acting. Any action beyond this range required an intervention by God, whose power alone it was to act in all ways possible. In the present article, Aquinas uses the example of the blind man to whom God miraculously grants the activity of seeing. Any earthly beatific vision, Aquinas envisioned along the same lines: Out of its natural powers, no creature could attain a vision of God's essence. But on the basis of God's miraculous intervention, that is, on the basis of His granting His power to a creature *against* its own nature, and not simply *beyond* its own nature as in the afterlife, the given creature could come to see God face to face in this life. Rather than any disposition or power inhering permanently in the creature, it would be God making the beatific vision possible transiently in this life. But how was this granting of His power to a creature possible?

The two themes that Aquinas interwove in his reasoning in article seven were those of the beatific vision and miracles, the theme of miracles being the key to answering the question. Earlier in his *Sentences*, Aquinas defined miracles to be subject to two conditions: (1) all miracles require a hidden cause, and (2) that upon which this hidden cause acts ought to be intended for another.[8] Both conditions certainly apply to the beatific vision in this life: God is the most hidden cause of all, and the intellect of the human being is intended for knowing through intelligible forms gathered from sense experience in this life. This is the reason that the beatific vision in this life is against nature (*contra naturam*), and not simply above nature (*supra naturam*) or beyond nature (*praeter naturam*).[9] In Aquinas's eyes, knowing through intelligible species is an act contrary to the beatific vision, which entails knowing through God's essence. To remove the contrariety of act, therefore, the human person necessarily must be taken out of the act of knowing through intelligible species before attaining the vision of God through His essence. This violence against nature is also the reason that the vision in this life cannot be permanent. It goes against the natural habit inherent in the creature and therefore cannot last.[10] But would both conditions

---

8. Thomas Aquinas, *Scriptum super libros Sententiarum*, l. 2, d. 18, q. 1, a. 3, ad 1 (ed. Mandonnet II, p. 456): "Ad primum dicendum, quod creatio, proprie loquendo, non est opus miraculosum, quia deficit una conditio miraculi: quamvis enim causam occultam habeat, tamen non est in re unde aliter esse deberet: immo esse rerum naturali quodam ordine a primo ente producitur, quamvis non per necessitatem naturae."

9. Id., *Scriptum super libros Sententiarum*, l. 2, d. 18, q. 1, a. 3 (ed. Mandonnet II, p. 456): "Contra naturam autem dicitur fieri, quando in re est aliquid contrarium ei quod fit, sicut si grave sursum moveretur, et quod virgo peperit, vel aliquid hujusmodi; ita quod miraculose sequatur actus manente contraria natura, quae scilicet est principium contrarii actus." For an explicit discussion of these three different states beyond nature in the direct context of rapture, see: Albertus Magnus, *Quaestio de raptu*, a. 1 (ed. Colon. 25/2, p. 87, v. 2–9): "Si vero attendamus actum intelligentiae in via, quo ipsa accipit cognitionem dei ex phantasmate imaginis et vestigii—et sine tali acceptione non habet actum cognitionis in via—contra naturam huiusmodi exitus ad actum erit non ex phantasmate, sed immediata inspectione videre. Et hoc attendens glossa dicit raptum esse elevationem contra naturam."

10. Thomas Aquinas, *Scriptum super libros Sententiarum*, l. 2, d. 11, q. 2, a. 4, ad 4 (ed. Mandonnet II, p. 291): "Ad quartum dicendum, quod Paulus in illo raptu secundum quid participavit statum comprehensorum, non tamen tanta gloria perfectus fuit ut lumen in angelos transfundere posset: quia, ut dicitur, factus est illius gloriae particeps miraculose quantum ad actum, et non quantum ad habitum, quod est lumen gloriae."

not equally apply to the beatific vision in the afterlife? Would it not be possible to maintain that the disembodied intellect of the blessed saint is intended for knowing through infused species? Although Aquinas did not address this matter here, it seems that knowing through infused intelligibles under the afterworldly conditions of immutability is not a contrary act to the blessed saint's intellectual activity of intuitive cognition. Rather, this act only requires perfection that lies beyond his natural ability. This is why it is to be considered supernatural (*supra naturam*), as we saw in article six. Just as in the case of the angels, the blessed saint would be given a new disposition, the light of glory, to exercise a new act under remaining circumstantial conditions.

In his replies to the objections, however, these two themes, the beatific vision and miracles, did not exhaust Aquinas's discussions. He also paid increasing attention to other supernatural visions of things divine that he considered to come in different grades in this life. Along the lines of the Augustinian division of corporeal visions, imaginative visions, and intellectual visions, Aquinas showed that all of them, which were thought to be had by certain biblical figures, were not visions of God's essence, with the exception of those of Moses and Paul, but rather visions of divine truths through created sensibles, images, or intelligibles.[11]

11. This threefold division stems from Augustine, and served as a common denominator for Latin medieval accounts of supernatural knowledge in this life. See, for instance: Augustinus Hipponensis, *De Genesi ad litteram*, l. XII, c. 6 (CSEL 28/1, p. 386, v. 22–p. 387 v. 4; PL 34, p. 458): "Quod autem non imaginaliter, sed proprie uidetur et non per corpus uidetur, hoc ea uisione uidetur, quae omnes ceteras superat. harum species atque differentias, quantum me dominus adiuuerit, explicare curabo. ecce in hoc uno praecepto cum legitur: diliges proximum tuum tamquam te ipsum, tria uisionum genera occurrunt: unum per oculos, quibus ipsae litterae uidentur, alterum per spiritum hominis, quo proximus et absens cogitatur, tertium per contuitum mentis, quo ipsa dilectio intellecta conspicitur." Petrus Lombardus, *Sententiae in IV libris distinctae*, l. 3, d. 23, c. 7 (ed. Grottaferrata, p. 146 v. 13–14). Solutions to the different visions along this threefold division that are parallel and strikingly similar to Aquinas's use in the present article are found in Albert the Great. See: Albertus Magnus, *De prophetia I*, a. 2, § 4 (ed. Colon. 25/2, p. 65 v. 10–p. 71 v. 48); id., *Commentarii in III Sententiarum*, d. 23, a. 16 (ed. Borgnet 28, p. 433–434); id., *Quaestio de raptu*, a. 2, § 1 (ed. Colon. 25/2, p. 90, v. 11–18): "Dicendum videtur, quod in visione corporali et imaginaria non sit raptus. Cuius ratio est, quia raptus principaliter consideratur penes excellentiam obiecti ad statum viae. Obiectum enim secundum illum modum quo beatificat beatos, excedit omnem statum viae et modum. Cum igitur in visione corporali et imaginaria nihil obiciatur super statum viae, in illis non erit raptus."

But Aquinas also returned to a theme he had discussed in article one: Avempace's account of how knowledge of separate substances can be achieved. In repeating Averroes's objection against Avempace—that there are no theoretical principles on whose basis anything beyond the empirically acquired universals can be known to humans in this life—Aquinas established generally speaking that the sciences never reach knowledge of those things that lie beyond the physical world. Later in his career, especially in his *Summa against the Gentiles*, Aquinas would develop this idea further, and it would become a hallmark of his conception of human epistemology.[12]

TRANSLATION

To the seventh article we proceed as follows. It seems that God can be seen through His essence in this life.

Objections

(1) For it is said in Isaiah 6:1–3: *I saw the Lord sitting upon a throne high and elevated. All the earth was full of His majesty. And the Seraphim cried out loudly.*[13] But He whose majesty fills the entire world is He who is God essentially. Therefore, Isaiah, living in this life, saw God through His essence.

(2) Furthermore, seeing God face to face is seeing God through His essence as is evident from I Corinthians 13:12.[14] For this is how the

---

12. Thomas Aquinas, *Summa contra gentiles*, l. 3, c. 39 (ed. Leon. 14, pp. 95–96): "Quod felicitas humana non consistit in cognitione Dei quae habetur per demonstrationem." Ibid., l. 3, c. 41 (ed. Leon. 14, pp. 102–104): "Utrum in hac vita homo possit intelligere substantias separatas per studium et inquisitionem scientiarum speculativarum." For a discussion on the Arabic context, see: Wirmer 2014.

13. Iesaias 6:1–3 (Vulgata 2007): *vidi Dominum sedentem super solium excelsum et elevatum et ea quae sub eo erant implebant templum seraphin stabant super illud sex alae uni et sex alae alteri duabus velabant faciem eius et duabus velabant pedes eius et duabus volabant et clamabant alter ad alterum et dicebant sanctus sanctus sanctus Dominus exercituum plena est omnis terra gloria eius.* Aquinas's citation of the passage here makes changes to the order of the biblical text and is abbreviated. It reads as follows in Latin (ed. Parma 7/2, p. 1209): "*Vidi Dominum sedentem super solium excelsum et elevatum; et plena erat omnis terra majestate ejus; et Seraphim clamabant*" (emphasis as in edition). In my adaptation of the Douay-Rheims translation (Douay-Rheims The Vulgate Bible 2010–2013), I follow Aquinas's wording.

14. Ad Corinthios I 13:12, see section II of the general introduction, note 1.

Apostle characterizes the blessed vision. But Jacob, living in this life, saw God face to face. Hence, he says in Genesis 32:30: *I have seen God face to face and my soul has been saved.*[15] Therefore, someone in this life can see God through His essence.

(3) Furthermore, <it is said> in Job 42:5: *With the hearing of the ear, I have heard thee, but now my eye seeth thee.*[16] Yet sight is of things present, whereas hearing is of things absent. Therefore, after Job had cognized God through hearing Him in absence, as it were, he nonetheless, while he still lived in this life, saw God through His essence in presence, as it were.

(4) Furthermore, it is said of Moses in Numbers 12:8: *Plainly, and not by riddles and figures doth he see the Lord.*[17] But any vision of God is either through a figure or through His essence, as is evident from I Corinthians 13:12.[18] Therefore, Moses, living in this life, saw God through His essence.

(5) Furthermore, <explaining> II Corinthians 12:2: *Such a one caught up to the third heaven,*[19] the Gloss says that "God discloses to the apostle the life in which He is to be seen in eternity." And in this way, "the apostle is caught up so that he sees God in Himself and not in some image."[20] And further on, <the Gloss> says that "in

---

15. Genesis 32:30 (Vulgata 2007): *vidi Deum facie ad faciem et salva facta est anima mea.*

16. Iob 42:5, see article two, note 10.

17. Numeri 12:8, see section II of the general introduction, note 2.

18. Ad Corinthios I 13:12, see section II of the general introduction, note 1.

19. Ad Corinthios II 12:2 (Vulgata 2007): *raptum eiusmodi usque ad tertium caelum.* Note that Aquinas here replaces *eiusmodi* with *huiusmodi* just as Albert the Great does in his *Quaestio de raptu.* I amend the Douay-Rheims translation according to Aquinas's version (Douay-Rheims The Vulgate Bible 2010–2013). For Albert's quotation of the passage, see: Albertus Magnus, *Quaestio de raptu*, a. 1 (ed. Colon. 25/2, p. 85, v. 32).

20. *Glossa interlin. et marg.* II Ad Cor. 12:2 (ed. Rusch, vol. IV, p. 358): "ostendit ei deus vitam in qua videndus est in eternum. <...> Ad hanc raptus est apostolus ut ipsum deum in se, non in figura aliqua videret." See also: Petrus Lombardus, *In epistulas Pauli*, II Ad Corinthios 12:2 (PL 192, p. 80B-D): "Tertium coelum spirituale, ubi angeli et sanctae animae fruuntur Dei contemplatione. Ad quod cum dicit se raptum, significat quod Deus ostendit ei vitam in qua videndus est in aeternum. [Augustinus] Vel tres coeli intelliguntur tria genera visionum. Et est sensus: Scio hominem hujusmodi raptum, id est contra naturam elevatum, usque ad tertium coelum, id est ad cognitionem deitatis. <...> Tertium coelum est intellectualis visio, quando nec corpora nec imagines eorum videntur, sed incorporeis substantiis intuitus mentis mira Dei potentia figitur.

the third order of the angels, there are the Thrones, the Cherubim, and the Seraphim, who contemplate God from nearby. In a way similar to them, the apostle is said to have seen God."[21] From all these things it is clearly disclosed that <the apostle> saw God through His essence. And in this way, the same follows as before.

(6) Furthermore, according to what Augustine <says> in his *The Literal Meaning of Genesis*, book XII, those things are seen with an intellectual vision that are in the soul through its essence. But an intellectual vision is of intelligible things themselves, not through any similitudes but through their essences, as Augustine says.[22] Therefore, since God is in the soul of a wayfarer through His essence, it seems that he sees Him through His essence.

(7) Furthermore, affect is more corrupted by sin than intellect because sin is in the will, as Augustine says.[23] But affect can love

---

Ad hanc raptus est Apostolus, ut ipsum Deum in se non in aliqua figura videret. Et haec visio duabus aliis multo excellentior est. Quod ergo non per corpus videtur nec imaginabiliter, sed proprie, hoc ea visione videtur quae omnes alias superat. Occurrunt enim tria genera visionum, unum per oculos quibus ipse litterae videntur; alterum, per spiritum hominis, quo proxima et absentia cogitantur; tertium, per contuitum mentis, quo ipsa dilectio intellecta conspicitur. In his tribus generibus illud primum manifestum est omnibus quo videtur coelum et terra, et omnia oculis conspicua." The same matter is discussed in similar terms in: Augustinus Hipponensis, *De Genesi ad litteram*, l. XII, c. 28 (CSEL 28/1, p. 422, v. 12–p. 423, v. 5; PL 34, p. 478): "Quapropter si hoc tertium uisionis genus, quod superius est non solum omni corporali, quo per corporis sensus corpora sentiuntur, uerum etiam omni illo spiritali, quo similitudines corporum spiritu, non mente cernuntur, tertium caelum appellauit apostolus, in hoc uidetur claritas dei, cui uidendae corda mundantur. unde dictum est: beati mundicordes, quia ipsi deum uidebunt, non per aliquam corporaliter uel spiritaliter figuratam significationem tamquam per speculum in aenigmate, sed facie ad faciem, quod de Moyse dictum est 'os ad os,' per speciem scilicet, qua deus est quidquid est, quantulumcumque eum mens, quae non est quod ipse, etiam ab omni terrena labe mandata, ab omni corpore et similitudine corporis alienata et abrepta capere potest: a quo peregrinamur mortali et corruptibili onere grauati, quamdiu per fidem ambulamus, non per speciem et cum hic iuste uiuimus. cur autem non credamus, quod tanto apostolo gentium doctori, rapto usque ad istam excellentissimam uisionem, uoluerit deus demonstrare uitam, in qua post hanc uitam uiuendum est in aeternum?"

21. *Glossa marg.* II Ad Cor. 12:2 (ed. Rusch, vol. IV, p. 359): "In tercio thronos cherubin et seraphin, quorum tercius vicinius deum contemplatur, ad quorum similitudinem vidisse deum apostolus dicitur."

22. Augustinus Hipponensis, *De Genesi ad litteram*, l. XII, c. 31 (CSEL 28/1, p. 425, v. 11–13; PL 34, p. 479): "Sic etiam in illo genere intellectualium uisorum alia sunt, quae in ipsa anima uidentur, uelut uirtutes, quibus uitia sunt contraria."

23. Augustinus Hipponensis, *Retractationum libri duo*, I. 1, c. 15 (CCSL 57, p. 46, v. 41–46; PL 32, p. 609): "Peccatum autem quod nusquam est nisi in uoluntate, illud praecipue intellegendum est,

God immediately in this life. Therefore, the intellect of the wayfarer (*intellectus uiatoris*) too can see God immediately.

(8) Furthermore, everything to which the intellect turns itself without being turned to anything else is immediately seen by the intellect. But the intellect of a wayfarer can be turned to God without being turned to something else. Therefore, the intellect of a wayfarer can see God immediately.

(9) Furthermore, that by which we judge things must be better known to us than the things are. But, according to Augustine in his book *On the True Religion*, we judge all things according to the uncreated Truth, consulting it with regard to all things in this life too.[24] Therefore, we see Truth itself. But uncreated Truth is the divine essence. Therefore, we can see God through His essence in this life.

(10) Furthermore, "whatever is the reason or cause of a thing, it is more the case for the reason or cause."[25] But all things that we cognize, we cognize by the divine light which is the divine essence itself because, as it is said in the book *On Spirit and Soul*, our mind cannot rise (*exire*) to an act of cognition unless it is imbued (*perfundatur*) with divine light.[26] Therefore, we see God Himself through His essence more than we see anything else.

(11) Furthermore, according to Augustine, our mind is informed by God with no creature placed in between.[27] But in every mediated

---

quod iusta damnatio consecuta est; hoc enim per unum hominem intrauit in mundum. Quamquam et hoc peccatum quo consentitur peccati concupiscentiae non nisi uoluntate committitur. Propter hoc et alio loco dixi: *non igitur nisi uoluntate peccatur*" (emphasis as in edition).

24. Augustinus Hipponensis, *De vera religione,* 30 (CCSL 32, p. 222, v. 1–p. 224, v. 77; PL 34, pp. 145–147).

25. Aristoteles, *Analytica posteriora*, l. I, c. 2 (72a29–30), trans. Iacobi (AL IV, 1/4, p. 9, v. 13–14): "semper enim propter quod est unumquodque, illud magis est."

26. Alcherus Claraeuallensis (pseudo-Augustinus), *De spiritu et anima*, c. 12 (PL 40, pp. 787–788): "Intellectus et intelligentia juvantur superius; quia Deus ignis et lux est (I *Joan*. I, 5). Lux ergo splendorem emittens ex se, quem retinet in se, illuminat intelligentiam ad cognitionem veritatis. Ignis vero calorem de se emittens, sed non amittens, inflammat affectum ad amorem virtutis. Et sicut solem non videt oculus nisi in lumine solis; sic verum ac divinum lumen non poterit intelligentia videre nisi in ipsius lumine. *Domine*, inquit propheta, *in lumine tuo videbimus lumen* (*Psal*. xxxv, 10)" (emphases as in edition).

27. Augustinus Hipponensis, *De diversis quaestionibus octoginta tribus*, q. 51 (CCSL 44A, p. 80, v. 48–49; PL 40, p. 33): "secundum ipsum <scil. Interiorem hominem> ita est ad imaginem,

vision something is placed in between. Therefore, even in this life, our mind sees God immediately.

(12) Furthermore, in any theoretical science, we cognize of a subject matter what it is (*quid est*). But God is the subject matter of some theoretical science, or at least in a part of a science, as in theology and also in metaphysics, which treats of God too, as is evident from the beginning of <Aristotle's> *Metaphysics*.[28] Therefore, it is known of God what He is (*quid est*) in some theoretical science. And this is to see Him according to His essence. Therefore, since we can have all the theoretical sciences in this life, we can see God through His essence in this life.

---

ut nulla natura interposita formetur, et ideo nihil sit deo coniunctius." Alcherus Claraeuellensis (pseudo-Augustinus), *De spiritu et anima*, c. 11 (PL 40, p. 786): "mentem dicimus, quae ita facta est ad imaginem Dei, ut nulla interposita natura ab ipsa veritate formetur." See also: Albertus Magnus, *Quaestio de raptu*, a. 1 (ed. Colon. 25/2, p. 85, v. 45–46); id., *Commentarii in I Sententiarum*, d. 16, a. 12 (ed. Borgnet 25, p. 457); id., *Commentarii in II Sententiarum*, d. 26, a. 1 (ed. Borgnet 27, p. 443); id., *Super Dionysius De divinis nominibus*, c. 4 (ed. Colon. 37, p. 131, v. 6–7).

28. Aristoteles, *Metaphysica*, l. 1, c. 1 (981b13–982a2), trans. media (AL XXV 2, p. 8, v. 28–p. 9, v. 12): "Primum quidem igitur conveniens est quamlibet artem invenientem ultra communem in hominibus sensum mirari non solum propter aliquam inventorum utilitatem sed sicut sapientem et ab aliis distinguentem; pluribus autem repertis artibus et aliis quidem ad necessaria et aliis vero ad introductionem existentibus, semper huiusmodi sapientiores illis esse arbitrandum est per id quod illorum scientie ad utilitatem non sunt. Unde omnibus huiusmodi partis hee non ad voluptatem neque ad scientiarum necessitatem reperte sunt, et primum reperte sunt in hiis locis ubi studuerunt, unde circa Egyptum mathematice artes primum substiterunt, ibi namque gens sacerdotum studere concessa est. In Moralibus autem que sit artis et scientie differentia et similium generum dictum est; cuius autem gratia nunc orationem facimus hoc est, quod denominatam sapientiam circa primas causas et principia esse videtur, artifex autem expertibus, architector autem manu artifice, speculative autem magis activis. Quod quidem igitur sapientia circa quasdam causas et principia scientia sit, manifestum est." Contrary to this see: Avicenna, *Liber de philosophia prima sive scientia divina*, tr. 1, c. 1 (ed. Van Riet 1977, p. 4, v. 58–68): "Inquiramus ergo quid sit subiectum huius scientiae, et consideremus an subiectum huius scientiae sit ipse Deus excelsus; sed non est, immo est ipse unum de his quae quaeruntur in hac scientia. Dico igitur impossibile esse ut ipse Deus sit subiectum huius scientiae, quoniam subiectum omnis scientiae est res quae conceditur esse, et ipsa scientia non inquirit nisi dispositiones illius subiecti, et hoc notum est ex aliis locis. Sed non potest concedi quod Deus sit in hac scientia ut subiectum, immo est quaesitum in ea, scilicet quoniam, si ita non est, tunc non potest esse quin sit vel concessum in hac scientia et quaesitum in alia, vel concessum in ista et non quaesitum in alia." See also: Albertus Magnus, *Super Ethica*, prol. (ed. Colon. 14/1, p. 3, v. 54–61): "Dicendum, quod sicut in prima philosophia subiectum potest dupliciter assignari, scilicet id de quo principaliter intenditur—et sic dicitur esse subiectum deus, unde et scientia divina dicitur, quamvis de eo non determinetur in qualibet parte eius, sed alia omnia determinantur propter ipsum—vel id de quo communiter determinatur in scientia, et sic ens est subiectum eius <...>."

(13) Furthermore, nothing is impeded except by its contrary. But the corruption of the body is not contrary to the disposition of the intellect since they are not in the same <genus>. Therefore, the disposition of the intellect is not impeded by the corruption of the body. But the soul which exists in an incorruptible body will see God through His essence. Therefore too, when it is united to a corruptible body, it can see God through His essence.

❂ ❂ ❂

(1) On the contrary, in Exodus 33:20 it is said: *Man shall not see me and live.*[29] The Gloss <explains>: "As long as one lives mortally, God can be seen through certain images, but He cannot <be seen> through the very species of His nature."[30]

(2) Furthermore, it is said in John 1:18: *No man hath seen God at any time.*[31] The Gloss <explains>: "No purely natural human being who lives in this body sees God as He is."[32]

(3) Furthermore, <as is said in> II Corinthians 5:6–7: *While we are in the body we are absent from the Lord. For we walk by faith and not by sight.*[33] The Gloss <explains>: "It cannot happen to humans who still lead a mortal life that they take possession of the most serene light of the immutable truth as long as it has been dispersed and is all broken up in a cloud of corporeal phantasms."[34]

(4) Furthermore, it belongs to Christ alone to be both a wayfarer and someone who comprehends. But anyone who sees God through

---

29. Exodus 33:20, see article one, note 47.

30. Gregorius Magnus, *Moralia in Iob*, l. XVIII, c. 54 (CCSL 143A, p. 951, v. 34–36; PL 76, p. 92B): "quamdiu hic mortaliter uiuitur, uideri per quasdam imagines Deus potest, sed per ipsam naturae suae speciem non potest <...>." Note that the Latin *species* here means the same as *essentia*, as is also the case in Augustine's writings.

31. Secundum Iohannem 1:18, see article one, note 23.

32. *Glossa marg.* Ioh. 1:18 (ed. Rusch, vol. IV, p. 231): "nullus purus homo vivens in hoc corpore vidit deum ut est."

33. Ad Corinthios II 5:6–7 (Vulgata 2007): *quoniam dum sumus in corpore peregrinamur a Domino per fidem enim ambulamus et non per speciem.*

34. *Glossa marg.* II Ad Cor. 5:6 (ed. Rusch, vol. IV, p. 349): "Homini enim vitam agenti adhuc mortalem non potest contingere ut dimoto et discusso omni nubilo fantasiarum corporalium secretissima incommutabilis veritatis luce potiatur."

His essence is someone who comprehends. Therefore, no one but Christ who lives as a wayfarer can see God through His essence.

(5) Furthermore, once a cause has been set, an effect is set <too>. But the cause by which the soul is blessed is the divine vision, as is evident from what has been said.[35] Therefore, if someone saw God through His essence in this life, he would be blessed in this life, which is absurd.

Response

It should be said that, since happiness is the ultimate end of the rational creature, the state of this life in any rational creature is said to be that in which it is devoid of happiness. Yet the happiness of every rational creature consists in the vision of God through His essence, as is evident from what has been said before. Yet the most delightful activity in which happiness consists must belong to a potency that is disposed and perfected in regard to the most dignified object, as is evident from the Philosopher in his *Nicomachean Ethics* X.[36] And for this reason, in order that a rational creature may be happy through the vision of God in His essence, it must be made capable of this vision by some disposition inhering in it, which we call the light of glory.

Yet in this way, no creature in its pure nature, living in this life, can see God through His essence. For humans, in virtue of all the dispositions they possess in this life, are unable to do anything

35. See article one above.

36. See: Aristoteles, *Ethica Nicomachea*, l. X, c. 4 (1174b18–20), trans. Grosseteste (AL XXVI 1–3, fasc. 3, p. 352, v. 16–18): "Secundum unumquodque optima est operacio optime dispositi ad potentissimum eorum que sub ipsam. Hec autem utique perfectissima erit et delectabilissima." Ibid., l. X, c. 10 (1178b7–10, 1178b22–27, 1179a22–24), trans. Grosseteste (AL XXVI 1–3, fasc. 3, p. 362, v. 17–19, p. 363, v. 3–8, p. 364, v. 5–7): "Perfecta autem felicitas quoniam speculativa quedam est operacio, et hinc utique apparebit. Deos enim maxime suspicati sumus beatos et felices esse. <...> Quare dei operacio beatitudine differens, speculativa utique erit; et humanarum utique que huic cognatissima, felicissima. Signum autem et non participare reliqua animalia felicitate, tali operacione privata perfecte. Diis quidem enim omnis vita beata, hominibus autem in quantum similitudo quedam talis operacionis existit. <...> Secundum intellectum autem operans et hunc curans et dispositus optime, et dei amantissimus videtur esse."

greater than to understand whatever they understand through species abstracted from the senses, because phantasms are to our intellect as sensible things are to the senses, as is evident from the Philosopher in his *De anima*, book III.[37] The intellect of an angel in this life too, in virtue of all its natural or even gratuitously given dispositions, is unable to do anything greater than to understand all that it understands through co-created forms to which its natural faculties of the intellect are limited, as is evident from what has been said before.[38] Yet God in His essence can neither be seen through some form abstracted from the senses nor through any created form, as is evident from what has been said before.[39] Hence, it is evident that no intellect of a purely natural creature living in this life is capable of the vision of God through His essence in virtue of any disposition inhering in it.

But it sometimes happens by divine power that a thing is miraculously led to something of which it is in no way capable by any dispositions inhering in it, just as that a virgin should give birth, or that fire should burn in water. And similarly, it can happen miraculously by the divine power that a created intellect which only has the dispositions of this life (*dispositiones uie*) can be elevated to the vision of God through His essence. Nonetheless, from such a vision it cannot be called happy completely (*simpliciter*), but only in a qualified way (*secundum quid*) inasmuch as it shares in the act of the blessed; also, as a body, which is in the state of gravity, can miraculously participate

---

37. Aristoteles, *De anima*, l. 3, lect. 4 (432a3–10), trans. vet. (ed. Gauthier 1985, p. 484): "Quoniam autem neque nulla extra magnitudines, sicut uidetur, sensibilia separata sunt, et in speciebus sensibilibus intelligibilia sunt, et quecunque abstractione dicuntur et quecunque sensibilium habitus et passiones. Et ob hoc neque non senciens nichil utique addiscet neque sciet, set cum speculetur, necesse est simul fantasmata speculari: fantasmata autem sicut sensibilia sunt preter quod sunt sine materia." For Michael Scot's translation from the Arabic, see: ibid., l. 3, tx. 39 (ed. Crawford 1953, p. 504, v. 1–p. 505, v. 10): "Et quia, secundum quod existimatur, magnitudo est esse sensibilia sensibilium, et est species sensibilium singulariter, intelligibilia autem sunt que dicuntur modo velocis, res autem existentes in sensibilibus sunt secundum modum habitus et passionis. Et ideo qui nichil sentit nichil addiscit et nichil intelligit. Si igitur viderit, necessario videt ymagines aliquas; ymagines enim similes sunt sensibilibus, sed sine materia. Ymaginatio enim aliud est ab affirmatione et negatione."

38. See article six above.

39. See article six above.

in the act of agility or impassibility, as we read of Habakkuk (in the last chapter of Daniel 14:32–38),[40] and of the three young men who were unscathed in the furnace (in the third chapter of Daniel 3).[41] Nonetheless, their bodies were not glorified. Still, what comes about miraculously is not called possible according to the nature in which it comes about, but solely according to the power of the one who brings it about. For we do not say, properly speaking, that a blind man can come to sight, but that God can grant him sight.

And for this reason, it should be said that no creature in its nature, living in this life, can see God through His essence, but that God can bring it about that it sees Him while still remaining in this life. Also, it is evident from what has been said that neither any human being in this life nor even an angel can cognize God through His essence, because He exceeds all sensible forms by which our intellect, living in this life, cognizes, and <He> also <exceeds> our

---

40. Daniel 14:32–38 (Vulgata 2007): *erat autem Abacuc propheta in Iudaea et ipse coxerat pulmentum et intriverat panes in alveolo et ibat in campum ut ferret messoribus dixitque angelus Domini ad Abacuc fer prandium quod habes in Babylonem Daniheli qui est in lacu leonum et dixit Abacuc domine Babylonem non vidi et lacum nescio et adprehendit eum angelus Domini in vertice eius et portavit eum capillo capitis sui posuitque eum in Babylone supra lacum in impetu spiritus sui et clamavit Abacuc dicens Danihel tolle prandium quod misit tibi Deus et ait Danihel recordatus es enim mei Deus et non dereliquisti diligentes te surgensque Danihel comedit porro angelus Dei restituit Abacuc confestim in loco suo.*

41. Daniel 3:17–23.91–94 (Vulgata 2007): *ecce enim Deus noster quem colimus potest eripere nos de camino ignis ardentis et de manibus tuis rex liberare quod si noluerit notum tibi sit rex quia deos tuos non colimus et statuam auream quam erexisti non adoramus tunc Nabuchodonosor repletus est furore et aspectus faciei illius inmutatus est super Sedrac Misac et Abdenago et praecepit ut succenderetur fornax septuplum quam succendi consuerat et viris fortissimis de exercitu suo iussit ut ligatis pedibus Sedrac Misac et Abdenago mitterent eos in fornacem ignis ardentem et confestim viri illi vincti cum bracis suis et tiaris et calciamentis et vestibus missi sunt in medium fornacis ignis ardentis nam iussio regis urguebat fornax autem succensa erat nimis porro viros illos qui miserant Sedrac Misac et Abdenago interfecit flamma ignis viri autem hii id est tres Sedrac Misac et Abdenago ceciderunt in medio camini ignis ardentis conligati <...> tunc Nabuchodonosor rex obstipuit et surrexit propere et ait optimatibus suis nonne tres viros misimus in medio ignis conpeditos qui respondentes dixerunt regi vere rex respondit et ait ecce ego video viros quattuor solutos et ambulantes in medio ignis et nihil corruptionis in eis est et species quarti similis filio Dei tunc accessit Nabuchodonosor ad ostium fornacis ignis ardentis et ait Sedrac Misac et Abdenago servi Dei excelsi egredimini et venite statimque egressi sunt Sedrac Misac et Abdenago de medio ignis et congregati satrapae magistratus et iudices et potentes regis contemplabantur viros illosquoniam nihil potestatis habuisset ignis in corporibus eorum et capillus capitis eorum non esset adustus et sarabara eorum non fuissent inmutata et odor ignis non transisset per eos.*

mind itself from whose similitude we cognize something of intellectual substances.

Replies to Objections

(1) To the first, therefore, it should be said that, according to Dionysius, chapter IV of his *Celestial Hierarchy*, when Scripture says that some blessed saint saw God, such as Isaiah or anyone else, this must not be understood to mean that some saw God through His essence, which is hidden from all wayfarers,[42] but that some forms, either corporeal or imaginative, were disclosed to them through which they were led to a cognition of God. And this came to pass by the ministry of the angels, by whose illumination the intellect of the prophet was strengthened so that it attained some kind of cognition of divine things from apparent forms. And because the angel did not intend to lead him to a cognition of itself primarily but rather to a cognition of God, the angel was not said to appear as the thing seen in this way, but as God, in whose role (*persona*) it appeared and from whose power it had the efficacy to illuminate the mind of the prophet. And in Scripture this is called "theophany," namely, an apparition of God.

Nonetheless, sometimes an angel is also said to be one who appeared because of the ministry he delivered. Hence, Gregory says: "The angel who is described as having appeared to Moses is sometimes remembered as an angel and sometimes as God: as an angel because it zealously served by speaking outwardly; as God because the One presiding within, conferred an efficacy over him

42. Pseudo-Dionysius Areopagita, *De caelesti hierarchia*, c. 4, sect. 60, trans. Eriugenae (Dionysiaca t. 2, pp. 808–811): "Si autem quis dixerit et inde immediate fuisse quibusdam sanctorum theophanias, discat et hoc sapienter ex sacratissmis eloquiis quomodo hoc quidem quid est Dei occultum, nemo vidit neque videbit; theophaniae autem sanctis factae sunt secundum decentes Deum perque quasdam sacras videntibus proportionalium visionum manifestationes. Ipsa igitur sapientissima theologia visionem illam, quae in ipsa est descripta revelavit divinam quasi in forma informium similitudinem, ex videntium in divinum reductione pulchre vocari theophaniam, quasi per ipsam videntibus divina facta illuminatione, et quidem divinis ipsis sancte perficientibus. Has autem divinas visiones gloriosi patres nostri perceperunt per medias caelestes virtutes." See also: Albertus Magnus, *Super Dionysium De caelesti hierarchia*, c. 4 (ed. Colon. 36/1, p. 68, v. 85–87; p. 70, v. 83–86); ibid. (ed. Colon. 36/1, p. 68, v. 72–p. 71, v. 42).

who spoke."[43] And these are also the words of Augustine in book II of his *On the Trinity*.[44]

(2) To the second, it should be said that the vision of Jacob was either imaginary or corporeal. Nonetheless, he is said to have seen face to face because he saw a figure face to face in which God appeared to him. Hence, the Gloss says on the same passage: "Not because God may be seen, but because he saw a form through which God spoke to him."[45] Nonetheless, in saying "face to face," a certain eminence of his vision is emphasized. For, as Moses Maimonides says in distinguishing grades of prophecy, the grade of prophecy is more eminent when something appears to the prophet in a wakeful vision than when it appears to him in sleep.[46] And in either of the two ways, if a revelation comes to be, it is of a more eminent grade when He Who speaks appears to sight in an image (*in aliqua figura uisui*) rather than when his speech alone is heard without anything being seen. It is an even more eminent grade, if He Who speaks, appears in the image of an angel rather than in the image of a human. And the apparition that Jacob had was of this eminence because it did not come to be in sleep but in wakefulness; he did not only hear the voice of the One Who spoke to him,[47] but also saw his image; but nonetheless, it was of a human. Hence, it is said that a man appeared to him etc., whom he took to be an angel (*quem angelum intellexit*). And in order to describe this eminence, it is said that he saw the Lord "face to face," calling the angel "Lord" on the account already given.

Or (*vel*), according to the Gloss of Gregory on the same passage, it can be said that this is understood (*intelligitur*) of a spiritual vision

---

43. Gregorius Magnus, *Moralia* in Iob, praefatio 1 (CCSL 143, p. 9, v. 50–54; PL 75, p. 517D): "angelus qui Moysi apparuisse describitur, modo angelus, modo Dominus memoratur. Angelus uidelicet propter hoc, quod exterius loquendo seruiebat; Dominus autem dicitur quia interius praesidens loquendi efficaciam ministrabat."

44. Augustinus Hipponensis, *De Trinitate*, l. 2, c. 13.17.18 (CCSL 50, p. 110, v. 1sqq.; p. 118, v. 32sqq.; p. 124, v. 27sqq.; PL 42, pp. 859sq., 864, 867).

45. *Glossa interlin.* Gen. 32:30 (ed. Rusch, vol. I, p. 87): "Non quod deus videri possit, sed formam vidit in qua deus locutus est."

46. See: Moses Maimonides, *Dux neutrorum*, II.37 (ed. Justinianus, Parisiis 1520, f. 63v).

47. Here I read *tantum* following the Parma edition.

by which also the minds of the blessed, once purged from their vices, contemplate God even in this life, aided by the divine light with which they are imbued.[48] However, even though the divine nature is not seen as it is because the received light is not a similitude sufficiently representing the divine essence, as has been said above,[49] a more perfect cognition of God is nonetheless had according to this vision since this light is a more distinct similitude of Him than the light of nature or of a sensible creature by which humans, in natural cognition, are led to the cognition of God. For, except in whatever way they did not behold Him, namely the uncreated Truth, they would not deem themselves (*se sentiret*) to be unable to behold Him, as is said in the same Gloss. And because we cognize someone by face, we call this cognition of God "by face."

(3) To the third, it should be said that the word of Job can be understood of an imaginary and an intellectual vision. For, if it is understood of an imaginary vision, it indicates Job's progress in the grade of prophecy since, at first, a revelation came to him through hearing the one who spoke only [or in a thing seen (*vel visu*)],[50] but later through seeing the one speaking. Yet, if it is understood of an intellectual vision, then his progress is shown from a cognition of faith to an understanding of divine things in the same way as it is had by the blessed through the aforementioned contemplation. And this is called a vision because, just as by seeing some things we cognize by receiving from these things, so too do the blessed in contemplating receive the light from God Himself through which they contemplate divine things in a loftier way than others. But, through the things heard, we cognize by assenting to those who have taken the species from the things themselves, when they report to us what they saw for themselves. And similarly, through faith, we adhere to the sayings of the apostles and prophets who were illumined by the

48. *Glossa marg*. Gen. 32:30 (ed. Rusch, vol. I, p. 87). Gregorius Magnus, *Moralia in Iob*, l. XVIII, c. 54 (CCSL 143A, p. 951, v. 18–p. 955, v. 165; PL 76, pp. 92–95).

49. See article six above.

50. Inserted by pre-ed. Leon.

divine light. And in this way, it must not be posited that he saw God through His essence.

(4) To the fourth, it should be said that a twofold preeminence of vision is ascribed to Moses. One in Exodus 33:11, where it is said that *the Lord spoke to Moses face to face, as a man is wont to speak to his friend.*[51] Nonetheless, from these words, it cannot be inferred that he saw God through His essence. This is evident from what he requested afterwards: *Shew me thy glory,*[52] because <the vision> was not granted to him then. Hence, it was said to him: *Thou canst not see my face.*[53] And for this reason, the Gloss says on the same passage: "Scripture speaks according to the opinion of the people who considered Moses to speak to God mouth to mouth, since He talked to him and appeared to him through a subjected creature, namely through an angel or through a cloud."[54] Yet this way of speaking can be understood to have been imaginary or corporeal. Hence, Augustine says in his *On the Trinity*, book II: "This way of speaking, which was coming to be in voices, was done in such a way as if it were of a friend speaking to a friend."[55] It can also be understood to be intellectual, according to which <Moses> viewed the intelligibles of divine things in a way of which it is said in Psalm 84:9: *I will hear what the Lord God will speak in me.*[56] And in both ways, it is shown to be a privileged revelation of his inasmuch as He revealed His secrets to <Moses> in a way more familiar than to the rest, like to a friend, as is said in John 15:15: *I have called you friends because all things whatsoever I have heard of my Father, I have made known*

51. Exodus 33:11, see section II of the general introduction, note 2.

52. Exodus 33:18, see article one, note 49.

53. Exodus 33:20, see article one, note 47.

54. *Glossa marg.* Exod. 33:11 (ed. Rusch, vol. I, p. 198): "Secundum opinionem populi loquitur scriptura, quod putabant moysen ore ad os loqui cum deo, cum per subiectam creaturam, id est per angelum et nubem ei loquretur et appararet."

55. Augustinus Hipponensis, *De Trinitate*, l. 2, c. 16 (CCSL 50, p. 116, v. 19–21; PL 42, p. 863): "Locutio quippe illa quae fiebat in uocibus sic modificabatur tamquam esset amici loquentis *ad amicum*" (emphasis as in edition).

56. Psalmi Iuxta LXX 84:9 (Vulgata 2007): *audiam quid loquatur Dominus Deus.*

to you.[57] And for this reason, it is said in Deuteronomy at the end: *And there arose no more a prophet in Israel like unto Moses, whom the Lord knew face to face.*[58]

The other eminence of the vision of Moses is shown in Numbers 12:8, where the Lord speaks of him to Aaron and Miriam: *For I speak to him mouth to mouth: and plainly, and not by riddles and figures doth he see the Lord,*[59] or, according to the Septuagint, <doth he see> *the glory of the Lord.*[60] From this, it emerges that his petition <of> *Shew me Thy face*, which he had made in Exodus, was fulfilled,[61] in such a way that he saw God through His essence before his death, as Augustine says in *The Literal Meaning of Genesis*, book XII, and in his book *On Seeing God.*[62] And for this reason, it is said

---

57. Secundum Iohannem 15:15 (Vulgata 2007): *vos autem dixi amicos, quia omnia quaecumque audivi a Patre meo nota feci vobis.*

58. Deuteronomium 34:10 (Vulgata 2007): *et non surrexit propheta ultra in Israhel sicut Moses, quem nosset Dominus facie ad faciem.*

59. Numeri 12:8, see section II of the general introduction, note 2.

60. Numeri 12:8 (Septuaginta): *στόμα κατὰ στόμα λαλήσω αὐτῷ, ἐν εἴδει καὶ οὐ δι' αἰνιγμάτων, καὶ τὴν δόξαν κυρίου εἶδεν· καὶ διὰ τί οὐκ ἐφοβήθητε καταλαλῆσαι κατὰ τοῦ θεράποντός μου Μωυσῆ.*

61. Exodus 33:18, see article one, note 49.

62. Augustinus Hipponensis, *De Genesi ad litteram*, l. XII, cc. 27–28 (CSEL 28/1, p. 421, v. 22–p. 422, v. 4; p. 422, v. 12–24; PL 34, pp. 477–478): "os ad os loquar ad illum <Moysen> in specie et non per aenigmata, et claritatem domini uidit. neque enim hoc secundum substantiam corporis, quae carnis sensibus praesentatur, intellegendum est; nam utique sic loquebatur ad Moysen facie ad faciem, contra in contra, quando tamen dixit ei: ostende mihi temet ipsum, et nunc etiam ad ipsos, quos obiurgabat et quibus Moysi meritum ita praeferebat, sic loquebatur per creaturam corporalem praesentatam sensibus carnis. <...> Quapropter si hoc tertium uisionis genus, quod superius est non solum omni corporali, quo per corporis sensus corpora sentiuntur, uerum etiam omni illo spiritali, quo similitudines corporum spiritu, non mente cernuntur, tertium caelum appellauit apostolus, in hoc uidetur claritas dei, cui uidendae corda mundantur. unde dictum est: beati mundicordes, quia ipsi deum uidebunt, non per aliquam corporaliter uel spiritualiter figuratam significationem tamquam per speculum in aenigmate, sed facie ad faciem, quod de Moyse dictum est 'os ad os,' per speciem scilicet, qua deus est quidquid est, quantulumcumque eum mens, quae non est quod ipse, etiam ab omni terrena labe mandata, ab omni corpore et similitudine corporis alienata et abrepta capere potest." For a partial quotation and translation of this passage, see section II of the general introduction, note 5. See also: id., *Epistulae,* ep. 147: De videndo Deo, c. 8 (CSEL 44/2, p. 294, v. 9–22; PL 33, p. 605): "unde, quod responsum est Moysi, uerum est, quia nemo potest faciem dei uidere et uiuere, id est nemo potest eum in hac uita uiuens uidere, sicuti est. nam multi uiderunt, sed quod uoluntas elegit, non quod natura formauit, et illud, quod Iohannes ait, si recte intellegitur: Dilectissimi, filii dei sumus et nondum apparuit, quid erimus; scimus, quia, cum apparuerit, similes ei erimus, quoniam uidebimus eum, sicuti est, non sicut eum homines uiderunt, quando uoluit, in specie, qua uoluit, non in natura, qua in semet ipso, etiam cum uideretur, latuit, sed sicut est, quod ab eo petebatur, cum ei diceretur: Ostende mihi temet ipsum ab eo, qui cum illo facie ad faciem loquebatur, non quia dei plenitudinem quisquam non solum oculis corporis sed uel ipsa mente aliquando comprehendit."

clearly: *I speak to him mouth to mouth*, which was not said in Exodus because the vision of God through His essence is not mediated by some higher spirit, but rather God shows Himself immediately. And this is to speak mouth to mouth. For, it is not to be understood to be the mouth of the body, but the mouth of the mind, as Augustine says.[63] But the contemplative vision of this life is mediated by an illumination of the angels, as is evident from Dionysius's *Celestial Hierarchy*, chapter IV.[64] And for this reason, the speaking cannot be called "mouth to mouth" in accordance with this, but a speaking through a messenger, as it were. Yet the vision by which <Moses> saw God through His essence before his death did not make him happy completely, since this vision did not remain in him permanently but for a certain amount of time, even though that time was not specified in Scripture.[65] For, it was not had on the basis of a

63. Ibid., c. 11 (CSEL 44/2, p. 302, v. 21–p. 303, v. 9; PL 33, p. 610): "ideo quippe inter illas beatitudines, cum omnia faciant, qui cor mundum habent, non est tamen alicubi positum: deum uidebunt, nisi ubi dictum est: beati mundo corde, quoniam mundo corde uidebitur, qui 'nec in loco uidetur nec oculis corporalibus quaeritur nec circumscribitur uisu nec tactu tenetur nec auditur affatu nec sentitur incessu.' deum enim nemo uidit umquam uel in hac uita, sicuti ipse est, uel etiam in angelorum uita, sicut uisibilia ista, quae corporali uisione cernuntur, quia unigenitus filius, qui est in sinu patris, ipse narrauit. unde non ad oculorum corporalium sed ad mentium uisionem dictum est pertinere, quod narrat."

64. See: Pseudo-Dionysius Areopagita, *De caelesti hierarchia*, c. 4, sect. 60, trans. Eriugenae (Dionysiaca, t. 2, p. 811): "Has autem divinas visiones gloriosi patres nostri perceperunt per medias caelestes virtutes." See also: Albertus Magnus, *Super Dionysium De caelesti hierarchia*, c. 4 (ed. Colon. 36/1, p. 70, v. 69–p. 71, v. 42, esp. p. 71, v. 12–40): "Dicimus, quod theophania quattuor modis dicitur: primo modo visio, quae est per corporales formas similitudine dissimili ducentes in deum, in qua necessarium non est lumen divinum esse, sed tantum ductio in deum; secundo modo dicitur, quando lumine divino, quod non est deus, videtur aliquid quod non est deus, sicut Ieremias vidit ollam succensam lumine divino, intelligens per hoc destructionem Ierusalem; tertio modo, ut est in usu loquentium, quando in lumine divino, quod non est deus, videtur obiectum, quod vere est deus, non in lumine sicut in medio, sicut videtur res in sua imagine, sed sub lumine confortante intellectum videtur immediate deus; quarto modo, quando in lumine, quod est deus, videtur obiectum, quod est deus, sicut dicit Hugo de Sancto Victore; sic deus ipse est in quolibet beato ut lumen quoddam, participatione sui faciens eum sui similitudinem, et in tali similitudine dei visio dicitur theophania; sic enim idem deus erit lumen et obiectum, sed obiectum, prout est in se, lumen vero, prout est participatus a beatis. Primis igitur duobus modis non videbitur deus in patria, et de illis tenet obiectio Magistri Hugonis; dicit enim: 'Quid est in theophaniis videri et praeter illas non videri nisi numquam vere videri et verum numquam videri?.' Sed aliis duobus modis erit in patria visio per theophanias, licet ipse Hugo non ponat nisi quartum, quia non attendit tertium, et ideo reprehendit alios aliter ponentes, qui tamen vera dicunt, intelligentes secundum tertium modum."

65. See Response to article above.

disposition existing in the intellect, but on the basis of the divine power alone, miraculously as it were, as has been said above.[66]

Yet, when a created nature is miraculously elevated to something above nature, it cannot simultaneously be in a contrary act, just as the body of Peter, when it had the act of the gift of agility for walking on water miraculously, did not simultaneously have the act of gravity whose nature is to pull downward.[67] And similarly, when the intellect of the wayfarer is miraculously elevated to the vision of God through His essence, it cannot simultaneously be in the act of the vision of this life by which the soul naturally perceives sensibles. And for this reason, the soul of the one seeing must be completely removed from the act of the senses in this state. And for this reason, Augustine says in *The Literal Meaning of Genesis*, book XII, that no one can see God through His essence, "unless one somehow passes away from this life, whether one goes out of the body completely or one is turned away and removed from the carnal senses."[68] And he says something similar in his book *On Seeing God*.[69] And in this

66. See also: Albertus Magnus, *De resurrectione*, tr. 4, q. 1, a. 9, § 2, ad 1 (ed. Colon. 26, p. 330, v. 18–21): "Ad hoc ergo quod obicitur, quod etiam hic est videre facie ad faciem, dicimus, quod hoc fit raptim et in raptu. Et ideo non est dos, quia dos est possessio quieta perpetua."

67. Secundum Matthaeum 14:28–29 (Vulgata 2007): *respondens autem Petrus dixit Domine si tu es iube me venire ad te super aquas at ipse ait veni et descendens Petrus de navicula ambulabat super aquam ut veniret ad Iesum.*

68. Augustinus Hipponensis, *De Genesi ad litteram*, l. XII, c. 27 (CSEL 28/1, p. 422, v. 6–9; PL 34, pp. 477–478): "nemo uiuens uidet uita ista, qua mortaliter uiuitur in istis sensibus corporis, sed nisi ab hac uita quisque quodammodo moriatur siue omnino exiens de corpore siue ita auersus et alienatus a carnalibus sensibus." See also: Petrus Lombardus, *In Ep. Pauli*, II Cor. 2:1 (PL 192, p. 82). Alexander Halensis, *Quaestiones disputatae 'antequam esset frater,'* q. 63 (ed. Quarrachi 21, p. 1548, v. 15–16). Albertus Magnus, *Quaestio de raptu*, a.1, § 1 (ed. Colon. 25/2, p. 94, v. 54–65): "Item, licet intellectus hominis secundum statum viae sit inferior angelo, tamen secundum quod est patriae, est aequalis, quia, sicut dicit Augustinus, inter mentem nostram et deum nihil est medium. Raptus autem est secundum quod est patriae. Quod probatur per Augustinum, qui dicit: 'Nisi ab hac vita quisque moriatur sive exiens a corpore sive alienatus et aversus a sensibus carnalibus, ut nesciat, sive in corpore sive extra corpus sit, non in illam rapitur visionem.' Sed constat, quod par in parem non habet potestatem; cum igitur angelus secundum visionem raptus par sit animae rationali, non habebit potestatem rapiendi eam."

69. See: Augustinus Hipponensis, *Epistulae:* ep. 147, De videndo Deo, c. 13 (CSEL 44/2, p. 305, v. 3–21; PL 33, p. 610): "Deinde potest mouere, quo modo iam ipsa dei substantia uideri potuerit a quibusdam in hac uita positis, propter illud, quod dictum est ad Moysen: nemo potest faciem meam uidere et uiuere, nisi quia potest humana mens diuinitus rapi ex hac uita ad angelicam uitam, antequam per istam communem mortem carne soluatur. sic enim raptus est,

way, it is not contrary to what is said in Exodus 33:20: *For man shall not see me and live.*[70] Hence, Gregory says on the same passage in his Gloss: "The brightness of the eternal God can be seen by some living in this flesh, but they have grown inestimably in their power. Nonetheless, humans will not see Him and live because whosoever sees the Wisdom which is God entirely dies to this world."[71]

(5) To the fifth, it should be said that, in this rapture, Paul saw God through His essence in the same way as it is said of Moses, as is evident from Augustine in his book *On Seeing God* and in his *The Literal Meaning of Genesis*, book XII, so that the teacher of the Gentiles and the master of the Jews attend to the same privilege.[72] Even though some say that this kind of vision was midway between a vision in this life and a vision in heaven,[73] meaning that God was not seen through His essence, but by the most eminent contemplation in life. Yet the words of the blessed seem to express the contrary about

---

qui audiuit illic ineffabilia uerba, quae non licet homini loqui, ubi usque adeo facta est ab huius uitae sensibus quaedam intentionis auersio, ut, siue in corpore siue extra corpus fuerit, id est utrum, sicut solet in uehementiore extasi, mens ab hac uita in illam uitam fuerit alienata manente corporis uinculo, an omnino resolutio facta fuerit, qualis in plena morte contingit, nescire se diceret. ita fit, ut et illud uerum sit, quod dictum est: nemo potest faciem meam uidere et uiuere, quia necesse est abstrahi ab hac uita mentem, quando in illius ineffabilitatem uisionis adsumitur, et non sit incredibile quibusdam sanctis nondum ita defunctis, ut sepelienda cadauera remanerent, etiam istam excellentiam reuelationis fuisse concessam."

70. Exodus 33:20, see article one, note 47.

71. Gregorius Magnus, *Moralia in Iob,* l. XVIII, c. 54 (CCSL 143A, p. 952, v. 59–65; PL 76, p. 93): "Sin uero a quibusdam potest in hac adhuc corruptibili carne uiuentibus, sed tamen inaestimabili uirtute crescentibus, quodam contemplationis acumine aeterna Dei claritas uideri; hoc quoque a beati Iob sententia non abhorret qui ait: *Abscondita est ab oculis omnium uiuentium*; quoniam quisquis sapientiam quae Deus est, uidet, huic uitae funditus moritur, ne iam eius amore teneatur."

72. See objection five and reply to objection four above.

73. See: Gregorius Magnus, *Moralia in Iob,* l. XVIII, c. 54 (CCSL 143A, pp. 952–953; PL 76, p. 93); id., *Homiliae in Hiezechihelem prophetam*, hom. 8 (CCSL 142, p. 119, v. 656–670; PL 76, p. 868): "Quid enim in uniuerso mundo sancti Spiritus gratia agat aspiciens, ait: *Hic erat aspectus splendoris per gyrum*. Quae uero interius eiusdem sancti Spiritus gloria maneat, considerare uolens, sed sicut erat non ualens, subiungit: *Et haec uisio similitudinis gloriae Domini.* Non enim ait: Visio gloriae, sed *similitudinis gloria*, ut uidelicet ostendatur quia quantalibet se intentione mens humana tetenderit, etiamsi iam phantasias imaginum corporalium a cogitatione compescat, si iam omnes circumscriptos spiritus ab oculis cordis amoueat, adhuc tamen in carne mortali posita uidere gloriam Dei non ualet sicut est. Sed quidquid de illa est quod in mente resplendet, similitudo, et non ipsa est. Vnde et ille praedicator qui raptus ad tertium caelum fuerat dicebat: *Videmus nunc per speculum in aenigmate*" (emphases as in edition).

this matter.[74] Nonetheless, in this regard, it can be said that it was midway between either of two cognitions: for the fact that <Paul> saw God through His essence, it was above the cognition of this life, but for the fact that from this vision he was not completely happy, this vision was below the cognition of heaven.

(6) To the sixth, it should be said that an intellectual vision is had of those things that are in the soul by their essence, yet not in every way. Rather, it is of those things that are in it as intelligible forms are in the intellect. Yet in this way, God is not in the soul of the wayfarer by His essence but by a similitude. Yet what Augustine says, that an intellectual vision is of those things whose similitudes are nothing other than themselves, must be ascribed to the object of vision, not to the medium by which He is seen.[75] For it is obvious that the medium by which a stone is understood is its species in the soul, which is not the essence of the very stone. But through the similitude of the stone, a cognition of the essence of the very stone is attained because the object of the intellect is the "what it is" (*obiectum intellectus est quid*). But this does not happen in an imaginary or corporeal vision because the object of imagination or the senses is not the very essence of the thing, but accidents which are outside of it, such as color, shape, and the like. Hence, in the intellectual vision of the wayfarer too, it is not necessary that the divine essence itself is a medium by which He is seen, but <it is necessary that> some kind of cognition of the divine essence is attained by some similitude of Him. What God is, is not known by this, yet what He is not, is known by it.

Or, it should be said that Augustine, in his *The Literal Meaning of Genesis*, book XII, where the words are summarized from the Gloss on II Corinthians 12, introduces them to show the difference between an intellectual vision and other visions.[76] For an intellectual vision has the advantage over the others that it can cognize things which are in the intellect by their essence, unlike the imagination and

74. See replies to objections four and five above.

75. See note 22 above.

76. See reply to objection five above.

the senses. Yet it does not follow on account of this that the intellect understands only through its essence and that it does not understand by some similitudes.

(7) To the seventh, it should be said that in all powers which are ordered to one another, it is necessary that where the act of the prior power ends, the act of the second power begins. Hence, since the will presupposes the intellect, the will is led to that in which the intellect ends. Yet, even though the intellect cognizes God in this life only through His effects, nonetheless, its activity ends in God Himself, according to any cognition, however small, that it takes from Him. And for this reason, in order to be uplifted to God, the affect need not revert a medium, but can be uplifted immediately to God, to Whom the intellect has reached.

(8) To the eighth, it should be said that, even when something is seen through the similitude of another thing, it can happen that the one seeing the thing through a medium considers (*cogitat*) it immediately without having his consideration (*cogitatio*) turned to some other thing. For it is not turned to the medium as a given thing, but rather as the image of the thing cognized by <the image>. Yet the motion of the intellect to the image, inasmuch as it is an image, is the same as <its motion> to the imagined, although the motion of the intellect to the image, inasmuch as it is a given thing, is not the same as <the motion of the intellect> to that of which it is an image. And for this reason, when the intellect, by the similitude of a creature which it has at its disposal, is not turned to a creature as a certain thing, but only as the similitude of a thing, then it considers (*cogitat*) God immediately, even though it does not see Him immediately.

(9) To the ninth, it should be said that, just as the Gloss says about Psalm 11:2: *Truths are decayed* etc.:[77] from the one uncreated Truth result many truths in our soul, just as from one face many similitudes in a fractured mirror or in many mirrors. And the truth which

77. *Glossa interlin.* Ps. 11:2 (ed. Rusch, vol. II, p. 473): "veritas una: sed in hominibus multe." Psalmi Iuxta LXX 11:2 (Vulgata 2007): *quoniam inminuti sunt fideles a filiis hominum.*

results in our intellect consists first and foremost in the first self-evident principles. And for this reason, when we judge all things by them, our judgment is in accordance with the First Truth, of which the truth of the aforementioned principles is a similitude.

(10) To the tenth, it should be said that something is cognized from another in two ways. In one way, just as someone proceeds from the cognition of one thing to the cognition of another. And in this way, that by which a thing is cognized is more known, just as the principles <are more known than> the conclusions. In another way, <something that proceeds from another is cognized> as perfecting the cognizer for cognizing. This is either a form, as the species of a stone in the eye that perfects the eye for seeing, or an efficient principle of this kind of form, as the eye is said to see by the sun.[78] And in this way, that by which something is cognized need not be more known. On the contrary, it is possible that it is not cognized. For, it is cognized through a certain bending (*reflexio*) of the intellect, proceeding away from the cognizable object to what was the principle of cognition. Yet in this way, we cognize all things in God; and for this reason the account does not follow.

(11) To the eleventh, it should be said that the reasoning of Augustine must be understood to mean that no creature is placed between our mind and God by means of which our mind mediately proceeds from God in being (*esse*) or by means of which it is mediately informed by grace or by glory as by an efficient medium.[79] Nonetheless, nothing prevents our mind from being informed by God by the mediation of some created form, just as by grace or by the habit of love. And in this way, the mind of the wayfarer is informed to a vision of God by a created species.

78. What Aquinas discusses in this passage is the difference between an objective form that perfects the power (as the species of the stone) or a subjective form (as the light of the sun which illuminates in parallel to the light that God bestows upon the agent intellect).

79. See: Albertus Magnus, *Quaestio de visione Dei in patria* (ed. Colon. 25/2, p. 98, v. 39–42): "Sicut enim nihil esse potuit medium in creatione, ita, ut dicit Hugo de s. Victore, nihil in gloria nos sistet usque ad deum, qui per se beatificat, sicut ipse per se creavit."

(12) To the twelfth, it should be said that Avempace posited that an understanding of the essences of separate substances can be achieved by humans through the theoretical sciences which we learn in this life.[80] But the Commentator disproves this position in his <*Long Commentary on Aristotle's*> *On the Soul*, book III: Because as yet no such principles have been found on whose basis one can attain this <understanding>, it would seem to be unlikely that one could attain this <understanding> through the principles of the theoretical sciences, and especially since all human cognition would be ordered to it. For, it would be unlikely that the human species would fall short of its natural perfection entirely.[81]

And for this reason, it should be said that this position is impossible. The reason for this is that the theoretical sciences proceed from self-evident principles which have been received from the senses, as is said in <Aristotle's> *Posterior Analytics*, book II.[82] And for this reason, we cannot, through them, arrive at the essences of those things that transcend all sensible forms. Hence, we do not know what God is or what an angel is by any of the theoretical sciences that we

---

80. For Avempace's doctrine on this matter, see: Averroes, *Commentarium magnum in Aristotelis De anima libros*, l. 3, com. 36 (ed. Crawford 1953, p. 494, v. 430–436): "In epistola autem Continuationis dixit: *Et cum Philosophus ascenderit alia ascensione, considerando in intellecto inquantum intellectum, tunc intelliget substantiam abstractam*. Et manifestum est ex hoc quod intelligere intellectum secundum ilium est pars scientiarum speculativarum, scilicet Scientia Naturalis; et hoc apparuit etiam in illa perscrutatione ab eo" (emphasis as in edition). See also: Wirmer 2006, pp. 569–590.

81. Averroes, *Commentarium magnum in Aristotelis De anima libros*, l. 3, com. 36 (ed. Crawford 1953, p. 494, v. 437–p. 495, v. 459): "Et cum ita sit, nos omnes homines, quod accidit nobis de ignorantie istius scientie aut erit quia adhuc non scimus propositiones que inducunt nos ad hanc scientiam (ut dicitur de multis artificiis que videntur esse possibilia sed sunt causarum ignoratarum, v. g. Alkimie), aut hoc intelligere hoc acquiritur per exercitium et usum in rebus naturalibus, sed nondum habemus de exercitio et usu tantum per quod possumus acquirere hanc intellectionem, aut erit hoc propter diminutionem nostre nature naturaliter. Si igitur hoc accidit propter diminutionem in natura, tunc nos et omnes qui innati sunt acquirere hanc scientiam dicimur homines equivoce. Et si hoc accidit propter ignorantiam propositionum inducentium in hanc scientiam, tunc scientia speculativa nondum perfecta est; et forte Avempeche dicit hoc esse inopinabile, sed non impossibile. Et si hoc accidit propter consuetudinem, tunc sermo erit propinquus sermoni dicenti quod causa in hoc est ignorantia propositionum inducentium in hanc scientiam. Et omne hoc dicitur cum hoc quod videtur esse remotum, licet non impossibile. Quomodo ergo potest evadere ab illis questionibus predictis?"

82. Aristoteles, *Analytica posteriora*, l. 2, c. 19 (99b15–100b17), trans. Gerardus Cremonensis (AL IV, 3, p. 94, v. 11–p. 98, v. 4).

acquire now—except, under certain similitudes, <when> we cognize of them much more 'what they are not' than 'what they are.' And because of this, the Philosopher says at the beginning of his *Metaphysics* that knowledge of God is not a human possession because it is obvious that we cannot have it to its full extent.[83]

(13) To the thirteenth, it should be said that the body can only be corruptible when the soul does not have full dominion over it. For if it were to have full dominion over it, it would bestow its incorruptibility upon it. And for this reason, in the state of corruption, the soul must cognize according to the demands of the body, namely by receiving from the senses. Yet, God cannot be seen through His essence by such a mode of cognition, as is evident from what has been said before.[84] And accordingly, the state of corruption is incompatible with the vision of God through His essence.

83. Aristoteles, *Metaphysica* l. 1, c. 2 (983a5–10), trans. media (AL XXV 2, p. 11, v. 12–17): "Nam maxime divina et maxime honoranda et talis dupliciter ea sola; quam enim maxime deus habet, divina scientiarum est, tamen et si qua sit divinorum. Ea tamen sola hec habet utraque, deus enim videtur causarum omnibus esse et principium quoddam, et talem aut solus aut maxime deus habet."

84. See Response above.

Bibliography

PRIMARY SOURCES

Albertus Magnus (ed. Borgnet 25), *D. Alberti Magni, Ratisbonensis Episcopi, Ordinis Prædicatorum, Commentarii in I Sententiarum (Dist. I–XXV)*, Augustus Borgnet (ed.), vol. 25, *B. Alberti Magni, Ratisbonensis Episcopi, Ordinis Prædicatorum, Opera Omnia*, Parisiis 1893.

———. **(ed. Borgnet 26)**, *D. Alberti Magni, Ratisbonensis Episcopi, Ordinis Prædicatorum, Commentarii in I Sententiarum (Dist. XXVI–XXXXVIII)*, Augustus Borgnet (ed.), vol. 26, *B. Alberti Magni, Ratisbonensis Episcopi, Ordinis Prædicatorum, Opera Omnia*, Parisiis 1893–4.

———. **(ed. Borgnet 27)**, *D. Alberti Magni, Ratisbonensis Episcopi, Ordinis Prædicatorum, Commentarii in II Sententiarum*, Augustus Borgnet (ed.), vol. 27, *B. Alberti Magni, Ratisbonensis Episcopi, Ordinis Prædicatorum, Opera Omnia*, Parisiis 1894.

———. **(ed. Borgnet 28)**, *D. Alberti Magni, Ratisbonensis Episcopi, Ordinis Prædicatorum, Commentarii in III Sententiarum*, Augustus Borgnet (ed.), vol. 28, *B. Alberti Magni, Ratisbonensis Episcopi, Ordinis Prædicatorum, Opera Omnia*, Parisiis 1894.

———. **(ed. Borgnet 30)**, *D. Alberti Magni, Ratisbonensis Episcopi, Ordinis Prædicatorum, Commentarii in IV Sententiarum*, Augustus Borgnet (ed.), vol. 30, *B. Alberti Magni, Ratisbonensis Episcopi, Ordinis Prædicatorum, Opera Omnia*, Parisiis 1894.

———. **(ed. Borgnet 31)**, *D. Alberti Magni, Ratisbonensis Episcopi, Ordinis Prædicatorum, Summa theologiae pars prima*, Augustus Borgnet (ed.), vol. 28, *B. Alberti Magni, Ratisbonensis Episcopi, Ordinis Prædicatorum, Opera Omnia*, Parisiis 1894.

———. **(ed. Borgnet 32)**, *D. Alberti Magni, Ratisbonensis Episcopi, Ordinis Prædicatorum, Summa theologiae, secunda pars (quaest. I–LXVII)*, Augustus Borgnet (ed.), vol. 32, *B. Alberti Magni, Ratisbonensis Episcopi, Ordinis Prædicatorum, Opera Omnia*, Parisiis 1895.

———. **(ed. Borgnet 34)**, *D. Alberti Magni, Ratisbonensis Episcopi, Ordinis Prædicatorum, Compendium theologicae veritatis in septem libros digestum, Prima pars Summae de creaturis*, Augustus Borgnet (ed.), vol. 34, *B. Alberti Magni, Ratisbonensis Episcopi, Ordinis Prædicatorum, Opera Omnia*, Parisiis 1895.

———. **(ed. Colon. 7/1)**, *Alberti Magni Ordinis Fratrum Praedicatorum, De anima*, Clemens Stroick (ed.), t. 7/1, *Sancti Doctoris Ecclesiae Alberti Magni Ordinis Fratrum Praedicatorum Episcopi Opera Omnia*, Monasterii Westfalorum 1968.

———. **(ed. Colon. 14/1)**, *Alberti Magni Ordinis Fratrum Praedicatorum, Super Ethica. Commentum et Quaestiones. Libri quinque priores*, Wilhelm Kübel (ed.), t. 14/1, *Sancti Doctoris Ecclesiae Alberti Magni Ordinis Fratrum Praedicatorum Episcopi Opera Omnia*, Monasterii Westfalorum 1968/1972.

———. **(ed. Colon. 14/2)**, *Alberti Magni Ordinis Fratrum Praedicatorum, Super Ethica Commentum et Quaestiones libros VI–X*, Wilhelm Kübel (ed.), t. 14/2, *Sancti Doctoris Ecclesiae Alberti Magni Ordinis Fratrum Praedicatorum Episcopi Opera Omnia*, Monasterii Westfalorum 1972.

———. **(ed. Colon. 25/2)**, *Alberti Magni Ordinis Fratrum Praedicatorum, Quaestiones*, Albert Fried, Wilhelm Kübel, Henryk Anzulewicz (eds.), t. 25/2, *Sancti Doctoris Ecclesiae Alberti Magni Ordinis Fratrum Praedicatorum Episcopi Opera Omnia*, Monasterii Westfalorum 1993.

———. **(ed. Colon. 26)**, *Alberti Magni Ordinis Fratrum Praedicatorum, De sacramentis*, Albertus Ohlmeyer (ed.), *De incarnatione*, Ignatius Backes (ed.), *De resurrectione*, Wilhelmo Kübel (ed.), t. 26, *Sancti Doctoris Ecclesiae Alberti Magni Ordinis Fratrum Praedicatorum Episcopi Opera Omnia*, Monasterii Westfalorum 1958.

———. **(ed. Colon. 27/2)**, *Alberti Magni Ordinis Fratrum Praedicatorum, De homine*, Henryk Anzulewicz, Joachim R. Söder (eds.), t. 27/2, *Sancti Doctoris Ecclesiae Alberti Magni Ordinis Fratrum Praedicatorum Episcopi Opera Omnia*, Monasterii Westfalorum 2008.

———. **(ed. Colon. 29/1)**, *Alberti Magni Ordinis Fratrum Praedicatorum, Super I librum Sententiarum, distinctiones 1–3*, Maria Burger (ed.), t. 29/1, *Sancti Doctoris Ecclesiae Alberti Magni Ordinis Fratrum Praedicatorum Episcopi Opera Omnia*, Monasterii Westfalorum 2015.

———. **(ed. Colon. 36/1)**, *Alberti Magni Ordinis Fratrum Praedicatorum Super Dionysium De caelesti hierarchia*, Paul Simon, Wilhelm Kübel (ed.), t. 36/1, *Sancti Doctoris Ecclesiae Alberti Magni Ordinis Fratrum Praedicatorum Episcopi Opera Omnia*, Monasterii Westfalorum 1993.

———. **(ed. Colon. 37/1)**, *Alberti Magni Ordinis Fratrum Praedicatorum Super Dionysium De divinis nominibus*, Paulus Simon (ed.), t. 37/1, *Sancti Doctoris Ecclesiae Alberti Magni Ordinis Fratrum Praedicatorum Episcopi Opera Omnia*, Monasterii Westfalorum 1972.

———. **(ed. Colon. 37/2)**, *Alberti Magni Ordinis Fratrum Praedicatorum Super Dionysii Mysticam theologiam et Epistulas*, Paulus Simon (ed.), t. 37/2, *Sancti Doctoris Ecclesiae Alberti Magni Ordinis Fratrum Praedicatorum Episcopi Opera Omnia*, Monasterii Westfalorum 1978.

Alcherus (Ps.-Augustinus) (PL 40), *[Ps.-]Augustinus [Alcherus], De spiritu et anima*, in: *Sancti Aureli Augustini Hipponensis Episcopi Opera omnia*, Jacques-Paul Migne (ed.), t. 40, Paris 1865, pp. 779–831.

Alexander Aphrodisiensis (ed. Théry 1926), *De intellectu et intellecto*, Gabriel Théry (ed.), *Autour du déctret de 1210: II.—Alexander d'Aphrodise*, Bibliothèque Thomiste VII, Saulchoir-Kain 1926, pp. 74–82.

Alexander Halensis (ed. Quaracchi 1), *Doctoris Irrefragabilis Alexandri de Hales Ordinis Minorum, Summa Theologica <Summa fratris Alexandri>*, Bernard Klumper (ed.), t. 1, Ad Claras Aquas 1924.

———. **(ed. Quaracchi 12)**, *Magistri Alexandri de Hales, Glossa in quatuor libros Sententiarum Petri Lombardi. I in librum primum*, PP. Collegii S. Bonaventurae (ed.), Bibliotheca franciscana scholastica medii aevi, t. 12, Quaracchi-Florence 1951.

———. **(ed. Quaracchi 13)**, *Magistri Alexandri de Hales, Glossa in quatuor libros Sententiarum Petri Lombardi. II in librum secundum*, PP. Collegii S. Bonaventurae (ed.), Bibliotheca franciscana scholastica medii aevi, t. 13, Quaracchi-Florence 1952.

———. **(ed. Quaracchi 21)**, *Magistri Alexandri de Hales, Quaestiones disputatae 'antequam esset frater,'* PP. Collegii S. Bonaventurae (ed.), Bibliotheca franciscana scholastica medii aevi, t. 21, Quaracchi-Florence 1960.

———. **(ed. Dondaine 1952)**, "*Glossa in IV libros Sententiarum*: l. II, dist. 8," in: Hyacinthe F. Dondaine, "L'objet et le 'medium' de la vision béatifique chez les théologiens du XIIIe siècle," *Recherches de théologie ancienne et médiévale* 19 (1952), pp. 60–130.

Ambrosius Mediolanensis (CCSL 14), *Sancti Ambrosii Mediolanensis, Opera Pars IV, Expositio evangelii secundum Lucam, Fragmenta in Esaiam*, Marcus Adriaen, Paolo Angelo Ballerini (eds.), Corpus Christianorum Series Latina, t. 14, Turnhout 1957; [*Sancti Ambrosii Mediolanensis Episcopi Opera omnia*, Jacques-Paul Migne (ed.), t. 15, Paris 1845.]

Anonymous, Douai MS 434 **(ed. Dondaine 1952)**, "Anonyme de *Douai 434*: question 9," in: Hyacinthe F. Dondaine, "L'objet et le 'medium' de la vision béatifique chez les théologiens du XIIIe siècle," *Recherches de théologie ancienne et médiévale* 19 (1952), pp. 60–130.

Anonymous (ed. Lafleur 1992), *Le "Guide de l'étudiant" d'un maître anonyme de le faculté des arts de Paris au XIIIe siècle, Édition critique provisoire du ms. Barcelona, Arxiu de la Corona d'Aragó, Ripoll 109, ff. 134ra-158va*, Claude Lafleur (ed.), Joanne Carrier (co-ed.), Québec, Faculté de philosophie, Université Laval 1992.

Aristoteles (ed. Gauthier 1985), *Anonymi, magistri artium (1245–1250) lectura in librum De anima a quodam discipulo reportata, Ms. Roma Naz. V.E. 828*, René Antoine Gauthier (ed.), Grottaferrata-Romae 1985.

———. **(ed. Crawford 1953)**, *Averrois Cordubensis Commentarium magnum in Aristotelis De anima libros*, F. Stuart Crawford (ed.), Cambridge, MA 1953.

———. **(AL I 1–5)**, *Categoriae vel Praedicamenta. Translatio Boethii—editio composita. Translatio Guillelmi de Moerbeka. Lemmata e Simplicii commentario decerpta Pseudo-Augustini Paraphrasis Themistiana*, Laurentius Minio-Paluello (ed.), Bruges / Paris 1961.

———. **(AL IV 1/4)**, *Analytica posteriora. Translatio Iacobi, Laurentius Minio-Paluello* (ed.), Bruges / Paris 1968.

———. **(AL IV 3)**, *Analytica posteriora. Gerardo Cremonensi interprete*, Laurentius Minio-Paluello (ed.), Bruges / Paris 1954.

———. **(AL VII)**, *Physica. Translatio Vetus*, F. Bossier, J. Brams (eds.); *Translatio Vaticana*, A. Mansion (ed.), 2 volumes, Leiden / New York 1990. (First ed. of VII by A. Mansion, Bruges / Paris 1957).

———. **(AL XXV 1–1a)**, *Metaphysica, lib. I–IV.4. Translatio Iacobi sive 'Vetustissima' cum Scholiis et Translatio Composita sive 'Vetus,'* G. Vuillemin-Diem (ed.), Bruxelles / Paris 1970.

———. **(AL XXV 2)**, *Metaphysica, lib. I–X, XII–XIV, translatio anonyma et 'media,'* Gudrun Vuillemin-Diem (ed.), Leiden 1976.

———. **(AL XXVI 1–3)**, *Ethica Nicomachea, (1) Praefatio, (2) Translatio Antiquissima libr. II–III sive 'Ethica Vetus' et Translationis Antiquioris quae supersunt sive 'Ethica Nova,' 'Hoferiana,' 'Borthesiana,' (3) Translatio Roberti Grosseteste Lincolniensis sive 'Liber Ethicorum,' A. Recensio Pura, (4) Translatio Roberti Grosseteste Lincolniensis sive 'Liber Ethicorum,' B. Recensio Recognita,* Renatus Antonius Gauthier (ed.), Leiden 1972.

Arnulfus Provincialis (ed. Lafleur 1988), "Arnulfi Provincialis, Magistri Artium Parisiensis, Divisio Scientiarum," Claude Lafleur (ed.), *Quatre introductions à la philosophie au XIIIe siècle. Textes critique et étude historique, Montreal: Institut d'études médiévales,* Paris 1988, pp. 295–355.

Augustinus Hipponensis (CSEL 28/1), *Sancti Aureli Augustini, De Genesi ad litteram libri duodecim eiusdem libri capitula, De Genesi ad litteram inperfectus liber, Locutionum in Heptateuchum libri septem,* Iosephus Zycha (ed.), Corpus Scriptorum Ecclesiasticorum Latinorum, t. 28/1, Pragae / Vindobonae / Lipsiae 1894. [**(PL 34)**, *Sancti Aureli Augustini Hipponensis Episcopi Opera omnia,* Jacques-Paul Migne (ed.), t. 34, Paris 1841].

———. **(CCSL 27)**, *Sancti Aureli Augustini, Confessionum libri XIII,* L. Verheijen (ed.), Corpus Christianorum Series Latina, t. 27, Turnhout 1981. [**(PL 32)**, *Sancti Aureli Augustini Hipponensis Episcopi Opera omnia,* Jacques-Paul Migne (ed.), t. 32, Paris 1841].

———. **(CCSL 29)**, *Sancti Aureli Augustini, Contra academicos, De beata vita, De ordine, De magistro, De libero arbitrio,* William M. Green, Klaus-Detlef Daur (eds.), Corpus Christianorum Series Latina, t. 29, Turnhout 1970. [**(PL 32)**, *Sancti Aurelii Augustini Hipponensis Episcopi Opera omnia,* Jacques-Paul Migne (ed.), t. 32, Paris 1841].

———. **(CCSL 32)**, *Sancti Aureli Augustini, De doctrina christiana, De vera religione,* K. D. Daur, J. Martin (eds.), Corpus Christianorum Series Latina, t. 32, Turnhout 1962. [**(PL 34)**, *Sancti Aureli Augustini Hipponensis Episcopi Opera omnia,* Jacques-Paul Migne (ed.), t. 34, Paris 1841].

———. **(CCSL 44A)**, *Sancti Aureli Augustini De diversis quaestionibus octoginta tribus, De octo dulcitii quaestionibus,* Almut Mutzenbecher (ed.), Corpus Christianorum Series Latina, t. 44 A, Turnhout 1975. [**(PL 40)**, *Sancti Aureli Augustini Hipponensis Episcopi Opera omnia,* Jacques-Paul Migne (ed.), t. 40, Paris 1865].

———. **(CSEL 44/2)**, *Sancti Aureli Augustini Hipponiensis Episcopi, Epistulae Pars III (ep. 124–184 A),* Alois Goldbacher (ed.), t. 44/2, Vindobonae / Lipsiae 1904. [**(PL 33)**, *Sancti Aureli Augustini Hipponensis Episcopi Opera omnia,* Jacques-Paul Migne (ed.), t. 33, Paris 1865].

———. **(CCSL 48)**, *Sancti Aureli Augustini, De civitate dei libri XI–XXII,* B. Dombart, A. Kalb (eds.), Corpus Christianorum Series Latina, t. 48, Turnhout 1955. [**(PL 41)**, *Sancti Aureli Augustini Hipponensis Episcopi Opera omnia,* Jacques-Paul Migne (ed.), t. 41, Paris 1864].

———. **(CCSL 50)**, *Sancti Aureli Augustini, De trinitate libri XV, libri I–XII,* W.J. Mountain, F. Glorie (eds.), Corpus Christianorum Series Latina, t. 50, Turnhout

1968. [(**PL 42**), *Sancti Aureli Augustini Hipponensis Episcopi Opera omnia*, Jacques-Paul Migne (ed.), t. 42, Paris 1865].

———. (**CCSL 57**), *Sancti Aureli Augustini, Retractationum libri II*, Almut Mutzenbecher (ed.), Corpus Christianorum Series Latina, t. 57, Turnhout 1984. [(**PL 32**), *Sancti Aureli Augustini Hipponensis Episcopi Opera omnia*, Jacques-Paul Migne (ed.), t. 32, Paris 1841].

———. (**PL 38**), *Sancti Aureli Augustini Hipponensis Episcopi Opera omnia*, Jacques-Paul Migne (ed.), t. 38, Paris 1865.

Averroes (ed. Venetiis 1562), *Aristotelis Metaphysicorum libri cum Averrois Cordubensis in eosdem Commentariis et Epitome*, Venice 1562.

———. (**ed. Darms 1966**): *In Aristotelis librum II (α) metaphysicorum commentarius, Die lateinische Übersetzung des Mittelalters auf handschriftlicher Grundlage mit Einleitung und problemgeschichtlicher Studie*, Gion Darms (ed.), Freiburg 1966.

———. (**ed. Crawford 1953**), *Averrois Cordubensis Commentarium magnum in Aristotelis De anima libros*, F. Stuart Crawford (ed.), Cambridge, MA 1953.

Averroes (trans. Taylor 2009), *Averroes (Ibn Rushd) of Cordoba, Long Commentary on the De Anima of Aristotle*, Richard C. Taylor (ed., tr.), New Haven, CT 2009.

Avicenna (ed. Van Riet 1968), *Avicenna Latinus Liber de Anima seu Sextus de Naturalibus, IV–V*, Édition critique de la traduction latine médiévale par S. Van Riet, Introduction sur la doctrine psychologique d'Avicenne par G. Verbeke, Louvain / Leiden 1968.

———. (**ed. Van Riet 1977**), *Avicenna Latinus Liber de Philosophia prima sive Scientia divina, I–IV*, Édition critique de la traduction latine médiévale par S. Van Riet, Introduction doctrinale par G. Verbeke, Louvain / Leiden 1977.

———. (**ed. Van Riet 1980**), *Avicenna Latinus Liber de Philosophia prima sive Scientia divina, V–X*, Édition critique de la traduction latine médiévale par S. Van Riet, Introduction doctrinale par G. Verbeke, Louvain / Leiden 1980.

Avicenna (ed. Marmura 2005), Avicenna, *The Metaphysics of The Healing*, Michael E. Marmura (ed.), Provo, UT 2005.

BOE núm. 211 (29 de julio de 1835), *Real Decreto de 25 de julio de 1835 suprimiendo los monasterios y conventos de religiosos que no tengan 12 individuos profesos, de los cuales las dos terceras partes a lo menos sean de coro*, <http://pares.mcu.es/ParesBusquedas20/catalogo/autoridad/6360>, last accessed: 28 Jan 2018.

BOE núm. 292 (14 de octubre de 1835), *Real Decreto de 11 de octubre de 1835 suprimiendo los monacales*, <http://pares.mcu.es/ParesBusquedas20/catalogo/autoridad/6360>, last accessed: 28 Jan 2018.

Bonaventura (ed. Quaracchi 1/1), *Doctoris Seraphici S. Bonaventurae, Commentaria in Quatuor Libros Sententiarum Magistri Petri Lombardi, t. 1/1, In primum librum Sententiarum,* Bernardinus a Portu Romatino (ed.), *Doctoris Seraphici S. Bonaventurae Opera omnia*, Ad Claras Aquas 1882.

———. (**ed. Quaracchi 1/2**), *Doctoris Seraphici S. Bonaventurae, Commentaria in Quatuor Libros Sententiarum Magistri Petri Lombardi, t. 1/2, In primum* *librum Sententiarum,* Bernardinus a Portu Romatino (ed.), *Doctoris Seraphici S. Bonaventurae Opera omnia,* Ad Claras Aquas 1883.

———. **(ed. Quaracchi 2)**, *Doctoris Seraphici S. Bonaventurae, Commentaria in Quatuor Libros Sententiarum Magistri Petri Lombardi, t. 2, In secundum librum Sententiarum,* Bernardinus a Portu Romatino (ed.), *Doctoris Seraphici S. Bonaventurae Opera omnia,* Ad Claras Aquas 1885.

———. **(ed. Quaracchi 4)**, *Doctoris Seraphici S. Bonaventurae, Commentaria in Quatuor Libros Sententiarum Magistri Petri Lombardi, t. 4, In quartum librum Sententiarum,* Bernardinus a Portu Romatino (ed.), *Doctoris Seraphici S. Bonaventurae Opera omnia,* Ad Claras Aquas 1889.

———. **(ed. Quaracchi 5)**, *Doctoris Seraphici S. Bonaventurae, Opuscula varia theologica,* Aloysius a Parma (ed.), *Doctoris Seraphici S. Bonaventurae Opera omnia,* t. 5, Ad Claras Aquas 1891.

CUP (ed. Denifle t. 1), *Chartularium Universitatis Parisiensis sub auspiciis consilii generalis facultatum Parisiensium ex diversis bibliothecis tabularisque collegit,* Henricus Denifle O.P. (ed.), t. 1, ab anno MCC usque ad annum MCCLXXXVI, Paris 1889.

———. **(ed. Denifle t. 2)**, *Chartularium Universitatis Parisiensis sub auspiciis consilii generalis facultatum Parisiensium ex diversis bibliothecis tabularisque collegit,* Henricus Denifle O.P. (ed.), t. 2, sect. prior, ab anno MCCLXXXVI usque ad annum MCCCL, Paris 1891.

Dionysius [Pseudo-Dionysius] Areopagita (Dionysiaca t. 1), *Dionysiaca. Recueil donnant l'ensemble des traductions latines des ouvrages attribués au Denys de l'Aréopage,* Philippe Chevallier (ed.), t. I, Bruges 1937.

———. **(Dionysiaca t. 2)**, *Dionysiaca. Recueil donnant l'ensemble des traductions latines des ouvrages attribués au Denys de l'Aréopage*, Philippe Chevallier (ed.), t. II, Bruges 1950.

Glossa (ed. Rusch), Biblia latina cum glossa ordinaria, Adolph Rusch (ed.), 4 vols., Strassburg 1480/81.

Gregorius Magnus (CCSL 142), *Homiliae in Hiezechielem prophetam,* Marcus Adriaen (ed.), Corpus Christianorum Series Latina t. 142, Turnhout 1971.

———. **(CCSL 143)**, *Moralia in Iob, Libri I–X,* Marcus Adriaen (ed.), Corpus Christianorum Series Latina t. 143, Turnhout 1979.

———. **(CCSL 143A)**, *Moralia in Iob, Libri XI–XXII,* Marcus Adriaen (ed.), Corpus Christianorum Series Latina t. 143 A, Turnhout 1979.

———. **(SC 260)**, *Grégoire le Grand: Dialogues, Livre IV,* Adalbert de Vogüé, Paul Antin (eds.), tables et index, t. II, Paris 1979.

———. **(SC 265)**, *Grégoire le Grand: Dialogues, Livre IV,* Adalbert de Vogüé, Paul Antin (eds.), tables et index, t. III, Paris 1980.

Guerricus de Sancto Quintino (ed. Dondaine 1952), "*Commentaire de l'évangile de saint Jean,* ch. 1," in: Hyacinthe F. Dondaine, "L'objet et le 'medium' de la vision béatifique chez les théologiens du XIIIe siècle," *Recherches de théologie ancienne et médiévale* 19 (1952), pp. 60–130.

Guillelmo de Tocco (ed. le Brun-Gouanvic 1996), *Ystoria sancti Thome de Aquino,* Claire le Brun-Gouanvic (ed.), Toronto 1996.

Guilielmus Alvernus (ed. Hotot 1674), *Guilielmi Alverni episcopi Parisiensis, mathematici perfectissimi, eximii philosophi, ac theologi praestantissimi, Opera omnia*, F. Hotot (ed.), t. 1, Londini 1674.

Haymo (PL 117), *Haymonis Halberstatensis Episcopi Opera omnia*, Jacques-Paul Migne (ed.), t. 117, Paris 1881.

Hieronymus (CCSL 73), *Commentariorum in Esaiam libri I–XI*, Marcus Adriaen (ed.), Corpus Christianorum Series Latina, t. 73, Turnhout 1963. [**(PL 24)**, *Sancti Eusebii Hieronymi Opera omnia,* Jacques-Paul Migne (ed.), t. 24, Paris 1865.]

———. **(PL 26)**, *Commentarius in Epistolam ad Ephesios*, in: *Sancti Eusebii Hieronymi Opera omnia,* Jacques-Paul Migne (ed.), t. 26, Paris 1845.

Hugo de Sancto Caro (ed. Lyon 1645), *Postillae in universa Biblia juxta quadruplicem sensum, litteralem, allegoricum, moralem, anagogicum*, Lyon 1645.

———. **(ed. Dondaine 1952)**, "Hugues de Saint-Cher, *Postille sur l'évangile de saint Jean*: ch. 1, v. 16," in: Hyacinthe F. Dondaine, "L'objet et le 'medium' de la vision béatifique chez les théologiens du XIIIe siècle," *Recherches de théologie ancienne et médiévale* 19 (1952), pp. 60–130.

Hugo de Sancto Victore (CCCM 178), *Hugonis de Sancto Victore, Super Ierarchiam Dionysii*, Dominic Poirel (ed.), Corpus Christianorum Continuatio Mediaevalis 178, Turnhout 2015. [**(PL 175)**, *Hugonis de Sancto Victore Opera omnia*, Jacques-Paul Migne (ed.), t. 175, Paris 1854.]

Iohannes Chrysostomus (ed. Dondaine 1952), "Saint Jean Chrysostome: *Homélie XV sur l'évangile de saint Jean*: n. 1–2," in: Hyacinthe F. Dondaine, "L'objet et le 'medium' de la vision béatifique chez les théologiens du XIIIe siècle," *Recherches de théologie ancienne et médiévale* 19 (1952), pp. 60–130.

Iohannes Damascenus (ed. Buytaert), *Saint John Damescene, De fide orthodoxa: Versions of Burgundio and Cerbanus*, Eligius M. Buytaert (ed.), St. Bonaventure, NY 1955.

Iohannes Pecham (BFSMA 28), *Iohannes Pecham, Quaestiones de beatitudine animae et corporis*, Hieronymus Spettmann, Girard J. Etzkorn (eds.), Bibliotheca Franciscana Scholastica Medii Aevi 28, Turnhout 2002.

Iohannes Scotus Eriugena (CCCM 161), *Iohannis Scotti seu Eriugenae Periphyseon, liber primus*, Corpus Christianorum Continuatio Medievalis 161, Turnhout 1996.

———. **(CCCM 162)**, *Iohannis Scotti seu Eriugenae Periphyseon, liber secundus*, Corpus Christianorum Continuatio Medievalis 162, Turnhout 1997. [**(PL 122)**, *Ioannis Scoti Opera omnia*, Jacques-Paul Migne (ed.), t. 122, Paris 1865.]

Isaac Israeli (ed. Muckle), "Isaac Israeli, Liber de Definicionibus," Joseph Thomas Muckle (ed.), *Archives d'histoire doctrinale et litteraire du Moyen Âge*, 12–13 (1937–1938), pp. 299–340.

Isidorus Hispalensis (CCSL 111), *Isidorus Hispalensis, Sententiae*, Pierre Cazier (ed.), Corpus Christianorum Series Latina, t. 111, Turnhout 1998. [**(PL 83)**, *Sancti Isidori Opera omnia,* Jacques-Paul Migne (ed.), t. 83, Paris 1862.]

Johannes von Paltz (ed. Burger/Stasch 1983), Johannes von Paltz, *Werke 1: Coelifodina*, Christoph Burger, Friedhelm Stasch (eds.), Berlin / New York 1983.

Leibniz, Gottfried Wilhelm, *New Essays Concerning Human Understanding*, Alfred Gideon Langley (trans.), New York / London 1896.

Liber de causis (ed. Pattin), "Le Liber de causis. Edition établie à l'aide de 90 manuscrits avec introduction et notes," Adriaan Pattin (ed.), *Tijdschrift voor Filosofie* 28 (1966), pp. 90–203.

Moses Maimonides (ed. Justinianus), Augustinus Justinianus (ed.), *Moses Maimonides, Dux neutrorum*, Paris 1520.

Petrus Lombardus (ed. Grottaferrata), *Magistri Petri Lombardi Parisiensis Episcopi Sententiae in IV libris distinctae*, Grottaferrata-Romae 1971.

———. **(PL 191),** *Petrus Lombardus Magister Sententiarum Parisiensis Episcopus Commentaria in Psalmos, Commentaria in Epistolas S. Pauli, P. Lombardi Magistri Sententiarum Parisiensis Episcopi Opera omnia*, Jacques-Paul Migne (ed.), t. 191, Paris 1854.

———. **(PL 192),** *Petrus Lombardus Magister Sententiarum Parisiensis Episcopus Collectaneorum in Epistolas S. Pauli continuatio, Sententiarum libri quatuor, P. Lombardi Magistri Sententiarum Parisiensis Episcopi Opera omnia,* Jacques-Paul Migne (ed.), t. 192, Paris 1855.

Ps.-Thomas Aquinas, *De visione divinae essentiae,* Wolfenbüttel, Herzog-August Bibliothek 59.1 Aug. fol. (Catal. 2609), ff. 1ra-3va (15th cent.).

Rabanus Maurus (PL 112), Rabanus Maurus, *Enarrationes in Epistolas Beati Pauli, Rabani Mauri Opera omnia,* Jacques-Paul Migne (ed.), t. 112, Paris 1852.

Richard Fishacre (ed. Ermatinger), Ermatinger, Charles J., "Richard Fishacre, *Commentum in librum I Sententiarum* (Dist. 2, Cap. 1)," *The Modern Schoolman* 35 (1958), pp. 213–235.

Strabo (ed. A. Meinecke 1877), *Strabonis Geographica*, A. Meineke (ed.), vol. 3, Leipzig 1877, at <http://www.perseus.tufts.edu/hopper/text?doc=Strab.+10.3.10&from doc=Perseus%3Atext%3A1999.01.0197>, last accessed: 19 Feb 2018.

Thomas Aquinas (ed. Parma 7/2), *Sancti Thomae Aquinatis Doctoris angelici ordinis praedicatorum Opera omnia ad fidem optimarum editionum accurate recognita t. 7.2 Commentum in quatuor libros Sententiarum magistri Petri Lombardi,* Parma 1858.

———. **(ed. Mandonnet 1),** *S. Thomae Aquinatis Ordinis Praedicatorum Doctoris Communis Ecclesiae Scriptum super libros Sententiarum Magistri Petri Lombardi Episcopi Parisiensis*, R.P. Mandonnet O.P. (ed.), t. 1, Paris 1929.

———. **(ed. Mandonnet 2),** *S. Thomae Aquinatis Ordinis Praedicatorum Doctoris Communis Ecclesiae Scriptum super libros Sententiarum Magistri Petri Lombardi Episcopi Parisiensis*, R. P. Mandonnet O.P. (ed.), t. 2, Paris 1929.

———. **(ed. Moos),** *S. Thomae Aquinatis Doctoris Communis Ecclesiae Scriptum Super Sententiis Magistri Petri Lombardi*, Maria Fabianus Moos (ed.), t. 3, Paris 1933.

———. **(ed. Leon. 12),** *Sancti Thomae de Aquino Opera omnia iussu Leonis XIII P.M. edita, t. 12, Tertia pars Summae theologiae, a quaestione LX ad quaestionem XC cum commentariis Thomae de Vio Caietani et supplemento eiusdem tertiae partis*, Cura et studio Fratrum Praedicatorum, Rome 1906.

———. **(ed. Leon. 14)**, *Sancti Thomae de Aquino Opera omnia iussu Leonis XIII P.M. edita, t. 14, Summa contra gentiles liber tertius*, Cura et studio Fratrum Praedicatorum, Rome 1926.

———. **(ed. Leon. 22/1)**, *Sancti Thomae de Aquino Opera omnia iussu Leonis XIII P.M. edita, t. 22, Quaestiones disputatae de veritate*, vol. 1 fasc. 2, qq. 1–7, Cura et studio Fratrum Praedicatorum, Rome 1970.

———. **(ed. Leon. 22/2)**, *Sancti Thomae de Aquino Opera omnia iussu Leonis XIII P.M. edita, t. 22, Quaestiones disputatae de veritate*, vol. 2, qq. 8–12, Cura et studio Fratrum Praedicatorum, Rome 1972.

———. **(ed. Leon. 25/2)**, *Sancti Thomae de Aquino Opera omnia iussu Leonis XIII P.M. edita, t. 25, Quaestiones de quodlibet*, vol. 2, Quodlibet I, II, III, VI, IV, V, XII, Indices, Cura et studio Fratrum Praedicatorum, Paris 1996.

———. **(trans. Mortensen 2018)**, Saint Thomas Aquinas, *Commentary on the Sentences Book IV, Distinctions 43–50*, Beth Mortensen, Peter Kwasneiwski, Dylan Schrader (trans.), vol. 10, Green Bay, WI 2018.

———. **(trans. Taylor)**, *In 4 Sent.*, d. 49, q. 2, a. 1, Richard Taylor (trans.), online at: <http://academic.mu.edu/taylorr/Aquinas_and_the_Arabs_Project_Translations/60_In_4_Sent._D._49,_Q.2,_A.1.html>, last accessed: 15 June 2018.

———. **(trans. Fathers of the English Dominican Province)**, *The Summa Theologiae of St. Thomas Aquinas*, Fathers of the English Dominican Province (trans.), 2nd ed., 1920, online at: <http://www.newadvent.org/summa/5092.htm>, last accessed: 15 June 2018.

Vulgata, *Biblia Sacra Vulgata*, Robert Weber, Roger Gryson (eds.), 5th ed., Stuttgart 2007.

Vulgate Douay-Rheims trans., *The Vulgate Bible*, 6 vols., Dumbarton Oaks Medieval Library, Cambridge, MA 2010–2013.

SECONDARY LITERATURE

Abram, Marieke, "Volkssprachliche Philosophie im Spieghel der volcomenheit von Hendrik Herp (1410–1477): Lektüre und Wirkungsgeschichte eines mystischen Wegweisers für Laien," unpubl. dissertation, Albert-Ludwigs-Universität Freiburg i. Br. 2017.

———, "Die irdische Gottesschau der erkennenden Seele. Wie Peter von Bergamo und Hendrik Herp im 15. Jahrhundert den *doctor sanctus* Thomas von Aquin lasen," in: M.J.F.M. Hoenen, M. Meliado, S. Negri (eds.), *Thomas Problematicus*, forthcoming.

Adamson, Peter, "Avicenna and his Commentators on Human and Divine Self-Intellection," in: Dag Hasse, Amos Bertolacci (eds.), *The Arabic, Hebrew and Latin Reception of Avicenna's Metaphysics*, Berlin / Boston 2012, pp. 97–122.

Albertus-Magnus-Institut (ed.), *Albertus Magnus und sein System der Wissenschaften. Schlüsseltexte in Übersetzung Lateinisch–Deutsch*, Münster 2011.

Altmann, Alexander, "Ibn Bâjjah on Man's Ultimate Felicity," in: *Harry Austryn Wolfson Jubilee Volume*, vol. I, Jerusalem 1965, pp. 47–87.

Anzulewicz, Henryk, De forma resultante in speculo. *Die theologische Relevanz des Bildbegriffs und des Spiegelbildmodells in den Frühwerken des Albertus Magnus*, vol. 2, Münster 1999.

———, "Die Denkstruktur des Albertus Magnus. Ihre Dekodierung und ihre Relevanz für die Begrifflichkeit und Terminologie," in: Jacqueline Hamesse, Carlos Steel (eds.), *L'Élaboration du Vocabulaire Philosophique au Moyen Âge. Actes du Colloque international de Louvain-la-Neuve et Leuven 12–14 septembre 1998 organisé par la SIEPM*, Turnhout 2000a, pp. 369–396.

———, "Pseudo-Dionysius Areopagita und das Strukturprinzip des Denkens von Albert dem Großen," in: Tzotcho Boiadjiev, Georgi Kapriev, Andreas Speer (eds.), *Die Dionysius-Rezeption im Mittelalter*, Turnhout 2000b, pp. 251–295.

———, "Entwicklung und Stellung der Intellektlehre im System des Albertus Magnus," *Archives d'histoire doctrinale et littéraire du Moyen Âge* 70 (2003), pp. 165–218.

———, "Die Emanationslehre des Albertus Magnus: Genese, Gestalt und Bedeutung," in: Ludger Honnefelder, Hannes Möhle, Susana Bullido del Barrio (eds.), *Via Alberti. Texte—Quellen—Interpretationen*, Münster 2009, pp. 219–242.

———, "Handschriftliche Überlieferung, Werkausgaben," in: Volker Leppin (ed.), *Thomas Handbuch*, Tübingen 2016, pp. 2–12.

Anzulewicz, Henryk and Krause, Katja, "Albert der Große und sein holistisches Konzept menschlicher Erkenntnis," in: Tengiz Iremadze, Udo Reinhold Jeck (eds.), *Veritas et Subtilitas. Truth and Subtlety in the History of Philosophy. Essays in Memory of Burkhard Mojsisch (1944–2015)*, Amsterdam 2018, pp. 158–194.

Anzulewicz, Henryk and Rigo, Caterina, "*Reductio ad esse divinum*. Zur Vollendung des Menschen nach Albertus Magnus," in: Jan Aertsen, Martin Pickavé (eds.), *Ende und Vollendung. Eschatologische Perspektiven im Mittelalter*, Berlin 2002, pp. 388–416.

Bataillon, Louis-Jacques, "Un traité «De visione divinae essentiae» attribué à saint Thomas d'Aquin," *Revue des sciences philosophiques et théologiques* 48 (1964), pp. 471–474.

Bazán, Bernardo C., "Intellectum Speculativum: Averroes, Thomas Aquinas and Siger of Brabant on the Intelligible Object," *Journal of the History of Philosophy* 19 (1981), pp. 425–446.

———, "A Body for the Human Soul," in: Luis Xavier López-Farjeat, Jörg Alejandro Tellkamp (eds.), *Philosophical Psychology in Arabic Thought and the Latin Aristotelianism of the 13th Century*, Paris 2013, pp. 243–277.

Beierwaltes, Werner (ed.), *Eriugena Redivivus. Zur Wirkungsgeschichte seines Denkens im Mittelalter und im Übergang zur Neuzeit*, Heidelberg 1987.

Bender, Melanie, *The Dawn of the Invisible: The Reception of the Platonic Doctrine on Beauty in the Christian Middle Ages: Pseudo-Dionysius the Areopagite—Albert the Great—Thomas Aquinas—Nicholas of Cusa*, Münster 2007.

Benjamin, Walter, "The Task of the Translator," in: Marcus Bullock, Michael W. Jennings (eds.), *Selected Writings: Volume 1, 1913–1926*, Cambridge, MA 1996, pp. 253–263.

Bianchi, Luca, *Censure et liberté intellectuelle à l'Université de Paris (XIIIe–XIVe siècles)*, Paris 1999.

Black, Deborah, "Conjunction and the Identity of Knower and Known in Averroes,' *American Catholic Philosophical Quarterly* 73 (1999), pp. 159–184.

———, "*Cognoscere Per Impressionem*: Aquinas and the Avicennian Account of Knowing Separate Substances," *American Catholic Philosophical Quarterly* 88 (2014), pp. 213–236.

Blankenhorn, Bernhard, *The Mystery of Union with God. Dionysian Mysticism in Albert the Great and Thomas Aquinas*, Washington, D.C. 2015.

Borgo, Marta, "Early Aquinas on Matter. Notes on the Reception of the Aristotelian Corpus in the 13th Century," *Topicos, Revista de Filosofía* 45 (2013), pp. 83–128.

Bradley, Denis, *Aquinas on the Twofold Human Good: Reason and Human Happiness in Aquinas'Moral Science*, Washington, D.C. 1997.

Brenet, Jean-Baptiste, "Vision béatifique et séparation de l'intellect au début du XIVe siècle. Pour Averroès ou contre Thomas d'Aquin?," *Freiburger Zeitschrift für Philosophie und Theologie* 53 (2006), pp. 310–342.

———, "S'unir à l'intellect, voir Dieu: Averroès et la Doctrine de la Jonction au Coeur du Thomisme," *Arabic Sciences and Philosophy* 21 (2011), pp. 215–247.

Brower, Jeffrey and Brower-Toland, Susan, "Aquinas on Mental Representation: Concepts and Intentionality," *Philosophical Review* 117 (2008), pp. 193–243.

Burger, Maria, "Codex 30 der Dombibliothek Köln. Ein Arbeitsexemplar für Thomas von Aquin als Assistent Alberts des Großen," in: H. Finger (ed.), *Mittelalterliche Handschriften der Kölner Dombibliothek. Erstes Symposion der Diözesan- und Dombibliothek Köln zu den Dom-Manuskripten (26.–27. November 2004)*, Cologne 2005, pp. 190–208.

———, "Thomas Aquinas's Glosses on the Dionysius Commentaries of Albert the Great in Codex 30 of the Cologne Cathedral Library," in: Ludger Honnefelder, Hannes Möhle, Susana Bullido del Barrio (eds.), *Via Alberti. Texte—Quellen—Interpretationen*, Münster 2009, pp. 561–582.

Burwick, Frederick, "Romantic Theories of Translation," *The Wordsworth Circle* 39 (2008), pp. 68–74.

Classen, Peter, *Burgundio von Pisa: Richter—Gesandter—Übersetzer*, Heidelberg 1974.

Corrigan, Kevin and Harrington, L. Michael, "Pseudo-Dionysius the Areopagite," in: Edward N. Zalta (ed.), *The Stanford Encyclopedia of Philosophy*, https://plato.stanford.edu/archives/sum2018/entries/pseudo-dionysius-areopagite/, Stanford 2018.

Cory, Therese Scarpelli, *Aquinas on Human Self-Knowledge*, Cambridge 2013.

———, "Rethinking Abstractionism: Aquinas's Intellectual Light and Some Arabic Sources," *Journal of the History of Philosophy* 53 (2015), pp. 607–646.

———, "Embodied vs. Non-Embodied Modes of Knowing in Aquinas: Different Universals, Different Intelligible Species, Different Intellects," *Faith and Philosophy* 35 (2018), pp. 417–446.

Cunningham, Francis L.B., *The Indwelling of the Trinity: A Historico-Doctrinal Study of the Theory of St. Thomas Aquinas*, Dubuque 1955.

D'Ancona, Cristina, "The *Theology* Attributed to Aristotle: Sources, Structure, Influence," in: K. El-Rouayheb, S. Schmidtke (eds.), *The Oxford Handbook of Islamic Philosophy*, Oxford / New York 2017, pp. 8–29.

———, "Elementi di neoplatonismo nella teoria della conoscenza umanadi Tommaso d'Aquino (Q. d. *De Veritate*, 10, 6 e *Super Librum de Causis*, prop. 13[14])," in: A. Bertolacci, A. Paravicini Bagliani (eds.), *La filosofia medievale tra antichità ed età moderna. Saggi in memoria di Francesco del Punta*, Florence 2017, pp. 325–362.

Davidson, Herbert, *Alfarabi, Avicenna, and Averroes on Intellect*, Oxford 1992.

de Contenson, Pierre Marie, "Avicennisme Latin et vision de Dieu au début du XIIIe siècle," *Archives d'histoire doctrinale et littéraire du Moyen Âge* 34 (1959a), pp. 29–97.

———, 'S. Thomas et l'avicennisme latin,' *Revue des sciences philosophiques et théologiques* 43 (1959b), pp. 3–31.

———, "La théologie de la vision de Dieu au début du XIIIe siècle: le «De Retributionibus Sanctorum» de Guillaume d'Auvergne et la condemnation de 1241," *Revue des sciences philosophiques et théologiques* 46 (1962), pp. 409–444.

Deferrari, Roy J., *A Lexicon of Saint Thomas Aquinas*, Fitzwilliam, NH 2004.

De Leemans, Pieter, "Aristotle Transmitted: Reflections on the Transmission of Aristotelian Scientific Thought in the Middle Ages," *International Journal of the Classical Tradition* 17 (2010), pp. 325–353.

Dod, Bernard, "Aristoteles Latinus," in: Norman Kretzmann, Anthony Kenny, Jan Pinborg (eds.), Eleonore Stump (associate ed.), *The Cambridge History of Later Medieval Philosophy: From the Rediscovery of Aristotle to the Disintegration of Scholasticism, 1100–1600*, Cambridge 1982, pp. 45–79.

Donato, Antonio, "Aquinas' Theory of Happiness in its Greek, Byzantine, Latin and Arabic Sources," *Al-Masaq* 18 (2006), pp. 161–189.

Dondaine, Hyacinthe F. OP, "L'objet et le 'medium' de la vision béatifique chez les théologiens du XIIIe siècle," *Recherches de théologie ancienne et médiévale* 19 (1952), pp. 60–130.

———, *Le Corpus Dionysien de l'université de Paris au XIIIe siècle*, Rome 1953.

———, "Cognoscere de Deo 'quid est,'" *Recherches de théologie ancienne et médiévale* 22 (1955), pp. 72–78.

Druart, Thérèse-Anne, "The Human Soul's Individuation and its Survival after the Body's Death: Avicenna on the Causal Relation between Body and Soul," *Arabic Sciences and Philosophy* 10 (2000), pp. 259–273.

———, "Averroes's *Long Commentary on Aristotle's De anima* and Direct Knowledge of Separate Beings," in: Ahmad Hasnawi (ed.), *La lumière de l'intellect. La pensée scientifique et philosophique d'Averroès dans son temps. Actes du IVe colloque international de la SIHSPAI, Cordoue, 9–12 décembre 1998*, Leuven 2011, pp. 371–379.

Duba, William Owen, "Seeing God: Theology, Beatitude and Cognition in the Thirteenth Century," unpubl. dissertation, University of Iowa 2006.

Fauser, Winfried, *Super librum IV Sententiarum*, Commissio Leonina 2014, <http://www.commissio-leonina.org//2014/07/thomas-daquin/>, last accessed: 28 Jan 2018.

Fladerer, L., *Augustinus als Exeget. Zu seinen Kommentaren des Galaterbriefes und der Genesis*, Vienna 2010.

Fries, Albert, "Prolegomena," in: *Alberti Magni Ordinis Fratrum Praedicatorum, Quaestiones*, Albert Fried, Wilhelm Kübel, Henryk Anzulewicz (eds.), t. 25/2, *Sancti Doctoris Ecclesiae Alberti Magni Ordinis Fratrum Praedicatorum Episcopi Opera Omnia*, Münster 1993, pp. V–VIII.

Gauthier, René, "Appendix: Saint Thomas et L'Ethique a Nicomaque," in: *Sancti Thomae de Aquino Opera Omnia Iussu Leonis XIII P.M. Edita, t. XLVIII, Sententia Libri Politicorum, Tabula Libri Ethicorum, Appendix: Saint Thomas et L'Ethique a Nicomaque*, Cura et studio Fratrum Praedicatorum, Rome 1971, pp. V–XXV.

———, "Le cours sur l'Ethica Noua d'un maître ès arts de Paris (1235–1240)," *Archives d'histoire doctrinale et littéraire du Moyen Âge* 42 (1975), pp. 71–141.

Gilson, Étienne, "Sur la problématique Thomiste de la vision béatifique," *Archives d'histoire doctrinale et littéraire du Moyen Âge* 31 (1964), pp. 67–88.

Greene-MacCreight, K., *Ad Litteram. How Augustine, Calvin and Barth Read the "Plain Sense" of Genesis 1–3*, New York 1999.

Hankey, Wayne, "*Participatio Divini Luminis*, Aquinas' doctrine of the Agent Intellect: Our Capacity for Contemplation," *Dionysius* 22 (2004), pp. 149–178.

Harrington, L. Michael, *A Thirteenth-Century Textbook of Mystical Theology at the University of Paris*, Leuven 2004.

Hasse, Dag Nikolaus, *Avicenna's De Anima in the Latin West. The Formation of a Peripatetic Philosophy of the Soul 1160–1300*, London / Turin 2000.

———, *Latin Averroes Translations of the First Half of the Thirteenth Century*, Hildesheim / Zürich / New York 2010.

Hoye, William, *Actualitas Omnium Actuum: Man's Beatific Vision of God as Apprehended by Thomas Aquinas*, Meisenheim am Glan 1975.

———, "Heil und Auferstehung nach Albert dem Großen," in: Albert Zimmermann (ed.), *Albert der Große. Seine Zeit, sein Werk, seine Wirkung*, Berlin 1981, pp. 61–77.

Jenkins, John, *Knowledge and Faith in Thomas Aquinas*, Cambridge 2007.

King, Peter, "Rethinking Representation in the Middle Ages: A Vade-Mecum to Mediaeval Theories of Mental Representation," in: Henrik Lagerlund (ed.), *Representation and Objects of Thought in Medieval Philosophy*, Aldershot 2007, pp. 81–100.

Kleber, Hermann, *Glück als Lebensziel. Untersuchungen zur Philosophie des Glücks bei Thomas von Aquin*, Münster 1988.

Krause, Katja, "Aquinas' Philosophy of the Beatific Vision: A Textual Analysis of his Commentary on the Sentences in Light of its Greek, Arabic, and Latin Sources," unpubl. dissertation, King's College London, 2014.

———, "Remodelling Ultimate Human Happiness: Thomas Aquinas' *Commentary on the Sentences* and Its Sources," *Divus Thomas* 118 (2015a), pp. 15–56.

———, "Transforming Aristotelian Philosophy: Alexander of Aphrodisias in Aquinas' Early Anthropology and Eschatology," *Przegląd Tomistyczny* 21 (2015b), pp. 175–217.

———, "Meaning Beyond Defining: Averroes's *Dispositio* in Thomas Aquinas's Account of Heavenly Beatitude," in: Yehuda Halper (ed.), *The Pursuit of Happiness in Medieval Jewish and Islamic Thought*, forthcoming.

Kübel, Wilhelm, "Prolegomena," in: *Alberti Magni Ordinis Fratrum Praedicatorum, Super Ethica. Commentum et Quaestiones. Libri quinque priores*, Wilhelm Kübel (ed.), t. 14/1, *Sancti Doctoris Ecclesiae Alberti Magni Ordinis Fratrum Praedicatorum Episcopi Opera Omnia*, Münster 1968/1972, pp. III–XIV.

———, "Prolegomena," in: *Alberti Magni Ordinis Fratrum Praedicatorum, De sacramentis*, Albertus Ohlmeyer (ed.), *De incarnatione*, Ignatius Backes (ed.), *De Resurrectione*, Wilhelmo Kübel (ed.), t. 26, *Sancti Doctoris Ecclesiae Alberti Magni Ordinis Fratrum Praedicatorum Episcopi Opera Omnia*, Monasterii Westfalorum 1958, pp. V–XIX.

Maillard, Pierre-Yves, *La vision de Dieu chez Thomas d'Aquin: Une lecture de l'In Ioannem à la lumière de ses sources augustiniennes*, Paris 2001.

Mainoldi, Ernesto Sergio, *Dietro «Dionigi l'Areopagita»: la genesi e gli scopi del* Corpus Dionysiacum, Rome 2018.

Marenbon, John, *From the Circle of Alcuin to the School of Auxerre: Logic, Theology and Philosophy in the Early Middle Ages*, Cambridge 1981.

McEvoy, James and Dunne, Michael (eds.), *History and Eschatology in John Scottus Eriugena and His Time. Proceedings of the Tenth International Conference for the Promotion of Eriugenian Studies, Maynooth and Dublin, August 16–20, 2000*, Leuven 2002.

Moran, Dermot, "John Scottus Eriugena," in: Edward N. Zalta (ed.), *The Stanford Encyclopedia of Philosophy* http://plato.stanford.edu/archives/fall2008/entries/scottus-eriugena/, Stanford 2018.

Müller, Jörn, *Natürliche Moral und philosophische Ethik bei Albertus Magnus*, Münster 2001.

Mulchahey, M. Michèle, *"First the Bow is Bent in Study. . . ." Dominican Education before 1350*, Toronto 1998.

———, "The *Studium* at Cologne and Its Role Within Early Dominican Education," *Listening. Journal of Religion and Culture* 43 (2008), pp. 118–147.

———, "The Dominican *Studium Romanae Curiae*: The Papacy, the *Magisterium* and the Friars," in: Kent Emery, Jr., William J. Courtenay, Stephen M. Metzger (eds.), *Philosophy and Theology in the Studia of the Religious Orders and at Papal and Royal Courts*, Turnhout 2012, pp. 577–599.

Oliva O.P., Adriano, *Les débuts de l'enseignement de Thomas d'Aquin et sa conception de la sacra doctrina*, Paris 2006.

———, personal email conversation, 23 Jan 2018.

———, "Philosophy in the Teaching of Theology by Thomas Aquinas," *The Thomist* 76 (2012a), pp. 397–430.

———, "La contemplation des philosophes selon Thomas d'Aquin," *Revue des sciences philosophiques et théologiques* 96 (2012b), pp. 585–662.

Pannacio, Claude, "Aquinas on Intellectual Representation," in: Dominik Perler (ed.), *Ancient and Medieval Theories of Intentionality*, Leiden / Boston / Cologne 2001, pp. 185–201.

Pasnau, Robert, *Theories of Cognition in the Later Middle Ages*, New York 1997.

———, *Thomas Aquinas on Human Nature. A Philosophical Study of* Summa theologiae *Ia 75–89*, Cambridge 2002.

———, "Id Quo Cognoscimus," in: Simo Knuuttila, Pekka Karkkainen (eds.), *Theories of Perception in Medieval and Early Modern Philosophy*, Dordrecht 2008, pp. 131–149.

Pegis, Anton, "The Separated Soul and Its Nature in St. Thomas," in: Armand Maurer (ed.), *St. Thomas Aquinas 1274–1974: Commemorative Studies*, vol. 1, Toronto 1974a, pp. 131–158.

———, "Between Immortality and Death: Some Further Reflections on the 'Summa Contra Gentiles,'" *Monist* 51 (1974b), pp. 1–15.

Perl, Eric, "Hierarchy and Participation in Dionysius the Areopagite and Greek Neoplatonism," *American Catholic Philosophical Quarterly* 68 (1994), pp. 15–30.

Perler, Dominik, *Theorien der Intentionalität im Mittelalter*, 2nd ed., Frankfurt am Main 2004.

Pines, Shlomo, "The Limitations of Human Knowledge according to al-Farabi, Ibn Bajjah, and Maimonides," in: I. Twersky (ed.), *Studies in Medieval Jewish History and Literature*, vol. 1, Cambridge, MA. 1979, pp. 82–109.

Polloni, Nicola, *The Twelfth-Century Renewal of Latin Metaphysics. Gundissalinus's Ontology of Matter and Form*, Toronto 2020.

Rigo, Caterina, "Zur Redaktionsfrage der Frühschriften des Albertus Magnus," in: Ludger Honnefelder (ed.), *Albertus Magnus und die Anfänge der Aristoteles-Rezeption im lateinischen Mittelalter. Von Richard Rufus bis zu Franciscus de Mayronis*, Münster 2005, pp. 325–374.

Rorem, Paul, *Eriugena's Commentary on the Dionysian Celestial Hierarchy*, Toronto 2005.

———, "The Early Latin Dionysius: Eriugena and Hugh of St Victor," *Modern Theology* 24 (2008), pp. 601–614.

Schleiermacher, Friedrich, "On the Different Methods of Translating," in: Lawrence Venuti (ed.), *The Translation Studies Reader*, London / New York 2000, pp. 43–63.

Smit, Houston, "Aquinas's Abstractionism," *Medieval Philosophy and Theology* 10 (2001), pp. 85–118.

Spruit, Leen, *Species intelligibilis: From Perception to Knowledge, vol. 1: Classical Roots and Medieval Discussions*, Leiden 1994.

Steel, Carlos, *Der Adler und die Nachteule. Thomas und Albert über die Möglichkeit der Metaphysik* (Lectio Albertina 4), Münster 2001.

Sweeney, Leo, *Divine Infinity in Greek and Medieval Thought*, 2nd ed., New York 1998.

Taylor, Richard, "Personal Immortality in Averroes' Mature Philosophical Psychology," *Documenti e studi sulla tradizione filosofica medievale* 9 (1998), pp. 87–110.

———, "The Agent Intellect as 'Form for Us' and Averroes's Critique of al-Fârâbî," *Tópicos* 29 (2005), pp. 29–51.

———, "Intellect as Intrinsic Formal Cause in the Soul According to Aquinas and Averroes," in: Maha Elkaisy-Friemuth, John M. Dillon (eds.), *The Afterlife of the Platonic Soul: Reflections of Platonic Psychology in the Monotheistic Religions*, Leiden / Boston 2009a, pp. 187–220.

———, "Introduction," Richard C. Taylor (ed., trans., and intr.), Thérèse-Anne Druart (subed.), *Averroes (Ibn Rushd) of Cordoba, Long Commentary on the 'De Anima' of Aristotle*, New Haven 2009b, pp. i–cix.

———, "Aquinas and the Arabs: Arabic / Islamic Philosophy in Thomas Aquinas' Conception of the Beatific Vision in his *Commentary on the Sentences* IV,49,2,1," *The Thomist* 76 (2012), pp. 509–550.

———, "Aquinas and 'the Arabs': Aquinas's First Critical Encounter with the Doctrines of Avicenna and Averroes on the Intellect, In 2 Sent. d. 17, q. 2, a. 1," in: Luis Xavier López-Farjeat, Jörg Alejandro Tellkamp (eds.), *Philosophical Psychology in Arabic Thought and the Latin Aristotelianism of the 13th Century*, Paris 2013, pp. 141–183.

———, "Remarks on the Importance of Albert the Great's Analyses and Use of the Thought of Avicenna and Averroes in the *De homine* for the Development of the Early Natural Epistemology of Thomas Aquinas," in: Günther Mensching, Alia Mensching-Estakhr (eds.), *Die Seele im Mittelalter. Von der Substanz zum funktionalen System*, Würzburg 2018, pp. 131–148.

Tellkamp, Jörg Alejandro, "*Vis estimativa* and *vis cogitativa* in Thomas Aqinas's *Commentary on the Sentences*," *The Thomist* 76 (2012), pp. 611–640.

Torrell, Jean-Pierre, "La vision de Dieu 'per essentiam' selon saint Thomas d'Aquin," *Micrologus* 5 (1997), pp. 43–68.

———, *Saint Thomas Aquinas. The Person and His Work*, vol. 1, Robert Royal (trans.), Washington, D.C. 2000.

———, "Nature et grâce chez Thomas d'Aquin," *Revue Thomiste* 101 (2001), pp. 167–202.

Trottmann, Christian, *La vision béatifique, des disputes scolastiques à sa definition par Benoît XII*, Rome 1995.

Trouillard, Jean, "La genèse de l'hylémorphisme selon Proclus," *Dialogue* 6 (1967), pp. 1–17.

Venuti, Lawrence (ed.), *The Translation Studies Reader*, London / New York 2000.

von Goethe, Johann Wolfgang, *Noten und Abhandlungen zu besserem Verständnis des west-östlichen Divans*, in: *Berliner Ausgabe. Poetische Werke, vols. 1–16*, vol. 3, Berlin 1961.

Waddell, Michael, "Aquinas on the Light of Glory," *Topicos* 40 (2011), pp. 105–132.

Wéber, Édouard-H., "Les Apports positifs de la noétique d'Ibn Rushd à celle de Thomas d'Aquin," in: Jean Jolivet, Rachel Arié (eds.), *Multiple Averroès. Actes du Colloque International organisé à l'occasion du 850e anniversaire de la naissance d'Averroès, Paris, 20–23 septembre 1976*, Paris 1978, pp. 211–248.

Weisheipl, James A., *Friar Thomas d'Aquino. His Life, Thought and Works*, 2nd ed., Washington, D.C. 1983.

White, Kevin, "The Quodlibeta of Thomas Aquinas in the Context of his Work," Christopher Schnabel (ed.), *Theological Quodlibeta in the Middle Ages: The Thirteenth Century*, Leiden 2006, pp. 49–133.

Wieland, Georg, *Ethica—Scientia Practica. Die Anfänge der philosophischen Ethik im 13. Jahrhundert*, Münster 1981.

———, "The Reception and Interpretation of Aristotle's Ethics," in: Norman Kretzmann, Anthony Kenny, Jan Pinborg (eds.), Eleonore Stump (associate ed.), *The Cambridge History of Later Medieval Philosophy: From the Rediscovery of Aristotle to the Disintegration of Scholasticism, 1100–1600*, Cambridge 1982, pp. 657–672.

Wicki, Nikolaus, *Die Lehre von der himmlischen Seligkeit in der mittelalterlichen Scholastik von Petrus Lombardus bis Thomas von Aquin*, Freiburg 1954.

Wilder, Alfred, "On the Knowing Species in St. Thomas: Their Necessity and Epistemological Innocence," *Angelicum* 68 (1991), pp. 2–32.

Williams, Anna Ngaire, *The Ground of Union: Deification in Aquinas and Palamas*, Oxford / New York 1999.

Williams, Steven J., "Defining the *corpus Aristotelicum*: Scholastic Awareness of Aristotelian Spuria in the High Middle Ages," *Journal of the Warburg and Courtauld Institutes* 58 (1995), pp. 29–51.

Wippel, John, "Thomas Aquinas on What Philosophers Can Know About God," *American Catholic Philosophical Quarterly* 66 (1992), pp. 279–297.

———, "Thomas Aquinas on the Separated Soul's Natural Knowledge," in: James McEvoy, Michael Dunne (eds.), *Thomas Aquinas: Approaches to Truth, The Aquinas Lectures at Maynooth, 1996–2001*, Dublin 2000, pp. 114–140.

Wirmer, David, "Avempace—'*ratio de quiditate*.' Thomas Aquinas's Critique of an Argument for the Natural Knowability of Separate Substances," in: Andreas Speer, Lydia Wegener (eds.), *Wissen über Grenzen. Arabisches Wissen und lateinisches Mittelalter*, Berlin 2006, pp. 569–590.

———, "Nachwort," in: David Wirmer (ed., trans., and introd.), *Averroes. Über den Intellekt. Auszüge aus seinen drei Kommentaren zu Aristoteles'* De anima. *Arabisch, Lateinisch, Deutsch*, Freiburg / Basel / Vienna 2008, pp. 287–409.

———, *Vom Denken der Natur zur Natur des Denkens. Ibn Bāǧǧas Theorie der Potenz als Grundlegung der Psychologie*, Berlin / Munich / Boston 2014.

Small Glossary of Technical Terms

LATIN – ENGLISH

abstractio	abstraction
abstrahere	to abstract
accidens	accident
acquisitus, a, um	acquired
actus purus	pure actuality
affectus	affect
analogia	analogy
angelus	angel
anima	soul
assistere	to appear before
astare (coram / juxta)	to serve (at someone's side)
auferre	to lift from, remove
beatitudo	happiness
beatus, a, um	blessed
calefactio	heating
calor	heat
capacitas	capacity
capax	capable
capere	to enclose
caritas	love (usually meaning a descending love that shares itself freely)
carnalis, is, e	carnal
caro	flesh
causa	cause
clarus, a, um	bright
claritas	brightness
cogitare	to think, consider
cognitio	cognition
cognitio matutina	morning cognition (applies to the angels)
cognitio vespertina	evening cognition (applies to the angels)
cognoscere	to cognize

Commentator	the Commentator (= Averroes)
communicare	to share, have in common
communis, is, e	shared
compositum (here as noun)	composite
comprehendere	to comprehend
conjungere	to conjoin
conspicere	to behold
contemplatio	contemplation
contendere	to confine
contineri	to be confined
continuum	space
corporalis, is, e	corporeal
corpus	body
corrumpere	to impair, corrupt, destroy
corruptio	corruption
creatus, a, um	created
debilis, is, e	insufficient
defectum	defect
degenerare	to decrease, deteriorate
demonstratio	demonstration
desiderium	desire
determinare	to limit
diabolus	devil
dictum	assertion, saying
dies iudicii	Judgment Day
dispositio	disposition
dispositio naturalis	natural disposition
dispositio ultima	ultimate disposition
dos	gift
effectivus, a, um	efficient
effectus	effect
eminentia	eminence
ens creatum	created being
equalis, is, e	equal
esse	being
essentia	essence
essentia divina	divine essence
excessus	excess
exire	to go out, to depart, to rise
existens in hac vita	living in this life

expressus, a, um	distinct
ex propriis naturalibus	by their own natural powers
ex puris naturalibus	by purely natural means
facie ad faciem	face to face
facultas	faculty
figura	figure, shape
finitus, a, um	finite
forma	form
forma concreata	co-created form (in the intellect of the angels)
forma creata	created form
forma proportionata	proportionate form
forma sensibilis	sensible form
forma subsistens	subsisting form
formare	to inform, give shape
frustra	in vain
frustrari	to be in vain
genus	genus
gloria	glory
gradus prophetiae	grade of prophecy
gratia	grace
habitudo	relation, disposition
habitus	habit
ignis	fire
ignorantia	ignorance
illuminatio	illumination
imago Dei	image of God
immaterialis, is, e	immaterial
impedimentum	impediment
impedire	to prevent, hinder
impressio	impression
improbare	to refute
in actu	in actuality
in patria	in the afterlife
in prima conditione	in original condition
in statu viae	in the present life
in via	in this life
includere	to enclose
incorporalis, is, e	incorporeal
incorporeus, a, um	incorporeal

increatus, a, um	uncreated
indare	to impart, infuse
indispositio	ill-disposed
inditus, a, um	infused
inequalitas	inequality
infinitus, a, um	infinite
informare	to inform, instruct
intellectus agens	agent intellect
intellectus possibilis	possible intellect
intelligentia	intelligence
intelligere	to understand
intelligibile	(an) intelligible
intensio	intensity
limbus	limbo
lumen	light (implied is light that has been emitted from its source)
lumen gloriae	light of glory
lumen intellectuale	intellectual light
lumen intelligibilis	intelligible light
lumen naturale	natural light
lux	light (implied is the light as it is found in its source)
magnitudo	magnitude
materia	matter
medium	medium
mensura	measure
modus	mode, way
modus essendi	mode of being
motus	motion
natura	nature
natus esse	to be natural
notitia simplicis intelligentiae	knowledge of a simple intelligence
notitia visionis	knowledge of vision
numerus	number
objectum	object
oculus corporalis	corporeal eye
oculus glorificatus	glorified eye
oculus spiritualis	spiritual eye
operatio	activity
opinio	opinion

ordo	order
ordo causarum	order of causes
ordo effectuum	order of effects
organum corporale	corporeal organ
participare	to participate
peccatum	sin
per essentiam	through (His) essence
per se subsistens	self-subsistent
perfectio	perfection
perfectus, a, um	perfect
perfundere	to imbue
phantasma	phantasm
Philosophus	the Philosopher (= Aristotle)
plenus, a, um	full
poenalitas	penalty
ponere	to posit
populus	people (sg.)
potentia	potency, power
potentia activa	active potency
potentia passiva	passive potency
premium	prize, reward
prendere	to seize
prima principia per se nota	first self-evident principles
principium	principle
privatio	privation
proportio	proportion
proprietas	property
providentia dei	God's providence
purgare	to purge
qualitas	quality
quantitas	quantity
quantitas dimensiva	dimensive quantity
quantitas virtualis	virtual quantity
quid est	what it is, quiddity
quiditas	quiddity
quies	rest
raptus, a, um	caught up
ratio	nature, measure, characteristic
ratio conjungibilis	measure of the ability to conjoin
ratio intelligibilis	intelligible characteristic

receptibilis, is, e	receptible
receptio	reception
recipere	to receive
reducere	to reduce
redundantia	overflow
resurrectio	resurrection
revelatio	revelation
sanctus	blessed saint
scientia	knowledge
scientia visionis	knowledge of vision
sensibile commune	common sensible
sensibile proprium	proper sensible
sensibilis, is, e	sensible, sensible thing
sensus	sense, the senses
sensus corporalis	corporeal sense
sensus exterior	external sense
sensus interior	internal sense
signum	indication
similitudo	similitude
simplex	simple
simpliciter	absolutely, completely
sol	sun
species	species
species intelligibilis	intelligible species
speculum	mirror
speculum increatum	uncreated mirror
speculum materiale	material mirror
spes	faith
spiritualis, is, e	spiritual
stare	to hold still, remain unmoved
subjectum	subject
substantia	substance
substantia separata	separate substance
substare	to stand under
superaddere	to superadd
tempus	time
terminatus, a, um	terminated
terminus	limit, end
theophania	theophany (Aquinas defines it as 'an apparition of God')

totaliter	completely
totus, a, um	entirely (adverbial meaning when an adjective in agreement with subject)
transferre	to turn into
unibilis, is, e	capable of union
unire	to unite
universalis, is, e	universal
ut est	as He is (synonym to describe the vision of God's essence)
Verbum	the Word (= Christ)
veritas	truth
veritas increata	uncreated Truth
viator	wayfarer
virtus	power
virtus aestimativa	estimative power
virtus cogitativa	cogitative power
virtus divina	divine power
vis	power
vis apprehensiva	apprehensive power
visibile	visible thing
visio beatifica	beatific vision
visio corporalis	corporeal vision
visio dei per essentiam	vision of God through His essence
visio intellectualis	intellectual vision
visio imaginaria	imaginary vision
visus	vision
vita	life
vitium	vice
voluntas	will

ENGLISH – LATIN

absolutely, completely	simpliciter
abstraction	abstractio
accident	accidens
acquired	acquisitus, a, um
active potency	potentia activa
activity	operatio
affect	affectus
agent intellect	intellectus agens
analogy	analogia
angel	angelus
apprehensive power	vis apprehensiva
as He is (synonym to describe the vision of God's essence)	ut est
assertion, saying	dictum
beatific vision	visio beatifica
being	esse
blessed	beatus, a, um
blessed saint	sanctus
body	corpus
bright	clarus, a, um
brightness	claritas
by purely natural means	ex puris naturalibus
by their own natural powers	ex propriis naturalibus
capable	capax
capable of union	unibilis, is, e
capacity	capacitas
carnal	carnalis, is, e
caught up	raptus, a, um
cause	causa
co-created form (in the intellect of the angels)	forma concreata
cogitative power	virtus cogitativa
cognition	cognitio
common sensible	sensibile commune
completely	totaliter
composite	compositum
contemplation	contemplatio
corporeal	corporalis, is, e
corporeal eye	oculus corporalis

corporeal organ	organum corporale
corporeal sense	sensus corporalis
corporeal vision	visio corporalis
corruption	corruptio
created	creatus, a, um
created being	ens creatum
created form	forma creata
defect	defectum
demonstration	demonstratio
desire	desiderium
devil	diabolus
dimensive quantity	quantitas dimensiva
disposition	dispositio
distinct	expressus, a, um
divine essence	essentia divina
divine power	virtus divina
effect	effectus
efficient	effectivus, a, um
eminence	eminentia
entirely (when in agreement with subject)	totus, a, um
equal	equalis, is, e
essence	essentia
estimative power	virtus aestimativa
evening cognition (applies to the angels)	cognitio vespertina
excess	excessus
external sense	sensus exterior
face to face	facie ad faciem
faculty	facultas
faith	spes
figure, shape	figura
finite	finitus, a, um
fire	ignis
first self-evident principles	prima principia per se nota
flesh	caro
form	forma
full	plenus, a, um
genus	genus
gift	dos

glorified eye	oculus glorificatus
glory	gloria
God's providence	providentia dei
grace	gratia
grade of prophecy	gradus prophetiae
habit	habitus
happiness	beatitudo
heat	calor
heating	calefactio
ignorance	ignorantia
ill-disposed	indispositio
illumination	illuminatio
image of God	imago Dei
imaginary vision	visio imaginaria
immaterial	immaterialis, is, e
impediment	impedimentum
impression	impressio
in actuality	in actu
in original condition	in prima conditione
in the afterlife	in patria
in the present life	in statu viae
in this life	in via
in vain	frustra
incorporeal	incorporalis, is, e
incorporeal	incorporeus, a, um
indication	signum
inequality	inequalitas
infinite	infinitus, a, um
infused	inditus, a, um
insufficient	debilis, is, e
intellectual light	lumen intellectuale
intellectual vision	visio intellectualis
intelligence	intelligentia
(an) intelligible	intelligibile
intelligible characteristic	ratio intelligibilis
intelligible light	lumen intelligibile
intelligible species	species intelligibilis
intensity	intensio
internal sense	sensus interior
Judgment Day	dies iudicii

knowledge	scientia
knowledge of a simple intelligence	notitia simplicis intelligentiae
knowledge of vision	scientia visionis, notitia visionis
life	vita
light (implied is light that has been emitted from its source)	lumen
light (implied is the light as it is found in its source)	lux
light of glory	lumen gloriae
limbo	limbus
limit, end	terminus
living in this life	existens in hac vita
love (usually meaning a descending love that shares itself freely)	caritas
magnitude	magnitudo
material mirror	speculum materiale
matter	materia
measure	mensura
measure of the ability to conjoin	ratio conjungibilis
medium	medium
mirror	speculum
mode, way	modus
mode of being	modus essendi
morning cognition (applies to the angels)	cognitio matutina
motion	motus
natural disposition	dispositio naturalis
natural light	lumen naturale
nature	natura
nature, measure, characteristic	ratio
number	numerus
object	objectum
opinion	opinio
order	ordo
order of causes	ordo causarum
order of effects	ordo effectuum
overflow	redundantia
passive potency	potentia passiva
penalty	poenalitas
people (sg.)	populus
perfect	perfectus, a, um

perfection	perfectio
phantasm	phantasma
possible intellect	intellectus possibilis
potency, power	potentia
power	virtus
power	vis
principle	principium
privation	privatio
prize, reward	premium
proper sensible	sensibile proprium
property	proprietas
proportionate form	forma proportionata
proportion	proportio
pure actuality	actus purus
quality	qualitas
quantity	quantitas
quiddity	quiditas
receptible	receptibilis, is, e
reception	receptio
relation, disposition	habitudo
rest	quies
resurrection	resurrectio
revelation	revelatio
self-subsistent	per se subsistens
sense, the senses	sensus
sensible form	forma sensibilis
sensible, sensible thing	sensibilis, is, e
separate substance	substantia separata
shared	communis, is, e
similitude	similitudo
simple	simplex
sin	peccatum
soul	anima
space	continuum
species	species
spiritual	spiritualis, is, e
spiritual eye	oculus spiritualis
subject	subjectum
subsisting form	forma subsistens
substance	substantia

sun	sol
terminated	terminatus, a, um
the Commentator (= Averroes)	Commentator
the Philosopher (= Aristotle)	Philosophus
the Word (= Christ)	Verbum
theophany (Aquinas defines it as 'an apparition of God')	theophania
through (His) essence	per essentiam
time	tempus
to abstract	abstrahere
to appear before	assistere
to be confined	contineri
to be in vain	frustrari
to be natural	natus esse
to behold	conspicere
to cognize	cognoscere
to comprehend	comprehendere
to confine	contendere
to conjoin	conjungere
to decrease, deteriorate	degenerare
to enclose	capere
to enclose	includere
to go out, depart, rise	exire
to hold still, remain unmoved	stare
to imbue	perfundere
to impair, corrupt, destroy	corrumpere
to impart, infuse	indare
to inform, give shape	formare
to inform, instruct	informare
to limit	determinare
to participate	participare
to posit	ponere
to prevent, hinder	impedire
to purge	purgare
to receive	recipere
to reduce	reducere
to refute	improbare
to remove, lift from	auferre
to seize	prendere
to serve (at someone's side)	astare (coram / juxta)

to share, have in common	communicare
to stand under	substare
to superadd	superaddere
to think, consider	cogitare
to turn into	transferre
to understand	intelligere
to unite	unire
truth	veritas
ultimate disposition	dispositio ultima
uncreated	increatus, a, um
uncreated mirror	speculum increatum
uncreated Truth	veritas increata
universal	universalis, is, e
vice	vitium
virtual quantity	quantitas virtualis
visible thing	visibile
vision	visus
vision of God through His essence	visio dei per essentiam
wayfarer	viator
what it is, quiddity	quid est
will	voluntas

Indexes

REFERENCES TO SCRIPTURE

All references given refer to the quotations of Scripture as they appear in the footnotes.

References to Authorities Quoted by Thomas Aquinas

References to Authorities Not Quoted by Thomas Aquinas

General Index

B

D

H

I

N

O

P

Q

U

V

W